The Longman Companion to
The Labour Party, 1900–1998

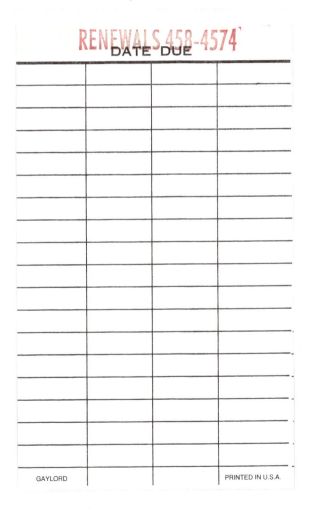

Longman Companions to History

General Editors: Chris Cook and John Stevenson

Now available

The Longman Companion to

The Labour Party 1900–1998

Harry Harmer

Longman
London and New York

Addison Wesley Longman Limited
Edinburgh Gate,
Harlow, Essex CM20 2JE,
United Kingdom
and Associated Companies throughout the world.

*Published in the United States of America
by Addison Wesley Longman, New York.*

© Addison Wesley Longman Limited 1999

First published 1999

ISBN 0–582–31214–0 CSD
ISBN 0–582–31215–9 PPR

Visit Addison Wesley Longman on the world wide web at
http://www.awl-he.com

British Library Cataloguing in Publication Data

A catalogue entry for this title is available from the British Library

Library of Congress Cataloging-in-Publication Data

Harmer, H.J.P.
    The Longman companion to the Labour Party, 1900–1998 / Harry
Harmer.
        p.   cm. — (Longman companions to history)
    Includes bibliographical references and index.
    ISBN 0–582–31215–9 (pbk.). — ISBN 0–582–31214–0 (hc.)
    1. Labour Party (Great Britain)—History—20th century. 2. Great
Britain—Politics and government—20th century.   I. Title.
II. Series.
JN1129.L32H32   1999
324.24107′09′04—dc21   98–51307
                                                                                CIP

Set by 35 in 9 Albert New Baskerville
Produced by Addison Wesley Longman Singapore (Pte) Ltd.,
Printed in Singapore

Contents

Preface

This *Companion* is intended to provide, in a concise and accessible format, the essential facts and figures on the Labour Party since its foundation. By its nature, a book of this kind cannot deal with the meat of political argument or the complexities of policy. The *Companion* does, however, attempt to give the reader the background that will help her or him get to grips with them.

Much of the *Companion* takes the form of chronologies of Labour's history in government and – more often – in opposition. In addition, there are chronologies on the important groups with which the party has been related. Among these are the trade unions (the interests of which played a central part in Labour's foundation), the revolutionary left (with a love-hate relationship in which it attempted to radicalise or destroy the party), women, and ethnic minorities.

I should like to thank Dr Chris Cook for suggesting that I contributed this *Companion* to the series, and for useful advice on the contents from him, Dr John Stevenson (both General Editors of the series), and from Hilary Shaw at Addison Wesley Longman. I should also like to thank Graham Bishop for his valued practical help and Arianna Silvestri for her patience while I struggled to complete it.

Harry Harmer
November, 1998

Abbreviations

ACAS	Advisory Conciliation and Arbitration Service
ASRS	Amalgamated Society of Railway Servants
BMA	British Medical Association
BSP	British Socialist Party
BUF	British Union of Fascists
CBI	Confederation of British Industry
CDS	Campaign for Democratic Socialism
CLP	Constituency Labour Party
CLPD	Campaign for Labour Party Democracy
CND	Campaign for Nuclear Disarmament
CPGB	Communist Party of Great Britain
CRE	Commission for Racial Equality
DEA	Department of Economic Affairs
DHSS	Department of Health and Social Security
EEC	European Economic Community
EMU	European Monetary Union
ETU	Electricians' Trade Union
FBI	Federation of British Industry
GLC	Greater London Council
GMC	General Management Committee
GMWU	General and Municipal Workers' Union
ICFTU	International Confederation of Free Trade Unions
ICI	Imperial Chemical Industries
ILEA	Inner London Education Authority
ILO	International Labour Organisation
ILP	Independent Labour Party
IMF	International Monetary Fund
IRA	Irish Republican Army
IRC	Industrial Reorganisation Corporation
KC	King's Counsel
LCC	London County Council
LCDTU	Liaison Committee for the Defence of Trade Unions
LRC	Labour Representation Committee
LSE	London School of Economics
MEP	Member of the European Parliament
MFGB	Miners' Federation of Great Britain

MP	Member of Parliament
MSP	Member of the Scottish Parliament
NATO	North Atlantic Treaty Organisation
NATSOPA	National Society of Operative Printers, Graphical and Media Personnel
NCCL	National Council for Civil Liberties
NDP	National Democratic Party
NEC	National Executive Committee
NEDC	National Economic Development Council
NHS	National Health Service
NUGMW	National Union of General and Municipal Workers
NUM	National Union of Mineworkers
NUPE	National Union of Public Employees
NUR	National Union of Railwaymen
NUS	National Union of Seamen
OEEC	Organisation of European Economic Co-operation
OMOV	One member one vote
PC	Plaid Cymru
PLP	Parliamentary Labour Party
QC	Queen's Counsel
SCL	Society of Christian League
SDF	Social Democratic Federation
SDL	Social Defence League
SDLP	Social Democratic and Labour Party
SDP	Social Democratic Party
SEATO	South East Asia Treaty Organisation
SLD	Social and Liberal Democratic Party
SLL	Socialist Labour League
SLP	Scottish Labour Party
SNP	Scottish National Party
SSC	Society of Socialist Churches
SSIP	Society for Socialist Inquiry and Propaganda
SWMF	South Wales Miners' Federation
TGWU	Transport and General Workers' Union
TUC	Trades Union Congress
UDC	Union of Democratic Control
UDI	unilateral declaration of independence
USDAW	Union of Shop, Distributive and Allied Workers
VFS	Victory for Socialism
WEA	Workers' Education Association
WFTU	World Federation of Trades Unions
WSPU	Womens' Social and Political Union
YCL	Young Communist League

1   The Labour Party –
Outline Chronology

This chronology provides a basic outline of the central events in the Labour Party's history since its foundation. More detailed information can be found in the theme chronologies, glossary and biographies.

1900   Labour Representation Committee (LRC) formed with Ramsay MacDonald as secretary.

1906   Twenty-two LRC candidates elected as candidates for the general election. LRC transformed into the Labour Party under Keir Hardie's chairmanship.

1907   Arthur Henderson succeeds Hardie as party chairman.

1908   MacDonald succeeds Henderson as party chairman; Henderson becomes secretary.

1914   Labour divides over Britain's participation in the First World War; among leading figures, Hardie, MacDonald and Snowden oppose, Henderson and Clynes support.

1918   New Constitution introduces individual party membership and commits the party to the socialist objectives of Clause Four. *Labour and the New Social Order* adopted by the party conference.

1922   Labour wins 142 seats at the general election and becomes the leading Opposition party.

1924   Labour wins 191 seats in December 1923 election and forms a minority government under MacDonald in January.

1929   Labour wins 288 seats and forms second minority government under MacDonald.

1931   Labour government collapses as Cabinet divides over unemployment benefit reductions and MacDonald forms a

National Government; Henderson becomes Labour leader; Labour suffers heavy defeat at general election and returns with only 52 MPs.

1932   George Lansbury succeeds Henderson as party leader; Independent Labour Party (ILP) disaffiliates from the Labour Party.

1935   Clement Attlee succeeds Lansbury as party leader; Labour wins 154 seats in general election revival.

1940   Labour joins wartime Coalition government under Churchill.

1942   Policy document *The Old World and the New Society* advocates post-war continuation of controls, planning of production and expansion in public ownership.

1945   Labour withdraws from the wartime Coalition, wins 393 seats at ensuing general election and forms its first majority government under Attlee.

1950   Labour wins 315 seats at the general election, reducing its majority to six.

1951   Conservatives win general election as Labour increases its vote but returns with 295 seats.

1955   Labour loses general election, returning with 277 seats; Gaitskell succeeds Attlee as party leader.

1959   Labour loses third successive general election to the Conservatives; Gaitskell thwarted in attempt to revise Clause Four.

1960   Labour conference adopts unilateral nuclear disarmament in defeat for party leadership.

1961   Policy of unilateral nuclear disarmament reversed. Policy document *Signposts for the Sixties* sets out social services expansion based on economic growth.

1963   Gaitskell dies and is succeeded as party leader by Wilson.

1964   Labour narrowly wins general election with 317 seats and forms a government under Wilson.

1966   Labour returns with 363 seats and wins general election.

1969   Labour government forced to drop *In Place of Strife* proposals for industrial relations reform following trade union and party opposition.

1970   Labour unexpectedly loses general election to the Conservatives, returning with 287 seats.

1974   Labour, with 301 seats, forms minority government following February general election; returns with 319 seats and a small majority in October.

1976   Wilson resigns and is succeeded as party leader and prime minister by James Callaghan.

1977–78   Labour retains office with a Lib-Lab pact.

1979   Labour returns with 268 seats and loses general election to the Conservatives.

1980   Michael Foot succeeds Callaghan as party leader.

1981   Special conference adoption of an electoral college for selecting the party leadership provokes the launch of the Social Democratic Party (SDP) by the 'Gang of Four'.

1983   Labour loses general election to the Conservatives with the party's lowest ever share of the vote; Neil Kinnock succeeds Foot as party leader.

1987   Labour loses third successive general election to the Conservatives.

1988   Labour initiates a policy review in attempt to make the party electable.

1992   Labour loses fourth successive general election to the Conservatives; John Smith succeeds Kinnock as party leader.

1993   Party conference adopts one member one vote (OMOV) for conference voting and the selection of the party leadership.

1994   Smith dies and is succeeded as party leader by Tony Blair.

1995   Special conference votes for drastic revision of Clause Four of the party constitution.

1997   Labour wins general election with overwhelming majority and forms government under Blair.

2 Leadership, Membership and Policy

The Party Leadership

From 1906 to 1921 the leading figures in the Labour Party were known as the Chairman and Vice Chairman of the Parliamentary Party, from 1922 to 1963 as the Chairman and Leader of the Parliamentary Party and Deputy Leader, from 1970 to 1978 as Leader of the Parliamentary Party and Deputy Leader, and from 1978 onwards as Leader and Deputy Leader of the Labour Party.

Leader

1906–8	Keir Hardie
1908–10	Arthur Henderson
1910–11	George Barnes
1911–14	James Ramsay MacDonald
1914–17	Arthur Henderson
1917–21	William Adamson
1921–22	Joseph Clynes
1922–31	James Ramsay MacDonald
1931–32	Arthur Henderson
1932–35	George Lansbury
1935–55	Clement Attlee
1955–63	Hugh Gaitskell
1963–76	Harold Wilson
1976–80	James Callaghan
1980–83	Michael Foot
1983–92	Neil Kinnock
1992–94	John Smith
1994–	Tony Blair

Deputy Leader

1906–8	David Shackleton
1908–10	George Barnes
1910–11	Joseph Clynes

1911–12	William Brace
1912–14	James Parker
1914–15	Arthur Gill
1915–18	John Hodge and George Wardle (joint)
1918–21	Joseph Clynes
1921–22	James Thomas and Stephen Walsh (joint)
1922–23	Stephen Walsh and Josiah Wedgwood (joint)
1923–31	Joseph Clynes
1931–35	Clement Attlee
1935–45	Arthur Greenwood
1945–56	Herbert Morrison
1956–59	James Griffiths
1959–60	Aneurin Bevan
1960–70	George Brown
1970–72	Roy Jenkins
1972–76	Edward Short
1976–80	Michael Foot
1980–83	Denis Healey
1983–92	Roy Hattersley
1992–94	Margaret Beckett
1994–	John Prescott

Elections to the Labour Party Leadership

Labour Party leader

Until 1981 the Parliamentary Party had the right to elect the leader and deputy leader annually while the party was in Opposition, although elections were contested on only eight occasions.

21 November 1922

James Ramsay MacDonald	61
Joseph Clynes	56

3 December 1935

	1st ballot	2nd ballot
Clement Attlee	58	88
Herbert Morrison	44	48
Arthur Greenwood	33	–

14 December 1955

Hugh Gaitskell	166
Aneurin Bevan	70

3 November 1960

Hugh Gaitskell	157
Harold Wilson	81

2 November 1961

Hugh Gaitskell	171
Anthony Greenwood	59

14 February 1963

	1st ballot	2nd ballot
Harold Wilson	115	144
George Brown	88	103
James Callaghan	41	–

5 April 1976

	1st ballot	2nd ballot	3rd ballot
James Callaghan	84	141	176
Michael Foot	90	133	137
Roy Jenkins	56	–	–
Tony Benn	37	–	–
Denis Healey	30	38	–
Anthony Crosland	17	–	–

3 November 1980

	1st ballot	2nd ballot
Michael Foot	83	139
Denis Healey	112	129
John Silkin	38	–
Peter Shore	32	–

Voting procedure for the leader and deputy leader was changed at the 1981 party conference. Election was no longer confined to members of the Parliamentary Party but was extended to the constituency parties and the trade unions, with MPs having 30% of the vote, the constituencies 30% and the trade unions 40%. In the tables that follow the results are given in percentages. PLP = Parliamentary Labour Party (MPs), CLP = constituency Labour parties, TU = Trade unions.

2 October 1983

	PLP	CLP	TU	Total
Neil Kinnock	14.778	27.452	29.042	71.272
Roy Hattersley	7.883	0.577	10.878	19.288
Eric Heffer	4.286	1.971	0.046	6.303
Peter Shore	3.103	0.000	0.033	3.137

2 October 1988

	PLP	CLP	TU	Total
Neil Kinnock	24.842	24.128	39.660	88.630
Tony Benn	5.158	5.872	0.340	11.370

18 July 1992

	PLP	CLP	TU	Total
John Smith	23.187	20.311	39.518	91.016
Bryan Gould	6.813	0.689	1.482	8.984

Voting procedures for the leader and deputy leader were altered once more at the 1993 party conference with the introduction of one member one vote (OMOV) under which trade unions and constituency Labour parties were required to ballot members individually, with the resulting votes then being allocated proportionately. In addition, the weights of votes in the electoral college were changed to one-third to each of the Parliamentary Labour Party, constituency Labour parties and the trade unions.

21 July 1994

	PLP	CLP	TU	Total
Tony Blair	60.5	58.2	52.3	57.0
John Prescott	19.6	24.4	28.4	24.1
Margaret Beckett	19.9	17.4	19.3	18.9

Labour Party deputy leader

11 November 1952

Herbert Morrison	194
Aneurin Bevan	82

29 October 1953

Herbert Morrison	181
Aneurin Bevan	76

2 February 1956

James Griffiths	141
Aneurin Bevin	111
Herbert Morrison	40

10 November 1960

	1st ballot	2nd ballot
George Brown	118	146
Frederick Lee	73	83
James Callaghan	55	–

12 November 1961

George Brown	169
Barbara Castle	56

8 November 1962

George Brown	133
Harold Wilson	103

8 July 1970

Roy Jenkins	133
Michael Foot	67
Frederick Peart	48

17 November 1971

	1st ballot	2nd ballot
Roy Jenkins	140	140
Michael Foot	96	126
Tony Benn	46	–

25 April 1972

	1st ballot	2nd ballot
Edward Short	111	145
Michael Foot	89	116
Anthony Crosland	61	–

21 October 1976

Michael Foot	166
Shirley Williams	128

1 September 1981

1st ballot	PLP	CLP	TU	Total
Denis Healey	45.369	5.367	24.696	45.369
Tony Benn	36.627	23.483	6.410	36.627
John Silkin	18.004	1.150	8.894	18.004

2nd ballot	PLP	CLP	TU	Total
Denis Healey	19.759	5.673	24.994	50.426
Tony Benn	10.421	24.327	15.006	49.574

2 October 1983

	PLP	CLP	TU	Total
Roy Hattersley	16.716	15.313	35.237	67.266
Michael Meacher	8.806	14.350	4.730	27.886
D. Davies	3.284	0.241	0.000	3.525
Gwynneth Dunwoody	1.194	0.096	0.003	1.323

2 October 1988

	PLP	CLP	TU	Total
Roy Hattersley	17.376	18.109	31.339	66.823
John Prescott	7.195	7.845	8.654	23.694
Eric Heffer	5.430	4.046	0.007	9.483

18 July 1992

	PLP	CLP	TU	Total
Margaret Beckett	12.871	19.038	25.394	57.303
John Prescott	9.406	7.096	11.627	28.129
Bryan Gould	7.723	3.866	2.979	14.568

21 July 1994

	PLP	CLP	TU	Total
John Prescott	53.7	59.4	55.6	56.5
Margaret Beckett	46.3	40.6	43.4	43.5

Labour Party General Secretary

Until 1959 the post was known as Secretary.

1906–12	J.R. MacDonald
1912–35	A. Henderson
1935–44	J. Middleton
1944–62	M. Phillips
1962–68	A. Williams
1968–72	H. Nicholas
1972–82	R. Hayward
1982–85	J. Mortimer
1985–94	L. Whitty
1994–98	T. Sawyer
1998–	M. McDonagh

Parliamentary Labour Party (PLP) Chairman

The PLP did not elect its own chairman until 1970. When Labour was in Opposition the party leader normally chaired PLP meetings. When Labour was in government the PLP elected a committee (under various names) to liaise with ministers.

Parliamentary Executive Committee, 1924

R. Smillie	1924

Consultative Committee, 1929–31

H. Snell	1929–30
J. Barr	1930–31

Administrative Committee, 1940–45

H. Lees-Smith	1940–42
H. Pethick-Lawrence	1942
A. Greenwood	1942–45

Liaison Committee, 1945–51

N. Maclean	1945–46
M. Webb	1946–50
W. Glenvill Hall	1950–51

Liaison Committee, 1964–70

E. Shinwell	1964–67
D. Houghton	1967–70

Parliamentary Labour Party, 1970–

D. Houghton	1970–74
I. Mikardo	1974
C. Hughes	1974–79
F. Willey	1979–81
J. Diamond	1981–88
S. Orme	1988–92
D. Hoyle	1992–97
C. Soley	1997–

Party Membership

Year	Individual members (thousands)[a]	Affiliated TU members (thousands)	Co-operative & Socialist Societies (thousands)	Total members (thousands)[b]
1900	—	353	23	376
1901	—	455	14	469
1902	—	847	14	861
1903	—	956	14	970
1904	—	855	15	900
1905	—	904	17	921
1906	—	975	21	998
1907	—	1,050	22	1,072
1908	—	1,127	27	1,159
1909	—	1,451	31	1,486
1910	—	1,394	31	1,431
1911	—	1,502	31	1,539

Year	Individual members (thousands)[a]	Affiliated TU members (thousands)	Co-operative & Socialist Societies (thousands)	Total members (thousands)[b]
1912	—	1,858	31	1,895
1913	—	[c]	33	[c]
1914	—	1,572	33	1,612
1915	—	2,054	33	2,093
1916	—	2,171	42	2,220
1917	—	2,415	47	2,465
1918	—	2,960	53	3,013
1919	—	3,464	47	3,511
1920	—	4,318	42	4,360
1921	—	3,974	37	4,010
1922	—	3,279	32	3,311
1923	—	3,120	36	3,156
1924	—	3,158	36	3,194
1925	—	3,338	36	3,374
1926	—	3,352	36	3,388
1927	—	3,239	55	3,294
1928	215	2,025	52	2,292
1929	228	2,044	59	2,331
1930	277	2,011	58	2,347
1931	297	2,024	37	2,358
1932	372	1,960	40	2,372
1933	366	1,899	40	2,305
1934	381	1,858	40	2,278
1935	419	1,913	45	2,378
1936	431	1,969	45	2,444
1937	447	2,037	43	2,528
1938	429	2,158	43	2,630
1939	409	2,214	40	2,663
1940	304	2,227	40	2,571
1941	227	2,231	28	2,485
1942	219	2,206	29	2,454
1943	236	2,237	30	2,503
1944	266	2,375	32	2,673
1945	487	2,510	41	3,039
1946	645	2,635	42	3,322
1947	608	4,386	46	5,040

Year	Individual members (thousands)[a]	Affiliated TU members (thousands)	Co-operative & Socialist Societies (thousands)	Total members (thousands)[b]
1948	629	4,751	42	5,422
1949	730	4,946	41	5,717
1950	908	4,972	40	5,920
1951	876	4,937	35	5,849
1952	1,015	5,072	21	6,108
1953	1,005	5,057	34	6,096
1954	934	5,530	35	6,498
1955	843	5,606	35	6,484
1956	845	5,658	34	6,537
1957	913	5,644	26	6,583
1958	889	5,628	26	6,542
1959	848	5,564	25	6,437
1960	790	5,513	25	6,328
1961	751	5,550	25	6,326
1962	767	5,503	25	6,296
1963	830	5,507	21	6,358
1964	830	5,502	21	6,353
1965	817	5,602	21	6,440
1966	776	5,539	21	6,336
1967	734	5,540	21	6,295
1968	701	5,364	21	6,087
1969	681	5,462	22	6,164
1970	680	5,519	24	6,183
1971	700	5,559	25	6,310
1972	703	5,425	40	6,197
1973	665	5,365	42	6,073
1974	692	5,787	39	6,406
1975	675	5,750	44	6,392
1976	659	5,800	48	6,499
1977	660	5,913	43	6,754
1978	676	6,260	55	6,990
1979	666	6,511	58	7,236
1980	348	6,407	56	6,811
1981	277	6,273	58	6,608
1982	274	6,185	57	6,516
1983	295	6,101	59	6,456

Year	Individual members (thousands)[a]	Affiliated TU members (thousands)	Co-operative & Socialist Societies (thousands)	Total members (thousands)[b]
1984	323	5,844	60	6,227
1985	313	5,827	60	6,200
1986	297	5,778	58	6,133
1987	289	5,564	55	5,908
1988	266	5,481	56	5,804
1989	294	5,335	53	5,682
1990	311	4,922	54	5,287
1991	261	4,811	54	5,126
1992	280	4,634	51	4,965

[a] There was no individual membership until 1918 and no count of individual members was made until 1928.

[b] The Co-operative Societies affiliated to the LRC in 1900 and the Co-operative Party (formed in 1917) to the Labour Party in 1926. Among Socialist Societies which are, or have been, affiliated are the Fabian Society, the SDF (disaffiliated 1901), the ILP (disaffiliated 1932), the Royal Arsenal Co-operative Society, the Socialist Medical Association, the Socialist Education Association, Poale Zion, the Society of Labour Lawyers, the National Organisation of Labour Students, and the Association of Labour Social Workers.

[c] The Osborne judgment prevented the compilation of membership figures.

(*Source*: Based on tables in H. Tracey (ed.), *The British Labour Party*, London, 1948; D.E. Butler and G. Butler, *British Political Facts, 1900–94*, Macmillan, London, 1994)

Party Organisation – Chronology of Main Events

1900   Labour Representation Committee (LRC) formed by trade unions and socialist societies.

1901   Social Democratic Federation (SDF) disaffiliates from the Labour Representation Committee (LRC).

1903   LRC annual conference votes to levy one penny a year from each member of affiliated organisations and to pay a maximum £200 a year maintenance to MPs.

1906   In February, the LRC is formally renamed the Labour Party.

1907   Party conference votes by 642,000 to 252,000 that its decisions are binding on Labour MPs but that 'the time and method of giving effect to those instructions be left to the party in the House, in conjunction with the National Executive'.

1914   J.R. Clynes declares at the party conference that: 'The conference – and no-one else – has the right to judge and decide what the Parliamentary and electoral activity should be.'

1918   Labour's new Constitution transforms the party from a loose federation of affiliated organisations to a national party with individual members in local constituency parties subject to central discipline. The party conference is to comprise delegates from national affiliated organisations and delegates from constituency parties in proportion to their affiliated membership. The National Executive is increased to 23 members, with 14 representing the trade unions and affiliated organisations, five the constituencies and four women. All National Executive posts are to be elected by the entire conference, confirming the influence of the trade unions. In February, the object of the party is declared to be 'to give effect as far as may be practicable to the principles from time to time approved by the Party Conference'.

1924   In October, the Labour Party conference bans Communists from membership and from adoption as candidates.

1925   In October, the Labour Party conference reaffirms ban on Communists from individual membership and requests trade unions not to allow Communists as delegates to national or local party conferences.

1926   Local Co-operative Parties become eligible for affiliation to divisional Labour Parties.

1928   In October, the Labour Party conference bans Communist Party members from attending the conference as trade union delegates. MacDonald declares to the conference that: 'As long as I hold any position in the Parliamentary Party – and I know I can speak for my colleagues – we are not going to take our instructions from any outside body unless we agree with them.'

1931   The October Labour Party conference votes against allowing Independent Labour Party (ILP) MPs to act as a separate party in the House of Commons and revises the Constitution not to allow the selection as a candidate anyone 'who does not undertake to accept and act in harmony with the Standing Orders of the Parliamentary Party'.

1932   In July the ILP votes to sever links with the Labour Party. The October Labour Party conference votes to disaffiliate the ILP.

1933   National Executive report *Labour and Government* sets out 15 guidelines on the conduct of a future Labour administration and declares that the 'policy to be pursued by the Labour government would be that laid down in Resolutions of the Annual Conference and embodied in the General Election Manifesto'. The King's Speech was to 'announce the instalments of the Party's policy with which the government proposed to deal'.

1937   The October party conference increases the number of constituency party representatives on the National Executive from five to seven and allows constituency parties the right to an exclusive vote for their representatives, removing the trade unions' direct participation in selection.

1946   In June, the Labour Party conference revises rules to prevent Communist Party requests for affiliation; agreement made to provide for the nomination of Co-operative and Labour Party candidates at elections.

1960   First ever challenge to incumbent party leader mounted by Wilson; he is defeated by Gaitskell by 166 votes to 81 in November. The number of Co-operative and Labour candidates standing at elections is limited to 30.

1973   Labour Party ends the 'proscribed list' of outside organisations which party members are barred from joining.

1979   The October party conference supports resolution for mandatory reselection of MPs during the lifetime of a Parliament and for placing control over the contents of the election manifesto in the hands of the National Executive.

1980   In September, the party conference votes for new leadership election procedure to be drawn up and reaffirms mandatory reselection of MPs.

1981   In January, a special party conference agrees on an electoral college to select leader and deputy leader; trade unions to have 40% of the votes, constituency parties 30% and MPs 30%. New electoral college procedure is used for first time in September in election for deputy leadership in which Healey narrowly defeats Benn.

1983   In October, the electoral college procedure is used for first time for leadership and deputy leadership elections in which Kinnock becomes leader and Hattersley deputy leader.

1992   The October Labour Party conference reduces trade unions' share of the vote at conference from 87% to 70% but retains trade union participation in the election of the party leadership and selection of candidates; increases constituency party share to almost 30%.

1993   In February, Labour leader Smith makes proposal to reduce the union share of the vote in party leadership elections and candidate selection in constituencies. One member one vote (OMOV) agreed by the party conference. Trade union and constituency party sections of electoral college must ballot members individually for party leadership and deputy leadership elections and allocate votes proportionally; in September, the electoral college voting weight is reproportioned to one-third each to MPs, trade unions and constituency parties.

1994   In July, Blair wins party leadership election against Prescott and Beckett with 57% of the vote in first contest conducted with OMOV; Prescott defeats Beckett for deputy leadership with 56.5% of the vote. The October Labour Party conference rejects Blair's proposal to revise Clause Four of the party Constitution by 50.9% to 49.1%; in December, the party National Executive votes by 20–4 to revise Clause Four.

1995   In April, a special Labour Party conference (with constituency parties having 30% of the vote and trade unions 70%) accepts the revised Clause Four by 65.23% to 34.77%. The October annual conference accepts reduction of trade union block vote at conference from 70% to 50%, making it equal with constituency parties from 1996.

1997   In September, the Labour Party annual conference adopts *Partnership into Power* programme with fundamental changes in the composition of the National Executive and the methods of its election and accepts the establishment of a National Policy Forum for a 'rolling programme' of policy formulation.

Major Party Conferences

This section sets out the most significant of the annual conferences held by the Labour Representation Committee from 1900 to 1905 and the Labour Party from 1906 to 1997 with brief notes on events and decisions.

Labour Representation Committee

27–28 Feb. 1900, London
Labour Representation Committee (LRC) formed at Memorial Hall by delegates from trade unions, the Independent Labour Party (ILP), the Fabian Society and the Social Democratic Federation (SDF).

19–21 Feb. 1903, Newcastle upon Tyne
Agrees on annual voluntary levy of one penny from members of affiliated societies; MPs elected with LRC support to be provided with a maximum of £200 a year maintenance; 70 trade unions already agree to do this.

Labour Party

15–17 Feb. 1906, London
Labour Representation Committee formally renamed the Labour Party.

24–26 Jan. 1907, Belfast
Attempts to define relations between the party and its parliamentary representatives. Votes by 642,000 to 252,000 that 'resolutions instructing the Parliamentary Party as to their action in the House of Commons be taken as the opinions of the Conference, on the understanding that the time and method of giving effect to those instructions be left to the Party in the House, in conjunction with the National Executive'.

20–22 Jan. 1908, Hull
Party conference votes by 514,000 to 469,000 that the party should have as its object 'the socialisation of the means of production, distribution

and exchange to be controlled by a democratic State in the interests of the entire community . . .'.

24–26 Jan. 1912, Birmingham
Approves by 1,323,000 votes to 155,000 a proposal from the Second International that each national party should 'investigate and report on whether and how far a stoppage of work, either partial or general, in countries about to engage in war would be effective in preventing hostilities'. Opposes any franchise reform that continues the exclusion of women.

29–31 Jan. 1913, London
After being requested to do so at the last two conferences, the Parliamentary party gives a formal report of its activities over the past year, instituting what becomes a regular practice.

27–30 Jan. 1914, Glasgow
J.R. Clynes declares that: 'The conference – and no one else – has the right to judge and decide what the Parliamentary and electoral policy should be.'

26–28 Jan. 1916, Bristol
Endorses, after some opposition within the National Executive and Parliamentary Party, the acceptance by Henderson and two colleagues in May 1915 of posts in the Coalition government by 1,622,000 votes to 495,000. Opposes the introduction of conscription by 1,716,000 votes to 360,000.

23–26 Jan. 1917, Manchester
Endorses decision to join the Lloyd George Coalition government by 1,849,000 votes to 307,000. Rejects ILP proposal to attend International Socialist Congress in Stockholm to discuss war aims. Agrees to revise procedures for elections to the National Executive by abolishing sectional voting and makes all positions subject to election by the whole conference, strengthening the position of the trade unions.

10 Aug. 1917, London
Special party conference agrees Labour should send a delegation to the International Socialist Conference in Stockholm by 1,846,000 votes to 550,000; Henderson resigns from the Coalition government that evening.

23–25 Jan. 1918, Manchester
Adopts without debate resolution proposing abolition of the House of Lords and opposition to any form of second chamber. Discusses new

Constitution which is adopted at a special conference in February. Individual membership and local constituency parties are established; trade unions and socialist societies are affiliated at local and national level; annual party conference to comprise delegates from national affiliated organisations and from local constituency parties with strength in proportion to affiliated membership; membership of the new National Executive (all members of which are to be elected by the conference) is increased to 23, with 13 allocated to the unions, five to constituency parties and four to women; object of the party is 'to give effect as far as may be practicable to the principles from time to time approved by the Party Conference'.

26–28 June 1918, London
Adopts *Labour and the New Social Order* as the party programme, committing Labour to socialism with a new social order based on the 'socialisation of industry' and planned production and distribution 'for the benefit of all who participate by hand or brain'.

25–27 June 1919, Southport
Votes by 1,893,000 to 935,000 in favour of 'direct action' to end military intervention in Russia.

22–25 June 1920, Scarborough
Votes to establish a commission into the activities of the Black and Tans and Auxiliaries in Ireland. Demands an end to armed intervention in Russia, the ending of the blockade and an encouragement of trade but rejects a call from the British Socialist Party for a general strike to end participation in 'open and covert' attacks. Clynes declares that there could be 'no authority exercised over the Parliamentary Party by an outside body' following the rejection of an attempt to refer back the Parliamentary report on the grounds that Labour MPs' attendance in the Commons had been unsatisfactory.

21–24 June 1921, Brighton
Endorses the rejection of the Communist Party's request for affiliation to Labour by 4,115,000 to 224,000.

26–29 June 1923, London
In his presidential address Sidney Webb speaks of the 'inevitability of gradualness' and forecasts that Labour would win a clear majority 'somewhere about 1926'.

7–10 Oct. 1924, London
Rejects a further Communist request for affiliation to Labour by 3,185,000 votes to 193,000; bans endorsement of Communists as Labour candidates

by 2,456,000 to 654,000, and bans Communists as individual party members by 1,804,000 votes to 1,546,000.

29 Sept.–2 Oct. 1925, Liverpool
Rejects Bevin's motion (which is opposed by MacDonald) that Labour should never take office as a minority. Reaffirms ban on Communists from party membership by 2,870,000 votes to 321,000 and requests trade unions not to allow Communists as delegates at local and national conferences.

1–5 Oct. 1928, Birmingham
Approves *Labour and the Nation* as the new party programme. Bans Communists from attending the conference as trade union delegates. MacDonald sets the relationship between the conference and the party leadership clear by declaring: 'As long as I hold any position in the Parliamentary Party – and I know I can speak for my colleagues also – we are not going to take our instructions from any outside body unless we agree with them.'

6–10 Oct. 1930, Llandudno
Mosley's motion that his proposals to deal with unemployment should be examined by the party's National Executive is narrowly defeated by 1,251,000 votes to 1,046,000.

5–8 Oct. 1931, Scarborough
Moves against allowing Independent Labour Party MPs to act, in effect, as a separate party by adopting a revision to the Constitution forbidding the selection as a candidate of anyone 'who does not undertake to accept and act in harmony with the Standing Orders of the Parliamentary Party'.

3–7 Oct. 1932, Leicester
Adopts without a debate a resolution that 'the leaders of the next Labour Government and the Parliamentary Labour Party be instructed by the National Conference that, on assuming office, either with our without power, definite Socialist legislation must be immediately promulgated, and that Party shall stand or fall in the House of Commons on the principles in which it has faith'. Reaffirms that 'the main objective of the Labour Party is to establish Socialism' and 'the common ownership of the means of production and distribution is the only means by which the producers by hand and brain will be able to secure the full fruits of their industry'. Accepts Bevin's motion that 'the claim of organised labour [is] that it shall have its place in the control and direction of publicly owned industries'.

2–6 Oct. 1933, Hastings

Accepts a resolution from Cripps that a future Labour government should immediately introduce socialism and that the Parliamentary Labour Party should not form a minority government without prior consultation with the National Joint Council. Adopts *Labour and Government* which provides for Parliamentary Labour Party consultation on Cabinet appointments and government adherence to conference decisions when framing legislation. Votes unanimously against rearmament and for action as far as a general strike to prevent war. Rejects a Communist invitation to form a United Front against Fascism.

1–5 Oct. 1934, Southport

Adopts *For Socialism and Peace*, the most radical document ever produced by the party, advocating a full, centrally-directed socialist planning, large-scale nationalisation of main industries and services, including the banks. Adopts *War and Peace*, calling for disarmament and collective security through the League of Nations but rejecting a general strike to prevent war. Gives National Executive powers to discipline party members who work with Communists in the United Front.

30 Sept.–4 Oct. 1935, Brighton

Supports sanctions against Italy following invasion of Abyssinia (Ethiopia) by 2,168,000 votes to 102,000, forcing Lansbury's resignation as leader after Bevin accuses him of 'taking your conscience round from body to body asking to be told what you ought to do with it'.

5–9 Oct. 1936, Edinburgh

Accepts the need for defence forces 'consistent with our country's responsibility as a member of the League of Nations' but rejects a 'purely competitive armament policy' by 1,738,000 votes to 657,000. Endorses the policy on non-intervention in the Spanish Civil War that had broken out in July by 1,836,000 votes to 519,000, provided the policy was effective on both sides. Rejects a renewed Communist request for affiliation by 1,728,000 votes to 592,000 and disbands the Labour League of Youth for supporting United Front activities.

4–8 Oct. 1937, Bournemouth

Adopts *Labour's Immediate Programme*, which forms the basis for the 1945 government's policies; advocates the nationalisation of coal, gas and electricity under public corporations, government control of local industry, and the co-ordination of transport. Rejects the United Front but elects three supporters – Cripps, Laski and Pritt – to the party National Executive. Adopts National Council of Labour report on foreign policy,

International Policy and Defence, supporting rearmament to strengthen Britain's defences but continuing a call for collective security through the League of Nations. Gives greater influence to constituency parties by expanding National Executive constituency section from five to seven, with direct election by the section rather than conference as a whole.

29 May–June 1939, Southport

Rejects participation in the Communist-dominated Popular Front by 2,360,000 votes to 248,000 and upholds the expulsion of Popular Front supporters – Bevan, Cripps and Trevelyan – by 2,100,000 votes to 402,000.

13–16 May 1940, Bournemouth

Approves acceptance of Churchill's invitation to join his wartime Coalition government following the invasion of the Low Countries by 2,450,000 votes to 120,000.

25–28 May 1942, London

Narrowly votes by 1,275,000 to 1,209,000 to accept the continuation of the wartime electoral truce. Accepts a resolution on the establishment of a comprehensive social security scheme, family allowances and a free health service.

11–15 Dec. 1944, London

Rejects National Executive report 'Economic Controls, Public Ownership and Full Employment', which opposes immediate nationalisation, in favour of a composite resolution calling for the public ownership of banking, heavy industry, land, fuel and power, and transport (the basis of the party's 1945 general election programme *Let Us Face the Future*).

21–25 May 1945, Blackpool

Refuses to accept the proposal by Attlee, Bevin and Morrison that the wartime Coalition government should remain until Japan is defeated, calls for immediate withdrawal, and adopts *Let Us Face the Future* as the party's programme.

29 Sept.–3 Oct. 1952, Morecambe

Motion calling for the National Executive to draw up a list of the key industries to be taken into public ownership is carried without a vote.

28 Sept.–2 Oct. 1953, Margate

Motion for worker participation in managing nationalised industries is defeated by 4,658,000 votes to 1,488,000 but a motion calling for the closer association of consumers and workers in their management, together with the supervision of private industry, is accepted.

27 Sept.–1 Oct. 1954, Scarborough
In key right–left contest for the post of party treasurer, Gaitskell defeats
Bevan by 4.3 million votes to 2 million. German rearmament is accepted
by 3.2 million votes to 3 million.

1–5 Oct. 1956, Blackpool
Bevan is elected party treasurer by 3 million votes to right-winger Brown's
2.7 million. Gaitskell warns against the use of force by Britain in the
Suez crisis.

30 Sept.–4 Oct. 1957, Brighton
Rejects motion calling for unilateral nuclear disarmament by 5,836,000
votes to 781,000 following Bevan's charge that it is an 'emotional spasm'
and would mean a British foreign secretary going 'naked into the conference chamber'. Adopts *Industry and Society* by 5,309,000 votes to
1,276,000 calling for the renationalisation of steel and road haulage,
taking into public ownership any industry 'found seriously to be failing
the nation', and public acquisition of shares in private industry.

28–29 Nov. 1959, Blackpool
Gaitskell's proposal to revise Clause Four – on the grounds that it would
counter the Conservatives' 'monstrous falsehood that we are a class party
and they are not' – is rejected.

3–7 Oct. 1960, Scarborough
Accepts unilateral nuclear disarmament by 3.3 million votes to 2.9
million, provoking party leader Gaitskell into accusing the resolution's
supporters of being 'pacifists, unilateralists and fellow-travellers' and
declaring that he will 'fight and fight and fight again' to save the party.

2–6 Oct. 1961, Blackpool
Rejects unilateral nuclear disarmament by 4.5 million votes to 1.7
million. Demands increased public ownership by 3.7 million votes to
2.4 million and adopts *Signposts for the Sixties*.

2–5 Oct. 1962, Brighton
Party leader Gaitskell wins backing from the left but loses the support of
his allies by attacking British entry to the European Economic Community as threatening 'the end of a thousand years of history'.

30 Sept.–4 Oct. 1963, Scarborough
In an atmosphere of unparalleled unity as a general election approaches,
party leader Wilson sets out planning and technology as socialism's mod-
ernised image.

27 Sept.–1 Oct. 1965, Blackpool
Supports the government's backing of United States policy in Vietnam by 3.6 million votes to 2.5 million.

3–7 Oct. 1966, Brighton
Supports government incomes policy by 3.8 million votes to 2.5 million votes. Rejects government support for the United States in Vietnam by 3.8 million votes to 2.6 million, provoking party leader Wilson into declaring that the government is not bound by conference decisions.

2–6 Oct. 1967, Scarborough
Calls for dissociation from the policies of the United States in Vietnam. Accepted continued wage restraint and Britain's application for entry into the European Economic Community.

30 Sept.–4 Oct. 1968, Blackpool
Votes by a five to one majority against a statutory incomes policy; Chancellor Jenkins and Employment Secretary Castle declare that the government will not be influenced by the conference decision. Rejects a motion calling for taking into public ownership 300 monopolies, banks, finance houses and insurance companies by 3,282,000 votes to 2,921,000.

29 Sept.–3 Oct. 1969, Brighton
Accepts policy document *Agenda for a Generation* providing for an extension of public ownership, the establishment of a National Investment Board and a wealth tax. Castle promises government will introduce legislation on equal pay for women.

1–5 Oct. 1973, Blackpool
Rejects a motion for the nationalisation of 250 major monopolies, land, banks, finance houses, insurance companies and building societies under workers' control. Votes to continue boycott of European Economic Community institutions until membership has been confirmed by a referendum or general election. Adopts radical party document *Labour's Programme, 1973* calling for 'a fundamental and irreversible shift in the balance of power and wealth in favour of working people'.

26 Apr. 1975, London
Special conference on Britain's membership of the European Economic Community (EEC) votes two to one for withdrawal after government White Paper has recommended remaining a member.

27 Sept.–1 Oct. 1976, Blackpool
Votes for the future nationalisation of the seven major insurance companies, four clearing banks and one merchant bank by 3,314,000 votes to 526,000.

3–7 Oct. 1977, Brighton
Votes to support Labour government's economic policy. Resolves that a future Labour government will abolish the House of Lords.

2–6 Oct. 1978, Blackpool
Votes against Labour government's 5% wage increase guidelines, foreshadowing the future 'Winter of Discontent'.

1–5 Oct. 1979, Brighton
Accepts policy of mandatory reselection of sitting MPs in each Parliament and the principle of establishing an electoral college to elect party leadership rather than leaving the decision in the hands of the Parliamentary Labour Party. Supports National Executive having the final decision on the wording of the party manifesto. Sets up a Committee of Enquiry into party organisation.

29 Sept.–3 Oct. 1980, Blackpool
Adopts the policy document *Peace, Jobs and Freedom* in an attempt to reconcile growing differences between the left and right of the party. Agrees by 3,909,000 votes to 3,511,000 on a new procedure for the election of the party leadership but fails to agree on the shape of an electoral college. Rejects by 3,625,000 votes to 3,508,000 a National Executive amendment that it should decide on the manifesto before each general election.

24 Jan. 1981, London
Special conference at Wembley accepts by 5,252,000 votes to 1,868,000 the establishment of an electoral college to elect party leader and deputy made up of 40% trade union delegates, 30% constituency party delegates and 30% MPs, provoking the setting up of the Council for Social Democracy which leads to the formation of the Social Democratic Party (SDP).

27 Sept.–2 Oct. 1981, Brighton
Votes overwhelmingly for a policy of unilateral nuclear disarmament. Refers back a proposal for a future Labour government to nationalise banking and insurance.

3–8 Oct. 1983, Brighton
Reaffirms unilateral nuclear disarmament as the party's policy.

29 Sept.–4 Oct. 1985, Bournemouth
Party leader Kinnock wins widespread support for his bitter attack on Militant actions on Liverpool City Council.

27 Sept.–2 Oct. 1987, Brighton
Accepts the leadership proposal to set up a total policy review following Labour's third successive general election defeat.

1–6 Oct. 1989, Brighton
Formally abandon the party's support for unilateral nuclear disarmament.

29 Sept.–4 Oct. 1991, Blackpool
Defeats leadership by calling with a two-thirds majority for defence spending to be reduced by a future Labour government to the average levels of other West European states; rejects the abandonment of the Trident nuclear submarine programme.

6–9 Oct. 1992, Brighton
Votes by 4,420,000 to 103,000 to reduce the trade union share of the vote at party conferences from 87% to 70% and to increase the constituency parties share to almost 30%; retains trade union participation in leadership election and selection of candidates by 3,193,000 votes to 2,118,000. Rejects the abandonment of Trident nuclear submarine programme by 2,484,000 votes to 2,699,999.

26 Sept.–1 Oct. 1993, Brighton
Accepts one member one vote (OMOV); leader and deputy leader to be elected in future by an electoral college made up of one-third constituency party delegates, one-third MPs and MEPs, and one-third trade union delegates, voting as individuals and not as a block; selection of parliamentary candidates to be by all constituency party members and trade unionists who pay a nominal sum to join the party.

2–7 Oct. 1994, Blackpool
Rejects party leader Blair's proposal to review Clause Four and replace it with 'a clear, up-to-date statement of the objects and objectives of the party' by reaffirming a 1993 party conference decision to confirm Labour's commitment to the original Clause Four by 50.9% to 49.1%.

29 April 1995, London
Special conference accepts a rewording of Clause Four by 65.23% to 34.77%; constituency parties (with 30% of the total vote) vote 90% for the change while the trade unions (with 70%) vote 54.6% in favour.

2–6 Oct. 1995, Brighton
Supports the appointment by a future Labour government of a Low Pay Commission to recommend a national minimum wage. Rejects an attempt to restore the main provisions of the old Clause Four by 88.7% to 11.3%. Supports moves to reduce the trade union block vote at the party conference from 70% to 50%, providing equal weight with constituency parties, in 1996.

10 Sept.–1 Oct. 1996, Blackpool
Approves the general election manifesto, *New Labour, New Life for Britain*, with five pledges for early fulfilment. Blair says a future Labour government will institute 'an age of achievement'.

Sept. 1997, Brighton
Adopts *Partnership into Power* programme to reform party decision-making processes; accepts wide-ranging changes in the National Executive and methods of election; accepts the establishment of a National Policy Forum for policy formulation. Accepts appeal from deputy prime minister Prescott not to demand renationalisation of the railways.

3   Labour and the Electorate

General Elections, 1900–97

1900
Date: 1–24 Oct.
Total electorate: 6,730,935
Votes cast: 3,523,482 (75.1%)

	Votes	% of vote	No. of candidates	Seats won
Conservative	1,767,958	50.3	579	402
Liberal	1,572,323	45.0	402	184
Irish Nationalist	91,055	2.6	101	82
Labour	62,698	1.3	15	2
Others	29,448	0.8	15	1

1906
Date: 12 Jan.–8 Feb.
Total electorate: 7,694,741
Votes cast: 5,626,091 (83.2%)

	Votes	% of vote	No. of candidates	Seats won
Liberal	2,751,057	49.4	539	400
Conservative	2,422,071	43.4	574	157
Labour	329,748	5.9	51	30
Irish Nationalist	35,031	0.7	87	83
Others	96,269	1.7	45	4

1910

Date: 15 Jan.–10 Feb.
Total electorate: 7,694,741
Votes cast: 6,667,400 (86.8%)

	Votes	% of vote	No. of candidates	Seats won
Liberal	2,866,157	43.5	600	273
Conservative	3,104,407	46.8	516	275
Labour	505,657	7.6	78	40
Irish Nationalist	91,055	2.6	104	82
Others	29,448	0.8	15	1

1910

Date: 3–19 Dec.
Total electorate: 7,709,981
Votes cast: 5,235,238 (81.6%)

	Votes	% of vote	No. of candidates	Seats won
Liberal	2,293,869	44.2	467	272
Conservative	2,420,169	46.6	548	271
Labour	371,802	6.4	56	42
Irish Nationalist	131,720	2.5	106	84
Others	17,678	0.3	14	1

1918

Date: 14 Dec.
Total electorate: 21,392,322
Votes cast: 10,786,818 (57.2%)

	Votes	% of vote	No. of candidates	Seats won
Coalition				
Conservative	3,472,738	32.5	362	332
Liberal	1,396,590	12.6	145	127
Labour	161,521	1.5	18	10
Others	166,108	1.6	19	10
Non-Coalition				
Labour	2,245,777	20.8	361	57
Liberal	1,388,784	13.0	276	36
Conservative	671,454	6.2	83	50
Sinn Fein	497,107	4.6	102	73
Irish Nationalist	238,197	2.2	60	7
Co-operative	57,785	0.6	10	1
Others	598,316	5.5	200	10

1922

Date: 15 Nov.
Total electorate: 20,874,456
Votes cast: 14,392,330 (73.0%)

	Votes	% of vote	No. of candidates	Seats won
Conservative	5,502,298	38.5	482	344
Labour	4,237,349	29.7	414	142
Liberal	2,668,143	18.9	334	62
National Liberal	1,471,317	9.9	151	53
Irish Nationalist	102,667	0.4	4	3
Communist	33,637	0.2	5	1
Others	376,919	2.4	51	10

1923

Date: 6 Dec.
Total electorate: 21,283,061
Votes cast: 14,547,695 (71.1%)

	Votes	% of vote	No. of candidates	Seats won
Conservative	5,514,541	38.0	536	258
Labour	4,439,780	30.7	427	191
Liberal	4,301,481	29.7	457	158
National	97,993	0.4	4	3
Communist	39,448	0.2	4	0
Others	154,452	1.0	18	5

1924

Date: 29 Oct.
Total electorate: 21,730,988
Votes cast: 16,640,279 (77.0%)

	Votes	% of vote	No. of candidates	Seats won
Conservative	7,854,523	46.8	534	412
Labour	5,489,087	33.3	514	151
Liberal	2,928,737	17.8	339	40
Constitutionalist	185,075	1.2	12	7
Communist	55,346	0.3	8	1
Others	127,511	0.6	20	4

1929

Date: 30 May
Total electorate: 28,854,748
Votes cast: 22,648,375 (76.3%)

	Votes	% of vote	No. of candidates	Seats won
Conservative	8,656,225	38.1	590	260
Labour	8,370,417	37.1	569	287
Liberal	5,308,738	23.5	513	59
Communist	50,634	0.2	25	0
Others	262,361	1.1	33	9

1931

Date: 27 Oct.
Total electorate: 29,952,361
Votes cast: 21,656,373 (76.4%)

	Votes	% of vote	No. of candidates	Seats won
National Government				
Conservative	11,905,925	55.0	518	470
Liberal	1,372,595	6.5	111	32
National Liberal	807,302	3.7	41	35
National Labour	341,370	1.5	20	13
National	100,193	0.5	4	4
Non-National Government				
Labour	6,649,630	30.9	516	52
Independent Liberals	103,528	0.5	6	4
Communist	74,824	0.3	26	0
New Party	36,377	0.2	24	0
Others	262,269	0.9	26	5

1935

Date: 14 Nov.
Total electorate: 31,374,449
Votes cast: 21,997,054 (71.1%)

	Votes	% of vote	No. of candidates	Seats won
National Government				
Conservative	10,496,300	47.8	515	387
National Liberal	866,354	3.7	44	33
National Labour	339,811	1.5	20	8
National	53,189	0.3	4	1
Non-National Government				
Labour	8,325,491	38.0	552	154
Liberal	1,443,093	6.7	161	21
ILP	139,577	0.7	17	6
Communist	27,117	0.1	2	1
Others	306,122	1.3	33	6

1945

Date: 5 July
Total electorate: 33,240,391
Votes cast: 25,095,195 (72.8%)

	Votes	% of vote	No. of candidates	Seats won
Labour	11,967,746	48.0	603	393
Conservative	9,101,099	36.2	559	197
Liberal	2,252,430	9.0	306	12
National Liberal	737,732	2.9	49	11
National	133,179	0.5	10	2
Commonwealth	110,634	0.5	23	1
Communist	102,780	0.4	21	2
ILP	46,769	0.2	5	3
Others	642,826	2.3	107	19

1950

Date: 23 Feb.
Total electorate: 34,412,255
Votes cast: 28,771,124 (83.9%)

	Votes	% of vote	No. of candidates	Seats won
Labour	13,266,176	46.1	617	315
Conservative	11,507,061	40.0	564	282
Liberal	2,621,487	9.1	475	9
National Liberal & Conservative	985,343	3.4	55	16
Others	391,055	1.5	157	3

1951

Date: 25 Oct.
Total electorate: 34,919,331
Votes cast: 28,596,594 (82.6%)

	Votes	% of vote	No. of candidates	Seats won
Conservative	12,660,061	44.3	562	302
Labour	13,948,883	48.8	617	295
National Liberal & Conservative	1,058,138	3.7	55	19
Liberal	730,546	2.6	109	6
Others	198,966	0.7	33	3

1955

Date: 26 May
Total electorate: 34,852,179
Votes cast: 26,759,729 (76.8%)

	Votes	% of vote	No. of candidates	Seats won
Conservative	12,468,778	46.6	579	324
Labour	12,405,254	46.4	620	277
National Liberal & Conservative	842,133	3.1	45	21
Liberal	722,402	2.7	110	6
Others	321,182	1.2	55	2

1959

Date: 8 Oct.
Total electorate: 35,397,304
Votes cast: 27,862,652 (78.7%)

	Votes	% of vote	No. of candidates	Seats won
Conservative	12,985,081	46.6	586	345
Labour	12,216,172	43.8	621	258
Liberal	1,640,760	5.9	216	6
National Liberal & Conservative	765,794	2.8	39	20
Plaid Cymru	77,571	0.3	20	0
Others	177,274	0.6	54	1

1964

Date: 15 Oct.
Total electorate: 35,894,054
Votes cast: 27,657,148 (77.1%)

	Votes	% of vote	No. of candidates	Seats won
Labour	12,205,808	44.1	628	317
Conservative	11,676,512	42.2	611	298
Liberal	3,099,283	11.2	365	9
National Liberal & Conservative	326,130	1.2	19	6
Plaid Cymru	69,507	0.2	23	0
Scottish National	69,044	0.2	15	0
Others	215,864	0.9	96	0

1966

Date: 31 Mar.
Total electorate: 35,957,245
Votes cast: 27,264,747 (75.8%)

	Votes	% of vote	No. of candidates	Seats won
Labour	13,096,629	48.0	622	364
Conservative	11,268,676	41.3	620	250
Liberal	2,327,457	8.6	311	12
National Liberal & Conservative	149,779	0.6	9	3
Scottish National	128,474	0.5	23	0
Plaid Cymru	61,071	0.2	20	0
Others	232,661	0.8	102	1

1970

Date: 18 June
Total electorate: 39,342,013
Votes cast: 28,344,798 (72.0%)

	Votes	% of vote	No. of candidates	Seats won
Conservative	13,145,123	46.4	628	330
Labour	12,208,758	43.1	625	288
Liberal	2,117,035	7.5	332	6
Scottish National	306,802	1.1	65	1
Plaid Cymru	175,016	0.6	36	0
Others	392,064	1.4	151	5

1974

Date: 28 Feb.
Total electorate: 39,753,863
Votes cast: 31,340,162 (78.8%)

	Votes	% of vote	No. of candidates	Seats won
Conservative	11,872,180	37.9	623	297
Labour	11,645,616	37.2	623	301
Liberal	6,059,519	19.3	517	14
Scottish National	633,180	2.0	70	7
Plaid Cymru	171,374	0.6	36	2
Others	958,293	3.0	266	14

1974

Date: 10 Oct.
Total electorate: 40,072,970
Votes cast: 29,189,104 (72.8%)

	Votes	% of vote	No. of candidates	Seats won
Labour	11,457,079	39.2	623	319
Conservative	10,462,565	35.8	622	277
Liberal	5,346,704	18.3	619	13
Scottish National	839,617	2.9	71	11
Plaid Cymru	166,321	0.6	36	3
Others	916,818	3.2	281	12

1979

Date: 3 May
Total electorate: 41,095,649
Votes cast: 31,221,362 (76.0%)

	Votes	% of vote	No. of candidates	Seats won
Conservative	13,697,923	43.9	622	339
Labour	11,532,218	36.9	623	269
Liberal	4,313,804	13.8	577	11
Scottish National	504,259	1.6	71	2
Plaid Cymru	132,544	0.4	36	2
Others	1,040,614	3.4	647	12

1983

Date: 9 June
Total electorate: 42,192,999
Votes cast: 30,671,137 (72.7%)

	Votes	% of vote	No. of candidates	Seats won
Conservative	13,012,316	42.4	633	397
Labour	8,456,934	27.6	633	209
Liberal	4,210,115	13.7	322	17
Social Democrat	3,570,834	11.7	311	6
Scottish National	331,975	1.1	72	2
Plaid Cymru	125,309	0.4	38	2
Others	963,654	3.1	569	17

1987

Date: 11 June
Total electorate: 43,180,753
Votes cast: 32,529,578 (75.3%)

	Votes	% of vote	No. of candidates	Seats won
Conservative	13,760,583	42.3	633	376
Labour	10,029,807	30.8	633	229
Liberal	4,173,450	12.8	327	17
Social Democrat	3,168,183	9.7	306	5
Scottish National	416,473	1.3	71	3
Plaid Cymru	123,599	0.4	38	3
Others	857,433	2.7	317	17

1992
Date: 9 Apr.
Total electorate: 43,240,084
Votes cast: 33,610,162 (77.7%)

	Votes	% of vote	No. of candidates	Seats won
Conservative	14,093,890	41.9	645	336
Labour	11,559,857	34.4	634	271
Liberal	5,995,712	17.8	632	20
Scottish National	629,552	1.8	35	3
Plaid Cymru	154,439	0.5	72	4
Others	1,176,692	3.5	366	17

1997
Date: 1 May
Total electorate: 43,784,559
Votes cast: 31,287,702 (71.5%)

	Votes	% of vote	No. of candidates	Seats won
Labour	13,517,911	43.2	639	418
Conservative	9,600,940	30.7	648	165
Liberal Democrats	5,243,440	16.8	639	46
Scottish National	622,260	22.1	72	6
Plaid Cymru	161,030	9.9	40	4
Others	2,142,621	6.8	1,686	20

Lost Deposits at General Elections, 1918–97

Year of election	No. of lost deposits*	No. of Labour candidates	% lost
1918	6	361	1.7
1922	7	414	1.7
1923	17	427	4.0
1924	28	514	5.4
1929	35	569	6.1
1931	21	516	4.1
1935	16	552	2.9
1945	2	603	0.3
1950	0	617	0.0
1951	1	617	0.2
1955	1	620	0.2
1959	1	621	0.2
1964	8	628	1.3
1966	3	622	0.5
1970	6	625	1.0
1974 (Feb.)	25	623	4.0
1974 (Oct.)	13	623	2.1
1979	22	623	3.5
1983	119	633	18.8
1987	0	633	0.0
1992	1	634	0.15
1997	0	639	0.0

* From the 1918 general election until October 1985, a candidate who failed to poll over one-eighth of total votes (excluding spoilt papers) forfeited a £150 deposit. From October 1985 this amount was increased to £500 but the proportion of votes a candidate was required to poll was reduced to one-twentieth (excluding spoilt papers).

European Parliamentary Elections

The first elections to the European Parliament were held in 1974. Before that date, members were nominated.

1979

Date: 7 June
Total electorate: 41,155,166
Votes cast: 13,446,091 (32.7%)

	Votes	% of vote	Seats won
Conservative	6,508,493	48.4	60
Labour	4,253,207	31.6	17
Liberal	1,690,599	12.6	0
Others	993,792	7.4	4

1984

Date: 14 June
Total electorate: 42,493,122
Votes cast: 13,998,190 (32.9%)

	Votes	% of vote	Seats won
Conservative	5,426,821	38.8	45
Labour	4,865,261	34.8	32
Liberal	1,358,145	9.7	0
Social Democratic	1,233,490	8.8	0
Others	1,114,473	7.9	4

1989

Date: 15 June
Total electorate: 42,590,060
Votes cast: 15,353,154 (35.9%)

	Votes	% of vote	Seats won
Labour	6,153,640	40.1	45
Conservative	5,331,077	34.7	32
Green	2,292,705	14.9	0
Liberal Democrat	986,292	6.2	1
Others	638,929	4.3	1

1994
Date: 9 June
Total electorate: 42,293,640
Votes cast: 15,267,550 (36.1%)

	Votes	% of vote	Seats won
Labour	6,753,863	44.2	62
Conservative	4,248,531	27.8	18
Liberal Democrat	2,552,730	16.7	2
Others	1,712,429	11.2	2

Major By-election Gains and Losses

The tables below set out the important Labour's gains and losses at by-elections since its formation, together with notes on the significance of the particular result.

Significant Labour by-election gains

Constituency	Won from	Date
Clitheroe	Liberal	1 Aug. 1902

The new Labour Representation Committee's first by-election victory. In 1903 the party went on to take Woolwich from the Conservatives and Barnard Castle from the Liberals.

Bothwell	Coalition Unionist	16 July 1919

The capture of a seat from the Coalition, the first of three in 1919 (Widness followed in August and Spen Valley in December), signalled Labour's advance in post-war electoral politics.

Dartford	Coalition Liberal	27 Mar. 1920

Inflicted one of the most decisive ever by-election defeats on a Coalition government candidate, turning a 9,370 majority into a 9,048 majority for Labour. The Coalition candidate's 71.5% 1918 general election share of the vote fell to 15.5%, while Labour increased its share from 26.6% to 50.2%.

Constituency	Won from	Date
South Norfolk	Coalition Liberal	20 July 1920

A significant victory, following a number of defeats, which brought
into question the Coalition Liberals' survival. Labour's decision
to contest the seat had come at the last moment. Labour went on
to capture Dudley from a Coalition Unionist and Kirkcaldy from
a Coalition Liberal in March 1921, Heywood and Radcliffe from a
Coalition Liberal in June 1921 and Southwark South East from a
Coalition Liberal in December 1921.

Camberwell North	Coalition Unionist	20 Feb. 1922

This victory for Labour was followed by the capture of Leicester East
from a Coalition Unionist in March 1922 and Pontypridd from a
Coalition Liberal in July.

Mitcham	Conservative	3 Mar. 1923

A sensational success for Labour but a contest in which the
Conservative candidate was also challenged by an Independent
Conservative.

Liverpool Edge Hill	Conservative	6 Mar. 1923

This by-election victory gave Labour its first seat in Liverpool but it
was captured on a low turn-out (70.5% down to 58.1%) and with the
benefit of Conservative abstentions.

Liverpool West Toxteth	Conservative	22 May 1924

One of the rare occasions on which a government candidate took an
Opposition seat at a by-election.

Hammersmith North	Conservative	28 May 1926

This victory came in a strongly working-class area of London two
weeks after the General Strike.

Northampton	Conservative	9 Jan. 1928

The capture of Northampton began a run of Labour victories over
the Conservatives as the 1929 general election approached. In April
Labour took Linlithgow, Ashton-under-Lyme in October, North
Midlothian in January 1929 and North Lanark in March 1929.

Constituency	Won from	Date
Wakefield	Conservative	21 Apr. 1932

The first of a series of by-election victories by a Labour Party that had been shattered by the formation of the National Government in 1931 and badly mauled at the October 1931 general election. Labour went on to take Wednesbury from the Conservatives in July and Rotherham in February 1933.

Fulham East	Conservative	25 Oct. 1933

A Labour candidate standing on a pacifist platform transformed a Conservative 1931 general election majority of 14,521 to a Labour majority of 4,840 to capture a seat never before held by Labour.

Hammersmith North	Conservative	24 Apr. 1934

The recapture of this seat from the Conservatives continued a run leading to the Labour revival at the 1935 general election. In May Labour took West Ham Upton from the Conservatives and in October had by-election victories over the Liberals (Lambeth North) and the Conservatives (Swindon).

Liverpool Wavertree	Conservative	6 Feb. 1935

Labour was assisted in this by-election by the presence of an Independent Conservative candidate who took 23.9% of the vote.

Liverpool West Toxteth	Conservative	16 July 1935

Labour took this seat on an 18.9% swing from the Conservatives in a straight contest. The result provided a further boost to Labour in the run-up to a general election.

Dunbartonshire	Conservative	18 Mar. 1936

This victory represented the beginning of a run of Labour successes over the Conservatives that continued up to the outbreak of the war in 1939. Labour captured Camberwell Peckham in May, Derby in July, Greenock in November, Wandsworth Central in April 1937, Islington North in October, Ipswich in February 1938, Fulham West in April, Lichfield in May, Dartford in November, Southwark North in May 1939. Also in May 1939 Labour captured Lambeth Kennington on an 11.2% swing from the Conservatives, the highest achieved by Labour since the 1935 general election. Brecnor and Radnor fell to Labour in August 1939.

Constituency	Won from	Date
Lewisham North	Conservative	14 Feb. 1957

The first Labour by-election gain from the Conservative Party for 17 years. Labour captured Carmarthen from the Liberals two weeks later.

South Dorset	Conservative	22 Nov. 1962

Labour's capture of the seat was aided by the intervention of an anti-Common Market candidate. A Conservative majority of 6,693 was turned into a Labour majority of 604.

Bristol South East	Conservative	20 Aug. 1963

Anthony Wedgwood Benn (formerly Viscount Stansgate) was elected without Conservative and Liberal opposition following his renunciation of his peerage.

Birmingham Northfield	Conservative	28 Oct. 1982

Labour's first by-election win from the Conservatives since 1971, the only such gain in the 1979–83 Parliament and, surprisingly, one that came shortly after Britain's victory in the Falklands War.

Fulham	Conservative	4 Apr. 1986

A victory – with a respectable moderate candidate – that encouraged over-confidence about Labour's prospects at a future general election.

Mid-Staffordshire	Conservative	22 Mar. 1990

A Labour by-election success that came in the midst of turmoil over the introduction of the community charge (poll tax) in England and Wales.

Dudley West	Conservative	15 Dec. 1994

Transformed a Conservative 1992 general election majority of 5,789 to a Labour majority of 20,694, increasing Labour confidence in the party's general election prospects. Labour went on to capture Staffordshire South East in April 1996 (transforming a Conservative 1992 general election victory of 7,192 into a Labour majority of 13,762) and Wirral South in February 1997.

Significant Labour by-election losses

Constituency	Lost to	Date
Woolwich East	Coalition Unionist	2 Mar. 1921

This loss by Labour was one of the few occasions on which
a government candidate won a seat from the Opposition at
a by-election. Labour's candidate was Ramsay MacDonald.

Fulham West	Conservative	6 May 1930

An early sign of the Labour government's unpopularity in the face
of rising unemployment. The defeat followed on from the cutting
of Labour's majority in Sheffield Brightside from 10,349 to 2,931
in a by-election in February. Labour went on to lose Shipley to the
Conservatives in February 1931.

Liverpool East Toxteth	Conservative	5 Feb. 1931

The Labour government's increasing unpopularity, combined with
the failure of the Liberals to field a candidate, gave victory to the
Conservatives. This was part of a pattern of Labour by-election losses
to the Conservatives, who went on to take Sunderland on 26 March
and Ashton-under-Lyme on 30 April 1931. These were, however,
Labour's last by-election losses until 1945.

Motherwell	Scottish Nationalist	12 Apr. 1945

Labour's 1935 general election majority of 430 was transformed into
a Scottish Nationalist majority of 617. In a period of wartime electoral
truce, no Conservative candidate stood.

Sunderland South	Conservative	13 May 1953

This loss by Labour was one of the few occasions on which a government
candidate won a seat from the Opposition at a by-election, the first
such victory since 1924.

Brighouse and Spenborough	Conservative	17 Mar. 1960

Another unusual loss of an Opposition seat to the government, at a
time of intense internal Labour division.

Constituency	Lost to	Date
Leyton	Conservative	21 Jan. 1965

Labour's 1964 general election majority of 7,926 was transformed into a Conservative majority of 205. Labour had attempted to find a seat for Foreign Secretary Patrick Gordon Walker who had been defeated at Smethwick in October 1964.

Carmarthen	Plaid Cymru	14 July 1966

Labour's March 1966 general election majority of 9,233 was overturned to produce a Plaid Cymru majority of 2,436. The Plaid Cymru candidate had come third at the general election. This by-election began a run of by-election defeats as the Labour government's unpopularity mounted.

Walthamstow West	Conservative	21 Sept. 1967

Labour's 1966 general election majority of 10,022 was overturned to produce a Conservative majority of 11,656. Labour lost Cambridge to the Conservatives on the same day.

Hamilton	SNP	2 Nov. 1967

Labour's 1966 general election majority of 16,576 was overturned to produce a Scottish National Party (SNP) majority of 1,799. The SNP had not contested the seat since 1959, when the party's candidate forfeited his deposit.

Acton	Conservative	28 Mar. 1968

Labour loss followed unpopular public expenditure cuts introduced in January following devaluation in November 1967. On the same day Labour lost Meriden and Dudley to Conservatives and went on to lose Oldham West and Nelson and Colne in June.

Birmingham Ladywood	Liberal	26 June 1969

Labour's 1966 general election majority of 5,315 was transformed into a Liberal majority of 2,713 in the midst of the turmoil over the government's *In Place of Strife* proposals for trade union reform.

Swindon	Conservative	30 Oct. 1969

Labour's 1966 general election majority of 10,443 became a Conservative majority of 478. The by-election defeat followed the Labour government's abandonment of trade union reform.

Constituency	Lost to	Date
Rochdale	Liberal	26 Oct. 1972

Labour's 1970 general election majority of 5,171 was overturned by
the Liberal Party with a majority of 5,093.

Lincoln	Democratic Labour	1 Mar. 1973

The seat was held by Dick Taverne, who had stood down as Labour
MP because of his objections to what he saw as the party's increasing
move to the left.

Glasgow Govan	SNP	8 Nov. 1973

Labour's 1970 general election majority of 7,142 was overturned to
produce an SNP majority of 571. At the 1970 general election the SNP
had forfeited its deposit.

Walsall North	Conservative	4 Nov. 1976

Labour's October 1974 general election majority of 15,885 was
transformed into a Conservative majority of 4,379. Labour lost
Workington to the Conservatives ten days later.

Birmingham Stechford	Conservative	31 Mar. 1977

Labour's October 1974 general election majority of 11,923 was
transformed into a Conservative majority of 1,949. The by-election
followed the resignation of Roy Jenkins to take up the post of
President of the European Commission.

Ashfield	Conservative	28 Apr. 1977

Labour's October 1974 general election majority of 22,915 in a mining
constituency was transformed into a Conservative majority of 264 as
union dissatisfaction with the 'social contract' intensified.

Liverpool Edge Hill	Conservative	29 Mar. 1979

Labour's October 1974 general election majority of 6,171 was
transformed into a Conservative majority of 8,133 as the Labour
government attempted to survive until an almost inevitable general
election defeat in May.

Constituency	Lost to	Date
Bermondsey	Liberal	24 Feb. 1983

Labour's 1979 general election majority of 19,338 (one of the largest) was transformed into a Liberal majority of 9,319 following inner-party turmoil over the adoption of a gay Marxist as candidate.

Greenwich	SDP	26 Feb. 1987

The local Labour Party's adoption of a candidate described as a 'left-winger' led to a vicious media campaign.

Local Government – Chronology of Main Events

1919   Labour makes large gains in London council elections, particularly from Liberals, and throughout the country, capturing Bradford – birthplace of the Independent Labour Party and the first major city to come under Labour control.

1922   Labour suffers heavy losses in local elections (defending seat won in 1919).

1926   Labour takes Sheffield, gaining control of its second major city.

1930   Labour suffers its first net losses in local elections since 1922.

1931   Labour's serious losses in local elections mirror the party's national decline.

1932   Labour loses its stronghold in Sheffield but makes some small gains in local elections.

1934   Labour takes control of London County Council (LCC) for the first time and retains control until 1949; captures 21 county boroughs and 18 non-county boroughs.

1936   Labour suffers its first serious losses in local elections since 1931.

1939–45   Wartime electoral truce.

1945   Labour makes widespread gains in local elections, reflecting the party's national success.

1946   Labour retains control of the LCC, having held it since 1934.

1947   Labour losses in municipal elections.

1949   Widespread labour losses to the Conservatives in local elections, including the loss of overall control of the LCC.

1952   Labour regains control of the LCC in sweeping local election gains.

1961   Labour suffers heavy losses in borough, county council and LCC elections.

1963   Widespread Labour gains in local elections at the expense of both Conservatives and Liberals. London Government Act, abolishing LCC and establishing Great London Council (GLC) and Inner London Education Authority (ILEA), passed against Labour opposition.

1964   Labour wins control of the new GLC in the first elections to the authority with 54 seats to the Conservatives' 36.

1965   Labour defeats at the hands of the Conservatives in local elections.

1967   Labour loses control of the GLC to the Conservatives in widespread local election losses.

1968   Labour suffers losses to Conservatives and the Scottish National Party in local authority elections.

1970   Labour fails to regain control of the GLC in April but makes large gains in May municipal elections.

1971   Labour gains in local government elections.

1972   Labour continues to make gains in local government elections, winning control of over 50 cities and boroughs in England and Wales.

1973   In the first elections to new local authorities in England and Wales in April Labour wins control of all six new metropolitan authorities and recaptures the GLC. In the first elections for new district councils in May, Labour is the most successful party.

1977   Labour suffers massive defeats in English and Welsh local elections, including the loss of the GLC to the Conservatives.

1980   Labour gains in local elections.

1981   In March, Labour recaptures GLC from Conservatives. In December, House of Lords overturns GLC's cheap public transport fares policy.

1985   In March, the GLC votes to set legal rate, breaking Ken Livingstone's links with left. In June, Militant-controlled Liverpool City Council sets illegal rate and in July left-wing Lambeth Council sets legal rate.

1986   In March, the High Court dismisses appeals by Lambeth and Liverpool councillors against surcharge for failing to set legal rate. Labour-controlled GLC and six metropolitan councils cease to exist in April. In May there are Labour successes against Conservatives in borough and district council elections.

1987   In February, Kinnock warns local authorities that a future Labour government will not be able to restore cuts made by Conservatives. In May there are widespread Labour losses to Conservatives and Alliance in local elections.

1993   Labour makes extensive gains in the county council elections.

1995   Labour makes further advances in local authority elections.

1998   Labour government introduces 'Best value', a new standard in local government services and threatens penalties for councils failing to meet standards. In March, Blair proposes citizen juries to monitor services, local referendums and a reformed committee structure.

4   Labour and its Precursors

Chronology of Main Events

1852   William Newton, founder member of the Amalgamated Society of Engineers, defeated as working-class candidate for Tower Hamlets in general election.

1857   George Jacob Holyoake defeated as working-class candidate in Tower Hamlets.

1867   Reform Act enfranchises bulk of male working class.

1868   Trades Union Congress (TUC) established.

1869   Labour Representation League formed by trades unions and working-class bodies in London to 'organise fully the strength of the operative classes as an electoral power . . . to secure the return to Parliament of qualified men . . .'.

1870   London Trades Council secretary George Odger defeated as Labour Representation League candidate at Southwark by-election.

1874   Two miners' leaders – Thomas Burt (Morpeth) and Alexander Macdonald (Stafford) – elected as Liberal MPs at general election.

1876   TUC Parliamentary Committee establishes Direct Labour Representation Association; members win council seats in Birmingham.

1879   TUC Parliamentary Committee issues first general election manifesto with nine demands, including legislation to provide for workmen's compensation, improvements in the factory inspectorate, electoral law reform and abolition of imprisonment for debt.

1880   Henry Broadhurst (Stoke on Trent) and Joseph Arch (Wilton) elected as working-class Liberal MPs at general election.

1881   Democratic Federation formed (June) by the Marxist H.M. Hyndman with support of Eleanor Marx, William Morris and Harry Quelch. TUC annual conference instructs Parliamentary Committee to encourage working-class candidates to run at local and Parliamentary elections.

1883   Democratic Federation renamed Social Democratic Federation (SDF) and begins publishing journal *Justice*. TUC annual conference rejects motion to set up local and national funds to support working-class MPs; Fabian Society founded.

1884   Socialist League breaks away from SDF; bulk of trade unionists remain with SDF.

1885   TUC general election manifesto includes demand for votes for women. Ten trade unionists elected to Parliament as Liberal MPs.

1886   TUC establishes Labour Electoral Association, organised in nine areas, to which only *bona fide* working-class bodies could affiliate. Four prominent socialists – H.M. Hyndman, H.H. Champion, John Burns and Jack Williams – are charged with sedition following unemployed riot in central London in February. Tom Mann founds Eight-Hours League to encourage co-operation between trade unionists and socialists.

1887   Keir Hardie sets out in the *Miner* a programme for a new party, including an eight-hour day, state unemployment insurance and nationalisation of the coal industry. In November, the police break up Trafalgar Square unemployed demonstration in events which become known as 'Bloody Sunday'.

1888   Bradford conference to discuss formation of an independent Labour Party; delegates include Keir Hardie, Tom Mann and John Hodge. Hardie defeated as Labour candidate at Mid-Lanark by-election in April. In May, Scottish Labour Party founded in Glasgow with Hardie as secretary and Liberal MP R. Cunninghame Graham as president.

1889   In August, the London strike for the 'dockers' tanner' signals rise of the New Unionism.

1891   TUC annual conference rejects proposal for setting up a fund to support an independent Labour party. The *Clarion* founded by Robert Blatchford in October.

1892   Three working-class MPs returned at general election in July – Hardie (West Ham South) as Independent Labour, Burns (Battersea) and J. Havelock Wilson (Middlesbrough) as Liberals.

1893   Independent Labour Party (ILP) established as a socialist party at Bradford conference in January; among the 120 delegates are five from the SDF and 12 members of the Fabian Society, although neither organisation joins the ILP. TUC annual conference votes to establish a fund to assist independent Labour candidates in local and Parliamentary elections.

1895   ILP fields 28 candidates at general election, winning 45,000 votes but no seats.

1898   West Ham becomes first British local authority with a majority of working-class councillors.

1899   TUC annual conference votes by 546,000 votes to 434,000 to convene a special congress of 'all the co-operative, socialistic, trade union, and other working-class organisations . . . to devise ways and means of securing the return of an increased number of Labour members to the next Parliament'.

5   Foundation to Government, 1900–23

Chronology of Main Events

1900   (Feb.)   Labour Representation Committee (LRC) formed at two-day conference held at Memorial Hall, London.
(Oct.)   LRC fields 15 candidates at general election, two of whom – Richard Bell and Keir Hardie – are elected. They are joined at later by-elections by David Shackleton (1902), Will Crookes (1903) and Arthur Henderson (1903).

1901   (Aug.)   Social Democratic Federation (SDF) withdraws from the LRC.

1902   LRC National Executive interprets Taff Vale case as a sign of growing hostility to the trade union movement.

1903   (Jan.)   Taff Vale case costs and damages totalling £30,000 encourage trade union affiliation to the LRC. LRC conference agrees on annual voluntary levy of one penny from members of affiliated societies; MPs elected with LRC support to be paid a maximum of £200 a year. Miners' Federation of Great Britain MPs begin co-operation with LRC in the Commons. Gladstone–MacDonald Pact gives LRC candidates a clear run in 30 seats.

1906   (Jan.–Feb.)   LRC fields 50 candidates in general election; 29 elected (including J.R. Clynes, Will Crookes, Keir Hardie, Arthur Henderson, Ramsay MacDonald, Philip Snowden and Will Thorne), mainly at the expense of Conservatives; 23 of the 29 MPs are trade unionists; 22 Lib-Labs also elected.
(Feb.)   LRC renamed the Labour Party.
(Sept.)   Liberal leadership suggests Lib-Lab MPs should form a National Liberal–Labour League and a separate Labour Party within the Liberal Party. Trades Disputes Act overturns Taff Vale judgment.

1907   Labour's Unemployed Workmen's ('Right to Work') Bill, introduced in the Commons by MacDonald with support from some Liberals to establish local and central employment schemes and to guarantee maintenance to the unemployed, is defeated at second reading; Hardie resigns as party chairman and is succeeded by Ramsay MacDonald. Labour, the ILP, BSP and the Fabians agree to Second International resolution on Militarism and International Conflicts to work to prevent the outbreak of war 'by whatever means seem to them most effective'.

1908   Parliamentary strength increases as Mines' Federation of Great Britain affiliates to the Labour Party.

1909   Osborne judgment bars the use of trade union funds for political purposes, cutting the Labour Party's main source of income. Fabian Beatrice Webb calls for establishment of a state medical service through reorganisation of existing public and poor law health provision.

1910   (Jan.–Feb.)   Seventy-eight Labour Party candidates stand at general election; 40 returned. Majority of the separate Trade Union group of MPs merges with Labour in the Commons. (Dec.)   56 Labour Party candidates stand at general election; 42 returned. Lloyd George's proposal to Ramsay MacDonald that he should join a coalition of moderate Liberals and Conservatives is rejected after opposition from Arthur Henderson.

1911   (Jan.)   MacDonald promises Labour support to government's National Insurance Bill in return for Liberal promise of a bill to introduce annual payment of £400 to MPs. *Daily Herald* begins publication as London printer's strike bulletin. MacDonald elected Parliamentary Labour Party (PLP) chairman.

1912   ILP pamphlet attacks inadequacies of private health provision and calls for the establishment of a state medical service.

1913   Trade Union Act partially reverses effect of Osborne judgment, providing for ballots on trade union political funds and contracting-out of political levy.

1914   (Mar.)   Labour Party National Executive rejects Liberal offer of a new electoral pact, concessions on policy and a Cabinet seat for MacDonald in return for supporting a Coalition government.

(Aug.)   Outbreak of the First World War. MacDonald (opposing the war with, among others, Snowden and Hardie) resigns as Parliament Labour Party chairman when the PLP agrees to vote for war credits and is succeeded by PLP secretary Henderson. Labour agrees to electoral truce for duration of war. ILP issues manifesto entitled *German Workers Are Our Comrades.* War Emergency Workers' National Committee formed.

1915   (May)   Henderson enters Asquith's Coalition government as President of the Education Board to act as adviser on relationship with organised labour.

(Sept.)   Labour pioneer Keir Hardie dies. National Democratic Party formed by anti-Socialist Labour movement members.

1916   (Jan.)   Labour Party conference endorses Henderson's decision to join the Asquith Coalition and opposes the introduction of military conscription.

(Dec.)   Henderson joins Lloyd George's War Cabinet as Minister without Portfolio, with Clynes, Hodges and Roberts in other government posts.

1917   (Jan.)   Labour Party conference rejects ILP proposal to attend International Socialist Congress in Stockholm to discuss war aims; endorses the decision to participate in Lloyd George's Coalition government.

(Feb.)   Revolution in Russia; trade unionist Ben Tillett wins North Salford on an 'Anti-Profiteering' platform.

(June)   Leeds Convention of 1,100 delegates from the Labour Party, ILP, BSP, trade unions, trades councils, women's and peace association votes in favour of formation of Workers' and Soldiers' Councils; the decision, which comes to nothing, is repudiated by the party National Executive.

(Aug.)   Special Labour Party conference agrees to send delegation to International Socialist Congress in Stockholm.

(Oct.)   Bolsheviks seize power in Russia.

(Nov.)   Henderson resigns from War Cabinet following dispute with Lloyd George over proposed attendance at Stockholm conference; Barnes takes his place and William Adamson succeeds as party chairman.

1918   (Jan.–Feb.)   New Labour Party Constitution is adopted at the Nottingham party conference; the Constitution transforms Labour from a loose association of trade unions and socialist societies (the Independent Labour Party and the Fabians) into a nationally organised party with individual members in local branches and adopts Clause Four as an objective.
(June)   Party conference adopts *Labour and the New Social Order* as the party programme; the document commits Labour to socialism with a new social order based on the 'socialisation of industry' and planned production and distribution 'for the benefit of all who participate by hand or brain'.
(Nov.)   Party delegate conference votes to withdraw from the Coalition and to contest the general election; Barnes and Roberts ignore this and remain in the government until 1920.
(Dec.)   Labour emerges from the 'Coupon Election' as the largest opposition party with 57 seats; among the leading Labour casualties are MacDonald, Snowden and Henderson.

1919   (Mar.)   *Memorandum on the Causes and Remedies for Labour Unrest* produced by G.D.H. Cole and Henderson.
(June)   Labour Party conference votes in favour of 'direct action' to end Allied military intervention in Russia.
(Nov.)   'Hands off Russia' committee formed.

1920   (May)   Labour Party and TUC delegation visits Russia to examine conditions and returns to report that the Bolshevik regime is a dictatorship.
(Aug.)   Labour Party executive, Parliamentary Labour Party and the TUC establish a Council of Action to organise demonstrations against military intervention in Russia and threaten industrial action.
(Oct.)   Labour Party sets up a commission of investigation after the rejection of its call in the House of Commons for an investigation into the activities of the Black and Tans and Auxiliaries in Ireland. Deputation of Labour London mayors visits Prime Minister Lloyd George expressing concern over rising unemployment and cost of relief to Boards of Guardians in the capital's most deprived areas.

1921   (Jan.)   Labour Party commission on Ireland criticises British actions, calls for withdrawal of troops and the convocation of an Irish Constitutional Assembly.
(Feb.)   Clynes replaces Adamson as Parliamentary Labour Party chairman.

(Sept.)   Lansbury and 29 Poplar councillors imprisoned for
refusing to pay London County Council precept in protest
against unfairness in financing relief of unemployed.
(Oct.)   Labour MPs withdraw from Commons in protest
against the level of dependants' allowances for the
unemployed.

1922   (Nov.)   Labour makes significant general election gains in
industrial areas of Scotland, South Wales, Northumberland
and Yorkshire, and in London, taking 142 seats and becoming
the second largest party in the Commons. MacDonald defeats
Clynes in election for leadership of Parliamentary Labour
Party (by 61 votes to 56) and becomes first officially
designated Labour leader.

1923   (Mar.)   Snowden presents a private members bill in the
House of Commons calling for 'the gradual supersession of
the capitalist system'.
(Apr.)   Labour MPs sing the 'The Red Flag' and force the
Commons to adjourn in a protest against Conservative
unemployment policy.
(June)   Four Labour MPs are suspended from the Commons
after the ILP's James Maxton accuses the government of the
'murder' of children for reducing grants to welfare centres.
(Nov.)   Labour Party general election manifesto promises a
'programme of national work' to counter unemployment and
to provide 'adequate maintenance' but makes no reference to
nationalisation.
(Dec.)   Labour wins 191 seats in general election to
Conservatives 258 and Liberals 158; party National Executive
votes that if the opportunity arises Labour should form a
government alone and not enter into a coalition.

6   Labour in Government and Opposition, 1924–29

Labour Government, 1924 – Principal Ministers

(All held office from January to November 1924.)

Prime Minister and Secretary of State for Foreign Affairs	J. Ramsay MacDonald
Lord President of the Council	Lord Parmoor
Lord Chancellor	Viscount Haldane
Lord Privy Seal	J.R. Clynes
Chancellor of the Exchequer	Philip Snowden
Secretary of State for Home Affairs	Arthur Henderson
Secretary of State for the Colonies	J.H. Thomas
Secretary of State for War	Stephen Walsh
Secretary of State for India	Lord Olivier
Secretary of State for Air	Lord Thomson
Secretary of State for Scotland	William Adamson
President of the Board of Trade	Sidney Webb
President of the Board of Education	Charles Trevelyan
First Lord of the Admiralty	Viscount Chelmsford
Minister of Agriculture and Fisheries	Noel Buxton
Minister of Health	John Wheatley
Minister of Labour	Thomas Shaw
Postmaster-General	Vernon Hartshorn
First Commissioner of Works	Frederick Jowett
Chancellor of the Duchy of Lancaster	Josiah Wedgwood
Chief Whip in the House of Commons	B. Spoor

Chronology of Main Events

1924   (Jan.)   Labour forms a minority government dependent on Liberal support following the defeat of the Conservatives in the Commons on a confidence motion by 328 votes to 256. MacDonald becomes Prime Minister and Foreign Secretary. Among other leading appointments are Snowden as Chancellor, Henderson as Home Secretary and J.R. Clynes as Lord Privy Seal; left-wingers are represented in the Cabinet by John Wheatley (Minister of Health) and F.W. Jowett (First Commissioner of Works); Lansbury refuses to accept the post of Transport Minister because it is not included in the Cabinet.

Although in a minority, and only in office for ten months, the government is able to pass some legislation useful to its supporters. The Old Age Pensions Act guaranteed a weekly pension of 10s (50p) to people over the age of 70 earning under 15s (75p) a week. Wheatley's Housing Act provided for central government subsidies of £9 per dwelling for 40 years to local authorities to build homes for rent at controlled rents (521,700 have been built when the subsidy is abolished in 1933); the Act is also intended to increase employment in the building trades. The Protection of Eviction Act protected tenants from eviction by landlords attempting to obtain 'decontrolled' status for their properties in order to increase rents.

Unemployment benefit is increased to 18s (90p) a week for men over the age of 18 and 15s (75p) for women. The 'genuinely seeking work' clause is abolished, the 'gap' between benefit periods is ended and uncovenanted benefit (paid when National Insurance contributions are exhausted) is made a statutory right. Wheatley cancels restrictions, imposed by the previous government, on spending by the Poplar Board of Guardians.

Snowden announces £28 million spending to alleviate unemployment on road building, standardisation of electricity frequencies, municipal and public works. The Agricultural Wages (Regulation) Act creates county committees to set wages. An attempt to establish a Central Wages Board to supervise wage awards is defeated at committee stage; agricultural wages rise.

Education spending restrictions imposed by the previous government are revised; local authorities are encouraged to increase free secondary school places and state scholarships to universities are revived. London Traffic Act regulates privately-owned public transport, setting timetables and safety standards.

(Jan.)   Liaison Committee of three ministers and 12 Labour backbenchers is established to maintain contact between the government and the Parliamentary Labour Party. The ILP calls for the government to adopt a full socialist programme.
(Feb.)   Labour government formally recognises the Soviet Union. The government announces the construction of five cruisers and five destroyers to alleviate unemployment; work

on strengthening the Singapore naval base is abandoned;
preparations are made to institute air raid precautions. The
government appoints the Balfour Committee on Industry and
Trade to enquire into export prospects for British industry
(issues report in 1929). The government prepares to use
troops under the Emergency Powers Act in a national dock
strike.

(Mar.)   Government prepares to meet a strike of London
tramworkers (supported by Underground workers) with the
use of troops.

(Apr.)   Snowden's budget (which he declares is 'vindictive
against no class and no interest') estimates a £38 million
surplus; duties halved on sugar, tea, cocoa and coffee and
reduced on dried fruit; entertainment tax reduced; the
McKenna duties on luxury goods abolished, basic rate income
tax reduced from 5s (25p) to 4/6 (23p) and corporation
profits tax abolished. Government is defeated by 221 votes
to 212 on second reading of the Rent Restriction Bill.

(May)   Government survives a Conservative confidence
motion with Liberal support.

(June)   Government threat to use troops under the
Emergency Powers Act persuades striking London
Underground workers to end strike. Government is defeated
on a clause of the London Traffic Bill by 189 votes to 126.

(July)   Campbell Case begins with the publication by the
Communist *Workers' Weekly* of an article calling on troops
to refuse to fire on workers in war or industrial disputes.
Acting editor J.R. Campbell is charged under the 1797
Incitement to Mutiny Act but the charge is soon withdrawn

(Aug.)   Government is defeated by 171 votes to 149 on an
amendment to the Unemployment Insurance Bill. Bill to
ban eviction in cases where rent arrears are caused by
unemployment is defeated at committee stage.

(July–Aug.)   MacDonald presides over London Conference
on German reparations and (despite Labour's traditional
opposition to reparations) persuades France and Germany to
accept the Dawes Plan setting out payment of 1,000 million
marks in the first year, rising to 2,500 marks in the fifth and
subsequent years. MacDonald announces an international
loan of 800 million marks (£40 million) is to be negotiated.

(Aug.)   Commercial treaty signed with the Soviet Union
granting most-favoured nation trading status; negotiations
to begin on a loan and settlement of British claims over
companies nationalised by Soviet government.

(Sept.)   MacDonald leads delegation to the League of
Nations in Geneva, the first British prime minister to attend
the assembly. Conservatives table a motion of censure over the
withdrawal of charges against Campbell over the *Workers' Weekly*
article; Cabinet decides to treat it as a confidence motion.
(Oct.)   British proposal for a Protocol for the Pacific
Settlement of International Disputes (including sanctions
against aggressors) and to convene a disarmament conference
in 1925 is accepted by the League of Nations (succeeding
Conservative government refuses ratification). In Commons
debate on the Campbell Case the Conservatives support
a Liberal amendment calling for a select committee of
enquiry; the government is defeated by 364 votes to 198 and
resigns. Among the proposed legislation to fall is a bill to
set up a National Minimum Wage Commission, ratification
of the International Labour Convention on a maximum
48-hour working week and price controls. The Labour Party
conference votes by 2,456,000 to 654,000 to ban Communists
from endorsement as Labour candidates and by 1,804,000
to 1,546,000 to prevent them from individual Labour Party
membership; trade unions are requested not to send
Communists as delegates to local or national party
conferences. General election manifesto *Labour's Appeal to
the People* calls for further steps towards a 'really Socialist
Commonwealth'. The publication of Zinoviev letter –
allegedly from the Communist International to British
Communists linking ratification of an Anglo-Soviet treaty with
an increase in revolutionary activity in Britain – embarrasses
Labour. In the general election Labour's vote increases from
4.3 million to 5.5 million but seats fall to 152; Conservatives
take 415 seats and Liberals 42. Labour's greatest losses are in
London, Scotland, Lancashire and Cheshire.

1925   (Oct.)   Bevin's motion at the Labour Party conference
calling on Labour to refuse to take office in future as a
minority government is defeated following opposition from
MacDonald. The ban on Communists joining Labour is
reaffirmed.

1926   Joint Labour Party/TUC evidence to the Blanesburgh
Committee on Unemployment Insurance advocates increased
benefit and dependants' allowances.
(May)   Miners are locked out by employers for refusing to
accept longer hours and lower wages (1st). TUC General

Council calls general strike in support of miners (3rd). At midnight, the first wave of workers strike in transport, the railways, printing, heavy industry, the docks, steel and power, and supply. MacDonald, Clynes and Henderson deny the strike has any revolutionary intent. TUC calls off strike without concessions from government after nine days (12th). Local strikes continue as returning workers are threatened with worsening conditions; miners remained locked out for refusing to accept employers' conditions but there is a gradual return to work until the miners' final surrender in December. They return to longer hours and reduced wages. (Nov.)   Labour takes control of its first major city, Sheffield. Right-wing Labour MP George Spencer negotiates a local settlement with mine owners and establishes a breakaway union from the Miners' Federation based in Nottinghamshire. The Labour Party dissolves joint departments with the TUC, including research and press and publicity.

1927   (May)   Conservative government's Trade Disputes and Trade Union Act replaces 'contracting-out' with 'contracting-in' to the political levy. Labour MPs walk out of the Commons in protest against the government's use of the guillotine at committee stage. Party income is reduced by 25% as affiliated trade union membership falls from 3,352,347 in 1926 to 2,025,139 in 1928.
(Oct.)   At the Labour Party conference MacDonald calls for a new programme of 'legislation and administrative action for a Labour government'.

1928   (May)   Transport House opened by MacDonald as the headquarters of the Transport and General Workers' Union, the Trades Union Congress and the Labour Party.
(Oct.)   Labour Party conference adopts *Labour and the Nation* (drafted by Tawney) as its programme. The document declares that Labour is a 'socialist party' aiming at the organisation of industry in the interest 'of all who bring their contribution of useful service to the common stock'.

1929   (May) Labour emerges from the general election as the largest party for the first time, with 287 seats to the Conservatives' 261 and the Liberals' 59. Labour gains are in Lancashire, Cheshire, London, Yorkshire and West Midlands. Trade union representation among Labour MPs increases from 88 to 114.

7 Labour in Government and Opposition, 1929–39

Labour Government, 1929–31 – Principal Ministers

(All held office from June 1929 to August 1931 unless otherwise indicated.)

Prime Minister	J. Ramsay MacDonald
Lord President of the Council	Lord Parmoor
Lord Chancellor	Lord Sankey
Lord Privy Seal	J.H. Thomas
	(June 1929–June 1930)
	Vernon Hartshorn
	(June 1930–Mar. 1931)
	Thomas Johnston
	(Mar.–Aug. 1931)
Chancellor of the Exchequer	Philip Snowden
Secretary of State for Home Affairs	J.R. Clynes
Secretary of State for Foreign Affairs	Arthur Henderson
Secretary of State for the Colonies	Lord Passfield
Secretary of State for the Dominions	Lord Passfield
	(June 1929–June 1930)
	J.H. Thomas
	(June 1930– Aug. 1931)
Secretary of State for War	Thomas Shaw
Secretary of State for India	Wedgwood Benn
Secretary of State for Air	Lord Thomson
	(June 1929–Oct. 1930)
	Lord Amulree
	(Oct. 1930– Aug. 1931)
Secretary of State for Scotland	William Adamson
President of the Board of Trade	William Graham
President of the Board of Education	Sir Charles Trevelyan
	(June 1929–Mar. 1931)
	H.B. Lees-Smith
	(Mar.–Aug. 1931)
First Lord of the Admiralty	A.V. Alexander

Minister of Agriculture and Fisheries	Noel Buxton (June 1929–June 1930) Christopher Addison (June 1930–Aug. 1931)
Minister of Health	Arthur Greenwood
Minister of Labour	Margaret Bondfield
First Commissioner of Works	George Lansbury
Minister of Transport	Herbert Morrison
Chief Whip in the House of Commons	Thomas Kennedy

Ministerial Resignations

1930   (May)   Sir Oswald Mosley resigned as Chancellor of the Duchy of Lancaster following the government's rejection of his Memorandum setting out proposals to relieve unemployment.

1931   (Mar.)   Sir Charles Trevelyan resigned as President of the Board of Education following the defeat of his Education Bill in the House of Lords.

Labour Government, 1929–31 – Political and Economic Chronology

1929   (June)   Labour forms a minority government dependent on Liberal support. MacDonald becomes Prime Minister, Snowden returns as Chancellor, Clynes is appointed Home Secretary and Henderson Foreign Secretary.

(July)   MacDonald suggests in debate on the King's Speech that the parties in the Commons should 'consider ourselves more as a Council of Action and less as arrayed regiments facing each other in battle . . .'.

(Oct.)   Wall Street Crash begins with collapse of share prices on 'Black Thursday' (24th), leading to bank failures and a business recession which spreads to Europe.

(Nov.)   Thomas announces £92 million expenditure on public works to counter unemployment; Snowden appoints Macmillan Committee on Finance and Industry to examine how far the financial system is an obstacle to industry and exports (reported Mar. 1931).

(Dec.)   Government sets up three-party conference under former Speaker Lord Ullswater to consider electoral reform (wound up in July 1931 following Labour and Conservative refusal to accept proportional representation).

1930   (Jan.)   MacDonald announces the formation of an Economic Advisory Council including ministers, economists, trade union leaders and other figures from outside politics.

(Feb.)   Mosley Memorandum on unemployment submitted to Cabinet by Mosley, Lansbury and Johnston. Government narrowly defeats amendment to the Coal Mines Bill with the support of four Liberal MPs.

(Mar.)   Cabinet, against MacDonald's advice, tells Liberals an electoral reform bill will be introduced. Coal Mines Act reduces working day from eight to seven-and-a-half hours, establishes a cartel scheme to allocate production quotas to pits under the control of a central council and creates Mines Reorganisation Commission to encourage efficiency through amalgamations.

(Apr.)   Snowden's budget increases income tax but introduces exemptions to protect the lower paid, raises surtax and death duties, does not renew safeguarding duties and announces future imposition of a land duties tax. There is a dramatic fall in the Labour majority at Sheffield Brightside by-election.

(May)   Mosley resigns as minister following Cabinet rejection of his Memorandum on unemployment. Labour loses West Fulham to Conservatives at by-election. Party National Executive instructs Labour representatives on Ullswater Committee to reject changes in electoral system.

(June)   Mosley defeated by 202 votes to 29 after attacking government unemployment policy at special meeting of Parliamentary Labour Party. MacDonald's invitation to opposition parties to discuss unemployment is rejected by Conservative leader Baldwin.

(Oct.)   Motion calling for Mosley's unemployment proposals to be examined by the Labour National Executive is narrowly defeated at party conference by 1,251,000 to 1,046,000. Mosley is elected to National Executive.

(Dec.)   Mosley publishes manifesto signed by 17 Labour MPs including Bevan and Strachey. National Executive and Parliamentary Labour Party vote for inclusion of alternative vote system of proportional representation in a forthcoming Electoral Reform Bill; unemployment reaches 2.5 million.

1931   (Jan.)   Government defeated on report stage of Education Bill on subsidy to Catholic schools by 282 votes to 249 as 41 Labour MPs vote against.

(Feb.)   Trade Union Bill to restore 'contracting-out' and repeal of 1927 Trade Disputes and Trade Union Act abandoned following Liberal wrecking amendment at committee stage. Electoral Reform Bill with provision for alternative vote at all elections introduced (radically amended by the House of Lords, it fell with the collapse of the government in July). Mosley announces formation of the New Party and is expelled from the Labour Party.

(Mar.)   Committee on National Expenditure under Sir George May appointed to examine government spending and recommend savings following Liberal amendment to Conservative censure motion (Committee reported in July). Government narrowly wins vote on the appointment of chairman of the Mines Reorganisation Commission by 173 votes to 168. Government defeated in attempt to abolish University seats as two Labour MPs vote with the opposition and 20 abstain.

(Apr.)   Snowden presents a balanced budget with increase on petrol duty and proposes to introduce tax on land values following valuation. Snowden plans second budget for the autumn to reduce public expenditure.

(June)   Snowden requests increase in unemployment insurance fund borrowing powers as unemployment reaches 2.7 million.

(July)   Macmillan Committee on Finance and Industry issues pessimistic report on Britain's export prospects. May Committee on National Expenditure estimates government deficit of £120 million by 1932 and proposes £96 million public spending reduction (including 20% unemployment benefit cut) and £24 million tax increases. Following European bank collapses, Britain loses £2.25 million a day from gold reserves and raises bank rate from 2.5 to 4.5%.

(Aug.)   Government enters final crisis; Cabinet agrees on provisional spending reduction of £56 million (19th); TUC General Council deputation warns Cabinet that unemployment benefits cuts are unacceptable (20th); Cabinet agrees on £68 million spending reduction, including 10% benefit cut (22nd); Cabinet divides on benefit cut, with 11 for, 10 against (23rd); MacDonald informs Cabinet that he is to head a temporary National Government of individuals and not parties to meet financial crisis (24th); MacDonald forms government with three other Labour members (Snowden, Thomas, Lord Sankey), four Conservatives and two Liberals; Henderson becomes leader of Labour opposition.

Labour in Opposition, 1931–40 – Political Chronology

1931   (Sept.)   National Government's first Commons vote of 309
includes 12 Labour MPs. TUC General Council, Labour Party
National Executive and Parliamentary Labour Party issue a
joint manifesto denouncing the cuts agreed by the former
Labour Cabinet. National Executive votes (with party leader
Henderson dissenting) to expel all Labour supporters and
members of the National Government.

(Oct.)   Labour's general election manifesto, *Labour's Call to
Action*, declares that capitalism has failed, calls for national
planning of trade and industry and the nationalisation of
banking, credit, transport, power and steel, and for the
reversal of the benefit cuts. Labour suffers massive reverses as
its vote falls to 6.6 million, with heaviest losses in Scotland
and the Midlands, and seats to 46. All former Labour
ministers except Lansbury and all former junior ministers
except Attlee and Cripps are defeated; Henderson is defeated
but remains leader, with Lansbury as party leader in the
Commons.

(Nov.)   National Joint Council (renamed the National
Council of Labour in 1934) is reconstituted by the National
Executive and Parliamentary Labour Party and dominated by
the TUC General Council.

1932   (Aug.)   ILP disaffiliates from Labour; Socialist League
formed as radical grouping in the Labour Party.

(Oct.)   Henderson resigns as party leader and is succeeded
by Lansbury.

1933   (Oct.)   Party conference accepts resolution from Cripps on
an immediate introduction of socialism by a future Labour
government and the recommendation that the Parliamentary
Labour Party should consult the National Joint Council before
forming a minority government.

1934   (Oct.)   Party conference adopts *For Socialism and Peace*, the
most radical policy document ever produced by Labour.

1935   (Nov.)   Labour's general election manifesto calls for public
ownership of banking, coal, cotton, electricity, iron and steel,
land and transport; planning to solve the problems of the
Distressed Areas, with national development schemes to
absorb the unemployed; an end to the means test; raising

of the school leaving age, with provision of maintenance allowances; development of health services, increased old age pensions and a reduction in the retirement age; programme to build housing at reasonable rents; abolition of the House of Lords. The party sees some recovery, particularly in London, Yorkshire and Scotland, with vote increasing to 8.3 million and seats to 154. Among the casualties of 1931 who return are Alexander, Clynes, Dalton and Morrison.
(Dec.)   Attlee, Morrison and Greenwood compete for party leadership; Attlee defeats Morrison by 88 votes to 48 in second ballot.

1937   (Oct.)   Party conference adopts *Labour's Immediate Programme* advocating government control of location of industry, co-ordination of transport, nationalisation of coal, gas and electricity under public corporations and collective security through the League of Nations. The programme forms the basis of the 1945 government's policies. Constituency parties are given more weight in elections to the party's National Executive.

1939   (Jan.)   Cripps, Bevan and other supporters of the Popular Front are expelled from the party; Bevan returns within a year but Cripps remains out until 1945.
(Sept.)   Labour Party refuses Prime Minister Chamberlain's invitation to join a Coalition government on the outbreak of war but agrees to an electoral truce. Following the replacement of Chamberlain by Churchill in May 1940, Labour agrees to join the Coalition.

Chronology of Social Policy

1929   (Nov.)   Unemployment Insurance Act abolishes 'genuinely seeking work' clause in unemployment benefit (reimposed by Conservatives in 1928), eases eligibility conditions, extends provision for the long-term unemployed, increases dependants' allowances, and introduces individual means test.

1930   (July)   Education Bill proposing raising of the school leaving age to 15 from April 1931, together with provision of maintenance grants, is substantially amended by Catholic Labour MPs and then defeated in the Lords.

1930   Housing Act and Housing (Scotland) Act provides local authorities with additional central government subsidies to build new homes for people who have been moved out of slum clearance areas. Poor Prisoners' Defence Act introduces criminal legal aid for appearances in magistrates' courts. National Health Insurance (Prolongation of Insurance) Act extends provision of health insurance to unemployed men whose entitlement has run out. Unemployment Fund borrowing powers increased successively to £50 million, £60 million and £70 million as unemployment rises. Royal Commission on Unemployment Insurance under Judge Holman Gregory is appointed to make recommendations on reducing the deficit.

1931   Unemployment Fund borrowing powers increased to £90 million and then £115 million. Gregory Commission on Unemployment Insurance interim report recommends benefit reduction of 12%, removal of right of married women and casual workers to claim; 'Anomalies' Act removes these rights. May Report recommends increased national insurance contributions and a benefit cut of 20%. Failure of Cabinet to agree on compromise 10% leads to collapse of government.

1934   Establishment of a comprehensive state health service becomes official Labour Party policy.

Chronology of Defence and Foreign Affairs

1929   (Aug.)   Government agrees to Young Plan on German reparations after Snowden negotiates guaranteed £2 million payment to Britain.
(Sept.)   Government signs Statute of Permanent Court of International Justice, pledging to restore most disputes to court's arbitration.
(Oct.)   Diplomatic relations with Soviet government, which had been broken by Conservatives in 1927, are resumed.

1930   (Jan.)   MacDonald presides over London Naval Conference at which Britain, the United States and Japan agree on 5:5:3 ratio of naval forces.
(Apr.)   Government signs a commercial agreement with the Soviet Union.
(Oct.)   White Paper on Palestine Mandate proposes limiting Jewish settlement to areas already occupied and end to Arab evictions.

1931   (Feb.)   MacDonald affirms Labour's commitment to the establishment of a Jewish homeland in Palestine and Britain's agreement to immigration and settlement in the area. Foreign Secretary Henderson is elected president of the World Disarmament Conference in Geneva.

1933   (Oct.)   Party conference commits itself to oppose future war by a general strike if necessary.

1934   (Oct.)   Party conference reverses previous year's decision by adopting policy document *War and Peace*, opposing general strike to prevent war.

1935   (June)   Peace Ballot, supported by Labour and the TUC, shows support for economic and military measures against aggressors.
(Oct.)   Lansbury resigns as party leader following conference support for sanctions against Italy following invasion of Abyssinia (Ethiopia).

1936   (Mar.)   Labour opposes government White Paper proposing expansion of armed forces.
(Oct.)   Labour adopts policy of non-intervention in Spanish Civil War following consultations with TUC and the French Socialist Party.

1937   (Oct.)   Labour Party conference unanimously adopts a resolution calling for a nation-wide campaign to force the government to end the policy of non-intervention in the Spanish Civil War as the extent of German and Italian involvement becomes clear.

1938   (Sept.)   As the Sudetenland crisis mounts, the National Council of Labour calls on the government to warn Germany that Britain will ally with France and the Soviet Union to resist any attack on Czechoslovakia. Labour Party reluctantly supports Munich agreement on dismembering Czechoslovakia negotiated by prime minister Chamberlain.

1939   (Mar.)   Labour Party supports British government's declaration of conditional support for Poland against possible German aggression.
(Apr.)   Labour opposes Military Training Bill which introduces six months military conscription for 20 and 21 year olds.

(June)   Labour Party conference calls for mutual aid pacts to be negotiated with France and the Soviet Union to prevent German aggression.

(Sept.)   Labour deputy leader Arthur Greenwood – called on to 'Speak for England' – accuses government of vacillation for apparent hesitation to declare war on Germany immediately on invasion of Poland.

8 Labour in Coalition and Government, 1940–51

Coalition Posts held by Labour, 1940–45

(Labour members of the Coalition government are divided between posts in the War Cabinet and posts outside it.)

War Cabinet

Clement Attlee
    Lord Privy Seal   May 1940–Feb. 1942
    Secretary of State for Dominions   Feb. 1942–Sept. 1943
    Lord President of the Council   Sept. 1943–May 1945
(Attlee was Deputy Prime Minister from Feb. 1942–May 1945)

Arthur Greenwood
    Minister without Portfolio   May 1940–Feb. 1942

Ernest Bevin
    Minister of Labour and National Service   Oct. 1940–May 1945

Herbert Morrison
    Home Secretary and Minister of
    Home Security   Nov. 1942–May 1945

Stafford Cripps
    Lord Privy Seal   Feb.–Nov. 1942

Ministers not in War Cabinet

A.V. Alexander
    First Lord of the Admiralty   May 1940–May 1945

Hugh Dalton
    Minister of Economic Warfare   May 1940–Feb. 1942
    President of the Board of Trade   Feb. 1942–May 1945

Ernest Bevin
    Minister of Labour and National Service   May–Oct. 1940

Herbert Morrison
    Minister of Supply   May 1940–Oct. 1940
    Home Secretary and Minister of
    Home Security   Oct. 1940–Nov. 1942

William Jowitt
    Solicitor General   May 1940–Mar. 1942
    Paymaster-General   Mar.–Dec. 1942
    Minister without Portfolio   Dec. 1942–Oct. 1944
    Minister for Social Security
    (later National Insurance)   Oct. 1944–May 1945

Thomas Johnston
    Secretary of State for Scotland   Feb. 1941–May 1945

Stafford Cripps
    Minister of Aircraft Production   Nov. 1942–May 1945

Ben Smith
    Minister Resident in Washington for Supply   Nov. 1943–May 1945

Labour Government, 1945–51 – Principal Ministers

(All held office from July 1945 to October 1951 unless otherwise indicated.)

Prime Minister	Clement Attlee
Lord President and Leader of the House of Commons	Herbert Morrison (July 1945–Mar. 1951) Viscount Addison (Mar.–Oct. 1951)
Lord Chancellor	Lord Jowitt
Lord Privy Seal	Arthur Greenwood (July 1945–Apr. 1947) Lord Inman (Apr.–Oct. 1947) Viscount Addison (Oct. 1947–Mar. 1951) Ernest Bevin (Mar.–Apr. 1951) Richard Stokes (Apr.–Oct. 1951)
Chancellor of the Exchequer	Hugh Dalton (July 1945–Nov. 1947)

	Sir Stafford Cripps (Nov. 1947–Oct. 1950) Hugh Gaitskell (Oct. 1950–Oct. 1951)
Minister of Economic Affairs	Sir Stafford Cripps (Sept.–Nov. 1947)

(Amalgamated with Exchequer in Nov. 1947)

Secretary of State for Foreign Affairs	Ernest Bevin (July 1945–Mar. 1951) Herbert Morrison (Mar.–Oct. 1951)
Secretary of State for Home Affairs	Chuter Ede
First Lord of the Admiralty	A.V. Alexander (July 1945–Oct. 1946)

(Office removed from the Cabinet in Oct. 1946)

Minister of Agriculture and Fisheries	Thomas Williams
Secretary of State for Air	Viscount Stansgate (July 1945–Oct. 1946)

(Office removed from the Cabinet in Oct. 1946)

Secretary for State for the Colonies	George Hall (July 1945–Oct. 1946) Arthur Creech Jones (Oct. 1946–Feb. 1950)

(Office removed from the Cabinet in Feb. 1950)

Secretary of State for the Dominions	Viscount Addison (July 1945–Oct. 1947)

(Secretary of State for Commonwealth Relations from July 1947)

	Philip Noel-Baker (Oct. 1947–Feb. 1950) Patrick Gordon Walker (Feb. 1950–Aug. 1951)
Minister of Defence	Clement Attlee (July 1945–Dec. 1946) A.V. Alexander (Dec. 1946–Feb. 1950) Emanuel Shinwell (Feb. 1950–Oct. 1951)
Minister of Education	Ellen Wilkinson (July 1945–Feb. 1947)

	George Tomlinson (Feb. 1947–Oct. 1951)

Minister of Fuel and Power

Emanuel Shinwell
(July 1945–Oct. 1947)

(Office removed from the Cabinet in Oct. 1947)

Minister of Health

Aneurin Bevan
(July 1945–Jan. 1951)

(Office removed from the Cabinet in Jan. 1951)

Secretary of State for India and Burma

Lord Pethick-Lawrence
(July 1945–Apr. 1947)
Earl of Listowel
(Apr. 1947–Jan. 1948)

(Secretary of State for Burma from Aug. 1947. Office abolished in Jan. 1948.)

Chancellor of the Duchy of Lancaster
(Minister but office not in the Cabinet)

Hugh Dalton
(May 1948–Feb. 1950)
Viscount Alexander
(Feb. 1950–Oct. 1951)

Paymaster-General
(office intermittently in the Cabinet)

Arthur Greenwood
(July 1946–Mar. 1947)
Viscount Addison
(July 1948–Apr. 1949)

Minister without Portfolio
(office intermittently in the Cabinet)

A.V. Alexander
(Oct.–Dec. 1946)
Arthur Greenwood
(Apr.–Sept. 1947)

Secretary of State for Scotland

Joseph Westwood
(July 1945–Oct. 1947)
Arthur Woodburn
(Oct. 1947–Feb. 1950)
Hector McNeil
(Feb. 1950–Oct. 1951)

Minister of Town and Country Planning
(Minister but office not in the Cabinet.
Minister of Local Government and
Planning from Jan. 1951)

Hugh Dalton
(Feb. 1950–Oct. 1951)

President of the Board of Trade

Sir Stafford Cripps
(July 1945–Sept. 1947)

Harold Wilson
(Sept. 1947–Apr. 1951)
Sir Hartley Shawcross
(Apr.–Oct. 1951)

Secretary of State for War   J. Lawson
                                        (July 1945–Oct. 1946)
(Office removed from the Cabinet in Oct. 1946)

Chief Whip in the House of Commons   William Whiteley

Ministerial Resignations

1947   (Nov.)   Hugh Dalton resigns as Chancellor of the Exchequer
            following a budget leak.

1948   (Dec.)   John Belcher resigns as Parliamentary Secretary,
            Board of Trade following criticism of his conduct by the
            Lynskey Tribunal.

1951   (Apr.)   Aneurin Bevan (Minister of Labour and National
            Service), Harold Wilson (President of the Board of Trade)
            and John Freeman (Parliamentary Secretary, Ministry of
            Supply) resign over the imposition of health charges to meet
            an expansion in defence spending.

Chronology of Labour in Coalition, 1940–45

1940   (May)   Following German invasion of Low Countries and
            replacement of Chamberlain by Churchill, Labour agrees
            to join Coalition. Attlee (Lord Privy Seal) and Greenwood
            (Minister without Portfolio) join five-man War Cabinet; other
            posts are taken by Alexander (First Lord of the Admiralty),
            Bevin (Minister of Labour), Dalton (Minister of Economic
            Warfare) and Morrison (Minister of Supply). Bevin becomes
            Minister of Labour and National Defence and Morrison is
            appointed Home Secretary and Minister for Home Security
            (Oct.); Labour Party conference approves decision by
            2,450,000 votes to 120,000.

1941   (Mar.)   Determination of Needs Act abolishes household
            means test, a central Labour demand.

1942   (Feb.)   Attlee appointed deputy prime minister, Cripps
            Leader of the House, and Greenwood leaves War Cabinet.
            Labour Party policy statement *The Old World and the New*

Society advocates post-war continuation of planning, controls and public ownership.

(May)   Coal nationalisation proposals produced by Dalton and Cripps abandoned following Conservative backbench opposition.

(Nov.)   Morrison appointed to the War Cabinet.

(Oct.)   Cripps resigns from the War Cabinet after unsuccessful attempt to usurp Churchill as leader.

(Dec.)   Labour War Cabinet members support Churchill's opposition to making a commitment to implement the Beveridge Report; an amendment demanding legislation is supported by all non-ministerial Labour MPs but defeated by 338 votes to 121.

1943   (Feb.)   Majority of Labour backbenchers support an unsuccessful amendment calling for legislation based on the Beveridge Report.

1944   (Mar.)   Morgan Phillips becomes Labour Party general secretary and retains office until 1962.

1945   (May)   War in Europe ends. Churchill, supported by Attlee, Bevin and Dalton, calls for continuation of Coalition until victory over Japan. Labour Party conference refuses and adopts *Let Us Face the Future* as party programme.

(June)   Churchill says a Labour government committed to socialism would establish a 'Gestapo'; Churchill accuses Labour National Executive chairman Harold Laski rather than Attlee of effectively being Labour leader.

(July)   Attlee reiterates constitutional independence of the Parliamentary Labour Party from the party's National Executive. Labour with 393 seats to the Conservatives' 213 wins a majority for the first time at the general election.

Chronology of the Labour Government, 1945–51

1945   (July)   Clement Attlee becomes prime minister of the first majority Labour government; Ernest Bevin is appointed Foreign Secretary, Hugh Dalton Chancellor of the Exchequer, Herbert Morrison Lord President of the Council and Aneurin Bevin Minister of Health.

(Aug.)   Labour MPs sing 'The Red Flag' at first sitting of the new Parliament. Attlee declares necessity to retain wartime controls to meet economic situation. Lend-Lease ends;

government seeks emergency loans from the United States and Canada.

(Oct.)   President of the Board of Trade Stafford Cripps says main industries will be administered by tripartite bodies representing unions, employers and the government. Minister of Health and Housing Bevan says housing shortage will be met by local authorities. Chancellor Dalton reduces income tax in supplementary budget.

(Dec.)   Twenty-three Labour MPs vote against the government request for approval for an American loan of $3.75 billion.

1946   (Jan.)   Bank of England is nationalised. National Insurance Bill proposing expansion in the Welfare State is introduced. Parliamentary Labour Party relaxes discipline by suspending Standing Orders for two years. A Cabinet committee agrees secretly to prepare for a nuclear weapons programme under the guise of a civil energy programme as Bevin rejects the objections of Dalton and Cripps that Britain cannot afford it.

(Feb.)   Housing Bill is introduced, increasing Treasury subsidies for local authority house construction in England and Wales.

(Mar.)   Cabinet mission arrives in India to discuss independence.

(Apr.)   Chancellor of the Exchequer Dalton announces small tax relief in budget following concern over inflation.

(May)   Trade Union Act repeals the 1927 Conservative Trades Disputes and Trade Union Act and restores 'contracting-out' to the political levy on which much of Labour's income depends.

(June)   Labour government's foreign policy is attacked at the party conference. Cabinet mission leaves India following breakdown of independence negotiations. World wheat shortage forces introduction of flour and bread rationing.

(July)   Coal Industry Nationalisation Act receives Royal Assent.

(Aug.)   National Insurance Bill receives Royal Assent.

(Nov.)   Fifty-two Labour backbenchers vote for an end to conscription to the armed forces; Transport Bill published, proposing nationalisation of rail and road transport, docks, harbours and inland waterways.

(Dec.)   British Medical Association (BMA) refuses to enter into negotiations on the establishment of a National Health Service (NHS).

1947 (Jan.) President of the Board of Trade Cripps announces rationing of coal for industrial and domestic use. BMA agrees to negotiations over the NHS. Attlee announces that there is to be a voluntary policy on wage increases. A secret Cabinet committee agrees to begin construction of a nuclear weapon, with Attlee and Morrison arguing it is necessary that the United States should not have a monopoly.

(Feb.) Minister of Fuel and Power Emanuel Shinwell orders electricity supply cuts to industry in parts of England, leading to the lay-off of 1,800,000 workers. The government promises that India will achieve independence by 1 August 1948.

(Mar.) Exchange Control Act is introduced to restrict the movement of capital.

(Apr.) Dalton's budget extends income tax relief and raises indirect taxes. Seventy-two Labour MPs vote against continuing conscription to the armed forces. The government suffers a 237 to 219 defeat on a motion to annul a rationing order.

(May) Cabinet agrees to partition India and Pakistan on independence.

(June) US Secretary of State George Marshall proposes aid for European Recovery Programme (the 'Marshall Plan'). Exchange crisis forces reduction in petrol, tobacco and newsprint supplies.

(July) Sterling made convertible as a condition for loans from the United States; Britain suffers a drain of dollars and suspends convertibility in August. Government of India Act receives Royal Assent. Minister of Labour George Isaacs imposes staggered hours on industry. Attlee Must Go (AMGO) movement organised in the Parliamentary Labour Party because of continuing economic problems. The government suffers a 157 to 141 defeat on a motion to annul a prices order and is defeated by 232 to 229 on an amendment to the Forestry Bill. Economic Planning Board established under Sir Edwin Plowden.

(Aug.) Attlee announces proposals for austerity measures. Government takes power to use defence regulations to increase industrial production. Agriculture Act makes agricultural protection and subsidies permanent. Electricity Act and Transport Act receive Royal Assent. India and Pakistan become independent.

(Sept.) Attlee refuses to resign following meeting with Morrison; Cripps becomes Minister of Economic Affairs and Harold Wilson President of the Board of Trade, in a Cabinet reshuffle. Labour retains Liverpool Edge Hill at by-election with majority which falls from 6,029 to 1,953.

(Oct.)   Control of Engagement Order allows government direction of labour. Bill to reduce the House of Lords' veto powers over legislation from three years to one is announced in the King's Speech. New house and factory building is reduced by Cripps's £200 million cut in capital spending.

(Nov.)   Dalton resigns as Chancellor following a budget leak and is succeeded by Cripps.

1948   (Jan.)   British Medical Association (BMA) calls for the government's National Health Service to be rejected by the medical profession.

(Feb.)   Bevan (the minister responsible for plans for a National Health Service) denounces BMA as a 'squalid political conspiracy'. Government White Paper on Incomes, Costs and Prices calls for a voluntary incomes policy. Cripps calls on the employers' organisation, the Federation of British Industry (FBI), to set up a voluntary prices and profits policy.

(Mar.)   Cripps accepts FBI proposals for voluntary dividend and price controls.

(Apr.)   Cripps's budget introduces capital levy on investment income and increases indirect taxes. $980 million becomes available to Britain under Marshall Aid, administered by the Organisation for European Economic Co-operation (OEEC). Bevan makes concessions on pay beds and contracts for general practitioners to gain doctors' support for NHS. House of Commons votes to suspend death penalty by 245 to 222.

(May)   Defence Minister Alexander reveals the existence of an atomic weapon programme to the Commons.

(June)   Parliament Bill, including reform of the second chamber, is rejected in House of Lords by 177 votes to 81. Bread and flour rationing ends.

(July)   National Health Service begins functioning. National Insurance Act comes into force. Representation of People Act abolishes plural voting through the business and university franchise, abolishes the six months' residence qualification, reduces number of MPs from 640 to 625 and establishes a permanent Boundaries Commission. The House of Lords votes to retain death penalty by 99 votes to 19. Monopolies Commission is established by Monopolies and Restrictive Practices (Inquiry and Control) Act. Bevan describes Conservatives as 'lower than vermin'.

(Sept.)   House of Lords rejects Parliament Bill for the second time by 204 votes to 34.

(Oct.)   Lynskey Tribunal is established to investigate allegations of corruption in the Board of Trade. Attlee says there will be no change in Northern Ireland's constitutional status without the population's consent.

(Nov.)   Cripps declares that prices and incomes policies have effectively dealt with economic crisis. President of the Board of Trade Wilson's 'bonfire of controls' abolishes a wide range of restrictions on business activity. Labour holds Edmonton at by-election with a majority which falls from 19,069 to 3,327.

(Dec.)   Forty Labour backbenchers vote against restoring the period of conscription to the armed forces from 12 to 18 months.

1949   (Jan.)   Lynskey Tribunal issues a report finding there has been no corruption; junior Board of Trade minister John Belcher is criticised for misjudgment and resigns.

(Feb.)   Clothes rationing ends. Northern Ireland Labour Party formally dissociates itself from the Irish Labour Party. Labour hold South Hammersmith at by-election with majority which falls from 3,458 to 1,613.

(Apr.)   Cripps announces in budget that increased spending on defence and social services must be met by greater indirect taxation and reductions in food subsidies.

(May)   Gas industry comes into public ownership.

(July)   Gold and dollar reserves continue falling but Cripps rules out devaluation.

(Aug.)   Cabinet agrees on need to devalue pound but delays making an announcement.

(Sept.)   Pound is devalued from $4.03 to $2.80.

(Oct.)   Attlee announces £250 million public expenditure cuts following devaluation, giving inflationary fears as the reason.

(Nov.)   Iron and Steel Act, taking the industries into public ownership, receives Royal Assent. The House of Lords rejects the Parliament Bill for the third time by 110 votes to 37 but it receives Royal Assent the following month.

1950   (Jan.)   Attlee calls general election for 23 February.

(Feb.)   Labour government is re-elected with a majority of five; Attlee remains as prime minister, Cripps as Chancellor and Bevin as Foreign Secretary. Attlee refuses to resign following government defeat in the fuel and power debate by 283 votes to 257.

(Apr.)   Cripps's budget reduces income tax and increases petrol tax.

(May)   Meeting in Dorking of the Cabinet, the Labour National Executive, the Co-operative Party and trade union representatives agree on the need for a period of consolidation and the importance of winning middle-class support. Petrol rationing ends.

(Oct.)   Labour Party conference adopts *Labour and the New Society*. An article in the *New Statesman* by Richard Crossman points to a gap between the government's policies and the aspirations of its supporters. Gaitskell becomes Chancellor of the Exchequer.

(Dec.)   Marshall Aid to Britain ends.

1951   (Feb.)   Iron and steel come into public ownership. Morrison succeeds Bevin as Foreign Secretary.

(Apr.)   Minister of Labour Bevan threatens resignation if NHS charges are imposed but Chancellor Gaitskell's budget imposes charges for teeth, spectacles and prescriptions to meet rearmament costs. Bevan resigns, followed by President of the Board of Trade Wilson and junior Supply Minister John Freeman in protest against extent of rearmament. The left-wing Bevanite group forms.

(July)   Gaitskell announces counter-inflationary price and dividends controls. Left-wing Labour publication *One Way Only* calls for reductions in arms spending and support for national liberation movements.

(Sept.)   Attlee calls general election for 25 October.

(Oct.)   Labour wins its highest ever share of the vote at the general election but the Conservatives return with a majority of 17.

Chronology of Social Policy, 1940–49

1940   (May)   Labour enters Churchill's wartime Coalition with Attlee (Lord Privy Seal) and Greenwood (Minister without Portfolio) becoming members of five-strong War Cabinet; Bevin (Minister of Labour) joins War Cabinet in October.

1941   In March, the Coalition government's Determination of Needs Act abolishes household means test, a long-term Labour demand.

1942   Beveridge Report on *Social Insurance and Allied Services* is published.

1943   Labour publishes *National Service for Health* and the Socialist Medical Association publishes *The Socialist Programme for Health*, both advocating a state medical service.

1944   Coalition government publishes White Paper, *A National Health Service*, setting out proposals for free, comprehensive health provision; White Papers, *Social Insurance* and *Employment Policy*, give a commitment to maintaining a high and stable level of employment.

1945   Coalition government's Family Allowance Act brings in 5s (25p) non-contributory weekly allowance paid to mothers for second and subsequent children.

1946   National Health Service Act (coming into effect in July 1948) introduces free, comprehensive medical care and places local authority and voluntary hospitals under regional health boards responsible to the Minister of Health. National Insurance Act introduces compulsory insurance for most adults and payments of benefits for unemployment, sickness, maternity, widows and a death grant. Furnished House Rent Control Act establishes rent tribunals to control private sector rents. New Towns Act establishes development corporations to build new towns. Police Act amalgamates or abolishes 45 small non-county police forces.

1947   Town and Country Planning Act instructs county councils to prepare development plans and provides compulsory purchase powers. The school leaving age is raised to 15.

1948   National Assistance Act repeals remaining Poor Law provisions, extends assistance for those outside National Insurance scheme and allows supplementing of low benefits. Criminal Justice Act restricts imprisonment for juveniles and brings in improvements to probation and remand centres system.

1949   Legal Aid and Advice Act introduces a new system of civil legal aid. Justices of the Peace Act extensively reforms magistrates courts. Landlord and Tenant Rent Control Act empowers rent tribunals to determine a 'reasonable rent' for unfurnished private properties. National Parks and Access to the Countryside Act establishes national parks and protection for areas of outstanding beauty.

Chronology of Defence and Foreign Affairs, 1945–51

1945   (Aug.)   War with Japan ends following use of atomic weapons on Hiroshima and Nagasaki.
(Dec.)   Britain reaches agreement with the US and USSR on the establishment of a provisional government in Korea.

1946   (Jan.)   Cabinet committee agrees to make preparations for a British nuclear weapons programme despite objections from Cripps and Dalton as to the expense.
(Mar.)   Attlee refuses to dissociate the Labour government from Conservative leader Churchill's 'iron curtain' speech in Fulton, Missouri.
(June)   The Labour government's foreign policy comes under attack at the party conference.
(July)   Irgun terrorists blow up King David Hotel in Jerusalem, killing 91 people.
(Dec.)   Britain and the US agree on the economic merging of their zones of occupation in Germany.

1947   (Jan.)   Secret Cabinet committee makes final decision on the construction of an atomic bomb.
(Feb.)   British proosal to create separate Arab and Jewish zones in the Palestine Mandate is rejected by both sides.
(Mar.)   Britain's inability to maintain support for royalists in Greek Civil War leads US President Truman to declare Truman Doctrine of US support against Communist expansionism. Mountbatten is appointed Viceroy of India with instructions to speed up move to independence.
(May)   Labour Party attacks Soviet policy in Europe and Middle East in *Cards on the Table*. Left-wing Labour MPs Michael Foot, Richard Crossman and Ian Mikardo issue *Keep Left*, advocating a non-aligned foreign policy. The period of conscription to the armed forces is reduced from 18 to 12 months.
(June)   US Secretary of State George Marshall announces a European Recovery Programme (the Marshall Plan), of which Britain will be a beneficiary.
(Aug.)   India and Pakistan become independent.

1948   (Jan.)   Labour prime minister Attlee asserts the distinctiveness of the British system in relation to the United States and USSR but warns of Communist threat. Foreign Secretary Bevin calls in the Commons for the establishment of a Western European Union to face feared Soviet expansionism.

(Mar.)   Britain signs Brussels Treaty on economic and military co-operation with Belgium, France, Luxembourg and the Netherlands.

(Apr.)   Britain begins to receive Marshall Aid, administered by the Organisation for European Economic Co-operation (OEEC).

(May)   Defence Minister Alexander reveals to the Commons that Britain is constructing an atomic weapon.

(June)   Rising by the Malay Communist Party opens the Malayan 'emergency'.

(July)   Soviet blocking of rail and road links between West Berlin and the Western sectors of Germany is met by the Berlin Airlift which lasts until May 1949.

(Dec.)   Duration of conscription to the armed forces increased from 12 to 18 months.

1949   (Apr.)   Britain signs the North Atlantic Treaty, establishing NATO, with Canada, Denmark, France, Italy, the Netherlands, Norway and the United States. Ireland leaves the Commonwealth after becoming a republic.

(May)   Soviet blockade of West Berlin ends.

1950   (Jan.)   Britain recognises the Communist government in China.

(June)   Attlee dissociates himself from the Labour Party National Executive document criticising proposals for a European economic union. North Korean invasion of the south triggers Korean War.

(July)   Labour Defence Minister Shinwell says British troops will be sent to Korea; they begin to arrive in September. Total British casualties when an armistice is negotiated in 1953 are 686 killed, 2,498 wounded and 1,102 missing.

(Sept.)   Junior Treasury minister Gaitskell says in defence debate that the consumer will have to pay for increased arms spending; duration of conscription to the armed forces is increased from 18 months to two years.

(Dec.)   Attlee flies to the United States to dissuade President Truman from using nuclear weapons in Korean War.

1951   (Jan.)   Three-year defence programme costing £4,700 million
is announced by Attlee.

(Apr.)   Costs of rearmament are reflected in the imposition
of charges for teeth, spectacles and precriptions in the
budget. Bevan resigns as Minister of Labour in protest,
followed by the President of the Board of Trade Wilson and
junior Supply Minister Freeman.

(May)   British oil assets in Iran are nationalised.

(June)   Burgess and Maclean, two British officials who have
been long-term spies for the Soviet Union, defect to Moscow.

9   Labour in Opposition, 1951–64

Chronology of Main Events

1951   (Sept.)   Attlee calls general election for 25 October.
(Oct.)   Labour wins its highest ever share of the vote at the general election but the Conservatives return with a majority of 17.

1952   (Mar.)   Labour opposition abstains in vote on Conservative government's defence programme but 57 left-wing Labour backbenchers vote against.
(Oct.)   Bevanite supporters win six National Executive constituency places at the Labour Party conference. The Parliamentary Labour Party votes for disbanding of all unofficial party groupings by 188 votes to 51.
(Nov.)   Morrison defeats Bevan's challenge for deputy leadership by 194 votes to 82.

1953   (May)   Labour loses Sunderland South in a by-election as a general election majority of 306 becomes a 1,175 Conservative majority.
(June)   Labour leader Attlee says that a future Labour government would abolish commercial television.
(Oct.)   Labour Party conference supports comprehensive education but rejects the abolition of grammar schools. Morrison defeats Bevan's challenge for deputy leadership by 181 votes to 76.
(Nov.)   Labour opposition's call for an annual review of the continuation of conscription to the armed forces is defeated in the Commons.

1954   (Feb.)   Parliamentary Labour Party narrowly votes to support proposals for German rearmament by 113 to 104.
(Apr.)   Labour's call for an international summit meeting to discuss tension over nuclear weapons is accepted by Conservative prime minister Churchill. Bevan resigns from Shadow Cabinet in protest against Labour's support for the

formation of the South East Asia Treaty Organisation (SEATO) and is replaced by Wilson.

(July)   Attlee criticises the unwillingness of the United States to recognise Communist China. The left-wing Labour publication *It Need Not Happen* continues opposition to German rearmament.

(Oct.)   Labour Party conference accepts German rearmament by 3.2 million votes to 3 million. Gaitskell defeats Bevan in contest for party treasurer by 4.3 million votes to 2 million; Bevan attacks party leadership and, by implication, accuses Gaitskell of being a 'desiccated calculating machine'.

1955   (Feb.)   Labour backbencher Sidney Silverman's bill to suspend capital punishment is defeated in the Commons by 245 votes to 214.

(Mar.)   Bevan criticises Labour leader Attlee in a Commons debate on nuclear deterrence and leads a rebellion by 62 Labour MPs. The Parliamentary Labour Party votes by 141 to 112 to withdraw party whip from Bevan (he is re-admitted in April); National Executive votes by 14 to 13 against expelling Bevan from the party.

(Apr.)   Bill to enable Labour backbencher Anthony Wedgwood Benn to renounce peerage on death of father Lord Stansgate is rejected by the House of Lords.

(May)   Conservative government is re-elected with an increased majority; Labour's vote falls by 1.5 million on a reduced turnout.

(June)   Labour National Executive appoints a sub-committee under Wilson to examine party organisation.

(Oct.)   Wilson blames Labour's May general election defeat on party organisation being 'at the penny farthing stage in a jet-propelled era'. Labour Party conference re-elects Gaitskell as treasurer with 5.4 million votes to Bevan's 1.2 million.

(Dec.)   Attlee announces his retirement as party leader; Gaitskell elected as his successor with 157 votes to Bevan's 70.

1956   (Feb.)   Gaitskell appoints Bevan as opposition Colonial spokesperson in a conciliatory gesture. James Griffiths is elected Labour deputy leader with 141 votes to Bevan's 111; Morrison wins a humiliating 40 votes. Labour motion for the abolition of capital punishment is passed in a Commons free vote by 293 to 262 (rejected by the House of Lords in June).

(Apr.)   Labour Treasury spokesman Wilson describes Conservative Chancellor Macmillan's introduction of Premium Bonds as a 'squalid raffle'.

(Aug.)   Gaitskell criticises President Nasser in a Commons debate on the developing crisis over Egypt's threat to take control of the Suez Canal but argues against a military response.

(Oct.)   Bevan is elected party treasurer by 3 million votes to 2.7 million for right-winger George Brown. Gaitskell repeats warning against the use of force over Suez crisis at the Labour Party conference and, as RAF bombs Egyptian airfields, attacks the Conservative government for undermining democracy while the Soviet Union is crushing freedom risings in Hungary and Poland.

(Nov.)   Labour vote of censure over British role in Suez crisis is defeated in Commons by 324 votes to 255. Gaitskell calls for Conservative Party to oust Eden as leader; 'Law not War' rally addressed by Bevan in Trafalgar Square ends in violence.

1957   (Feb.)   Labour captures Lewisham from Conservatives in a by-election.

(July)   Odham's Press takes over control of the *Daily Herald* from the Trades Union Congress and the paper ceases its traditional automatic support of Labour and the trade union movement.

(Oct.)   Labour foreign affairs spokesman Bevan opposes unilateralist motion at the party conference on the grounds that it would send a British foreign secretary 'naked into the conference chamber'.

1958   (Feb.)   Labour captures Rochdale from Conservatives in a by-election. Labour criticises the Conservative government's reliance on nuclear weapons in a Commons defence debate.

(June)   Labour calls for abolition of the 11-plus examination in *Learning to Live*.

(Oct.)   Labour Party conference calls for partnership between the government, employers and unions to encourage the investment necessary for industrial expansion.

1959   (Mar.)   Twenty thousand attend a CND demonstration in Trafalgar Square.

(Apr.)   Bevan declares in the Commons that a future Labour government would end testing of nuclear weapons.

(Sept.)   Gaitskell promises the abolition of purchase tax and, as the general election approaches, that there will be no income tax increases under a Labour government.

(Oct.)   Labour suffers a third successive general election defeat as the Conservatives return with an increased majority.

Labour MP Douglas Jay advocates ending the party's identification with the working class to win middle-class support. Bevan is elected party deputy leader.

(Dec.)   Labour National Executive approves the establishment of the Young Socialists in an effort to broaden the party's appeal.

1960   (Mar.)   Forty-four Labour backbenchers defy leadership by abstaining on an Opposition Commons amendment supporting multilateral nuclear disarmament. Labour loses Brighouse and Spenborough to the Conservatives at a by-election.

(June)   Labour backbencher Kenneth Robinson's private member's bill on homosexual law reform is defeated in the Commons by 213 votes to 99.

(July)   Labour deputy leader Bevan dies. Labour National Executive reaffirms independence of Parliamentary Labour Party from other party bodies.

(Aug.)   Committee of 100 is formed to undertake non-violent agitation for unilateral nuclear disarmament.

(Oct.)   Passing of a motion supporting unilateral nuclear disarmament at the Labour Party conference by 3.3 million votes to 2.9 million provokes Gaitskell into declaring he will 'fight and fight and fight again' to save the party. William Rodgers issues *Victory for Sanity* to rally support for Gaitskell. Wilson announces he will mount first ever challenge to an incumbent party leader.

(Nov.)   Campaign for Democratic Socialism (CDS) is established to support Gaitskell's campaign against unilateralism. Gaitskell is re-elected party leader by 166 votes to Wilson's 81. George Brown defeats unilateralist candidate Fred Lee in party deputy leadership contest by 146 votes to 83. Labour backbencher Wedgwood Benn refuses to accept title of Lord Stansgate on father's death.

(Dec.)   Thirteen Labour backbenchers refuse to support the party leadership in a Commons' defence debate.

1961   (Mar.)   Michael Foot and four other Labour backbenchers defy the party leadership and vote in the Commons against Army and Air estimates; Foot accuses the leadership of mounting a witch-hunt when the party whip is withdrawn from the rebels.

(Apr.)   House of Commons denies admittance to Wedgwood Benn by 221 votes to 152, following his rejection of his father's title.

(May)   Wedgwood Benn returned with increased majority at Bristol South East by-election but Commons continues to refuse him admittance.

(Aug.)   Gaitskell leaves Labour's position on entry to the European Economic Community unclear in a Commons debate following Conservative prime minister Macmillan's announcement that Britain will seek membership.

(Oct.)   Labour Party conference overturns previous year's decision and rejects unilateral nuclear disarmament by 4.5 million votes to 1.7 million; a demand for wider public ownership is accepted by 3.7 million votes to 2.4 million.

(Nov.)   Gaitskell defeats Greenwood's challenge for party leadership by 171 votes to 81; Brown retains deputy leadership with 169 votes against Castle's 56.

1962   (Jan.)   Morgan Phillips stands down as party general secretary on health grounds and is succeeded by Len Williams.

(Mar.)   Labour MP Leo Abse's private member's bill to reform law on homosexuality is defeated in the Commons.

(May)   Young Socialists disrupt Gaitskell speech in Glasgow.

(July)   Labour-controlled London County Council (LCC) withholds co-operation from government proposals for a Greater London Council (GLC) on the grounds that it is intended to make it easier for Conservatives to win control.

(Sept.)   Gaitskell and other Commonwealth Labour leaders oppose Britain's application for entry to the European Economic Community.

(Oct.)   Gaitskell wins support from the left, but disappoints his allies by denouncing Britain's proposed entry to the European Economic Community as 'the end of a thousand years of history'. Labour National Executive attacks President Kennedy's mounting of a blockade on Cuba following the discovery of Soviet missiles.

(Nov.)   Brown defeats Wilson in deputy leadership contest by 133 votes to 103; Labour takes South Dorset from Conservatives in a by-election.

1963   (Jan.)   Labour leader Gaitskell dies suddenly at the age of 56.

(Feb.)   Wilson takes lead over Brown in first round of party leadership election as the right's vote is split between Brown and Callaghan and defeats Brown in the second round by 144 votes to 103.

(Mar.)   Labour defence spokesman Denis Healey declares in the House of Commons that a future Labour government would abandon Polaris.

(July)   Labour is unsuccessful in its opposition to the London Government Act (establishing the Greater London Council and the Inner London Education Authority). The Peerage Act enables Anthony Wedgwood Benn to renounce title of Viscount Stansgate (he is returned as an MP in August).

(Oct.)   New Labour leader Wilson sets out technology and planning as part of a new image of socialism at the party's annual conference, emphasising efficiency and modernisation rather than poverty and grievances.

1964   (Jan.)   Wilson advocates greater state involvement in industrial investment.

(Apr.)   Labour wins control of new Greater London Council (GLC).

(Oct.)   Labour wins general election with a majority of four seats.

10 Labour in Government and Opposition, 1964–79

Labour Government, 1964–70 – Principal Ministers

(All held office from October 1964 to June 1970 unless otherwise indicated.)

Prime Minister	Harold Wilson
Lord President of the Council	Herbert Bowden (Oct. 1964–Aug. 1966) Richard Crossman (Aug. 1966–Oct. 1968) Fred Peart (Oct. 1968–June 1970)
Lord Chancellor	Lord Gardiner
Lord Privy Seal	Earl of Longford (Oct. 1964–Dec. 1965) Sir Frank Soskice (Dec. 1965–Apr. 1966) Earl of Longford (Apr. 1966–Jan. 1968) Lord Shackleton (Jan.–Apr. 1968) Fred Peart (Apr.–Oct. 1968) Lord Shackleton (Oct. 1968–June 1970)
Chancellor of the Exchequer	James Callaghan (Oct. 1964–Nov. 1967) Roy Jenkins (Nov. 1967–June 1970)
Secretary of State for Economic Affairs	George Brown (Oct. 1964–Aug. 1966) Michael Stewart (Aug. 1966–Aug. 1967)

Peter Shore
(Aug. 1967–Oct. 1969)

(Office abolished in Oct. 1969)

Secretary of State for Foreign Affairs   Patrick Gordon-
Walker
(Oct. 1964–Jan. 1965)
Michael Stewart
(Jan. 1965–Aug. 1966)
George Brown
(Aug. 1966–Mar. 1968)
Michael Stewart
(Mar. 1968–June 1970)
(Amalgamated with the Commonwealth Office in Oct. 1968)

Secretary of State for Home Affairs   Sir Frank Soskice
(Oct. 1964–Dec. 1965)
Roy Jenkins
(Dec. 1965–Nov. 1967)
James Callaghan
(Nov. 1967–June 1970)

Secretary of State for the Colonies   Anthony Greenwood
(Oct. 1964–Dec. 1965)
Earl of Longford
(Dec. 1965–Apr. 1966)
Fred Lee
(Apr.–Aug. 1966)
(Absorbed into the Commonwealth Affairs Department in Aug. 1966)

Secretary of State for Commonwealth Relations Arthur Bottomley
(Oct. 1964–Aug. 1966)
Herbert Bowden
(Aug. 1966–Aug. 1967)
George Thomson
(Aug. 1967–Oct. 1968)
(Office renamed Commonwealth Affairs in Aug. 1966 and
amalgamated with the Foreign Office in Oct. 1968)

Secretary of State for Defence   Denis Healey

Secretary of State for Education and Science   Michael Stewart
(Oct. 1964–Jan. 1965)
Anthony Crosland
(Jan. 1965–Aug. 1967)

	Patrick Gordon-Walker (Aug. 1967–Apr. 1968) Edward Short (Apr. 1968–June 1970)
Minister of Labour	Ray Gunter (Oct. 1964–Apr. 1968) Barbara Castle (Apr. 1968–June 1970)

(Renamed Department of Employment and Productivity from
Apr. 1968)

Secretary of State for Health and Social Security	Richard Crossman (Oct. 1968–June 1970)
Secretary of State for Scotland	William Ross (Oct. 1964–June 1970)
Secretary of State for Wales	James Griffiths (Oct. 1964–Apr. 1966) Cledwyn Hughes (Apr. 1966–Apr. 1968) George Thomas (Apr. 1968–June 1970)
President of the Board of Trade	Douglas Jay (Oct. 1964–Aug. 1967) Anthony Crosland (Aug. 1967–Oct. 1969) Roy Mason (Oct. 1969–June 1970)
Minister of Agriculture, Fisheries and Food	Fred Peart (Oct. 1964–Apr. 1968) Cledwyn Hughes (Apr. 1968–June 1970)
Chancellor of the Duchy of Lancaster	Douglas Houghton (Oct. 1964–Apr. 1966)

(Office removed from the Cabinet in Apr. 1966)

Minister of Housing and Local Government	Richard Crossman (Oct. 1964–Aug. 1966) Anthony Greenwood (Aug. 1966–Oct. 1969)

(Office removed from the Cabinet in Oct. 1969)

Minister of Overseas Development	Barbara Castle (Oct. 1964–Dec. 1965) Anthony Greenwood (Dec. 1965–Aug. 1966) Arthur Bottomley (Aug. 1966–Aug. 1967)

(Office removed from the Cabinet in Aug. 1967)

Paymaster-General	Lord Shackleton (Apr.–Nov. 1968) Judith Hart (Nov. 1968–Oct. 1969) Harold Lever (Oct. 1969–June 1970)

(Minister in the Cabinet but not office)

Minister with Portfolio	Douglas Houghton (Apr. 1966–Jan. 1967) Patrick Gordon-Walker (Jan.–Aug. 1967) George Thomas (Oct. 1968–Oct. 1969) Peter Shore (Oct. 1969–June 1970)

(Minister in the Cabinet but not office)

Minister of Power	Fred Lee (Oct. 1964–Apr. 1966) Richard Marsh (Apr. 1966–Apr. 1968) Ray Gunter (Apr.–July 1968) Roy Mason (July 1968–Oct. 1969)

(Office abolished in Oct. 1969)

Minister of Technology	Frank Cousins (Oct. 1964–July 1966) Tony Benn (July 1966–June 1970)

Minister of Transport	Tom Fraser (Oct. 1964–Dec. 1965) Barbara Castle (Dec. 1965–Apr. 1968)

Richard Marsh
(Apr. 1968–Oct. 1969)

(Office removed from the Cabinet in Oct. 1969)

Chief Whip in the House of Commons

Edward Short
(Oct. 1964–July 1966)
John Silkin
(July 1966–Apr. 1969)
Robert Mellish
(Apr. 1969–June 1970)

Labour Government, 1974–79 – Principal Ministers

(All held office from March 1974 to May 1979 unless otherwise indicated.)

Prime Minister

Harold Wilson
(Mar. 1974–Apr. 1976)
James Callaghan
(Apr. 1976–May 1979)

Lord President of the Council

Edward Short
(Mar. 1974–Apr. 1976)
Michael Foot
(Apr. 1976–May 1979)

Lord Chancellor

Lord Elwyn-Jones

Lord Privy Seal

Lord Shepherd
(Mar. 1974–Sept. 1976)
Lord Peart
(Sept. 1976–May 1979)

Chancellor of the Exchequer

Denis Healey

Secretary of State for Foreign and
  Commonwealth Affairs

James Callaghan
(Mar. 1974–Apr. 1976)
Anthony Crosland
(Apr. 1976–Feb. 1977)
David Owen
(Feb. 1977–May 1979)

Secretary of State for Home Affairs

Roy Jenkins
(Mar. 1974–Sept. 1976)
Merlyn Rees
(Sept. 1976–May 1979)

Secretary of State for Defence

Roy Mason
(Mar. 1974–Sept. 1976)

Fred Mulley
(Sept. 1976–May 1979)

Secretary of State for Education and
    Science

Reg Prentice
(Mar. 1974–June 1975)
Fred   Mulley
(June 1975–Sept. 1976)
Shirley Williams
(Sept. 1976–May 1979)

Secretary of State for Employment

Michael Foot
(Mar. 1974–Apr. 1976)
Albert Booth
(Apr. 1976–May 1979)

Secretary of State for Energy

Eric Varley
(Mar. 1974–June 1975)
Tony Benn
(June 1975–May 1979)

Secretary of State for the Environment

Anthony Crosland
(Mar. 1974–Apr. 1976)
Peter Shore
(Apr. 1976–May 1979)

Secretary of State for Health and Social
    Security

Barbara Castle
(Mar. 1974–Apr. 1976)
David Ennals
(Apr. 1976–May 1979)

Secretary of State for Industry

Tony Benn
(Mar. 1974–June 1975)
Eric Varley
(June 1975–May 1979)

Secretary of State for Northern Ireland

Merlyn Rees
(Mar. 1979–Sept. 1976)
Roy Mason
(Sept. 1976–May 1979)

Secretary of State for Prices and Consumer
    Protection

Shirley Williams
(Mar. 1974–Sept. 1976)
Roy Hattersley
(Sept. 1976–May 1979)

Secretary of State for Scotland

William Ross
(Mar. 1974–Apr. 1976)

	Bruce Millan (Apr. 1976–May 1979)
Secretary of State for Wales	J. Morris
Secretary of State for Trade	Peter Shore (Mar. 1974–Apr. 1976) Edmund Dell (Apr. 1976–Nov. 1978) John Smith (Nov. 1978–May 1979)
Chancellor of the Duchy of Lancaster	Harold Lever
Minister of Agriculture, Fisheries and Food	Fred Peart (Mar. 1974–Sept. 1976) John Silkin (Sept. 1976–May 1979)
Chief Whip in the House of Commons	Robert Mellish (Mar. 1974–Apr. 1976) Michael Cocks (Apr. 1976–May 1979)

Ministerial Resignations

1966   (Feb.)   Christopher Mayhew resigns as Minister for the Navy in protest against defence estimates and in particular over the failure to order the construction of a new aircraft carrier.
(July)   Frank Cousins resigns as Minister of Technology over the imposition of an incomes policy which his background as general secretary of the Transport and General Workers' Union made unacceptable.

1967   (July)   Margaret Herbison resigns as Minister of Social Security over the government's social services policies.

1968   (Jan.)   Earl of Longford resigns in protest against the postponement of the raising of the school leaving age to 16 as a result of spending cuts.
(Mar.)   George Brown resigns as Foreign Secretary, ostensibly because he is not consulted over the temporary closure of the London foreign exchange, but later complains about his dissatisfaction with Wilson's overall conduct of government. He remains deputy leader.

(July)   Ray Gunter resigns as Minister of Power, complaining of general dissatisfaction with government policy.

1975   (Apr.)   Eric Heffer resigns as Minister of State at the Department of Industry following his open opposition in the House of Commons to the government's policy towards Europe.
(June)   Judith Hart resigns as Minister of Overseas Development in protest against what she sees as the government's right-wing stance. She returns to office in 1977.

1976   (Feb.)   Joan Lestor resigns in protest against education spending reductions.
(Dec.)   Reg Prentice resigns because he is out of sympathy with government policy. He goes on to join the Conservatives.

1977   (Nov.)   Joe Ashton resigns as a whip over the government's handling of a power dispute.

Political and Economic Chronology

1964   (Oct.)   Harold Wilson becomes prime minister of the first Labour government for 13 years; George Brown is appointed deputy prime minister and Secretary of State for the newly established Department of Economic Affairs, James Callaghan Chancellor of the Exchequer, and Patrick Gordon-Walker Foreign Secretary. Callaghan attempts to meet £800 million balance of payments deficit with the immediate levying of a 15% imports surcharge (reduced to 10% in Apr. 1965 and ended in Nov. 1966).
(Nov.)   Callaghan's first budget increases income tax and petrol duty, abolishes prescription charges and raises pensions. Wilson (having agreed against devaluation with Brown and Callaghan) tells a City of London audience that the government is determined to defend the value of sterling; bank rate is increased to 7% and $3,000 million loan is arranged from overseas banks to preserve level of sterling.

1965   (Jan.)   Foreign Secretary Patrick Gordon-Walker (defeated at the general election in Smethwick) loses Leyton at by-election and resigns; he is succeeded by Michael Stewart.
(Feb.)   Brown announces establishment of a National Board for Prices and Incomes.
(Apr.)   Callaghan's budget increases direct and indirect taxes, introduces capital gains and corporation taxes and cancels order for TSR–2 aircraft on grounds of expense.

Wilson announces in New York that his government will not devalue the pound.

(May)   Britain exercises the right to draw $1,400 from the International Monetary Fund. Government White Paper on steel nationalisation is narrowly approved in the House of Commons by 310 votes to 306.

(June)   Conservative opposition attempt to delay introduction of corporation tax is defeated on the Speaker's casting vote. Liberal leader Jo Grimond calls for Lib-Lab coalition in view of the government's precarious majority. Bank of England calls for policy to control income increases to meet balance of payments problems.

(July)   Government introduces further deflationary measures in which domestic public spending is cut by £350 million and the defence budget is reduced by £100 million; exchange controls tightened; clause of Finance Bill defeated in the Commons.

(Aug.)   Fall in reserves to £140 million leads to run of rumours that government is planning devaluation. Trades Disputes Bill receives Royal Assent, reversing 1964 *Rookes v Barnard* case and extending trade union immunities.

(Sept.)   Economic Affairs Secretary Brown introduces a National Economic Plan proposing a 25% increase in gross national product by 1970.

(Oct.)   Labour Party conference approves government's support of US policy in Vietnam by 3.6 million votes to 2.5 million. Callaghan declares Britain's balance of payment deficit will be cleared in a year. Dr Horace King becomes first Labour MP to be elected Speaker of the House of Commons.

1966   (Jan.)   Government issues a White Paper proposing the establishment of an Industrial Reorganisation Corporation to assist in the rationalisation of British industry. Labour holds Hull North in a by-election with an increased majority despite the intervention of a candidate opposing the government's support for US war in Vietnam.

(Feb.)   Wilson calls general election for 31 March; Labour's manifesto *Time for Decision* calls for more extensive economic planning.

(Mar.)   Labour returned at general election with overall majority of 97 seats; Callaghan remains Chancellor and Stewart Foreign Secretary.

(May)   Budget introduces selective employment tax to encourage employment in manufacturing industry rather than

services and ends import surcharge from November. A Royal
Commission is appointed under the chairmanship of Sir John
Maud to review local government in England and Wales.
Government declares state of emergency to meet seamen's
strike which seriously affects the economy and which Wilson
blames on Communists and left-wingers.

(June)   Motion at Parliamentary Labour Party meeting
calling for a British withdrawal from East of Suez is defeated
by 233 votes to 29.

(July)   Seamen's strike ends. Thirty-two Labour backbenchers
abstain in a Commons vote on the government's support
for US policy in Vietnam. Labour lose Carmarthen to Plaid
Cymru in a by-election. Government's 'July measures' impose
six months wages, prices, profits and dividends increase
'standstill', restrain credit and increase bank rate. Brown's
offer of his resignation as Economic Affairs Secretary because
of the thwarting of his hopes for an expansionist policy is
rejected. Technology Minister and Transport and General
Workers' Union leader Frank Cousins's resignation in protest
against incomes policy is accepted.

(Aug.)   Twenty-six Labour backbenchers abstain in vote on
Prices and Incomes Bill which includes a freeze on pay
increases. Stewart replaces Brown as Economic Affairs
Secretary and Brown becomes Foreign Secretary.

(Oct.)   Labour Party annual conference supports
government's incomes policy by 3.8 million votes to 2.5
million despite criticisms by Technology Minister and
Transport and General Workers' Union leader Frank
Cousins. Wilson declares that the government is not bound
by conference decisions when support for US policy in
Vietnam is defeated by 3.8 million votes to 2.6 million.

1967   (Jan.)   The government announces that a period of 'severe
restraint' will follow the six months wage and prices freeze
imposed in July 1966.

(Mar.)   Following a spate of Labour backbench rebellions
over economic, defence and foreign policy, Wilson issues a
warning in his 'every dog is allowed one bite' speech.

(May)   Following Wilson's announcement that the Cabinet
has agreed to seek entry to the European Economic
Community, 34 Labour MPs vote against the government
(including seven Parliamentary Private Secretaries) and
51 abstain following a three-day debate on application
(government wins the vote by 488 votes to 62).

(June)   Government announces a 'period of moderation' to follow period of 'severe restraint' on incomes; increases are not to exceed 3–3.5%.

(July)   Twenty-two Labour MPs abstain in vote on government restraint on income rises, reducing majority to 56. Callaghan rejects devaluation as a 'way out of Britain's difficulties' but introduces higher charges for school meals combined with an increase in family allowances. Nineteen Labour backbenchers abstain in a vote on a Defence Policy Statement reducing Britain's responsibilities 'East of Suez'. Nationalised British Steel Corporation comes into operation.

(Aug.)   Wilson announces he is 'overlord' of the Department of Economic Affairs (with Peter Shore as minister) in Cabinet reshuffle.

(Sept.)   Labour loses Walthamstow West and Cambridge to Conservatives in by-elections.

(Oct.)   Labour Party conference calls for the government to dissociate itself from US involvement in Vietnam but supports wage restraint and application for entry to the European Economic Community. Queen's Speech proposes the abolition of the hereditary basis of the House of Lords. Former Labour prime minister Clement Attlee dies at the age of 84.

(Nov.)   Pound devalued from $2.80 to $2.40, bank rate raised to 8% and cuts in bank lending imposed. Roy Jenkins and James Callaghan switch offices of Home Secretary and Chancellor of the Exchequer. Labour loses Hamilton to the Scottish National Party in a by-election. Forty-six Labour MPs criticise government's deflationary economic policies.

(Dec.)   Eighteen Labour backbenchers vote against and 16 abstain in vote on government Letter of Intent to the International Monetary Fund promising further deflationary policies. Brown leads opposition to Wilson in Cabinet over embargo on arms sales to South Africa but the policy is retained and Wilson emerges with his dominance confirmed.

1968   (Jan.)   Government introduces spending cuts of £716 million following devaluation, including a reduction in the house building programme, the re-introduction of NHS prescription and dental charges, a deferment of the raising of the school leaving age to 16, cancellation of the purchase of the F–111 fighter aircraft and a withdrawal of the British presence 'East of Suez' by 1971. Twenty-five Labour backbenchers abstain in a vote on the cuts in the Commons and one resigns the whip over defence reductions.

(Mar.)   Brown dramatically resigns from the government, ostensibly because of dissatisfaction over how the Cabinet reaches decisions, but he remains party deputy leader. Jenkins's deflationary budget imposes £923 million extra indirect taxes and promises 'two years of hard slog'. Labour lose Acton, Meriden and Dudley to the Conservatives in by-elections.

(Apr.)   Wilson gives up control over Economic Affairs Department and Castle is appointed Secretary of State for Employment and Productivity in government restructuring.

(May)   International Publishing Chairman Cecil King calls for the replacement of Wilson as party leader in the *Daily Mirror*. Thirty-four Labour backbenchers abstain in second reading of Prices and Incomes Bill; 49 Labour backbenchers vote against restoration of NHS prescription charges.

(June)   Wilson threatens 'comprehensive and radical' reforms of the second chamber after the House of Lords rejects economic sanctions against the illegal white Rhodesian regime by 193 votes to 184.

(July)   Harry Nicholas succeeds Sir Len Williams as Labour Party general secretary.

(Oct.)   Labour Party annual conference votes five to one against statutory incomes policy but Chancellor Jenkins and Employment and Productivity Secretary Castle insist that the government will not be influenced. An attack on a peaceful civil rights march in Londonderry opens a crisis in Northern Ireland; government appoints Cameron Commission to enquire into the causes of the crisis. Forty-nine Labour backbenchers vote against and over 100 abstain on Wilson's offer to allow white Rhodesian prime minister Smith to remain in office during negotiations.

(Nov.)   Government imposes a credit squeeze and strengthens hire purchase restrictions in the face of a trade imbalance. Wilson guarantees the constitutional status of Northern Ireland as part of the United Kingdom but calls for drastic improvements in Catholic civil rights. The House of Commons and House of Lords approve a government White Paper on reform of the second chamber.

1969   (Jan.)   Castle introduces government proposals to regulate the trade unions – *In Place of Strife* – in the Commons; compulsory strike ballots will be introduced and a 'cooling off period' imposed in unofficial strikes; both will be underpinned by sanctions. The document opens up a serious crisis in relations with the Trades Union Congress.

(Mar.)   Fifty-five Labour backbenchers vote against and 39 abstain in a vote in the Commons on *In Place of Strife*, which is accepted by 224 votes to 62. The Labour Party National Executive rejects the proposals by 16 votes to 5, with party Treasurer Callaghan among the objectors. Callaghan ends his revolt when the Cabinet reaffirms its support for the document's proposals but he is excluded from further discussions of the issue.

(Apr.)   Jenkins presents a budget continuing the government's deflationary policies, imposing £340 million tax increases; he blames industrial action for Britain's uncompetitive economic position and says that the government's proposed trade union legislation is a remedy. Wilson tells the Parliamentary Labour Party that legislation is essential 'to the government's continuance in office'. Castle denies that the sanctions legislation arising from *In Place of Strife* will involve imprisonment. Wilson announces the abandonment of House of Lords reform. Fighting between police and Catholics in Belfast and Londonderry is followed by the resignation of Terence O'Neill as Northern Ireland prime minister.

(May)   Parliamentary Labour Party chairman Douglas Houghton warns the Cabinet that backbenchers would not support a trade union bill; the government agrees to delay publication of a bill following discussions with the Trades Union Congress on alternatives to legislation but rejects TUC proposals for voluntary action as insufficient.

(June)   A TUC special conference rejects the *In Place of Strife* proposals. Wilson announces two weeks later that legislation is to be abandoned in favour of the TUC's proposals for voluntary intervention by the General Council in industrial disputes.

(Aug.)   Troops deployed in Londonderry following three days of rioting in which ten people are killed, 100 wounded and Catholics set up 'no go' areas to prevent further Protestant attacks. Wilson and Northern Ireland prime minister Chichester-Clark issue a Downing Street Declaration which promises rapid civil rights reforms, the extension of employment and housing opportunities to Catholics, and reaffirms the commitment that Northern Ireland will remain British. The Royal Ulster Constabulary B-Specials are replaced by a non-sectarian Ulster Defence Regiment.

(Oct.)   The Department of Economic Affairs (DEA) – established in 1964 in a spirit of optimistic expansionism – is wound up. Labour's new programme *Agenda for a Generation,* which includes proposals for a new wealth tax, is endorsed at the Labour Party conference by 3.5 million votes to 2.2 million.

(Dec.) $100 million lost from reserves on 'Mad Friday' as rumours spread that the pound is to be devalued and that Wilson and Jenkins have resigned. Forty-nine Labour backbenchers vote against the government and 44 abstain over the issue of support for the United States in Vietnam.

1970   (Jan.)   Employment Secretary Castle introduces a bill providing for equal pay for women from 1975.

(Mar.)   Jenkins's budget gives minimal tax concessions despite surplus of £2,444 million as part of policy of encouraging growth, and concentrates on creating a balance of payments surplus rather than a pre-election boom. Thirty-six Labour backbenchers abstain in vote on the government's defence White Paper.

(Apr.)   The Conservatives win control of the Greater London Council.

(May)   Wilson calls a general election for 18 June. Labour manifesto *Now Britain's Strong Let's Make It Great To Live In,* praises government's record but says little about future plans.

(June)   Labour suffers a surprising general election defeat at the hands of the Conservatives who win 330 seats to Labour's 287; Brown is among those who lose their seats and he resigns as deputy leader.

(July)   Jenkins wins party deputy leadership election with 133 votes against Foot's 67 and Peart's 48.

(Aug.)   Social Democratic and Labour Party (SDLP) formed in Northern Ireland as the voice of moderate nationalism; affiliates to the Socialist International.

(Oct.)   Labour Party annual conference rejects any incomes policies by future Labour government by 3.1 million votes to 2.8 million; Jenkins calls for the party to be free from trade union control.

(Dec.)   Conservative government's Industrial Relations Bill is vehemently opposed by the Labour Opposition.

1971   (Apr.)   Labour leader Wilson warns of too premature an entry to the European Economic Community on unfavourable terms.

(May)   One hundred and twenty Labour MPs support a backbench motion opposing entry to the European Economic Community. Labour wins Bromsgrove from the Conservatives in a by-election.

(July)   Labour holds special conference on entry to the European Economic Community; Wilson attacks terms negotiated by Conservative government while his deputy, Jenkins, denounces his stand as 'narrow' at a private Parliamentary Labour Party meeting.

(Oct.)   Labour Party conference votes to oppose entry to the European Economic Community by five to one; calls for widespread nationalisation, including banking and insurance. Labour MPs ordered by the Chief Whip to vote against British entry to the European Economic Community under a three-line whip; 69 Labour MPs, led by the party's deputy leader Roy Jenkins, vote in favour of entry.

(Nov.)   Jenkins is re-elected as Labour deputy leader at a second ballot with 140 votes to Foot's 126. Wilson attempts to find solution to Northern Ireland crisis by proposing that the Irish Republic declares its allegiance to the British monarchy as a preliminary to a united Ireland.

(Dec.)   Two leading opponents of entry to the European Economic Community – Michael Foot and Peter Shore – are given responsibility for European affairs in Labour's Shadow Cabinet.

1972   (Jan.)   Liaison Committee established by Parliamentary Labour Party, Party National Executive and TUC membership, under joint TUC–Labour Party chairmanship.

(Mar.)   Labour Shadow Cabinet announces support for a Conservative backbench motion demanding a referendum before entry to the European Economic Community.

(Apr.)   Jenkins resigns as Labour deputy leader in protest against support for a referendum; Short wins the position in second ballot with 145 votes to Foot's 116.

(Oct.)   Labour Party conference votes for further nationalisation, including banking, insurance and shipbuilding. Labour loses Rochdale to the Liberals in a by-election.

(Dec.)   The Parliamentary Labour Party refuses to select representatives to attend the European Parliament as nominated members.

1973   (Jan.)   Britain becomes a member of European Economic Community; Labour refuses to send delegates to the first sitting of the European Parliament at which Britain is represented.

(Feb.)   Joint Labour Party/TUC document, *Economic Policy and the Cost of Living*, introduces the concept of the 'Social Contract' under which a future Labour government would impose price controls, retain free collective bargaining, encourage industrial democracy and a policy of economic expansion.

(Mar.)   Labour MP Dick Taverne resigns in protest against left-wing influence in the party and forces a by-election in Lincoln which he wins under the Democratic Labour label.

(June)   Labour Party National Executive *Programme for Britain* calls for nationalisation of the top 25 companies; this is removed following criticisms from party leader Wilson. Campaign for Labour Party Democracy is formed to make the party leadership more accountable to activists.

(Oct.)   Labour Party conference votes to continue boycott of European Economic Community institutions until membership has been confirmed by a referendum or general election. Radical party document *Labour's Programme, 1973* calls for 'a fundamental and irreversible shift in the balance of power and wealth in favour of working people'.

(Nov.)   Labour loses Glasgow Govan to the Scottish National Party in a by-election. Labour leader Wilson calls on front bench spokesmen to submit speeches to party headquarters and not to criticise one another publicly.

1974   (Feb.)   Conservative government calls a 'Who governs Britain?' general election as a miners' strike begins. Labour manifesto *Get Britain Back to Work* calls for state intervention in the economy but rejects any statutory incomes policy. Wilson announces that a future Labour government will have a 'Social Contract' with the unions. Labour returns with more seats (301) than the Conservatives (296), but fewer votes.

(Mar.)   Wilson forms a minority government; Healey is appointed Chancellor of the Exchequer, Callaghan Foreign Secretary and former Bevanite Foot becomes Employment Secretary. From March to October the government is defeated 17 times in the Commons. The government ends the three-day week and power restrictions imposed by the previous Conservative government and offers the miners a £103 million pay deal which is accepted.

(Apr.)   The government declares that it will insist on a renegotiation of the terms of British entry to the European Economic Community.

(May)   Ulster Workers' Council strike against the Sunningdale Agreement (negotiated by the Conservatives in December 1973) leads to the suspension of the Northern Ireland Assembly and restoration of direct rule from London; the Irish Republican Army (IRA) opens a bombing campaign in Britain.
(June)   Government defeated by 311 votes to 290 following a debate on its industrial policy, and an Opposition motion on rates is carried by 298 votes to 289.
(July)   Government repeals the Conservative Industrial Relations Act 1971, ending statutory incomes policy. Industry Secretary Benn proposes support to workers' co-operatives as a weapon against unemployment.
(Oct.)   Labour is returned with a majority of three at the general election; Wilson re-appoints Healey as Chancellor, Callaghan as Foreign Secretary and Jenkins as Home Secretary. Five people are killed and 70 injured in an IRA pub bombing in Guildford.
(Nov.)   Following IRA pub bombing in Birmingham in which 21 are killed and 120 injured, government introduces the Prevention of Terrorism Act (described by Jenkins as temporary and 'draconian'); the IRA is proscribed, the police are given powers to hold suspects for five days and there are provisions for deportation to Northern Ireland.
(Dec.)   Government announces that it is to give financial aid to the motor manufacturer British Leyland to maintain its survival.

1975   (Jan.)   The government introduces an industry bill which includes the creation of a National Enterprise Board. A referendum on whether the UK is to remain in the European Economic Community is announced. The government is defeated on its Social Security Bill by 280 votes to 265 as nine Labour MPs withhold support.
(Mar.)   Labour government issues a White Paper, *Membership of the EEC: Report on Renegotiation*, in which it comes out against withdrawal from the Common Market.
(Apr.)   Special party conference votes by two to one for withdrawal from the EEC. The government accepts proposal in Ryder report for an eight-year £1,400 investment programme to support British Leyland.
(June)   Labour ministers are allowed to break Cabinet unity by campaigning on either side in the European Economic Community (EEC) referendum; 17,378,000 (67.2%) vote to remain in the EEC and 8,470,000 (32.8%) vote against.

(July)   Government White Paper, *The Attack on Inflation*, announces an incomes policy under which there is to be an upper limit of £6 on pay increases until August 1976. The government is defeated on an Opposition amendment to the Finance Bill by 108 votes to 106.

(Aug.)   Annual inflation rate reaches 26.9%. The government is defeated on an amendment to the Housing Finance Bill by 268 votes to 261.

(Nov.)   Conference held by the government and representatives of the Trades Union Congress (TUC), the employers' Confederation of British Industry (CBI) and the National Economic Development Council (NEDC) on industrial development. The government requests a £975 million loan from the International Monetary Fund (IMF) and announces cash limits will be imposed on 1976–77 public spending.

(Dec.)   Internment without trial in Northern Ireland (imposed by the previous Conservative government) is ended.

1976   (Feb.)   Government White Paper announces public expenditure will be cut by £1 billion in 1977–78 and £2.4 billion in 1978–79.

(Mar.)   Wilson makes a sudden announcement of resignation as prime minister. Government is defeated on motion approving public expenditure programme by 297 to 280 votes but wins subsequent confidence vote by 310 votes to 308. Sterling reaches an historic low of US$2. Direct rule in Northern Ireland continues following abortive negotiations on re-establishing an assembly.

(Apr.)   Six candidates – Callaghan, Foot, Jenkins, Benn, Healey and Crosland – run for party leadership; Callaghan defeats Foot in third ballot by 176 votes to 137. Callaghan appoints Foot as Lord President of the Council, Crosland as Foreign Secretary. Budget provides for £1.3 billion in tax reductions provided the TUC accepts continuation of pay restraint.

(May)   Stage 2 of the government's anti-inflationary wages policy sets pay limit of £2.50 minimum and £4.00 maximum a week; TUC agrees at special conference.

(June)   US and European central banks allow UK further standby credits.

(July)   Government announces a further £1,000 million spending reduction for 1977–78.

(Sept.)   Jenkins resigns as Home Secretary to accept post of European Commission president. Government asks for $3.9

billion standby credit from the International Monetary Fund. George Thomas becomes first Labour Speaker of the House of Commons.

(Oct.)   Minimum lending rate is increased to 15% as sterling reaches lowest ever point against dollar at $1.5675. Foot defeats Williams in party deputy leadership election by 166 votes to 128.

(Nov.)   Two Labour abstentions bring about government defeat on major clause in Dock Labour Bill.

(Dec.)   Government announces further £1,000 million spending cut for 1977–78, £1,500 million for 1978–79 and the sale of shares in British Petroleum under IMF pressure.

1977   (Feb.)   Bullock Report recommends an extension in industrial democracy. The government is defeated in an attempt to impose a guillotine on the Scotland and Wales Bill as 22 Labour MPs vote against and 23 abstain. Owen is appointed Foreign Secretary following the sudden death of Crosland. Government attempt to maintain British Leyland's survival is threatened by a strike.

(Mar.)   Government defeats Conservative censure motion by 322 votes to 298 with Liberal support following the negotiation of a Lib-Lab pact.

(June)   Loyalist strike organised by the Ulster United Action Council to put pressure on the government is abandoned.

(July)   Stage 3 of government incomes policy provides for a 10% limit on wage rises; Chancellor Healey threatens financial penalties on employers who breach the limit.

(Nov.)   Fire-fighters begin strike for a 30% pay increase in breach of government incomes policy (troops are deployed and the strike ends in January 1978). The government suffers a 199 to 184 vote defeat on the first clause of the Scotland Devolution Bill.

(Dec.)   Government recommendation for proportional representation in elections to European Parliament is defeated as 115 Labour MPs vote against in a free vote.

1978   (Jan.)   Government is defeated by 291 votes to 281 on motion to devalue Green Pound by 7.5%. An amendment is passed to Scotland Devolution Bill to create a 40% threshold in favour as 34 Labour MPs vote against government. The government is forced to exclude Orkney and Shetland from the bill by 204 to 118 votes. Liberals agree to continue the Lib-Lab Pact.

(Feb.)   Inflation falls below 10% for the first time in five years.

(May)   Callaghan refuses to resign following the passing of Conservative amendments to reduce the standard rate of income tax from 34% to 33% and to raise the threshold for higher tax to £8,000. Liberal leader Steel announces the end of the Lib-Lab Pact from August.

(July)   Government announces the next stage of its income policy will be a 5% guideline on pay increases. An amendment to the Wales Bill to prevent MPs standing for a Welsh Assembly is carried against the government by 293 votes to 260.

(Oct.)   Labour Party conference votes against acceptance of the government's 5% pay guideline.

(Nov.)   TUC General Council announces its rejection of the 5% pay guideline.

(Dec.)   Government is defeated on retaining sanctions against companies breaching pay policy by 285 votes to 283, but goes on to win ensuing vote of confidence. Britain is convicted by the European Court of Human Rights of 'inhuman and degrading conduct' towards Republican prisoners in Northern Ireland.

1979   (Jan.)   'Winter of discontent' threatens government's incomes policy (and survival) as 150,000 are laid off as a result of a road haulage strike. The government survives a confidence vote on its industrial relations policy.

(Mar.)   Wales votes against devolution in referendum and Scotland's vote in favour fails to reach the threshold of 40% of the total electorate. The government loses vote of confidence (the first such defeat since that of the Labour government in 1924) by 311 votes to 310; Callaghan calls a May general election.

(Apr.)   Labour manifesto, *The Labour Way is the Better Way*, ignores left-wing proposals.

(May)   Labour – returning with 269 seats and 36.9% of the vote – is defeated by the Conservatives' 339 seats and 43.9% share.

Chronology of Social Policy

1964   (Dec.)   Protection from Eviction Act outlaws evictions of tenants without a court order. Industrial Training Act establishes an Industrial Training Board to encourage training for people in work. Murder (Abolition of the Death Penalty) Bill is introduced by Labour backbencher Sidney Silverman; it receives a second reading by 355 votes to 170.

1965   (Jan.)   NHS prescriptions charges abolished.

(Apr.)   Education Secretary Crosland announces binary system of higher education with division into universities and polytechnics.

(May)   Private member's bill to legalise homosexual activity in private passes in the House of Lords by 94 votes to 49. The government refuses to permit Labour backbencher Leo Abse to introduce a bill in the Commons legalising homosexual activity.

(July)   Crosland issues Circular 10/65 to local authorities to encourage comprehensive secondary education and the end of the 11-plus examination. Certificate of Secondary Education (CSE) introduced.

(Oct.)   Government White Paper proposes the establishment of an Ombudsman (Parliamentary Commissioner).

(Nov.)   Murder (Abolition of the Death Penalty) Act suspends death penalty until 1970 and brings in mandatory life sentence.

(Dec.)   Rent Act introduces registration of rents, extends security of tenure and protection from eviction for private tenants.

1966   (Feb.)   Government announces its intention to set up a 'University of the Air' (later the Open University). The National Insurance Act introduces earnings-related supplements to sickness and unemployment benefits. Ministry of Social Services is established to pay benefits as a right to people on low incomes.

(July)   Labour backbencher Leo Abse's bill to legalise homosexual acts between consenting adults over 21 passes by 244 to 100 on a free vote.

1967   (Apr.)   An Ombudsman (Parliamentary Commissioner) is appointed to consider complaints against government departments and to impose remedies.

(Oct.)   The Abortion Act, a private member's bill supported by the government, allows abortion if danger is posed to the physical or mental health of a woman or another child, or in the case of a substantial risk that the child will be physically or mentally disabled. The Family Planning Act empowers local health authorities to establish family planning service with free advice and means-tested provision of contraceptive devices. The Criminal Justice Act introduces suspended prison sentences and allows a 10 to 2 majority vote for jury decisions. The Housing Subsidies Act provides financial assistance to local authorities for improvements and conversions, and reforms the standard of fitness for human habitation. The Leasehold Reform Act allows tenants on low-rent long leases to purchase freehold or extend lease.

1968   (Jan.)   Raising of school leaving age from 15 to 16 is deferred to 1973 following spending cuts.
(May)   Forty-nine Labour MPs vote against restoration of NHS prescription charges and 150 abstain, but prescriptions charges are reintroduced in June.
(July)   Clean Air Act extends powers to control air pollution.
(Nov.)   Department of Health and Social Security (DHSS) is formed through the merger of the Ministries of Health and of Social Security.

1969   (June)   The Open University is granted a Charter to provide degrees through part-time broadcast and correspondence courses.
(July)   Children and Young Persons Act reforms juvenile court system and extends local authority duties to provide community homes for juvenile offenders.
(Oct.)   Divorce Reform Act is passed.
(Dec.)   Censorship of plays by the Lord Chamberlain is abolished. Parliament votes on a free vote for the permanent suspension of the death penalty.

1970   (Jan.)   Age of majority is reduced from 21 to 18.
(Feb.)   Government introduces a bill giving powers to order local authorities to end the 11-plus examination and expand comprehensive provision.
(May)   Chronically Sick and Disabled Persons Act sets out local authority powers and duties to assist the chronically sick and disabled.

1974   (Apr.)   Circular 4/74 renews pressure for comprehensive education stalled under the 1970–74 Conservative government.

(July)   The Housing Finance Act increases aid to local authorities for slum clearance, introduces rent rebates for council tenants and introduces a system of 'fair rents' in public and private sector unfurnished accommodation. The Housing Act extends the role of the Housing Corporation, provides increased aid to housing associations and improves the renovation grants scheme. The Rent Act extends security of tenure to tenants of furnished properties and allows access to rent tribunals.

1975   (Jan.)   Education Secretary Reg Prentice announces the phasing out direct-grant grammar schools from September 1976.

(Aug.)   The Social Security Pensions Act introduces earnings-related supplement to retirement pensions. The Child Benefits Act replaces family allowance by child benefit paid to the mother for each child and introduces extra payment for lone parents.

(Nov.)   Community Land Act allows taking of development land into public control.

1976   (Aug.)   The Police Act establishes a Police Complaints Board to formalise the procedure for dealing with public complaints.

(Nov.)   The Bail Act introduces major reform in bail conditions with courts having to explain refusal of bail. The Rent (Agriculture) Act gives security of tenure for agricultural workers in tied accommodation. The Education Act requires all local education authorities which have failed to do so to submit proposals for comprehensive schools and limits taking up of independent and direct-grant school places. Callaghan calls for a 'great debate' over educational standards.

1977   (July)   The Housing (Homeless Persons) Act extends local authority responsibility to provide accommodation for homeless people in their area.

1978   The Health Services Act provides for the withdrawal of all private patients from NHS hospitals. Proposals are published for the establishment of a fourth television channel to

concentrate on minority and educational interests and a
Welsh language service.

Chronology of Defence and Foreign Policies

1964   (Oct.)   Wilson issues warning to white Rhodesians not to
declare independence unilaterally.
(Nov.)   Government declares that arms sales to South Africa
will be banned but proceeds with sale of 16 Buccaneer
aircraft; policy, in effect, is not to enter into new contracts
but to allow expansion of existing agreements.
(Dec.)   Wilson announces to the House of Commons that
the Polaris base at Holy Loch will remain. Wilson proposes
an Atlantic Nuclear Force with British Polaris missiles under
NATO control following a meeting with US President
Johnson.

1965   (Jan.)   British troops deployed in Kenya, Tanganyika and
Uganda to put down army mutinies.
(Feb.)   Wilson announces British support for a 'measured
response' by the United States in Vietnam.
(Apr.)   Foreign Secretary Michael Short defends US policy in
Vietnam against Labour backbench attacks.
(July)   British government representative is despatched to
North Vietnam in an attempt to initiate peace talks.
(Oct.)   Wilson meets Rhodesian prime minister Ian Smith
in an attempt to avert a white unilateral declaration of
independence but tells African leaders that Britain will not
use force if it does take place.
(Nov.)   White Rhodesian government makes illegal
declaration of independence; the government responds with
Southern Rhodesia Act imposing economic sanctions.
(Dec.)   Oil sanctions imposed on Rhodesia.

1966   (Jan.)   Wilson declares at Commonwealth Conference that
sanctions will bring down the Rhodesian regime in 'weeks
rather than months'; all trade with Rhodesia is banned.
(Feb.)   Government White Paper on defence retains Britain's
'East of Suez' role but reduces defence spending by 16% over
four years; Britain will not conduct military operations outside
Europe without allied co-operation; no overseas bases will
be maintained without the consent of the host country; the
base at Aden is to be evacuated by the end of 1968 but
some facilities in the Persian Gulf are to be increased; the

Territorial Army is to be reduced to a smaller Territorial and Army Volunteer Reserve.

(Apr.)   Government announces in Queen's Speech that Britain will join the European Economic Community provided Commonwealth interests are protected.

(June)   Wilson dissociates the Labour government from US bombing of civilian targets in North Vietnam.

(Oct.)   Proposal by Foreign Secretary Brown to convene Geneva Conference to end the war in Vietnam is rejected by South and North Vietnam.

(Nov.)   Government announces that it is to begin formal negotiations for entry into the European Economic Community.

(Dec.)   Wilson meets illegal Rhodesian regime premier Smith for unsuccessful constitutional discussions on *HMS Tiger*.

1967   (Jan.)   Prime Minister Wilson and Foreign Secretary Brown begin European Economic Community entry process by visiting Rome; Wilson warns on need for collective Cabinet responsibility on the issue following criticisms by President of the Board of Trade Douglas Jay. The renegotiated Simonstown Agreement with South Africa leads to a withdrawal of the last British naval vessel.

(Feb.)   Downing Street–Kremlin 'hotline' agreed on during visit to London by Soviet prime minister Kosygin.

(Mar.)   Commonwealth Relations Secretary Herbert Bowden claims that sanctions against Rhodesia are 'biting very deeply'.

(Apr.)   Britain and the United States agree on joint use of British Indian Ocean Territory for defence purposes.

(May)   Government makes its formal application for entry into the European Economic Community.

(July)   Government defence policy statement announces a reduction in Britain's 'East of Suez' commitments; British troops to withdraw from Aden and South Arabia by January 1968, naval and air units to remain. There will be a total British withdrawal from Malaysia and Singapore by the mid-1970s.

(Oct.)   Britain's first nuclear submarine *HMS Resolution* comes into service.

(Nov.)   Commonwealth Relations Secretary George Thomson has unsuccessful discussions with Smith in Salisbury, Rhodesia. British withdrawal from Aden completed. British entry into the European Economic Community vetoed by French President de Gaulle.

1968   (Jan.)   Government announces spending cuts including withdrawal from 'East of Suez' by 1971 and cancellation of purchase of F–111 aircraft; all British bases outside Europe and the Mediterranean (except Hong Kong) to be evacuated by 1971; Far East amphibian force to be redeployed in the Mediterranean; defence agreements with Persian Gulf states to be renegotiated and bases given up; Britain no longer to commit troops to the South East Asia Treaty Organisation (SEATO).
(Apr.)   Britain ends the Anglo–Kuwait defence agreement.
(Oct.)   Wilson offers to allow Smith to remain in office during fruitless negotiations over Rhodesia on *HMS Fearless.*

1969   (Jan.)   Wilson rejects Commonwealth Prime Ministers' demand for the overthrow by force of the white Rhodesian regime.
(Feb.)   Defence Secretary Denis Healey tells the Commons that the Defence White Paper confirms Britain's 'transformation from a world power to a European power' and emphasises a concentration on NATO.
(Mar.)   Wilson fails in attempt to persuade combatants to end Nigerian civil war.
(Dec.)   Following the resignation of French President de Gaulle in April, a European Economic Community summit agrees that negotiations should begin for Britain's entry by June 1970.

1970   (Feb.)   Government issues White Paper on possible results of entry to the European Economic Community, with vague projections of the effect on balance of payments, industrial costs and agricultural prices.

1974   (Apr.)   Government announces that it will proceed with renegotiation of the terms of Britain's entry to the European Economic Community agreed by the Conservatives before entry in 1973.
(Dec.)   Government announces further reductions in defence expenditure.

1975   (Jan.)   Government announces that a referendum will be held on the UK's continuing membership of the European Economic Community.
(Feb.)   Wilson meets Soviet leader Brezhnev in Moscow.
(Mar.)   Government announces that it has accepted new terms for European Economic Community membership.

(June)   Referendum on continuing membership of the European Economic Community shows two to one in favour. Simonstown Agreement with South Africa ended.

1976   (Mar.)   Britain withdraws final troops from Singapore but continues to contribute to air defence system with Australia, New Zealand and Malaysia.

1978   (Nov.)   Callaghan attacks EEC Common Agricultural Policy and announces Britain will not join the European Monetary System.

11 Labour in Opposition, 1979–97

Chronology of Main Events

1979 (May)   Labour defeated in general election.
(Oct.)   Labour Party conference accepts resolution to provide for the reselection of every MP during the life of a Parliament and agrees that the party National Executive should have the final say over the contents of a general election manifesto. A committee of enquiry is to be set up to investigate the party's organisation.

1980 (May)   Special party conference adopts policy document *Peace, Jobs and Freedom* in attempt to reconcile right–left differences.
(June)   Labour wins 17 seats in the first direct elections to the European Parliament and the Conservatives 60. The left-dominated committee of enquiry into party organisation set up at the 1979 conference begins operation.
(Oct.)   Labour Party conference accepts proposals for revised procedure for electing the party leader under which an electoral college rather than MPs alone will decide. Conference reverses its 1979 decision on National Executive control over general election manifesto. Callaghan announces his resignation as leader.
(Nov.)   Michael Foot defeats Denis Healey by 139 votes to 129 in a second ballot for the party leadership.

1981 (Jan.)   Changes in procedure for electing leader and deputy leader give trade unions 40% of the vote, constituency parties 30% and MPs 30% in the electoral college. 'Gang of Four' Jenkins, Owen, Williams and Rodgers form Council for Social Democracy in response.
(Feb.)   Williams resigns from party National Executive. One hundred Labour MPs form Solidarity Group under chairmanship of Hattersley to counter left-wing influence.
(Mar.)   'Gang of Four' form the Social Democratic Party (SDP); 12 Labour MPs and nine peers join and 29 Labour MPs eventually become members.

(Apr.)   Benn declares that he will challenge Healey for the party's deputy leadership.

(Sept.)   Formation of Liberal–SDP Alliance poses a potential threat to Labour as the main alternative to the Conservatives. Healey defeats Benn in contest for party deputy leadership by narrow margin of 50.43% to 49.57%; Benn later claims that SDP defectors who supported Healey mean he is rightfully deputy leader. Labour Party conference votes overwhelmingly for unilateral nuclear disarmament. The party National Executive begins an enquiry into the activities of Militant entryists.

1982   (Feb.)   Labour is further discredited in the Bermondsey by-election in which the party leadership dissociates itself from the candidate (a gay Marxist) during the campaign; the seat is lost to the Liberals.

(Apr.)   Foot attacks government military unpreparedness but supports resistance to Argentine seizure of the Falklands.

(Oct.)   Labour Party conference votes by substantial majority for unilateral nuclear disarmament.

1983   (June)   Labour's general election manifesto *The New Hope for Britain* makes sweeping promises to counter unemployment with an 'emergency prgramme of action', to repeal Conservative trade union legislation, increase benefits, extend the rights of women and ethnic minorities, unilateral nuclear disarmament, and is later dubbed 'the longest suicide note in history'. Labour wins 209 seats with 27.6% of the vote, the Liberal–SDP Alliance take 26% and the Conservatives win 397 seats.

(Oct.)   Following Foot's resignation, Kinnock wins party leadership contest against Hattersley, Heffer and Shore, defeating Hattersley in third ballot with 71% of the vote to 19%. Hattersley becomes deputy leader and both form a 'dream ticket', uniting left and right in the party. Party conference reaffirms policy on unilateral disarmament.

1984   (Mar.)   Announcement by National Coal Board of intention to close pits and discharge 20,000 miners.

(Apr.)   Miners' strike begins (ends April 1985), proving to be a major embarrassment as Kinnock attempts to divest Labour of its left-wing rhetoric; scenes of picket-line violence are used to discredit Labour.

1985   (Jan.)   Labour leader Kinnock criticises miners' leader
Scargill for his conduct of the strike, accusing him of acting
like a First World War general.
(June)   Larry Whitty appointed general secretary to
modernise party's organisation.
(Oct.)   Labour Party conference votes for non-nuclear
defence policy by 80% majority. Kinnock attempts to regain
the centre ground by attacking Scargill's conduct of the
miners' strike and the confrontationist tactics of Militant-
dominated Liverpool City Council. The National Executive
begins an investigation of the Liverpool party.
(Dec.)   Kinnock declares that the re-nationalisation of
privatised enterprises will not be a priority for a future Labour
government.

1986   (Mar.)   Lambeth and Liverpool councillors who have refused
to set a rate are ordered to pay a surcharge by the High
Court.
(Apr.)   Labour replaces the red flag as party symbol with
European socialist red rose. Labour captures Fulham from
Conservatives in by-election.
(July)   Labour holds Newcastle-under-Lyme in a by-election
with a reduced majority.
(Sept.)   Labour Party conference votes for the removal of US
nuclear bases in Britain by a future Labour government.
(Oct.)   National Executive recommends that the leaders of
the Liverpool district party should be expelled. Liverpool and
Lambeth councillors facing a surcharge for refusing to set a
rate on time propose that a future Labour government should
indemnify them.
(Nov.)   Deputy leader Hattersley says controlling inflation
must be at centre of Labour policy.

1987   (Jan.)   Kinnock declares Labour will reverse any tax cuts
made by Conservatives in budget.
(Mar.)   Former leader Callaghan attacks party policy on
unilateral abandonment of Trident. Labour policy document,
New Industrial Strength for Britain, calls for the establishment of
a British Investment Bank to encourage economic expansion.
(May)   Kinnock pledges instant withdrawal of Polaris
submarines from patrol on election of a Labour government.
(June)   Labour, attempting to demonstrate that it rather
than the Alliance is the main alternative to the Conservatives,
fights an impressive general election campaign with its

manifesto *Britain Will Win*; it increases its share of the vote to 30.8% and wins 229 seats, is particularly successful in the north of England and Scotland, but is defeated for a third time by the Conservatives.

(Sept.)   Labour Party conference overwhelmingly endorses Kinnock's proposals for an extensive review of party policy.

1988   (Oct.)   Benn mounts challenge to Kinnock for the party leadership but is defeated by 88.63% to 11.37%; Hattersley is re-elected deputy leader with 66.82% of the vote against Prescott and Heffer.

1989   (May)   Labour makes a significant revival in the European Parliament elections, winning 45 seats to the Conservatives' 31.

(Oct.)   Labour Party conference reverses policy of unilateral disarmament.

1990   (Mar.)   Kinnock attacks 'toy town revolutionaries' following spate of anti-poll tax riots through Britain.

1991   (Sept.)   Kinnock denies reports that he is under pressure to resign from party leadership to improve Labour's electoral prospects.

1992   (Apr.)   Labour's general election manifesto, *It's Time to get Britain Working Again*, promises an extra £1 billion for the National Health Service, £600 million for education, increases in retirement pensions and child benefit, a minimum wage of £3.40 an hour, a 50% higher rate of income tax, the abolition of the National Insurance ceiling, and the replacement of the House of Lords by an elected second chamber. Despite optimistic opinion polls, Labour loses its fourth election in a row, winning 271 seats, but the Conservative majority is reduced to 21. Kinnock and Hattersley resign from the leadership.

(July)   John Smith defeats Bryan Gould by 91% to 9% in contest for party leadership; Margaret Beckett is elected deputy leader with 57% of the vote against John Prescott (28%) and Gould (14.5%). Smith appeals for a more conciliatory tone in internal party debate so as not to alienate supporters and promises to reform the party's relationship with the trade unions.

(Sept.)   Labour Party conference reduces trade unions' share of the vote at conference from 87% to 70%.

1993   (Feb.)   Labour leader Smith proposes a reduction in the union's share of the vote in leadership elections and the selection of candidates at constituency level.
(Sept.)   Labour Party conference agrees on the introduction of 'one member one vote' (OMOV) by which trade union and constituency party sections of electoral college must ballot members individually for party leadership and deputy leadership elections and allocate votes proportionally. The electoral college voting weight is reproportioned to one-third each to MPs, trade unions and constituency parties (reducing the trade union share from 40%).

1994   (May)   Smith dies suddenly; Beckett becomes acting party leader pending a leadership election.
(June)   Labour makes further gains in election to the European Parliament, winning 62 seats to the Conservatives' 18.
(July)   Blair wins party leadership election against Prescott and Beckett with 57% of the vote in first contest conducted with one member one vote; Prescott defeats Beckett for deputy leadership with 56.5% of the vote.
(Oct.)   Labour Party conference rejects Blair's proposal to revise Clause Four by 50.9% to 49.1%.
(Dec.)   Labour Party National Executive votes by 20 to 4 to revise Clause Four.

1995   (Apr.)   Special Labour Party conference (with constituency parties having 30% of the vote and trade unions 70%) accepts the new revised Clause Four.

1996   (July)   Blair declares in an introduction to Labour's consultative document, *The Road to the Manifesto*, that the party's approach is 'based on stakeholding, not an old-fashioned war between bosses and workers'.
(Oct.)   Labour Party conference votes to end the National Health Service internal market, votes in favour of a minimum wage and to sign up to the European Social Charter by 1 January 1998. It rejects the re-nationalisation of the privatised utilities.
(Dec.)   The Parliamentary Labour Party votes by 86 to 27 (with 24 abstentions) to change standing orders to include a

clause making it a disciplinary offence to 'bring the party into disrepute' in return for a promise of closer communication between ministers and backbenchers.

1997   (Jan.)   Blair promises that a Labour government will not increase income tax during its first term and will show 'zero tolerance' towards minor crimes. Brown says that Labour will stick to Conservative spending plans.

(Feb.)   Labour captures Wirral South from the Conservatives in a by-election on a 17% swing.

(Mar.)   The previously staunchly Thatcherite tabloid *The Sun* declares its support for the Labour Party. The party outlines Welfare to Work plans to create 250,000 jobs for the young unemployed based on a £3 billion windfall tax on privatised utilities.

(Apr.)   Labour's general election manifesto, *New Labour because Britain Deserves Better*, promises increased National Health Service spending in real terms each year, reduction in class sizes for five, six and seven year olds to 30, a phasing out of assisted places, to retain the basic state retirement pension and increase it in line with prices, a minimum wage (with the level to be set by an independent pay commission), no rise in the basic rate of income tax in the life of the Parliament, reform of the House of Lords, a referendum on a reformed voting system, a Scottish Parliament and a Welsh Assembly.

(May)   Labour wins an overwhelming general election victory, taking 43.2% of the vote and returning with 418 MPs, 101 of whom are women.

12 Labour in Government from 1997

Labour Government from 1997 – Principal Ministers

(All held office from May 1997 unless otherwise indicated.)

Prime Minister — Tony Blair

Deputy Prime Minister (and Secretary of State for the Environment, Transport and the Regions) — John Prescott

Chancellor of the Exchequer — Gordon Brown

Foreign Secretary — Robin Cook

Lord Chancellor — Lord Irvine of Lairg

Home Secretary — Jack Straw

Education and Employment Secretary — David Blunkett

President of the Board of Trade — Margaret Beckett (May 1997–July 1998)
Peter Mandelson (July 1998–)

(Post reverted to title of Secretary of State for Trade and Industry)

Minister of Agriculture, Fisheries and Food — Jack Cunningham (May 1997–July 1998)
Nick Brown (July 1998–)

Secretary of State for Scotland — Donald Dewar

Secretary of State for Defence — George Robertson

Secretary of State for Health — Frank Dobson

President of the Council and Leader of the House of Commons — Ann Taylor (May 1997–July 1998)
Margaret Beckett (July 1998–)

Secretary of State for Culture, Media and Sport (National Heritage until July 1997)	Chris Smith
Secretary of State for Social Security	Harriet Harman (May 1997–July 1998) Alistair Darling (July 1998–)
Secretary of State for Northern Ireland	Marjorie Mowlem
Secretary of State for Wales	Ron Davies (May 1997–Oct. 1998) Alun Michael (Oct. 1998–)
Secretary of State for International Development	Clare Short
Lord Privy Seal and Leader of the House of Lords	Lord Richard (May 1997–July 1998) Baroness Jay (July 1998–)
Chancellor of the Duchy of Lancaster	David Clark (May 1997–July 1998) Jack Cunningham (July 1998–)
Minister of Transport	Gavin Strang (May 1997–July 1998) John Reid (July 1998–)
Chief Secretary to the Treasury	Alistair Darling (May 1997–July 1998) Stephen Byers (July 1998–)
Chief Whip of the House of Commons	Nick Brown (May 1997–July 1998) Ann Taylor (July 1998–)

Chronology of Main Events

1997   (May)   Blair forms the first Labour government for 18 years, with Prescott as deputy prime minister and Secretary for the Environment, Transport and the Regions, Brown as Chancellor, Cook as Foreign Secretary, Straw as Home Secretary, Beckett as President of the Board of Trade and Harman as Social Security Secretary. Brown announces that the Bank of England will take responsibility for setting interest rates through a new monetary policy committee. Cook announces that the UK will sign up to the European Social Charter. Blair offers Sinn Fein a meeting with officials on the Northern Ireland peace process without the precondition of a renewed ceasefire. The Queen's Speech sets out 26 proposed bills, including far-reaching constitutional reform and a commitment to a minimum wage.

(June)   Task forces are established on NHS efficiency and youth justice. Hong Kong is returned to China.

(July)   Brown's first budget cuts corporation tax; reduces VAT to 5% on fuel and mortgage tax relief; levies a £5.2 billion windfall tax on privatised utilities to fund a Welfare to Work programme to reduce youth and long-term unemployment by 250,000; provides £3.5 billion extra spending on health and education; sets out a five-year deficit reduction plan. The government announces that the Liberal Democrats have been invited to take seats on a Cabinet committee to discuss constitutional reform and other mutual interests. Proposals are issued to charge undergraduates for tuition and to replace the grant system with loans to raise £1.7 billion for higher education expansion. The IRA announces an 'unequivocal ceasefire'; Sinn Fein representatives are allowed to enter Stormont but not to participate in peace-process discussions; arms decommissioning issue left in abeyance. Former party deputy leader Hattersley declares he feels no loyalty to Labour because of what he describes as Blair's 'apostasy' on poverty and equality.

(Aug.)   Diana, Princess of Wales dies; Blair describes her as the 'People's Princess' and encourages the modernisation of the Royal Family.

(Sept.)   Blair declares at Labour Party conference that his ambition is for his administration to be 'one of the great reforming governments in British history'. On the economy, Brown says that the government's objective is 'employment opportunities for all'. Party conference adopts *Partnership into Power* to transform Labour's decision-making processes. Scotland accepts devolution and tax-raising proposals in a referendum and Wales accepts an assembly by a narrow majority.

(Oct.)   Following confusion over Labour's position on entry into the European Monetary Union (EMU), Brown announces that the government favours eventual entry but not in the lifetime of this Parliament and only if agreed in a referendum. Blair meets Sinn Fein leader Gerry Adams, the first British prime minister to meet an Irish Republican leader since 1921. Full-scale negotiations, including Republican and Loyalist representatives, begin. Proposals are announced to replace the first-past-the-post system with a proportional representation system in 1999 European Parliament elections and for a Greater London Authority (GLA) and a directly elected mayor for London.

(Nov.)   Labour government is embarrassed by allegations that its attitude to ending tobacco sponsorship of Formula One motor racing had been influenced by a million pound donation to party funds; Blair asks to be trusted and announces that the donation has been returned. A Lib-Lab Cabinet committee agrees to encourage a more positive national consensus on British attitudes towards Europe. Chancellor Brown's pre-budget report pledges a fundamental reform of the Welfare State and proposes a tax credit scheme for poor working families.

(Dec.)   The government faces its first rebellion when 47 Labour MPs defy a three-line whip to vote against a reduction in lone-parent benefit and 14 abstain; the vote is won by 457 votes to 107 with Conservative support. Electoral Reform Commission, under chairmanship of former Labour minister (and SDP co-founder) Lord Jenkins, is set up to devise a system of proportional representation for Westminster elections in preparation for a referendum on the issue. A ten-year programme to reform the National Health Service announced. The government issues a White Paper on a proposed Freedom of Information Act, covering national and local government, quangos, the NHS and privatised utilities. Sinn Fein leader takes the first Republican delegation into Downing Street since 1921.

1998   (Jan.)   New Deal begins for unemployed 18–24 year olds, giving a choice of work with subsidised private employers, education or training, voluntary sector work experience, environmental task force, or self-employment; the programme is to be extended to long-term unemployed adults and lone parents. Brown declares the aim is to eliminate unemployment in the twenty-first century.

(Mar.)   Brown introduces a redistributive budget which includes a Working Family Tax Credit to be introduced in October 1999, a Disabled Person's Tax Credit, increases in child benefit, subsidies for employers to take on the long-term unemployed, an extra £500 million spending on public transport, £500 million on health, £250 million on education, a reduction in Corporation Tax and increased duties on cigarettes and alcohol, and proposals to close offshore tax loopholes. The government announces it will oppose European Union legislation requiring employers to establish procedures for consultation with their workforces.

(Apr.) Agreement on the Irish peace process includes provision for a Northern Ireland Assembly, a North–South Ministerial Council and a Council of the Isles, including representatives from Westminster, Belfast, the Scottish Parliament and the Welsh Assembly.

(May) London votes in favour of a Greater London Authority (GLA) and an elected mayor in a referendum. The government announces a minimum hourly wage of £3.60 for adults and £3.00 for 18–21 year olds, from which two million low-paid workers (8% of the workforce) will benefit.

(July) Chancellor Brown unveils three-year Comprehensive Spending Review with an extra £21 billion spending on health, £19 billion on education, £4.4 billion on urban regeneration and increased expenditure on transport, science, the arts and overseas aid. Public sector wages curbs are to continue. Social Security Secretary Harman leaves in Blair's first cabinet reshuffle.

(Oct.) Blair welcomes Electoral Reform Commission's recommendations for an Alternative Vote Top-Up system of proportional representation for parliamentary elections.

(Nov.) Labour and Liberal Democrat leaders issue a joint statement extending cross-party co-operation to education, health, reform of the welfare state and Europe, but deny this is a prelude to a possible future coalition or merger of the two parties.

13 Labour, the Economy and Nationalisation

Unemployment Rates under Labour Governments

There have been changes over the years in the ways in which unemployment is defined and measured. The tables that follow should therefore be used as an illustration of trends.

Rates of unemployment immediately before, during and after periods of Labour in office for comparative purposes

	Minimum during year (thousands)	Maximum during year (thousands)
1924 Labour government		
1923	1,229 (Dec.)	1,525 (Jan.)
1924	1,087 (June)	1,374 (Jan.)
1925	1,243 (Dec.)	1,443 (Aug.)
1929–31 Labour government		
1928	1,127 (Mar.)	1,375 (Aug.)
1929	1,164 (June)	1,466 (Jan.)
1930	1,520 (Jan.)	2,500 (Dec.)
1931	2,578 (May)	2,880 (Sept.)
1932	2,309 (Nov.)	2,955 (Jan.)
1945–51 Labour government		
1944	N/A	84 (Jan.)
1945	N/A	111 (Jan.)
1946	360 (Jan.)	408 (Jan.)
1947	262 (Sept.)	1,916 (Feb.)
1948	299 (June)	359 (Dec.)
1949	274 (July)	413 (Jan.)
1950	297 (July)	404 (Jan.)
1951	210 (July)	367 (Jan.)
1952	379 (Jan.)	468 (Apr.)
1964–70 Labour government		
1963	449 (July)	878 (Feb.)
1964	318 (July)	501 (Jan.)

	Minimum during year (thosands)	Maximum during year (thosands)
1965	276 (June)	376 (Jan.)
1966	261 (June)	564 (Dec.)
1967	497 (July)	603 (Feb.)
1968	515 (July)	631 (Jan.)
1969	499 (June)	595 (Jan.)
1970	547 (June)	628 (Jan.)
1971	655 (Jan.)	868 (Dec.)
1974–79 Labour government		
1973	486 (Dec.)	785 (Jan.)
1974	515 (June)	628 (Aug.)
1975	738 (Jan.)	1,152 (Dec.)
1976	1,220 (June)	1,440 (Aug.)
1977	1,286 (May)	1,567 (Aug.)
1978	1,364 (Dec.)	1,608 (Aug.)
1979	1,299 (May)	1,464 (July)
1980	1,471 (Jan.)	2,244 (Dec.)

(*Source*: See main source at end of section, p. 139)

Balance of Trade under Labour Governments

Net balance of payments on current account in £ million immediately before, during and after each Labour government. Deficits are in brackets.

1924 Labour government

1923	169
1924	72
1925	46

1929–31 Labour government

1928	123
1929	103
1930	28
1931	(104)
1932	(51)

1945–51 Labour government

1944	(659)
1945	(875)
1946	(230)

1947	(381)
1948	26
1949	(1)
1950	307
1951	(369)
1952	163

1964–70 Labour government

1963	129
1964	(358)
1965	(45)
1966	109
1967	(294)
1968	(286)
1969	463
1970	731
1971	1,090

1974–79 Labour government

1973	(979)
1974	(3,728)
1975	(1,523)
1976	(846)
1977	53
1978	1,162
1979	(525)
1980	3,629

(*Source*: See main source at end of section, p. 139)

Devaluation under Labour Governments

	Pre-devaluation ($ to £)	Post-devaluation ($ to £)
1949 19 Sept.	4.03	2.80
1967 18 Nov.	2.79	2.40

Basic Rates of Income Tax under Labour Governments

Basic rates of income tax in the £ immediately before, during and after each Labour government. (Post-1971 decimalisation rates are given as a percentage.)

1924 Labour government
1923   5s (25p)
1924   5s (25p)
1925   4s 6d (22.5p)

1929–31 Labour government
1928   4s (20p)
1929   4s (20p)
1930   4s (20p)
1931   4s 6d (22.5p)
1932   5s (25p)

1945–51 Labour government
1944   10s (50p)
1945   10s (50p)
1946   10s (50p)
1947   9s (45p)
1948   9s (45p)
1949   9s (45p)
1950   9s (45p)
1951   9s (45p)
1952   9s 6d (47.5p)

1964–70 Labour government
1963   7s 9d (39p)
1964   7s 9d (39p)
1965   8s 3d (41p)
1966   8s 3d (41p)
1967   8s 3d (41p)
1968   8s 3d (41p)
1969   8s 3d (41p)
1970   7s 9d (39p)
1971   38.75% (expressed as % in the £ following currency decimalisation)

1974–79 Labour government
1973   30%
1974   33%
1975   35%
1976   35%
1977   34%
1978   33%

1979   30%
1980   30%

(*Source*: Compiled from information in tables on economic indicators in D.E. Butler and G. Butler, *British Political Facts, 1900–94*, Macmillan, London, 1994)

Labour and Nationalisation

Chronology of main events

1908   Labour Party conference votes by 514,000 to 469,000 that the party's objective is 'the socialisation of the means of production, distribution and exchange to be controlled by a democratic State in the interests of the entire community'.

1918   Clause Four of the Labour Party Constitution declares that the party's objective is 'the common ownership of the means of production' ('distribution and exchange' are added in 1928). The party programme, *Labour and the New Social Order*, calls for the nationalisation of land, railways, mines, electricity production, industrial insurance, harbours and shipping, and the manufacture and sale of alcohol.

1922   Labour Party general election manifesto calls for the nationalisation of the mines and railways.

1923   Labour Party general election manifesto makes no reference to nationalisation.

1928   Party programme *Labour and the Nation* calls for the nationalisation of agricultural and urban land, the production and distribution of coal and power, communications and transport networks and industrial life insurance.

1931   Labour Party general election manifesto calls for the public ownership and control of banking and credit and the reorganisation of basic industries as public services owned and controlled in the national interest.

1932   Labour Party conference passes resolution declaring that 'the common ownership of the means of production and distribution is the only means by which the producers by hand or brain will be able to secure the full fruits of their labour' and calls for the nationalisation of joint stock banks.

1933   Labour Party conference calls for the right of workers 'to an effective share in the control and direction of socialised industries which their labour sustains' and for direct trade union representation on boards of directors of nationalised industries.

1934   Labour Party policy document *For Socialism and Peace* calls for the taking into public ownership of banking and credit, transport, water, coal, electricity, gas, agriculture, iron and steel, shipping and shipbuilding, engineering, textiles, chemicals and insurance, and for an effective share in control and direction by employees.

1935   Labour Party general election manifesto calls for the nationalisation of banking, coal and ancillary products, transport, electricity, iron and steel, cotton and land.

1937   Party policy document *Labour's Immediate Programme* advocates the nationalisation of coal, electricity and gas under public corporations.

1944   Labour Party conference votes for the nationalisation of land, large-scale building, heavy industry, the banks, transport, fuel and power under the democratic control of workers and consumers.

1945   (Apr.)   Party document *Let Us Face the Future* proposes economic planning and divides industries into 'basic industries ripe and over-ripe for public ownership', 'big industries not yet ripe' and smaller businesses 'which can be left to go on with their useful work'.
(Oct.)   Bill is introduced to nationalise the Bank of England.
(Nov.)   Morrison warns that obstruction of the government's nationalisation plans could affect compensation paid to former owners.
(Dec.)   Coal Industry Nationalisation Bill is introduced.

1946   (Feb.)   Bank of England Bill receives Royal Assent.
(Apr.)   Government issues proposals to take iron and steel into public ownership.

(July) Coal Nationalisation Act establishes the National Coal Board.

(Oct.) Cripps rejects the possibility and practicability of workers' control of nationalised industries.

(Nov.) Cable and Wireless Bill and the National Health Services Bill receive Royal Assent.

1947 (Jan.) National Coal Board comes into operation. Electricity Bill for nationalisation of the electricity industry is introduced.

(May) Morrison warns Labour Party conference of the danger of too hasty moves towards socialism.

1948 (Jan.) Nationalisation of railways comes into effect.

(Mar.) Labour Party policy document *Public Ownership: The Next Step* advocates partial public ownership to prevent monopolies in a mixed economy.

(Apr.) Electricity industry is taken into public ownership.

(May) Shinwell calls for partial democracy in nationalised industries to encourage support for socialism. National Coal Board chairman resigns with complaints about 'cumbersome organisation'. At Labour Party conference Morrison calls for 'consolidation' and a slower pace in expanding public ownership.

(July) Gas Act takes gas into public ownership.

(Oct.) Bill is introduced to take iron and steel into public ownership.

1949 (Oct.) Churchill declares that a future Conservative government will reverse most of Labour's nationalisation.

(Nov.) Iron and Steel Bill to take the industry into public ownership receives Royal Assent. Minister of Supply Strauss offers to postpone implementation until after a general election.

1950 (Jan.) Labour Party general election manifesto *Let Us Win Through Together* proposes taking cement, chemical and sugar industries into public ownership.

(Aug.) Party document *Labour and the New Society* mentions only water as a candidate for future public ownership.

1951 (Feb.) Iron and steel industry is taken into public ownership.

(Sept.)   Labour Party general election manifesto makes no proposals for further nationalisation.

1952   (Sept.)   TUC annual conference votes for 'the extension of social ownership to other industries and services, particularly those now subject to monopoly' and calls for moves towards industrial democracy in nationalised industry.
(Oct.)   Labour Party conference calls on the National Executive to draw up a list of key industries to be taken into public ownership by a future Labour government.

1953   Labour Party policy document, *Challenge to Britain*, calls for the re-nationalisation of steel and parts of road transport (both restored to private ownership by the Conservatives), of water supply, sectors of engineering and the machine tool industry, and other industries in which 'private enterprise fails to act in the public interest'.

1955   (Apr.)   Special Labour Party conference on Clause Four abandons the project of wholesale public ownership. General election manifesto, *Forward with Labour*, promises the re-nationalisation of steel and road haulage and the taking into public ownership of sections of the chemical and machine tool industries.

1956   Crosland's book, *Future of Socialism*, argues that public ownership is irrelevant to the party's objective of equality.

1957   Labour Party conference adopts *Industry and Society*, changing the emphasis in Clause Four from socialism to an acceptance of a mixed economy with private industry made publicly accountable by state investment in individual companies.

1959   (Nov.)   Gaitskell is attacked at the Labour Party conference for advocating the abandonment of Clause Four.

1960   Labour Party conference agrees that the party's objective is an expansion of common ownership, substantial enough to 'give the community power over the commanding heights of the economy', that Clause Four should be retained, but that future nationalisation should be decided 'according to circumstances'.

1964   Labour Party general election manifesto proposes to re-nationalise the steel industry.

1965   (May)   Labour government survives threat from two backbenchers to oppose White Paper on steel nationalisation and wins Commons vote by 310 to 306.

1966   (Oct.)   Industrial Reorganisation Act establishes Industrial Reorganisation Corporation (IRC) to direct private sector investment.

1967   (Apr.)   Iron and Steel Bill, taking the industry back into public ownership, receives Royal Assent.

1968   (Oct.)   Labour Party conference rejects a motion calling for the nationalisation of 300 monopolies, banks, finance houses and insurance companies.

1969   The status of the Post Office is changed by the Labour government from that of government department to public corporation.

1970   Labour Party general election manifesto proposes the nationalisation of ports, state investment (with an element of control) in private companies and the establishment of a National Enterprise Board.

1973   Labour Party National Executive *Programme for Britain* calls for nationalisation of the top 25 companies but this is removed following criticisms from party leader Wilson in June. The party conference adopts programme to nationalise all land required for development, minerals, ports, shipbuilding, aircraft construction, North Sea gas and oil, and sections of the pharmaceutical, machine tool, construction and road haulage industries; this becomes a central part of the February 1974 general election manifesto.

1975   The British National Oil Corporation is established by the Labour government through the Petroleum and Submarine Pipelines Act 1975.

1976   (Oct.)   Labour Party annual conference votes for the nationalisation by a future government of the major insurance companies and clearing banks, together with one merchant bank.

1977   (Mar.)   Aircraft and Shipbuilding Industries Bill, which will take these industries into public ownership, receives Royal Assent.
(Sept.)   TUC annual conference calls for increased public ownership as part of an alternative economic strategy.

1980   (May)   Benn calls for an extension of public ownership and re-nationalisation, without compensation, of industries privatised by the Conservative government.

1981   Labour Party annual conference refers back a proposal for a future Labour government to nationalise banking and insurance. Labour leader criticises Benn for calling, in the Commons, for the nationalisation of the oil industry without compensation.

1982   Labour Party annual conference narrowly rejects proposals for nationalisation of the banks.

1985   Labour leader Kinnock declares that the re-nationalisation of industries privatised by the Conservative government will not be a priority for a future Labour government.

1986   Deputy Labour leader Hattersley's proposals for a variety of forms of social ownership rather than nationalisation are accepted by the party conference.

1987   Labour Party general election manifesto proposes the 'social ownership' of British Gas and British Telecom, both privatised by the Conservative government.

1996   Labour Party annual conference rejects a motion calling for the re-nationalisation of the privatised utilities.

1997   (June)   Chancellor Brown announces the proposed privatisation of the Tote, the Royal Mint, London Transport, the Commonwealth Development Corporation and air traffic control.
(Oct.)   Deputy prime minister Prescott persuades the Labour Party annual conference not to demand the re-nationalisation of the railways.

Industries and services taken into public ownership by Labour governments

Industry/service	Year nationalised
Bank of England	1946
Civil aviation	1946
Coal	1946
Electricity	1947
Canals	1948
Gas	1948
Railways	1948
Road haulage	1948
Iron and steel (de-nationalised by the Conservatives in 1953, and re-nationalised in 1967)	1951
British Leyland (majority shareholding vested in National Enterprise Board)	1975
Oil	1975
Aerospace	1977
Shipbuilding	1977

14 Labour and the Trade Unions

Chronology of Main Events, 1899–1998

1899   (Sept.)   TUC annual conference votes by 546,000 votes to 434,000 in favour of convening a special congress of 'all the co-operative, socialistic, trade union, and other working class organisations . . . to devise ways and means of securing the return of an increased number of Labour members to the next Parliament'.

1900   (Feb.)   Trade unionists are the majority of delegates at the founding conference of the Labour Representation Committee (LRC) in London with 67 unions represented with a total membership of 570,000, over a quarter of existing union members.
(Oct.)   One of the two Labour MPs returned at the general election is a trade unionist, Richard Bell, secretary of the Amalgamated Society of Railway Servants (ASRS).

1903   (Jan.)   Costs and damages awarded against the Amalgamated Society of Railway Servants in the Taff Vale decision total £30,000, and the extent of the penalty encourages trade union affiliation to the Labour Representation Committee.

1908   Labour's parliamentary strength is boosted by the affiliation of the Miners' Federation of Great Britain to the party.

1917   Trade union position is strengthened by the Labour Party conference decision to abolish sectional elections to the National Executive, making all posts subject to election by conference as a whole.

1918   (Feb.)   Labour Party's new Constitution provides for greater trade union representation on the National Executive and for a larger financial contribution from the unions to party funds.
(Dec.)   Forty-nine of the 60 Labour MPs returned at the general election are trade unionists and 25 of these are sponsored by the Miners' Federation.

1919   (Jan.)   Trade unions join with the Clyde Workers' Committee in organising Clydeside demonstrations, demanding the 40-hour week to prevent unemployment. The demonstrations are suppressed by troops.

1920   (May)   The TUC and the Labour Party send a joint delegation to Russia to examine post-revolutionary conditions. On its return, it reports that the Bolshevik regime is a dictatorship.
(Aug.)   The TUC joins with the Labour Party to establish a Council of Action to organise protests against military intervention in Russia and to threaten a possible general strike if British involvement in the war between Poland and Bolshevik Russia continues.

1924   First Labour Cabinet of 20 members includes five trade union representatives. The government declares that it will use troops, under the Emergency Powers Act, to counter strikes in the docks and on London tramways and the Underground. The threat is criticised by a joint meeting of the TUC General Council and the Labour Party Executive Committee. The Agricultural Wages (Regulation) Act creates county committees to set wages and a Central Wages Board to supervise the awards. Agricultural wages rise.

1926   Joint Labour/TUC evidence to Blanesburgh Committee on Unemployment Insurance proposes an increased unemployment benefit and dependants' allowances.
(Apr.)   TUC General Council delegation to the Cabinet, accompanied by Labour leaders MacDonald and Snowden, is unsuccessful in its attempt to prevent the General Strike by persuading mine owners to withdraw lock-out notices.
(May)   Labour leader MacDonald tells TUC General Council that the party will support the unions although he opposes general strikes. The strike is called off by the TUC after nine days.
(Nov.)   Right-wing Labour MP George Spencer negotiates a local settlement with mine owners and establishes a breakaway union from the Miners' Federation based in Nottinghamshire. The Labour Party dissolves joint departments with the TUC, including research and press and publicity.

1927   (Jan.)   Three trade union members of Blanesburgh Committee support the Report's recommendation of a reduction in unemployment benefit and tightening of 'genuinely seeking work' clause.

(Apr.)   Trade unions and the Labour Party establish a National Trade Union Defence Committee, formed to campaign for a repeal of the Conservative government's post-general strike Trade Union and Trades Disputes Act.

1928   (May)   Transport House is opened by party leader MacDonald as the headquarters of the Transport and General Workers' Union (led by Ernest Bevin), the Trades Union Congress and the Labour Party.

1930   TUC general secretary Walter Citrine and the Transport and General Workers' Union general secretary, Ernest Bevin, become members of MacDonald's Economic Advisory Council. The Coal Mines Act reduces miners' working day from eight to seven and a half hours.

1931   (Apr.)   The government abandons its attempt to repeal partially the 1927 Trade Disputes and Trade Union Act, following Liberal opposition.

(Aug.)   The TUC resistance to cuts in unemployment benefits provokes a Cabinet collapse and the ensuing formation of the National Government by MacDonald.

(Sept.)   The TUC calls for a reconstitution of the National Joint Council (renamed the National Council of Labour in 1934) to exert greater control over the Labour Party.

1940   (May)   Transport and General Workers' Union general secretary Bevin is appointed Minister of Labour and National Service in Churchill's wartime Coalition government.

1945   (Mar.)   The TUC General Council calls for Labour Party support for repeal of the 1927 Trade Union and Trades Disputes Act.

(Sept.)   The TUC annual conference calls on the Labour government to speed up the demobilisation of the armed forces.

1946   (Mar.)   Trade union leaders give the Labour government a pledge to assist in improving industrial productivity.

(May)   The Labour government repeals the 1927 Trades Disputes and Trade Union Act.

(Aug.)   National Insurance (Industrial Injuries) Act introduces benefits for all workers affected by injury or disease caused at work.

(Sept.)   TUC annual conference calls for a 40-hour week and pledges increased productivity and an end to 'restrictive practices'.

(Oct.)   Labour President of the Board of Trade Stafford Cripps rejects calls for workers' control in nationalised industries.

1947   (Jan.)   Road haulage strike begins a wave of industrial conflict which besets the Labour government.

(Sept.)   TUC annual conference gives support to the Labour government proposals for direction of labour. The Control of Engagement Order comes into force in October.

(Dec.)   Labour Party general secretary Morgan Phillips urges the trade unions to take action against Communist infiltration.

1948   (Feb.)   The TUC backs the government's call for a voluntary incomes policy.

(Mar.)   TUC delegate conference supports the Labour government's proposal for voluntary wage restraint by 5.4 million votes to 2 million despite vigorous left opposition.

(June)   The Labour government declares a state of emergency to meet unofficial docks strikes in London and Liverpool which continue until the end of the month. Attlee appeals to dockers' loyalty to their unions to end the dispute.

(Sept.)   TUC annual conference supports government proposals on wage restraint.

(Nov.)   TUC General Council issues guidance to unions on removing Communists from office.

(Dec.)   Transport and General Workers' Union, the largest union, bans Communists from holding office.

1949   (Jan.)   The TUC leaves the World Federation of Trades Unions (WFTU) because of the presence of Communist-controlled unions and works to establish the International Federation of Free Trade Unions (ICFTU).

(June)   Labour Party conference criticises wage restraint and the lack of industrial democracy in the nationalised industries.

(July)   The Labour government declares a state of emergency as troops are deployed to break dock strikes in London and Bristol.

(Sept.)   Attlee tells the TUC annual conference that wage rises cannot be justified without increases in productivity.
(Nov.)   TUC General Council announces an agreement to wage restraint if it is accompanied by curbs on price rises.

1950   (Apr.)   Trade union representatives agree at a meeting with the Cabinet, the Labour Party National Executive Committee and the Co-operative Party on the need for a period of consolidation to help win middle-class support. The Labour government deploys troops to break strikes in the London docks which last into the next month.
(July)   Attlee warns that Britain faces a Communist 'enemy within', particularly in the unions.
(Sept.)   The TUC annual conference rejects the Labour government's proposals for wage restraint but supports profits controls. The Transport and General Workers' Union general secretary Arthur Deakin calls for the Communist Party to be banned to counter increasing unofficial strikes.

1951   (Feb.)   Dock strikes begin in Liverpool and then in London which last until the end of the month. The committal for trial of seven dockers under Order 1305 provokes a nation-wide 24-hour dock strike.
(Aug.)   The Labour government replaces Order 1305 with a less strenuous Industrial Disputes Order following the unsuccessful prosecution of dock strikers.
(Sept.)   The TUC annual conference backs the Labour government's controversial expansion in arms spending (the effect of which on NHS charges caused the resignation of three ministers), but calls for an end to wage restraint.

1952   (Sept.)   The TUC annual conference votes for 'the extension of social ownership to other industries and services, particularly those now subject to monopoly' and calls for moves towards industrial democracy in nationalised industry.

1953   (Sept.)   The TUC annual conference votes to accept a General Council recommendation against any further public ownership by a future Labour government.

1959   (June)   The General and Municipal Workers' Union annual conference votes in favour of unilateral nuclear disarmament. Although reversed in August, this opens up a period of bitter controversy in the Labour Party. A joint TUC–Labour Party

statement rejects unilateralism but calls for the formation of a British-led movement of non-nuclear states.
(July)   The Transport and General Workers' Union annual conference votes in favour of unilateral nuclear disarmament.
(Sept.)   The TUC annual conference rejects unilateralism by 5.1 million votes to 2.8 million.

1960   (May)   The Amalgamated Engineering Union annual conference votes in favour of unilateral nuclear disarmament.
(July)   Trade union protests force the Labour Party National Executive Committee to agree that Clause Four will remain in the party Constitution; Gaitskell hopes that by doing so trade union leaders will back him against unilateralism.
(Sept.)   The TUC annual conference votes in support of both a unilateralist and a multilateralist motion.

1961   (Jan.)   A joint TUC–Labour Party statement on defence fails to reconcile differences between unilateral nuclear disarmers and multilateralists.
(Sept.)   The TUC annual conference votes to reject the policy of unilateral nuclear disarmament.

1963   (July)   Labour leader Harold Wilson describes an incomes policy as a 'great adventure' in a speech to the Transport and General Workers' Union annual conference.
(Sept.)   The Amalgamated Engineering Union and Transport and General Workers' Union leaders at the TUC annual conference oppose pay restraint under a future Labour government and call for more extensive public ownership.

1964   (Jan.)   Trade union right to strike – protected by the 1906 Trades Disputes Act – is threatened by the *Rookes v Barnard* judgment; the TUC annual conference in September calls for the judgment to be reversed by a future Labour government (Labour does this with the 1965 Trades Disputes Act).
(June)   Labour MP Ray Gunter (appointed as Minister of Labour in October) angers trade unions in an article in *Socialist Commentary* in which he threatens government action if they fail to reform themselves.
(Oct.)   Transport and General Workers' Union general secretary Frank Cousins is appointed Minister of Technology in the Labour government.
(Nov.)   The TUC, the Labour government and employers' organisations sign a Joint Statement of Intent on planned economic growth, wage and price restraint.

(Dec.)   Labour prime minister Wilson attacks backwardness of 'luddites' among trade union leaders and employers at the party conference.

1965   (Feb.)   The Labour government appoints a Royal Commission under Lord Donovan to examine the role of trade unions in bargaining, unofficial action and the growing influence of shop stewards.

(Apr.)   A White Paper on prices and incomes proposes 3–3.5% annual pay increase norm. A special TUC conference accepts prices and incomes policy by 6.6 million votes to 1.8 million but the Transport and General Workers' Union (led by Technology Minister Cousins) opposes the decision.

(Aug.)   Redundancy Payments Act orders many employers to make payments to redundant workers and to establish a redundancy fund to which all employers must contribute. The Trades Disputes Act reverses the effect of the 1964 *Rookes v Barnard* case and further extends unions' legal immunities.

(Sept.)   The compulsory early warning of pay increases is accepted at the TUC annual conference by 5.2 million votes to 3.3 million.

1966   (May)   The Labour government declares a state of emergency as the National Union of Seamen begin strike action for higher pay and a 40-hour week.

(June)   Labour prime minister Wilson blames a 'tightly-knit group of politically motivated men' (a euphemism for Communists) for the seamen's strike. He names six Communists and left-wing activists in the Commons. The strike ends in July.

(July)   Technology Minister (and Transport and General Workers' Union leader) Frank Cousins resigns over government pay restraint proposals. The TUC General Council accepts the policy by 20 votes to 12 but TUC general secretary George Woodcock declares it is impracticable.

(Aug.)   Twenty-seven Labour backbenchers vote against the Labour government's proposal to take statutory powers to refer wage and price increases to the Prices and Incomes Board.

(Sept.)   The TUC annual conference supports the government's pay policy by 5 million votes to 3.9 million despite opposition from the Transport and General Workers' Union.

1967   (Sept.)   The TUC annual conference votes to oppose the
Labour government's wage restraint policy. Dock strikes
in London and Liverpool begin and last until November,
threatening balance of payments position.

1968   (May)   The Amalgamated Engineering Union mounts a
one-day strike against the Labour government's statutory
pay policy.
(June)   Donovan Report on trade unions (appointed 1965)
calls for the establishment of a Commission on Industrial
Relations but opposes legal action against unofficial strikers.
(Sept.)   The TUC annual conference opposes the Labour
government's statutory incomes policy by 7.7 million votes to
one million and accepts a proposed voluntary policy by only
a 54,000 majority.
(Oct.)   The TUC and the employers' organisation, the
Confederation of British Industry, issue a joint statement
agreeing on the Donovan Report's recommendation of the
establishment of a Commission on Industrial Relations.

1969   (Jan.)   Employment Secretary Barbara Castle introduces
a controversial White Paper on trade union legislation, *In
Place of Strife*, opening up the most serious crisis of relations
between the two wings of the Labour movement since 1931.
The Commission on Industrial Relations is established under
the chairmanship of former TUC general secretary George
Woodcock.
(Mar.)   Forty Labour MPs abstain and 55 vote against a
motion to approve *In Place of Strife*, which is passed by 224
votes to 62. The Labour National Executive Committee
(including party treasurer James Callaghan) rejects *In Place
of Strife* by 16 votes to 5. The government remains determined
to go ahead with an industrial relations bill.
(Apr.)   Wilson tells the Parliamentary Labour Party that
industrial relations legislation is essential if the government
is to remain in office. Chancellor Jenkins blames Britain's
uncompetitive economic position on irresponsible strikes and
says the government is determined on legislation to reform
the trade unions. Castle denies that the proposed bill will
involve the imprisonment of strikers, though they may be
fined.
(May)   100,000 workers mount strike against the government's
industrial relations proposals. Wilson agrees to delay trade
union legislation following a discussion of possible voluntary

measures with the Trades Union Congress, but initially rejects TUC proposals set out in its document, *Programme for Action*, as inadequate.

(June)   TUC special conference on the government's proposed industrial relations legislation rejects financial penalties against unofficial strikers but welcomes provisions to strengthen unions. The legislation is dropped after the TUC offers the government a 'solemn and binding' undertaking to take firm voluntary action in industrial disputes, leaving the government's industrial relations policy in ruins. The Conservative Opposition pledges to bring in legislation.

(Sept.)   The TUC annual conference demands the repeal of the Prices and Incomes Act by 4.6 million votes to 4.2 million.

1971   (Oct.)   Labour deputy leader Roy Jenkins tells the party conference that the party should be free from trade union control.

1972   (Jan.)   Liaison Committee is established with equal TUC, Parliamentary Labour Party and party National Executive membership, under joint TUC–Labour Party chairmanship.

1973   (Feb.)   Joint TUC–Labour Party document, *Economic Policy and the Cost of Living*, refers to a 'Social Contract' under which the unions would retain the right to free collective bargaining while a future Labour government would impose price controls and encourage industrial democracy and economic expansion. The document has wide-ranging proposals on pensions, land, health service charges and the European Economic Community (EEC) which will figure in the party's 1973 programme.

1974   (Jan.)   The TUC and the Labour Party announce an agreement on a 'Social Contract' during the general election campaign; trade unions would encourage voluntary pay restraint in return for government food subsidies, a freeze in rent increases and the repeal of Conservative industrial relations legislation.

(Mar.)   The new Labour government's offer to striking miners of a £130 million pay package is accepted and the strike ends.

(July)   The Labour government's Trade Union and Labour Relations Act repeals the Conservatives' Industrial Relations Act 1971, terminating the Pay Board, ending the statutory pay policy and abolishing the National Industrial Relations Court. The Health and Safety at Work Act establishes a Health and Safety Commission and Executive and establishes a legal framework for health and safety at work.

1975   (July)   The TUC accepts a Labour government White Paper, *The Attack on Inflation*, which sets a maximum increase limit of £6 a week until August 1976, with no increase for those earning over £8,500 a year.

(Nov.)   The TUC attends a conference with the government, the National Economic Development Council and the employers' Confederation of British Industry to formulate proposals for industrial development. The Employment Protection Act provides redress against unfair dismissal, extends the redundancy payments scheme, enlarges the rights of unions and employees and establishes the Advisory, Conciliation and Arbitration Services (ACAS) to arbitrate in industrial disputes.

1976   (Apr.)   The Labour government announces £1.3 billion tax cuts in the budget in return for a TUC agreement to a Stage 2 policy limiting wage increases to 4.5%, with a minimum increase of £2.50 a week and a maximum of £4.00.

(July)   A TUC special conference accepts a 4.5% wage increase ceiling.

1977   (Jan.)   The Bullock Report on Industrial Democracy recommends workers' representation on company boards. The Labour government decides not to legislate following objections from the employers' organisation, the CBI.

(Mar.)   Transport and General Workers' Union general secretary Jack Jones calls for prices freeze to prevent the need for wage increases.

(Apr.)   The TUC calls for a return to free collective pay bargaining. The TUC and Labour government renew the Social Contract with a document entitled *The Next Three Years and into the Eighties*, setting out plans for a 3% annual growth and the creation of a million jobs.

(Sept.)   The TUC annual conference votes for a return to free collective bargaining with wage increases limited to single figures.

(Nov.)   The Labour government deploys troops to counter firefighters' strike for higher pay. The TUC condemns the strike which ends in January 1978.

1978   (May)   The Labour government proposes a 5% maximum pay guideline to take effect in August.
(Oct.)   The TUC annual conference rejects the Labour government's proposed 5% pay limit and renewal of the Social Contract.
(Dec.)   Unions' refusal to accept the 5% pay increase limit sets the scene for the 'Winter of Discontent' which begins with a road haulage strike in which secondary picketing forces the lay-off of substantial numbers of workers.

1979   (Jan.)   The 'Winter of Discontent' – a wave of strikes in the public and private sectors (particularly among local authority and hospital workers) – intensifies, laying the ground for Labour's general election defeat. Labour prime minister Callaghan withdraws the 5% maximum pay limit for lower-paid workers.
(Feb.)   Following clashes on picket lines, joint TUC–Labour Party guidelines are produced on the conduct of strikes, including secondary picketing. The government guarantees to the TUC that inflation will be reduced to 5% in three years.
(Dec.)   A TUC–Labour Party liaison committee promises the repeal of Conservative employment legislation by a future Labour government.

1981   (Jan.)   Trade unions receive 40% of the vote in the electoral college to select the party leader and deputy leader.

1983   (Mar.)   A joint TUC–Labour Party document, *Partners in Rebuilding Britain*, rejects a statutory incomes policy in favour of an annual tri-partite income assessment.

1984   (Apr.)   Miners' strike begins (and lasts for a year); the effect of the tactics adopted by National Union of Mineworkers' leader Scargill is to embarrass the TUC and Labour Party leadership and to open up divisions between the left and right in the unions and the party.
(June)   Labour leader Neil Kinnock criticises violence by both police and pickets in the miners' strike.
(Sept.)   Labour deputy leader Roy Hattersley says a voluntary incomes policy will be necessary under a future Labour government.
(Oct.)   Labour leader Kinnock attacks confrontational tactics of NUM leader Scargill in the miners' strike.

1985   (Mar.)   Labour leader Kinnock refuses NUM request for amnesty for miners convicted of serious crimes in the strike.
(Aug.)   A joint TUC–Labour Party document, *A New Partnership: A New Britain,* calls for gradual economic expansion and a role for workers in formulating company policies.

1986   (Mar.)   Members of 37 unions, who are forced by Conservative legislation to hold ballots on political funds, vote to retain them.
(Sept.)   A joint TUC–Labour Party document, *People at Work: New Rights, New Responsibilities,* includes strike ballots in proposed new legal framework for unions.

1989   (Dec.)   Shadow employment spokesman Tony Blair announces that the Labour Party is abandoning its support for the trade union closed shop.

1992   (July)   New Labour leader John Smith announces that he intends to reform the party's relationship with the trade unions and to abolish the union block vote at party conferences.
(Oct.)   The Labour Party conference reduces the strength of trade union delegates' votes from 87% to 70% but retains union participation in leadership elections and the selection of candidates.

1994   (July)   Tony Blair wins 52.3% of the trade union vote in the Labour Party leadership contest.
(Sept.)   Labour leader Blair refuses to support the rail signallers' strike despite trade union leaders' pressure, saying that politicians should remain neutral.
(Oct.)   Tom Sawyer, a leading trade union ally of Labour leader Tony Blair, is appointed party general secretary. Of the trade union delegates at the Labour Party conference, 241 support the leadership's proposal to revise Clause Four while 200 vote against.

1995   (Mar.)   Three trade union representatives on Labour's National Executive abstain on a vote on the party Constitution's new Clause Four; trade unions divide over their attitudes to the changes with the Transport and General Workers' Union, the public service union, Unison, and the National Union of Mineworkers opposing.

(Apr.)   The trade unions (with 70% of total representation) vote by 54.6% to 46.4% in favour of the revision of Clause Four of the Labour Party Constitution.

(Sept.)   The TUC conference calls for a minimum wage of £4.26 an hour (despite being asked by the Labour leadership not to propose a specific figure) and calls for an employment package including a restored right to take secondary action and a ban on the sacking of strikers.

(Oct.)   The Labour Party conference changes the rules on trade union membership for party members from 'if eligible' to 'if applicable' and reduces the trade union block vote at party conference from 70% to 50% (equal with constituency parties) from 1996.

1997   (Feb.)   The TUC offers to help minimise industrial disputes under a future Labour administration as part of a social partnership with government and employers, and to co-operate on European issues, training and public sector pay.

(May)   The Labour government restores the right to trade union membership for staff at Government Communications Headquarters, Cheltenham.

(June)   The United Kingdom signs the European Social Charter on workers' rights.

(Sept.)   Chancellor Brown fails to give the Labour Party conference a commitment to full employment but says that the government's objective is 'employment opportunities for all'.

(July)   New Left in New Labour group proposals call for the retention of a substantial role for the trade unions in party organisation.

(Sept.)   Labour leader Blair calls on the TUC at its annual conference to work in partnership with employers and to 'modernise your political structures as we have done in the Labour Party'.

1998   (Mar.)   The Labour government announces that it will oppose new European Union legislation requiring employers to extend workers' councils and to establish procedures for consultation with their workforces over, for example, major lay-offs.

(May)   Unions welcome the announcement of a minimum hourly wage but some protest at its level of £3.60, with a lower £3.00 rate for 18–21 year olds; the unions had proposed a single rate of between £4.00 and £4.61.

15 Labour and the Left

Throughout Labour's history there has been a political relationship with
a left wing in the party and left organisations – often self-proclaimed as
Marxist and revolutionary – outside the party. The chronologies that
follow set out these relationships. The Independent Labour Party (ILP),
which was a constituent part of the Labour Representation Committee
(LRC) at its foundation in 1900 but which disaffiliated from Labour in
1932, appears in each of the chronologies. Detailed information on the
organisations in these chronologies can be found in the Glossary.

Chronology of the Labour Left

1901 Blatchford declares in the *Clarion* that by joining the Labour
Party the Independent Labour Party (ILP) has ceased to be a
socialist party.

1907 (Oct).   Victor Grayson is elected as an Independent Socialist
MP for Colne Valley at a by-election supported by the local
but not national ILP. He calls for the establishment of a
specifically socialist party.

1909 Motion at ILP national conference for disaffiliation from
Labour is heavily defeated.

1914 (Aug.)   The ILP produces an anti-war *Manifesto on
International Socialism* in which it declares: 'Across the roar
of guns, we send sympathy and greetings to the German
socialists.'

1920 The ILP conference in Glasgow votes to secede from the
Second International but rejects affiliation to the Third
(Communist) International. The Labour Party conference
overwhelmingly rejects the British Socialist Party (BSP)
proposal that Labour should leave the Second International
and affiliate to the Third International.

1921 The ILP conference rejects affiliation to the Third
(Communist) International and votes for the removal of

Communist sympathisers. The ILP affiliates to the 'Two and a half International'.

1922   (Oct.)   The ILP National Administrative Council ends MacDonald's regular column in the *Socialist Register* because of his criticisms of ILP policy. The new ILP constitution commits the party to parliamentary socialism with a guild socialist tone. (Nov.)   Left-wing members of an organisation that became known as the Clydesiders are returned at the general election. These include Maxton, Shinwell, Wheatley and Buchanan.

1924   (Jan.)   Left-wing ILP members John Wheatley and F.W. Jowett are appointed to the Labour Cabinet as Minister of Health and First Commissioner of Works respectively. An unofficial group of left-wing ILP MPs (the Clydesiders) is established which criticises the Labour government's actions. Lansbury moves an amendment to the Army and Air Force Annual Bill allowing servicemen to refuse any duty in connection with trade disputes.

1925   The ILP declares its role in the Labour Party is to 'develop in detail the Socialist objectives of the movement' and appoints seven committees to formulate detailed policies for a future government. Reports are published on agriculture, the Empire, India, trade unions and industrial policy, and parliamentary reform. The party unsuccessfully attempts to impose a whip on its members in the Commons.

1926   (Apr.)   The ILP moves to the left with the election at its annual conference of Maxton as chairman.
(Sept.)   The ILP publishes a 'living wage' programme in *Socialism In Our Time*. Labour leader Macdonald attacks the proposals as attempting to give orders to Labour MPs and future ministers.

1927   The ILP ends the traditional selection of MacDonald as one of its delegates to the Labour Party conference. Snowden resigns from the ILP.
(Oct.)   The ILP's *Socialism in Our Time* is effectively dismissed by reference back to the National Executive at the Labour Party conference.

1928   (June)   The Cook–Maxton Manifesto proposes a new ILP/ Labour left alliance.

1929   (June)   MacDonald fails to offer any ILP member a seat in the new Labour government.

1930   (Apr.)   Eighteen left-wing ILP MPs form an unofficial committee to oppose the government's policies, particularly on unemployment.

1931   (June)   The Society for Socialist Inquiry and Propaganda (SSIP) is formed.
(Oct.)   The Labour Party conference votes against allowing ILP MPs to ignore Labour's Standing Orders and act as a separate party in the House of Commons.

1932   The ILP Easter conference votes against disaffiliation from the Labour Party but votes in July to disaffiliate by 241 votes to 142.
(Aug.)   The Scottish Socialist Party (ILP members who opposed disaffiliation) affiliates to the Labour Party.
(Oct.)   The Socialist League (including many former ILP members who opposed disaffiliation) is formed and affiliates to the Labour Party in 1933.

1933   (Oct.)   The Labour Party conference supports a resolution from Stafford Cripps calling for the immediate abolition of the House of Lords by an incoming Labour government and the passing of an Emergency Powers Act to rapidly introduce socialism.

1936   (July)   The Spanish Civil War breaks out; the ILP ends policy of pacifism to support the Republic.

1937   (Jan.)   The Socialist League is expelled from the Labour Party for working with the Communists. The League dissolves itself in March. *Tribune* – the voice of the Labour left – is founded by Bevan, Cripps, Mellor, Wilkinson and Strauss.

1940   (Dec.)   ILP motion calling for a compromise peace with Germany is defeated in the House of Commons by 341 votes to 4.

1944   Victory for Socialism (VFS) is established by Labour Party activists to press for left-wing policies.

1945   (Jan.)   The Labour Party refuses affiliation to the Common Wealth.

(Feb.)   Sir Stafford Cripps (expelled in 1939 for supporting a Popular Front) is re-admitted to the Labour Party.

1947   (May)   Left-wing Labour MPs Michael Foot, Richard Crossman and Ian Mikardo issue *Keep Left*, advocating a non-aligned foreign policy.

1948   (Feb.)   The Communist Party congress calls on the Labour left to oppose the Labour government.

(Apr.)   MP John Platts-Mills is expelled from the Labour Party for anti-government statements and 21 other Labour MPs are warned.

1949   (Apr.)   The Socialist Fellowship is founded by Fenner Brockway and Ellis Jones to agitate for a more active socialist policy.

(May)   Left-wing Labour MPs Konni Zilliacus and Leslie Solley are expelled from the party for opposing the government's foreign policy.

1951   (Apr.)   Bevan resigns as Minister of Labour in protest against NHS charges. President of the Board of Trade Wilson resigns in protest against rearmament costs, followed by junior Supply Minister John Freeman. The Bevanite group is established by Bevan, Wilson and 13 other Labour MPs. The Socialist Fellowship is proscribed and dissolves itself.

(July)   The left-wing Labour publication *One Way Only* calls for arms reductions and support for national liberation movements.

(Sept.)   The left-wing Labour group criticises right-wing trade union leaders in *Going Our Way*.

1955   (Oct.)   The Labour League of Youth is wound up because of fears of left-wing influence.

1958   (Feb.)   Victory for Socialism (VFS) is strengthened by an influx of Bevanite MPs, including Michael Foot and Ian Mikardo. Labour leader Gaitskell attacks the VFS as a 'professional, anti-leadership' group within the party. The Campaign for Nuclear Disarmament (CND) is launched.

(May)   The leader of St Pancras Council Labour group is suspended from the party membership following the flying of the red flag over the town hall.

1960   (Apr.)   One hundred thousand people attend CND demonstration in Trafalgar Square.
(May)   Labour leader Gaitskell attacks unilateralism in a speech in Leeds.
(June)   A 15-strong VFS group of Labour MPs calls for Gaitskell's resignation as leader on the unilateralism issue. The party National Executive statement on defence policy calls for unilateral nuclear disarmament but a retention of US bases in Britain. The publication of *Appeal for Unity in Support of Conference Decisions* by left-wing activists is followed by the formation of the Unity Group, the successor to VFS.

1962   (June)   CND accepts Michael Foot's proposal that it should not field candidates at elections, the effect of which would be to weaken Labour.

1964   The Unity Group of left-wing Labour MPs is formally dissolved but continues sporadic activity until 1967.

1965   (Mar.)   Fifty Labour MPs call on the government to dissociate itself from US involvement in Vietnam.

1966   (Aug.)   Twenty-seven Labour backbenchers vote against the Labour government's proposal to take statutory powers to refer wage and price increases to the Prices and Incomes Board.

1968   Socialist Charter is formed to mobilise the constituency and parliamentary left.
(Mar.)   Forty Labour MPs abstain and 55 vote against a motion to approve the government policy document on industrial relations, *In Place of Strife*.

1979   (May)   Tony Benn refuses to stand for the Shadow Cabinet following the general election defeat and goes to the backbenches to lead a left-wing campaign.
(Oct.)   The Labour Party conference accepts a policy for the mandatory reselection of sitting MPs in the life of each Parliament, a left-wing demand to retain activist control over MPs.

1980   (Jan.)   A left-wing dominated committee of enquiry begins an examination of the Labour Party's organisation.

(Oct.)   The Labour Party conference agrees to remove the right to elect the leader and deputy leader from MPs alone and to set up an electoral college comprising representatives of the trade unions, constituency parties and MPs.

1981   (Jan.)   A special Labour Party conference at Wembley gives trade unions 40%, constituency parties 30% and MPs 30% of the votes in the electoral college to choose party leadership. As a result, the right-wing 'Gang of Four' leave to form the Social Democratic Party (SDP) in March.

(May)   Ken Livingstone ousts right-wing Labour group leader to become leader of Greater London Council after its capture from the Conservatives. Seventy-one Labour MPs vote against a defence White Paper in defiance of the leadership.

(Oct.)   Benn is narrowly defeated by Denis Healey in the contest for the Labour Party deputy leadership; Benn's candidacy marks the growth of the left in the party.

(Dec.)   Left-wing former minister Eric Heffer calls for Labour to become a socialist party.

1982   (Oct.)   The hard left is weakened in elections to the party's National Executive.

1983   (Oct.)   Labour Party conference reaffirmation of unilateral nuclear disarmament demonstrates continuing left influence.

1984   (Oct.)   Left influence continues as Labour Party conference overwhelmingly condemns police violence against striking miners, votes for police to be kept out of industrial disputes, and continues support for unilateral nuclear disarmament.

1985   (Oct.)   Kinnock's denunciation at the Labour Party conference of Militant activities is attacked by members of the hard left.

1989   (Oct.)   Labour Party conference's formal abandonment of unilateral nuclear disarmament underlines Kinnock's strengthened position against the left.

1995   (Jan.)   Thirty-two Labour MEPs sign an open letter opposing Blair's proposals to revise Clause Four.

(Apr.)   Special Labour Party conference acceptance of rewording of Clause Four demonstrates the weakening of the traditional left, particularly in constituency parties which vote 90% in favour of the change.

1996   (May)   National Union of Mineworkers president Arthur
Scargill leaves Labour to form the Socialist Labour Party.

1997   (May)   The Socialist Labour Party fields 64 candidates at the
general election, all of whom lose their deposit.
(July)   New Left in New Labour group proposals call for the
retention of a substantial role for the trade unions in party
organisation and for genuine debate at party conferences.
(Sept.)   Benn criticises the policy-making reforms embodied
in *Partnership into Power* (accepted by the Labour Party
conference) as 'part of a strategy for the creation of a new
political party'.
(Oct.)   Four MEPs are suspended from the European
Parliamentary Labour Party for refusing to apologise for
breaking the code forbidding public criticism of party policy.

Chronology of Labour and Communism

1919   Labour Party leadership warns members against working with
Workers' and Soldiers' Councils formed in response to the
Russian Revolution. The ILP enters into unsuccessful 'Socialist
Unity' negotiations with the British Socialist Party (BSP) and
the Socialist Labour Party (SLP).

1920   (July)   The Communist Party of Great Britain (CPGB) is
formed in London by 160 delegates from the BSP, SLP,
South Wales Socialist Society and other organisations.
(Sept.)   The Labour National Executive rejects the
Communist Party's request for affiliation.

1921   (Jan.)   Lenin advocates a Communist tactical alliance with
Labour.
(June)   The Labour Party conference rejects the Communist
Party request for affiliation.

1922   (June)   The Labour Party conference rejects a renewed
Communist Party request for affiliation.
(Nov.)   Two Communists are returned as Labour MPs –
J.T. Walton Newbold (Motherwell) and S. Saklatvala (North
Battersea) – at the general election.

1923   (Oct.)   The Labour National Executive accepts London
Labour Party leader Herbert Morrison's proposal to move
against Communists in local parties and trade unions.

1924   (July)   J.R. Campbell calls, in the Communist *Workers' Weekly*, for soldiers to refuse to fire on workers; Campbell is charged under the Incitement to Mutiny Act but the Attorney-General withdraws charges, precipitating the fall of the Labour government and a general election in which Labour loses office.

(Oct.)   The Labour Party conference bans Communists as members and from adoption as candidates, and rejects a further Communist request for affiliation. The Zinoviev letter is used against Labour at the general election.

1925   (Oct.)   The Labour Party conference reaffirms its ban on Communists from individual membership and requests trade unions not to allow Communists as delegates to national or local party conferences. Twelve Communist leaders are arrested and imprisoned for seditious libel and incitement to mutiny as the Conservative government prepares for a general strike.

(Dec.)   Communists form a National Left Wing Movement to gain influence in constituency Labour parties.

1926   (May)   Communists claim the General Strike presents a revolutionary opportunity and condemn the Labour Party leadership for its failure.

(Oct.)   The Labour Party conference agrees on the disbanding of a dozen constituency parties for accepting Communists as members; 48 constituency parties support the Communist affiliation campaign.

1927   (Sept.)   Fifty-four local constituency Labour parties are represented at the National Left Wing Movement conference despite Labour's anti-Communist policy.

1928   (Sept.)   Communists adopt a 'Class against Class' policy, effectively ending the possibility of links with the Labour Party (which it denounces as 'social fascist') and the trade unions. Over 75 local Labour parties send delegates to the National Left Wing Movement conference.

(Oct.)   The Labour Party conference bans Communists from attending as union delegates.

1929   (May)   The Communist Party unsuccessfully fields 25 candidates against leading Labour figures at the general election.

1930   (Jan.)   The *Daily Worker* is founded under Comintern instructions with Soviet funds.

1931   The Labour Party bars members from working with the Communist 'United Front from Below'.

1933   (Mar.)   The Labour Party publishes *The Communist Solar System*, warning members against joining Communist Party front organisations.
(Oct.)   The Labour Party conference rejects a resolution arguing for the party to support a United Front against fascism with the ILP and the Communists.

1934   (Oct.)   TUC Circular 16 (Black Circular) bars Communists (and fascists) from membership of trades councils and from trade union office. The Labour Party conference reaffirms incompatibility of party membership with working with Communists in the United Front.

1935   *Soviet Communism: A New Civilisation?*, by the Fabian Webbs, is published; a second edition is published in 1937 without the question mark.
(Oct.)   The Labour Party conference rejects a further Communist Party request for affiliation.
(Nov.)   William Gallacher is returned as Communist MP for West Fife at the general election.

1936   (July)   The Fabian Society, the Socialist League and the Miners' Federation of Great Britain support the Communist campaign for affiliation to Labour.
(Dec.)   Communist Party leader Harry Pollitt appeals for volunteers to fight in defence of the Spanish Republic against Franco. Many Communists and Labour Party members join the International Brigade. The Labour Party disbands the Labour League of Youth because of Communist influence.

1937   (Jan.)   The Labour Party refuses an appeal from the Communists, the ILP and the Socialist League to join a Popular Front against fascism; it is estimated that in London alone one-fifth of Labour Party members support the Front's activities.

1938   (May)   The Labour Party National Executive warns that working in a Popular Front with the Communists would lose Labour votes at a general election.

1939   (Aug.)   The Soviet Union signs a pact with Germany.
Communists lose credibility by supporting a declaration of
war against Germany in September and then opposing it on
Comintern instructions.

1940   (May)   Ten resolutions at the Labour Party conference
support the Communist Party's opposition to the war; four
London constituency parties are disbanded for being under
Communist influence.

1941   (Jan.)   *Daily Worker* is suppressed by Home Secretary Herbert
Morrison.
(June)   Communists support war following German attack on
the Soviet Union.

1942   Communist membership reaches all-time high of 56,000. The
ban on *Daily Worker* is lifted.

1943   (June)   The Labour Party conference rejects a Communist
request for affiliation.

1945   (July)   Two Communist MPs, William Gallacher (West Fife)
and Phil Piratin (Mile End), are returned at the general
election. The TUC withdraws the 1934 Black Circular barring
Communists from trade councils.

1946   (June)   The Labour Party conference rejects the Communist
request for affiliation and revises rules to prevent any further
applications.
(Sept.)   Communists lead a squatting campaign in London
in protest against what they say is the Labour government's
failure to deal with housing shortages.

1947   Labour proscribes Communist front organisations, making
Labour Party membership incompatible with participation in
their activities.

1948   (Feb.)   The Communist Party congress calls on the Labour
left to oppose the Labour government.
(Mar.)   The Labour government bans Communists (and
fascists) from work of importance to state security.

1950   (Feb.)   The two Communist MPs lose their seats at the
general election.

(July)   Labour prime minister Attlee warns that Britain faces a Communist 'enemy within'.

(Sept.)   Minister of Labour George Isaacs accuses Communists of planning to disrupt British industry. The TGWU general secretary Arthur Deakin calls for the outlawing of Communists to counter unofficial strikes.

1951   (Feb.)   The new Communist programme, *The British Road to Socialism*, abandons the dictatorship of the proletariat and advocates parliamentary socialism.

1952   (Oct.)   Labour leader Gaitskell accuses one-sixth of Labour Party constituency delegates of being Communists or fellow-travellers.

1956   (Oct.)   The Soviet suppression of the Hungarian Revolution divides Communists and provokes a membership slump.

1957   (May)   *The New Reasoner* is published by former Communists, advocating a New Left outside both the Labour and Communist parties.

1961   (July)   The High Court finds that Communists rigged the Electrical Trades Union executive elections.

1966   (June)   Labour prime minister Wilson accuses Communists (a 'tightly-knit group of politically motivated men') of attempting to destabilise the Labour government by their involvement in the seamen's strike which begins in May and ends in July. Communists are prominent in establishing a left-wing Liaison Committee for the Defence of Trade Unions (LCDTU). *Daily Worker* is renamed *Morning Star* in an attempt to broaden its popularity.

1968   (Aug.)   The Communist Party criticises the Soviet invasion of Czechoslovakia but suffers further decline in membership. Communist dominance on the left is weakened by Trotskyists, Maoists and Anarchists.

1969   The left-wing Liaison Committee for the Defence of Trade Unions (LCDTU), in which Communists are prominent, leads the opposition to the Labour government's *In Place of Strife* proposals to reform trade unions.

1972   The TUC lifts its ban on Communists attending trades council conferences.

1977   A Eurocommunist faction gains strength in the Communist Party. The Communist-inspired Alternative Economic Strategy is adopted by the TUC.

1978   A new version of the Communist programme outlines a 'broad democratic' alliance of the working class, the women's movement, environmentalists and ethnic minorities.

1991   (Nov.)   Following the collapse of the Soviet Union, the Communist Party dissolves itself and is reconstituted as the Democratic Left.

Chronology of Labour and Trotskyism

1932   The Trotskyist 'Balham Group' is expelled from the Communist Party and forms a Communist League.

1934   The Trotskyist Communist League disbands and advises supporters to join the Independent Labour Party (ILP).

1944   The Revolutionary Communist Party is formed by the merger of the Revolutionary Socialist League and the Workers' International League.

1947   The Revolutionary Communist Party divides over the policy of entryism into the Labour Party but by 1949 most active Trotskyists have joined Labour.

1957   The Revolutionary Socialist League (forerunner to Militant) is founded by Ted Grant and Jimmy Deane, centred in Liverpool. It begins an immediate tactic of entryism into Labour Party (June).

1959   The Socialist Labour League (the forerunner to the Workers' Revolutionary Party) is established by Gerry Healy in May. The SLL is immediately proscribed by the Labour Party. The SLL soon wins control of the newly established Labour youth wing, the Young Socialists.

1960   The International Socialism group (later the Socialist Workers' Party) is established with an initial policy of entry into the Labour Party (it withdraws in 1965).

1964   The Revolutionary Socialist League sets up an entryist propaganda newspaper entitled *Militant: For Labour and Youth*. In the future, Militant members will masquerade as 'supporters' of the paper (June). The Labour Party disbands the Young Socialists because of their capture by the Socialist Labour League.

1965   The Labour Party forms the Labour Party Young Socialists; by 1970 Militant has a majority on the organisation's national committee.

1967   (Oct.)   Anti-Vietnam War demonstration in London signals emergence of a largely student-based Trotskyist and Anarchist extra-parliamentary left which builds on disillusion with the Labour government.

1968   Violent anti-Vietnam War demonstrations in March and October show growing support for the Trotskyist International Marxist Group, International Socialism (later the Socialist Workers' Party) and Anarchist and Maoist groupings.

1972   The setting up of a place for the Labour Party Young Socialists on the party's National Executive provides Militant with a key position.

1973   The abolition of the 'proscribed list' of organisations which Labour Party members are barred from joining has the effect of easing Militant entryism into the party.

1974   Militant wins control of the National Organisation of Labour Students until it is ousted by the broad left Clause Four coalition in 1975.

1975   (Nov.)   The Labour Party National Executive fails to take action on a report by national agent Reg Underhill on the extent of Militant infiltration into the party and the Labour Party Young Socialists. Militant membership is estimated at 1,000.

1976   Militant member Andy Bevan is appointed Labour Party National Youth Officer.

1980   (Mar.)   A report by Lord Underhill reveals the extent of Militant infiltration of the Labour Party.

1982   The Labour Party National Executive moves against
Trotskyists in the party by proposing a register of acceptable
non-affiliated organisations. Militant is denounced as a
'well-organised caucus, centrally controlled' in June.

1983   (Feb.)   The Labour Party National Executive votes to expel
five members of *Militant* editorial board from the party.
(May)   Labour wins control of Liverpool City Council with
51 seats, 16 of which are held by Militant members. Militant
effectively takes control of the council with Derek Hatton as
deputy leader.
(June)   Two Militant members, Terry Fields (Kirkdale) and
Dave Nellist (Coventry South East), are elected as Labour
MPs.

1984   (Mar.)   Liverpool City Council adopts an illegal deficit
budget as part of its Militant policy of confrontation with the
Conservative government.
(May)   Labour increases the number of seats in Liverpool at
the May local elections.

1985   (Sept.)   Liverpool City Council announces a projected 31,000
redundancies in an attempt to force concessions from the
government.
(Oct.)   Kinnock wins support at the Labour Party conference
in a bitter attack on Militant control of Liverpool City
Council. The Liverpool Labour Left Group is formed to
oppose Militant.

1986   (Feb.)   Labour Party National Executive issues a report on
the extent of Militant influence; 40 constituency parties expel
Militant supporters.
(June)   Seven Liverpool Militant members, including council
deputy leader Derek Hatton, are expelled from the Labour
Party.
(Oct.)   The Labour Party conference endorses the expulsion
of all members of Militant by 6,146,000 to 325,000 votes.

1992   The expulsion of Labour MPs Terry Fields and Dave Nellist
for membership of Militant marks the final purging of the
organisation. Militant – renamed Militant Labour – splits
between those favouring a new party and those wanting to
continue entryism.

1997   (Jan.)   Militant relaunches itself as the Socialist Party.

16 Scotland, Wales and Devolution

Labour Votes and Seats in General Elections in Scotland, 1900–97

Election	Votes	% of vote	No. of candidates	Seats won
1900	–	–	–	–
1906	16,897	2.3	4	2
1910 (Jan.)	37,852	5.1	10	2
1910 (Dec.)	24,633	3.6	5	3
1918	265,744	22.9	39	6
1922	501,254	32.2	43	29
1923	532,450	35.9	48	34
1924	697,146	41.1	63	26
1929	937,300	42.3	66	36
1931	696,248	32.6	57	7
1935	863,789	36.8	63	20
(ILP	111,256	5.0	11	4)
1945	1,144,310	47.6	68	32
(ILP	40,725	1.8	3	3)
1950	1,259,410	46.2	71	37
1951	1,330,244	47.9	71	35
1955	1,188,058	46.7	71	34
1959	1,245,255	46.7	71	38
1964	1,283,667	48.7	71	43
1966	1,273,916	49.9	71	46
1970	1,197,068	44.5	71	44
1974 (Feb.)	1,057,601	36.6	71	40
1974 (Oct.)	1,000,581	36.3	71	41
1979	1,211,445	41.6	71	44
1983	990,654	35.1	72	41
1987	1,258,132	42.4	72	50
1992	1,142,911	39.0	72	49
1997	1,283,353	45.6	72	56

Labour Votes and Seats in General Elections in Wales, 1900–97

Election	Votes	% of vote	No. of candidates	Seats won
1900	9,598	3.9	2	1
1906	11,865	3.5	2	1
1910 (Jan.)	60,496	14.9	5	5
1910 (Dec.)	47,027	17.8	7	5
1918	163,055	30.8	25	9
1922	363,568	40.8	28	18
1923	355,172	42.0	27	19
1924	320,397	40.6	33	16
1929	937,300	42.3	66	36
1931	479,547	44.1	30	16
1935	395,830	45.4	33	18
1945	779,184	58.5	34	25
1950	887,984	58.1	36	27
1951	925,848	60.5	36	27
1955	825,690	57.6	36	27
1959	841,450	56.4	36	27
1964	837,022	57.8	36	28
1966	863,692	60.7	36	32
1970	781,941	51.6	36	27
1974 (Feb.)	745,547	46.8	36	24
1974 (Oct.)	761,447	49.5	36	23
1979	795,493	48.6	36	22
1983	603,858	37.5	38	20
1987	765,209	45.1	38	24
1992	865,633	49.5	38	27
1997	885,935	54.7	40	34

Devolution – Chronology of Main Events

1925   Plaid Cymru (PC – Party of Wales) established.

1928   National Party of Scotland established.

1933   National Party of Scotland merges with the Scottish Party (formed 1930) to establish the Scottish National Party (SNP).

1945   (Apr.)   First SNP MP is elected in a by-election (defeated in July general election).

1946   (Sept.)   Attlee refuses Welsh Labour demands for appointment of a Secretary of State for Wales.

1948   (Apr.)   Standing Committee on Scottish Bills is established as a measure of devolution; the committee's role is to debate Scottish legislation before it is taken to a formal Second Reading in the Commons.

1949   (Apr.)   Council of Wales is formed to provide forum for Welsh interests.

1950   (July)   Labour government rejects demand for plebiscite on home rule for Scotland.

1958   (June)   Labour Party Scottish Council opposes proposals for a Scottish Parliament.

1964   (Oct.)   Labour government appoints the first Secretary of State for Wales.

1966   (Mar.)   Plaid Cymru (PC) wins its first parliamentary seat in the general election (the seat is lost at the 1970 general election).

1967   (Nov.)   Scottish National Party (SNP) captures Hamilton from Labour in a by-election (the seat is lost at the 1970 general election).

1970   (June)   Six SNP but no PC MPs are returned at the general election.

1973   (Oct.)   Kilbrandon Commission (set up by previous Labour government) rejects Scottish independence or a federal arrangement but supports a directly elected Scottish Assembly. (Nov.)   SNP wins Glasgow Govan in a by-election (the seat is lost at the February 1974 general election).

1974   (Jan.)   Labour general election manifesto promises substantial devolution to Scotland and a lesser amount to Wales.
(Feb.)   Seven SNP and two PC MPs are returned at the general election.
(June)   Privy Council Office publishes consultation document *Devolution in the UK*.

(Sept.)   Labour government announces proposal for elected assemblies to be established in Scotland and Wales.
(Oct.)   Eleven SNP and three PC MPs are returned at general election.

1975   (Nov.)   Labour government issues proposals for Scottish and Welsh devolution in *Our Changing Democracy.*

1976   (Jan.)   Four-day debate on devolution held in the House of Commons; Labour dissidents in Scotland, including two MPs, form a breakaway Scottish Labour Party (SLP) to oppose devolution proposals.
(Dec.)   Labour government issues *Devolution: The English Dimension.* The Scotland and Wales Bill passes its second reading by 292 votes to 247.

1977   (Feb.)   Labour government fails to secure guillotine on the Scotland and Wales Bill by 312 votes to 283.
(Mar.)   Labour Party in Scotland calls for a referendum on devolution.
(June)   Government withdraws the Scotland and Wales Bill following failure of all-party discussions.
(Nov.)   Scotland Bill receives second reading by 307 votes to 263 and the Wales Bill by 295 votes to 284; proportional representation for Scottish Assembly elections is rejected by 290 votes to 107.

1978   Labour Campaign for a Scottish Assembly formed.
(Jan.)   'Cunningham amendment' to the Scotland Bill makes it necessary for 40% of the total electorate to vote 'Yes' for the devolution referendum to pass.
(July)   Scotland Bill and Wales Bill receive Royal Assent.

1979   (Mar.)   Scotland votes by 33% to 31% (with 36% abstaining) for the devolution proposals but fails to reach the 40% threshold; Wales votes against by 47% to 12% (with 41% abstaining).
(May)   Two SNP and two PC MPs are returned at the general election.

1983   (June) Two SNP and two PC MPs are returned at the general election.

1987   (June)   Three SNP and three PC MPs are returned at the general election.

1988   Scottish Labour Action formed to campaign for home rule, greater autonomy for the party in Scotland and for greater internal party democracy.

1989   Cross-party Scottish Constitutional Conventional is formed on the initiative of the Labour Campaign for a Scottish Assembly.

1992   (Apr.)   Three SNP and four PC MPs are returned at the general election; Women's Caucus is set up by the Labour Party in Scotland to campaign for 50% women's representation in a future Scottish Parliament.

1994   (Sept.)   Labour leader Blair promises at the party conference that a future Labour government will establish a Scottish Parliament and a Welsh Assembly.

1996   (June)   Labour leader Blair says a future Labour government will hold referendums in Scotland and Wales on its proposals for devolution within six months of taking office.
(July)   Labour Campaign for a Scottish Parliament is formed to work with the Scottish Constitutional Convention on the referendum campaign.

1997   (May)   Six SNP and four PC MPs are returned at the general election; Labour government's Queen's Speech includes referendums in Scotland and Wales on devolved assemblies.
(July)   Government White Paper, *A Voice for Wales*, outlines the proposed Welsh Assembly; *Scotland's Parliament* outlines proposals to establish the first elected parliament for almost 300 years.
(Sept.)   Referendums are held on the government's proposals. Scotland is offered a 129-member parliament to deal with matters devolved to the Scottish Office (including education, health, law and order, local government, economic development, roads, the environment and the arts); 73 MSPs are to be elected by the first-past-the-post system and 56 by proportional representation. The Scots are asked whether the parliament should have tax-raising powers. There would continue to be a Secretary of State for Scotland and 72 MPs would continue to be sent to the House of Commons.
    Wales is offered a 60-seat assembly to deal with issues currently covered by the Welsh Office (including education, health, agriculture, roads and planning); 40 members would be elected by the first-past-the-post system and 20 by proportional representation.

Scotland votes in favour of a parliament by 74.3% to 25.7% and in favour of tax-raising powers by 63.5% to 36.5%. Wales votes in favour of an assembly by 50.3% to 49.7%.

1998   (May)   Scottish Secretary Dewar announces that the opening of the Scottish Parliament would be brought forward from 2000 to July 1999.

Referendums on Devolution for Scotland and Wales

1 Mar. 1979

	Yes	No
Scotland	1,230,937 (32.9%)	1,153,502 (30.8%)

(As fewer than 40% of the total electorate voted 'Yes' the proposal failed)

	Yes	No
Wales	243,948 (11.9%)	956,330 (46.9%)

Scotland

11 Sept. 1997

	Yes	No
Parliament	1,775,045 (74.3%)	614,400 (25.7%)
Tax-raising powers	1,512,889 (63.5%)	870,263 (36.5%)

Wales

18 Sept. 1997

	Yes	No
Assembly	559,419 (50.3%)	552,698 (49.7%)

17 Labour and Women

Women Labour Candidates standing in General Elections, 1918–97

Women were not granted the right to vote until 1918, and then only when they reached the age of 30. Women were allowed the vote at the age of 21 in 1928.

Year of election	No. of women Labour candidates	Women as % of Labour candidates
1918	4	1.1
1922	10	2.4
1923	14	3.3
1924	22	4.3
1929	30	5.3
1931	36	7.0
1935	33	5.6
1945	41	7.0
1950	42	6.8
1951	41	6.6
1955	43	7.0
1959	36	5.8
1964	33	5.2
1966	30	4.8
1970	29	4.6
1974 (Feb.)	40	6.4
1974 (Oct.)	50	8.0
1979	52	8.3
1983	78	12.3
1987	92	14.5
1992	136	21.5
1997	158	24.7

Women Labour Candidates elected in General Elections, 1918–97

Women were not admitted to Parliament until the passage of the Sex Disqualification Removal Act in 1919.

Year of election	No. elected	Women as % of Labour MPs	Women Labour MPs as % of all women MPs
1918	0	0.0	0.0
1922	0	0.0	0.0
1923	3	1.6	37.5
1924	1	0.7	25.0
1929	9	3.1	69.2
1931	0	0.0	0.0
1935	1	0.6	11.1
1945	21	5.3	87.5
1950	14	4.4	66.7
1951	11	3.7	64.7
1955	14	5.0	58.3
1959	13	5.0	52.0
1964	18	5.7	62.1
1966	19	5.2	61.5
1970	10	3.5	38.5
1974 (Feb.)	13	4.3	56.5
1974 (Oct.)	18	5.6	66.7
1979	11	4.1	57.9
1983	10	4.8	43.5
1987	21	9.2	51.2
1992	37	14.3	61.9
1997	101	24.2	84.2

Chronology of Main Events

1884   TUC conference votes in support of female suffrage.

1888   TUC conference calls for equal pay for women.

1893   Independent Labour Party (ILP) founded at Bradford conference. Many women, including Mary Macarthur, Margaret Bondfield, Enid Stacey, Katherine St John Conway (later Glasier), Margaret Macmillan, Caroline Martin and Emmeline Pankhurst, are among later prominent members.

1894   ILP conference votes in support of female suffrage.

1902   I.O. Ford of Leeds ILP becomes the first woman delegate at a Labour Representation Committee (LRC) conference.

1904   LRC conference supports a Women's Enfranchisement Bill to grant limited female suffrage.

1905   LRC conference rejects the Women's Enfranchisement Bill on the grounds that it would benefit middle and upper-class women while many men remain disenfranchised.

1906   Women's Labour League is established to secure direct representation for women in Parliament and local councils.

1912   ILP member Emmeline Pankhurst proposes Labour MPs should withhold support from Liberal government until it grants votes to women. Labour conference agrees to oppose any franchise bill that extends vote to more men but excludes women. Lansbury resigns as MP for Bow and Bromley to fight a by-election in support of female suffrage and is defeated. MacDonald attacks violent methods used by supporters of female suffrage.

1916   Standing Joint Committee of Working Women's Organisations, including the Labour Party National Executive, TUC and Co-operative Union, is set up to formulate policy, mount campaigns, secure representation of women on government committees.

1918   Women's Labour League amalgamates with the party to form basis of Women's Sections established under Labour's new Constitution.

1919   Beatrice Webb's *Men and Women's Wages: Should they be Equal?* is published.

1922   Following Labour's successes in the general election, Beatrice Webb forms the Half-Circle Club for the wives of Labour MPs to maintain a distance from the governing parties; the body is later absorbed into the Parliamentary Labour Club.

1923   Margaret Bondfield and Susan Lawrence are elected as the
         first women Labour MPs at general election in December.

1924   In January, three women MPs are made members of the 12-
         strong Liaison Committee to maintain contact between the
         Parliamentary Labour Party and the first Labour government.
         In May, a Labour women's deputation asks the Minister of
         Health to end ban on local authorities giving information on
         contraception. One woman Labour MP returns at October
         general election.

1925   Labour Party National Executive, aware of Catholic
         sensitivities, reports to annual conference that contraception
         is an individual matter on which the party cannot have a view.

1929   Nine women Labour MPs return at May general election;
         Margaret Bondfield becomes first woman minister as Minister
         of Labour; Susan Lawrence becomes first woman chair of the
         Labour National Executive Committee.

1931   No women Labour MPs return at October general election
         which follows formation of National Government.

1935   One woman Labour MP returns at November general election
         in Labour revival.

1936   Labour MP Ellen Wilkinson leads Jarrow unemployed march
         in October.

1945   Twenty-one women Labour MPs return at July general
         election in Labour landslide; Bessie Braddock is the first
         woman to be elected to a Liverpool seat; Ellen Wilkinson
         becomes first woman Minister of Education.

1947   Labour government institutes 'women must work' publicity
         campaign to encourage women to return to work in
         manufacturing, textiles and catering. Labour Party National
         Executive opposes party conference demands for equal pay
         for women.

1948   In May, the National Assistance Act allows support for
         unmarried mothers and children. In July, the British
         Nationality of Women Act allows British women the right to
         retain citizenship when marrying foreign men but withdraws

right of foreign women to automatic citizenship when marrying British men.

1949   Party programme *Labour Believes in Britain* proposes equal pay for women.

1950   Fourteen women Labour MPs return at February general election.

1951   TUC annual conference calls for equal pay for women in September. Eleven women Labour MPs return at October general election.

1952   Bessie Braddock becomes the first woman MP to be suspended from a Commons sitting.

1955   Fourteen women Labour MPs return at May general election.

1959   Thirteen Labour women MPs return at October general election.

1964   Eighteen women Labour MPs return at October general election; Barbara Castle is appointed to the Cabinet as Minister of Overseas Development.

1966   Nineteen women Labour MPs return at March general election.

1967   Margaret Herbison resigns as Minister of Social Security because of objections to curbs on the Welfare State demanded by measures to defend the pound. Abortion Act, a private member's bill supported by the government, allows abortion if danger is posed to physical or mental health of woman or another child, or in the case of a substantial risk that the child will be physically or mentally disabled. Family Planning Act empowers local health authorities to establish family planning services with free advice and means-tested provision of contraceptive devices.

1968   Barbara Castle is appointed Secretary of State for Employment and Productivity in April. In September, the TUC annual conference calls for equal pay for women.

1969   In September, Barbara Castle promises the Labour Party annual conference that the government will introduce legislation on equal pay for women.

1970   Equal Pay Act provides for equal pay for women carrying out comparable work and outlaws discrimination in terms and conditions of employment (to come into effect in 1975). Matrimonial Proceedings and Property Act allows courts to order provision for either spouse and recognises contribution to the joint home made during marriage. Ten women Labour MPs return at June general election.

1972   Labour Party issues a report on discrimination against women and recommends policies to achieve equal rights; forms the basis for policies in government.

1974   Thirteen women Labour MPs return at February general election; Barbara Castle is appointed to the Cabinet as Secretary of State for Health and Social Security and Shirley Williams for Education and Science. At the October election the number of women Labour MPs rises to 18.

1975   Social Security Act establishes a maternity allowance fund in March. In August, Social Security Pensions Act establishes equal treatment in pensions schemes and abolishes contributions test which limited state pensions for women. In November, Employment Protection Act outlaws dismissal for pregnancy and provides for paid maternity leave. Sex Discrimination Act outlaws direct and indirect discrimination on gender grounds and establishes Equal Opportunities Commission. Equal Pay Act comes into operation in December.

1979   Eleven women Labour MPs return at May general election.

1983   Labour National Executive publishes a *Charter to Establish Equality for Women within the Party* in April. Ten women Labour MPs return at general election in June.

1987   In April, Labour Party announces it will create a Ministry for Women when it forms a government. Twenty-one women Labour MPs return at general election in June.

1989   Party rule change for annual election to the Parliamentary Committee increases number of members to 18, at least three of whom must be women.

1991   In March, Labour Party issues a policy document entitled *A New Ministry for Women.*

1992   Thirty-seven women Labour MPs return at April general election; Betty Boothroyd, Labour MP for West Bromwich, is elected first woman Speaker of the House of Commons. Margaret Beckett becomes first woman Labour deputy leader in October.

1993   Party rule change for annual election to the Parliamentary Committee increases the minimum number of women members to four.

1994   Margaret Beckett serves as Labour acting leader on death of John Smith.

1996   An industrial tribunal rules that all-women short lists to select Labour parliamentary candidates represents discrimination on grounds of sex. Labour Party annual conference votes to take measures to increase the representation of women in the Parliamentary Labour Party to 50% within ten years.

1997   In May, 101 women Labour MPs return at general election; five are appointed to Cabinet – Margaret Beckett becomes President of the Board of Trade, Ann Taylor President of the Council and Leader of the House of Commons, Harriet Harman Secretary for Social Security, Marjorie Mowlam Northern Ireland Secretary and Clare Short Secretary for International Development; a Minister for Women is appointed for the first time. In June, Social Security Secretary Harman announces formation of a Cabinet sub-committee for women and a women's unit for cross-departmental co-ordination on women's issues.

1998   In May, the government announces all policy documents, programmes, plans of action and legislative changes will include specific assessments of the impact on women. Government announces target of 50% women's representation on 1,100 quangos and public bodies in June. Appointment announced of Margaret McDonagh as Labour's first woman general secretary in July.

18 Labour, Decolonisation, Immigration and Ethnic Minorities

Chronology of Main Events

1906   Black Labour Party member John Archer elected to Battersea Council in South London.

1907   MacDonald's *Labour and the Empire* criticises Conservative and Liberal Imperialism and declares that Labour would attempt to 'democratise the personnel of the Imperial structure'.

1913   John Archer becomes mayor of Battersea.

1922   Indian Communist Party member Shapurji Saklatvala returned as Labour MP at the November general election; he remains an MP until 1929.

1924   Labour government releases Indian independence activist Mahatma Gandhi from prison following his serious illness.

1930   After clashes between Arabs and Jews in the British mandate of Palestine, a White Paper proposes restrictions on new Jewish settlement and a ban on further evictions of Arabs. Jewish immigration to Palestine is later restricted. MacDonald presides over a Round Table Conference on the future government of India which is boycotted by the Congress Party.

1946   Gold Coast becomes first British African colony with black majority membership of legislature under new constitution.

1947   India and Pakistan become independent.

1948   Burma and Ceylon (now Sri Lanka) become independent. Britain gives up mandate in Palestine and withdraws troops; state of Israel proclaimed. State of emergency in Malaya following opening of Communist guerrilla campaign. Labour government White Paper declares aim of colonial policy to be 'to guide the colonial territories to responsible self-government within the Commonwealth'. *Empire Windrush* brings 492 Jamaican ex-servicemen to Britain, opening post-war Caribbean immigration. British Nationality Act confers British subject status on Commonwealth citizens and divides British citizens between those of independent Commonwealth countries and those of UK and Colonies.

1949   Ireland Act gives Irish citizens in Britain the rights of British citizens; Eire leaves the Commonwealth and becomes the Republic of Ireland.

1950   India becomes the first republic within the Commonwealth. Labour backbencher Reginald Sorensen unsuccessfully introduces private member's bill to introduce legislation to counter racial discrimination.

1955   Labour Party National Executive Commonwealth sub-committee declares party's opposition to racial discrimination.

1956   Labour backbencher Fenner Brockway unsuccessfully introduces private member's bill to counter racial discrimination; Labour Party conference condemns racial discrimination.

1958   Labour Party conference promises legislation against racial discrimination following race riots in Notting Hill in which black population defends itself against white attacks. Labour backbencher calls for restrictions on Commonwealth immigration.

1961   Conservative government's Commonwealth Immigration Bill denounced by Labour leader Gaitskell in the House of Commons as a 'plain anti-colour measure'.

1964   Labour prime minister Wilson denounces Tory MP elected for Smethwick following an allegedly racist general election campaign as a 'parliamentary leper'.

1965   Labour Home Secretary Frank Soskice claims that immigration controls are being widely evaded. Wilson announces a mission under Lord Mountbatten is to be despatched to the Commonwealth to investigate methods of regulating immigration. White regime in Southern Rhodesia unilaterally declares illegal independence. The Gambia becomes independent. Race Relations Act outlaws direct discrimination on grounds of colour, race, national or ethnic origin in some public places and establishes Race Relations Board. Government White Paper on Commonwealth Immigration proposes limiting of immigration to 8,500 professional and skilled workers annually through allocation of vouchers.

1966   Labour government brings in Section 11 of the Local Government Act allowing local authorities to claim grants to employ extra staff to meet special needs of Commonwealth immigrants. Basutoland (now Lesotho), Bechuanaland (Botswana), British Guiana (Guyana) and Barbados become independent.

1967   Aden becomes independent.

1968   Labour Home Secretary James Callaghan speeds Commonwealth Immigration Bill through Parliament in seven days to prevent entry of Asians with British passports expelled from Kenya; immigrants to be free from control only if at least one parent or grandparent is born in Britain; 35 Labour backbenchers abstain in vote in February. Conservative MP Enoch Powell makes anti-immigration 'rivers of blood' speech in April. Race Relations Act extends the 1965 Act into non-discrimination in employment and the provision of services and housing and establishes the Communication Relations Commission in October. Swaziland and Mauritius become independent.

1969   West Indies cricketer Sir Learie Constantine appointed a life peer.

1971   Labour Opposition denounces the Conservative government's Immigration Bill, which gives freedom of entry to 'patrials' whose parents or grandparents were born in Britain, as being overtly racist.

1974   Grenada becomes independent.

1975   David Pitt, black chairman of the Greater London Council, appointed a life peer. Papua New Guinea becomes independent.

1976   Race Relations Act outlaws indirect racial discrimination, sets out measures of positive action to combat effects of discrimination, and establishes the Commission for Racial Equality to oversee the working of the Act. Illegal white Rhodesian government accepts British–US proposals for majority rule within two years (but goes on to reject them in January 1977). Seychelles become independent.

1978   White regime in Rhodesia reaches an 'internal settlement' with three black nationalist leaders. House of Commons select committee recommends firmer control on immigration. Dominica becomes independent.

1984   Black Section movement launched at conference in Birmingham to establish separate black sections in the Labour Party and trade unions.

1985   Labour Party conference in October votes overwhelmingly against establishment of Black Sections.

1987   Sharon Atkins is suspended as candidate for Nottingham East after calling Labour a racist party for refusing to accept establishment of separate Black Sections. Black party members are leaders of three London boroughs – Linda Bellos (Lambeth), Bernie Grant (Haringey), Merle Amory (Brent); four ethnic minority MPs – Diane Abbott (Hackney North and Stoke Newington), Paul Boateng (Brent South), Bernie Grant (Tottenham) and Keith Vaz (Leicester East) – are returned for Labour at June general election.

1990   Labour Party conference agrees to establish a Black Socialist Society, affiliated to the party; formed the following year.

1992   Piara Khaba returned for Ealing South at April general election as Labour's fifth ethnic minority MP.

1996   Transport and General Workers' Union general secretary Bill Morris accuses the Labour Party failing to give adequate support to Black Socialist Society.

1997   Of Labour candidates 1.9% are from ethnic minorities at the May general election (compared with 1.7% Conservatives and 2.5% Liberal Democrats); nine ethnic minority Labour MPs are elected. Paul Boateng appointed Parliamentary Under Secretary, Department of Health.

19 Labour and the International Movement

The Socialist International

The Socialist International, of which the Labour Party is a founding member, dates its origins to 1864 when Karl Marx established the International Working Men's Association (the First International). The First International was dissolved in 1876 following protracted arguments between Marxists and Anarchists. With the growth of socialist parties in Europe seeking power through parliamentary action (although retaining a generally nominal commitment to Marxism), a Second International was formed in Paris in 1889. The Second International acted primarily as a forum for the exchange of information between member parties. At the Second International's conference in 1907, delegates (including representatives from the Labour Party and the Independent Labour Party) passed a resolution on Militarism and International Conflicts pledging that they would work to prevent the outbreak of war 'by whatever means seem to them most effective'. The outbreak of war in 1914, and the support given by the majority of socialist parties to their governments, effectively ended the Second International.

In 1919, following the successful seizure of power by the Bolsheviks in Russia in 1917, a Third International (the Communist International, or Comintern) was formed in Moscow. The majority of socialist parties in Western Europe refused to accept the conditions – particularly the necessity for a revolutionary seizure of power – required for membership of the Third International. Radicals in a number of socialist parties seceded to form Communist parties. The Comintern was dissolved in 1943.

In 1921 the French, Italian and Spanish socialist parties formed a 'Two-and-a-Half International' (the International Working Union of Socialist Parties) in an unsuccessful attempt to bridge the divisions between democratic and reformist socialism and the revolutionary model represented by the Comintern. The British Independent Labour Party (ILP) became a member. This was dissolved in 1923. In May 1923 the non-Communist socialist parties established a Labour and Socialist International at a conference in Hamburg, with the Labour Party as a founding member.

The Labour and Socialist International withered with the success of fascism in Italy, Germany and Spain and the occupation of Western

Europe in the Second World War. But in June 1951 the organisation was revived as the Socialist International at a conference in Frankfurt, with the Labour Party and the Scandinavian social democratic parties as the prime movers. The Socialist International was essentially an instrument in the Cold War with the Soviet bloc. Its ideological document, *Aims and Tasks of Democratic Socialism*, emphasised member parties' commitment to parliamentary democracy, civil liberties and the defence of the West against Communism. Although it envisaged a move from capitalism towards socialism, attempts to retain an element of Marxist rhetoric were rejected. The Socialist International was particularly active in assisting in the development of socialist parties in Portugal and Spain in the 1950s and 1960s and in sustaining their growth in the transition to democracy in both countries in the mid-1970s. This effectively prevented Communist parties from becoming the main forces on the left.

The Socialist International's Stockholm Declaration of 1989 – in line with the modernising tendencies of its most influential members – removed any reference to the abolition of capitalism and declared the organisation's central concerns to be freedom, solidarity and social justice. With the collapse of the Soviet bloc, reformed Communist parties – notably what was formerly the strongest and most influential in Western Europe, the Italian Communist Party (now the Democratic Party of the Left) – have become members of the Socialist International.

The Socialist International – the headquarters of which is in London – functions as a focus for political action, policy discussion and the exchange of ideas between democratic socialist, labour and social democratic parties and works with the International Confederation of Free Trades Unions (ICFTU). The International holds a congress every three years, its council meets twice a year and there are regular conferences of member party leaders. Among associated bodies are the Confederation of Socialist Parties of the European Community, the Socialist Group of the European Parliament and the Socialist Women International.

Member Parties of the Socialist International

Albania	Social Democratic Party (PSD)
Algeria	Socialist Forces Front (FFS)
Argentina	Popular Socialist Party (PSP)
Aruba	People's Electoral Movement (MEP)
Australia	Australian Labor Party (ALP)
Austria	Social Democratic Party of Austria (SPÖ)
Barbados	Barbados Labour Party (BLP)
Belgium	Belgian Socialist Party (PSB), Socialist Party (BSP)
Bolivia	Revolutionary Left Movement (MIR)

Brazil	Democratic Labour Party (PDT)
Bulgaria	Bulgarian Social Democratic Party (BSDP)
Burkina Faso	Party for Democracy and Progress (PDP)
Canada	New Democratic Party (NDP/NPD)
Cape Verde	African Independence Party of Cape Verde (PAICV)
Chile	Social Democratic Radical Party (PRSD), Socialist Party of Chile (PS)
Costa Rica	National Liberation Party (PLN)
Curaçao	Movement for a New Antilles (MAN)
Cyprus	Socialist Party of Cyprus (EDEK)
Czech Republic	Czech Social Democratic Party (CSSD)
Denmark	Social Democrats (SD)
Dominican Republic	Dominican Revolutionary Party (PRD)
Ecuador	Democratic Left Party (PID)
Egypt	National Democratic Party (NDP)
Estonia	Moodukad
Finland	Finnish Social Democratic Party (SDP)
France	Socialist Party (PS)
Germany	Social Democratic Party of Germany (SPD)
Greece	Panhellenic Socialist Movement (PASOK)
Guatemala	Social Democratic Party (PSD)
Haiti	Party of the National Congress of Democratic Movements (KONAKOM), Revolutionary Progressive Nationalist Party of Haiti (PANPRA)
Hungary	Hungarian Socialist Party (MSzP)
Iceland	Social Democratic Party
Ireland	Labour Party
Israel	Israel Labour Party, United Workers' Party of Israel (MAPAM)
Italy	Democratic Party of the Left (PDS), Italian Democratic Socialist Party (PSDI), Italian Socialists (SI)
Ivory Coast	Ivory Coast Popular Front (FPI)
Jamaica	People's National Party (PNP)
Japan	Social Democratic Party (SD)
Latvia	Latvian Social Democratic Workers' Party (LSDSP)
Lebanon	Progressive Socialist Party (PSP)
Lithuania	Lithuanian Social Democratic Party (LSDP)
Luxembourg	Luxembourg Socialist Workers' Party (LSAP/POSL)
Malaysia	Democratic Action Party (DAP)

Malta	Malta Labour Party
Mauritius	Mauritius Labour Party
Mexico	Party of Democratic Revolution (PRD)
Mongolia	Mongolian Social Democratic Party (MSDP)
Morocco	Socialist Union of Popular Forces (USFP)
Netherlands	Labour Party (PvdA)
New Zealand	New Zealand Labour Party (NZLP)
Nicaragua	Sandinista National Liberation Front (FSLN)
Northern Ireland	Social Democratic & Labour Party (SDLP)
Norway	Norwegian Labour Party (DNA)
Paraguay	Revolutionary Feberista Party (PRF)
Poland	Social Democracy of the Republic of Poland (SdRP), Union of Labour (UP)
Portugal	Socialist Party (PS)
Puerto Rico	Puerto Rican Independence Party (PIP)
San Marino	San Marino Socialist Party (PSS)
Senegal	Socialist Party (PS)
Slovak Republic	Party of the Democratic Left (SDL), Social Democratic Party of Slovakia (SDSS)
Slovenia	United List of Social Democrats of Slovenia (ZL)
Spain	Spanish Socialist Workers' Party (PSOE)
Sweden	Social Democratic Party (SAP)
Switzerland	Social Democratic Party of Switzerland (SPS)
Tunisia	Constitutional Democratic Assembly (RCD)
Turkey	Republican People's Party (CHP)
United States	Democratic Socialists of America (DSA), Social Democrats USA (SDUSA)
Venezuela	Democratic Action (AD)

(*Source*: Socialist International, London)

Notes on Major Fraternal Parties

Australia – Australian Labor Party (ALP)

The Australian Labor Party (ALP) emerged from the trade union movement in 1890–91 in response to the pressures of economic recession. The ALP briefly formed a minority government – the first in the world – in Queensland in 1901 and formed its first national government (for four months) in 1904. A history of internal splits kept the ALP out of office for much of the twentieth century.

In 1916 the party divided over the issue of military conscription in the First World War, with the leader and much of the parliamentary membership leaving to join the opposition in a new National Party. In 1932, weakened (like the Labour government in Britain) by its inability to cope with the effects of the depression, the ALP government elected in 1929 collapsed as some parliamentary members left to form an anti-Labor United Australia Party. The ALP government of 1941–49 instituted a number of progressive social welfare, economic management and immigration policies but in 1957 an anti-Communist and predominantly Catholic group left to form the Australian Democratic Labor Party. Returned to office in 1972, prime minister Gough Whitlam was dismissed by the governor Sir John Kerr in 1975 following Whitlam's refusal to call a general election after losing a supply vote in the Senate. The dismissal encouraged republican sentiment in the ALP. ALP governments in the 1980s and 1990s, while moving to the right on economic and social issues, made the break with the British Crown a central issue.

Austria – Social Democratic Party of Austria (SPÖ)

The Social Democratic Party of Austria (SPÖ) was formed as a Marxist party in Lower Austria in 1888. In the First Republic, established following Austria's defeat in the First World War, the SPÖ was identified with 'Austro-Marxism', an attempt to bridge the division between revolutionary and parliamentary socialism. However, despite its radical rhetoric, the party was in practice reformist. The party was extinguished during the civil war of 1934 and an underground group known as the Revolutionary Socialists was established. In the Second Republic, established after the Second World War, the SPÖ was renamed the Socialist Party of Austria. Taking on a less radical emphasis than its pre-war counterpart, the party entered into governing coalitions with the more conservative Austrian People's Party. This had the effect of increasing electoral support for the party. In 1991 the SPÖ reverted to its original title.

Belgium – Belgian Socialist Party (PSB/BSP)

The Belgian Socialist Party (PSB/BSP) is divided into two wings, representing the linguistic division of Belgium, with the PSB as the Francophone element and the BSP the Flemish. The party was founded as the Belgian Workers' Party in 1885 and won significant influence through its leadership of a general strike which achieved manhood suffrage in 1894. In the inter-war years the party was a member of coalition governments with the Catholic Party and Liberals. In 1944 the Belgian Workers' Party renamed itself the Belgian Socialist Party. The election of two party presidents in 1971, and contested elections between the two wings on competing lists, highlighted the linguistic divisions in the party. This culminated in 1978 in a formal break. The two wings of the party, however, continue to co-operate on national policy formulation and on participation in coalition governments through a formal co-ordinating committee.

Denmark – Social Democrats (SD)

The Social Democrats (SD) were established in 1871 as a party with Marxist principles but with a concentration on trade unionism. The party's first parliamentary representative was elected in 1884. SD participated in a coalition government from 1916 to 1920 and in 1924 became the largest party in parliament. In coalition with the Liberals from 1929 to 1943, the SD laid the foundation for the welfare state. The party has been in office for the bulk of the period since the end of the Second World War with a programme of equality, solidarity and economic democracy.

France – Socialist Party (PS)

The Socialist Party (PS) derives from the French Section of the Workers' International (SFIO), founded in 1905 by the amalgamation of a number of rival working-class organisations. Although claiming to be a class-based party with a socialist objective, the SFIO was in practice reformist. In 1920, the majority of delegates at the SFIO congress voted to join the Third International and formed the Communist Party, creating a significant rival for working-class support. By the end of the Second World War, despite participation in the 1930s Popular Front, the SFIO had become relatively insignificant.

Under new leadership in 1969, the SFIO was renamed the Socialist Party (PS) and attempted to realign the non-Communist left. However, with the amalgamation into the PS of François Mitterrand's Republican Institutions Federation in 1971 and the Unified Socialist Party in 1974, a move was made to create a 'Union of the Left' including the Communists. In 1981 Mitterrand was elected President with Communist support and in the 1980s and 1990s PS formed governments in which Communist influence was negligible.

Germany – Social Democratic Party of Germany (SPD)

The Social Democratic Party of Germany (SPD) was formed in 1875 by the merger of the non-Marxist German Workers' Association and the strongly Marxist Social Democratic Party. By 1912 the SDP was the strongest party in the Reichstag and the dominant party in the Second International. Following defeat in the First World War, the SPD formed a provisional government and then played a significant part in coalition governments of the 1920s and the defence of parliamentary democracy. Radicals split from the party in 1919 to form the Communist Party (KPD).

The SPD was declared illegal on the Nazi seizure of power in 1933 but retained an existence in exile. The party was re-established in 1945 but the party in the Russian-occupied zone was forcibly merged with the Communist Party in 1946 to form the Socialist Unity Party. In Western Germany, the SDP remained in opposition. In 1959, with the Godesberg Programme, the party abandoned its by-now nominal Marxism and declared itself to be a party of the people rather than the working class and a supporter of the market system. In 1966 the SPD entered into a coalition with the Christian Democrats and in 1969 formed its first post-war government with the Federal Democrats. The SPD was out of office from 1983. In 1990, with the reunification of the two states, both wings of the SDP amalgamated. Following the 1998 general election, the SPD formed a coalition government with the Greens.

Ireland – Labour Party

The Labour Party – the oldest of the major parties in Ireland – was formed in 1912 as an ancillary of the Trades Union Congress (TUC) and following independence was a junior partner in the relationship. In 1930 the party became relatively more autonomous as the industrial and parliamentary wings of the movement separated. The party, which has never achieved more than 20% of the vote, was weakened by an internal dispute over Communism in 1943. Labour participated in Coalition governments from 1948 to 1951 and 1954 to 1957, and intermittently from the 1970s to the 1990s. In the late 1960s, a new leadership attempted to distance the party further from the trade unions by taking on a more classical social democratic stance. In 1990, Labour merged with the Democratic Socialist Party (which itself had been formed in 1982).

Netherlands – Labour Party (PvdA)

The Labour Party (PvdA) was founded in 1946 but was based on the Social Democratic Workers' Party which had been established as a Marxist party in 1894. The PvdA was intended to be a more broadly based grouping and included left-wing Liberals and progressive Catholics and Protestants. The party worked in governing coalitions with the Catholic People's Party until forming an administration at the head of a centre–left coalition in 1973.

Norway – Norwegian Labour Party (DNA)

The Norwegian Labour Party (DNA) was formed in 1887 in close association with the trade union movement. At the end of the First World War, the party leadership was captured by radicals who provoked a split by affiliating to the Third International. Following its revival in the 1920s, the party became the most significant force in Norwegian politics for over a half a century. Elected in 1935, the party retained power for 30 years, with only the German occupation as an interruption. From 1945 to 1961 the party had an absolute parliamentary majority and in 1971 headed a minority government. In office, the party abandoned its early radicalism but remained committed to gradual reform built on full employment and an extensive welfare state within a mixed economy.

Spain – Spanish Socialist Workers' Party (PSOE)

The Spanish Socialist Workers' Party (PSOE) was established in the country's industrial regions in 1874. The PSOE participated in a coalition government following the establishment of the Second Republic in 1931 and played a leading role in the 1936–39 Popular Front government. Declared illegal following the defeat of the Republic by Franco, the PSOE splintered and declined in exile. However, with the backing of the Socialist International, the party emerged as the significant force on the left following the restoration of democracy in the mid-1970s. At its first congress in Spain for almost half a century, the PSOE declared itself in 1976 to be a class-based party with Marxist objectives. The leadership was less radical. The party merged with the Socialist People's Party in 1978. At the first post-Franco elections the party captured 29% of the vote and – with a shift to the centre attracting progressive middle-class support – won the 1982 and 1986 general elections. The party was returned to office in 1993 but without an absolute majority. However, increasing dissatisfaction with the government's economic policies – and allegations of corruption – led to the party's defeat in 1996.

Sweden – Social Democratic Party (SAP)

The Social Democratic Party (SAP) was founded in 1889 and its first parliamentary representative was elected (on the Liberal ticket) in 1896. Although the SAP adopted a modified Marxist programme in 1897, it was from the beginning a party of reform and worked in co-operation with the Liberals. By 1914 the SAP was capturing over one-third of the vote and from 1932 became the dominant party in Swedish politics, holding office until 1976, though occasionally in coalition. The party retained a commitment to egalitarianism and economic democracy. In opposition from 1976 to 1982, the SAP remained the largest party in parliament. In 1998, despite winning the smallest share of the vote since 1921, the SAP formed a coalition government with the Left Party and the Greens.

20 Biographies

Abbott, Diane Julie (born 1953) First black woman MP. Educated Harrow County Girls' Grammar School and Cambridge. Civil servant; National Council for Civil Liberties (NCCL) race relations officer; television researcher and reporter; trade union equality officer; press officer, Greater London and Lambeth Councils. Westminster City councillor, 1982–86. MP for Hackney North and Stoke Newington since 1987. Secretary, Campaign Group of Labour MPs since 1992.

Adamson, William (1863–1936) Cabinet minister. Educated Dame School. Miner for 27 years. Assistant secretary of Fife, Kinross and Clackmannan Miners' Association, 1902–8; general secretary, 1908. MP for West Fife, 1910–31. Parliamentary Labour Party chairman, 1917–18. Party leader in the Commons, 1918–21. Secretary of State for Scotland, 1924, 1929–31.

Addison, Christopher (1st Viscount) (1869–1951) Cabinet minister and prominent recruit from the Liberals. Educated Trinity College School, Harrogate, and St Bartholomew's Hospital. Professor of Anatomy, Sheffield University. Liberal MP for Hoxton, 1910–18; Shoreditch, 1918–22. Parliamentary Secretary, Board of Education, 1914–15. Parliamentary Secretary, Ministry of Munitions, 1915–16. Minister of Munitions, 1916–17. Minister of Reconstruction, 1917–19. President of Local Government Board, 1919. First Minister of Health, 1919–21. Minister without Portfolio, 1921. Resigned from Coalition government, accusing Lloyd George of betraying housing pledges, 1921. Joined Labour Party, 1922. MP for Swindon, 1929–31, 1934–35. Parliamentary Secretary, Ministry of Agriculture, 1929–30. Minister of Agriculture, 1930–31. Created Baron, 1937; Viscount, 1945. Leader of Labour peers, 1940–51. Leader of the House of Lords, 1945–51. Secretary of State for the Dominions, 1945–47; for Commonwealth Relations, 1947. Lord Privy Seal, 1947–51. Paymaster-General, 1948–49. Lord President of the Council, 1951. Among his publications are *Politics from Within 1911–18* (1925), *Four and a Half Years* (1934).

Alexander, Albert Victor (1st Earl Alexander of Hillsborough) (1885–1965) Cabinet minister. Left school at 13; clerk and Baptist lay preacher.

Army service in the First World War. Secretary, Co-operative Congress parliamentary committee, 1920. Labour and Co-operative MP for Sheffield Hillsborough, 1922–31, 1935–50. Parliamentary Secretary, Board of Trade, 1924. First Lord of the Admiralty, 1929–31, 1940–46. Negotiated London Naval Treaty, 1930. Declined to serve in National Government, 1931. Minister of Defence, 1946–50. Chancellor of the Duchy of Lancaster, 1950–51. Member of Cabinet delegation to India, 1946. Labour leader in the House of Lords, 1955.

Allen, (Reginald) Clifford (Baron Allen of Hartwood) (1889–1939)   Leading Independent Labour Party (ILP) figure. Educated Berkhamsted and Cambridge. Led the No Conscription Fellowship in the First World War. ILP treasurer, 1922; part of the ILP's inner leadership with Attlee and Brockway; ILP chairman, 1923. Under his leadership in the mid-1920s the ILP became increasingly influential. Resigned leadership in opposition to attacks on MacDonald, 1925. Supported MacDonald on the formation of the National Government, 1931.

Angell, (Sir) Norman (Lane, Ralph Norman Angell) (1872–1967)   Writer and peace campaigner. Educated Lycée St Omer and University of Geneva. Traveller and journalist; general manager continental *Daily Mail*, 1904–12. Co-founder of Union of Democratic Control in the First World War. Joined Labour Party, 1920. Unsuccessful candidate in 1922, 1923 and 1935 general elections. MP for Bradford North, 1929–31. Awarded Nobel Peace Prize, 1933. Abandoned socialism in mid-1930s. Anti–appeasement activist, 1937–39. Among his many publications are *Patriotism under Three Flags: A Plea for Rationalism in Politics* (1903), *The Great Illusion* (1910), *After All* (1951).

Archer, John Robert (1863–1932)   Black Labour and Pan-African activist. Worked as a photographer. Labour Party Battersea Borough councillor, 1906; mayor of Battersea, 1913. Founding president, African Progress Union, 1918; delegate to Pan-African Conference, 1919. Deputy leader of Battersea Council at death.

Attlee, Clement Richard (1st Earl Attlee) (1883–1955)   Prime minister of first majority Labour government. Educated Haileybury and Oxford. Called to the Bar, 1905. Joined Fabian Society, 1907; Independent Labour Party (ILP), 1908. Social worker; secretary of Toynbee Hall, 1910. Lecturer, London School of Economics, 1912–23. Army service in the First World War. First Labour mayor of Stepney, 1919. MP for Limehouse, 1922–50, West Walthamstow, 1950–55. Parliamentary Private Secretary to Ramsay MacDonald, 1922–24. Under Secretary for War, 1924. Appointed member of Commission of Enquiry on Industry, 1927. Member of Simon Commission on India, 1927–30. Chancellor of the Duchy of Lancaster, 1930–31. Postmaster-General, 1931. Deputy party leader in the House of Commons, 1931–35. First chair of the New Fabian Research Bureau, 1931–37. Defeated Morrison and Greenwood to become party leader, 1935–55. Leader of the Opposition, 1935–40. Lord Privy Seal and deputy Leader of the Commons, 1940–42; deputy prime minister and Dominions Secretary, 1942–43; Lord President of the Council, 1943–45. Prime minister, 1945–51. Minister of Defence, 1945–46. Leader of the Opposition, 1951–55. Among his publications are *The Labour Party in Perspective* (1937), *Twelve Years After* (1949), *As It Happened* (1954).

Barnes, George Nicoll (1859–1940)   Coalition government minister who left Labour to establish his own party. Elementary education; became an engineer at the age of 12. Amalgamated Society of Engineers executive member, 1889–96; assistant secretary, 1892–96; general secretary, 1896–1908. Led strike for the eight-hour day, 1897–98. Delegate at Labour Representation Committee founding conference, 1900. President, National Committee of Organised Labour on Old Age Pensions. Labour MP for Glasgow Blackfriars, 1906–18. National Democratic MP for Gorbals, 1918–22. Party vice-chairman in Commons, 1908–10; chairman, 1910–11. Chairman of Independent Labour Party (ILP) organising department, 1909. First Minister of Pensions, 1916–18. War Cabinet member on resignation of Henderson, 1917–19; Cabinet member, 1919–20. Left Labour Party to remain in the government; formed and led National Democratic Party, 1918. Delegate at the first League of Nations Conference, 1920; prominent in establishment of the International Labour Organisation (ILO). Among his publications is *From Workshop to War Cabinet* (1924).

Beckett, John Warburton (1894–1964)   Left-wing and later fascist activist. Educated Latymer Secondary School and the Regent Street Polytechnic. Shop assistant; advertising specialist; journalist. First World War service in army, 1914–17. Chairman, National Union of Ex-Servicemen, 1918–19. Hackney Borough councillor, 1919–22. MP for Gateshead, 1924–29; Peckham, 1929–31. Joined Independent Labour Party (ILP) in 1931; defeated at election by official Labour candidate. Joined British Union of Fascists (BUF), 1934; organiser on Tyneside; editor of *Action*, 1936–37. Left BUF to form National Socialist League with William Joyce ('Lord Haw Haw'), 1937. Co-founded British People's Party with Duke of Bedford, 1938. Imprisoned under Defence of Realm Act 1940.

Beckett, Margaret Mary (born 1943)   Party leader and Cabinet minister. Educated Notre Dame High School, Manchester, and Manchester University. Metallurgist; television researcher, 1979–83. MP for Lincoln, 1974–79; Derby South since 1983. Assistant government whip, 1975–76.

Parliamentary Secretary, Department of Education and Science, 1976–79. Party NEC member, 1980–81, 1985–86, 1988–. Opposition spokesperson on social security, 1984–88; Shadow Chief Secretary to the Treasury, 1989–92. Deputy leader of the Opposition, 1992–94; acting leader, 1994. Shadow leader of the House of Commons and campaign co-ordinator, 1992–94. Unsuccessful candidate for party leadership and deputy leadership, 1994. Shadow Secretary of State for Health, 1994–95; for Trade and Industry, 1995–97. President of the Board of Trade, 1997–98. Lord Privy Seal and Leader of the House, 1998–.

Benn, Anthony Neil Wedgwood (Tony) (born 1925)   Cabinet minister who became a leading figure on the left in the 1980s. Educated Westminster and Oxford. Second World War service in Royal Air Force Volunteer Reserve and Royal Navy Volunteer Reserve. Active in the Movement for Colonial Freedom and the Fabian Colonial Bureau. Campaigned to renounce hereditary title Viscount Stansgate, 1960–63. MP for Bristol East, 1950–60, 1963–83; Chesterfield since 1984. Party National Executive member 1959–60, 1962–94; chairman, 1971–72. Postmaster-General, 1964–66; Minister of Technology, 1966–70; Secretary of State for Industry and Minister for Posts and Telecommunications, 1974–75; Secretary of State for Energy, 1975–79. Unsuccessful candidate for party leadership, 1976, 1988; for deputy leadership, 1971, 1981. President, Campaign Group of Labour MPs since 1987. Among his many publications are *The Regeneration of Britain* (1964), *Arguments for Socialism* (1979), *Out of the Wilderness: Diaries 1963–67* (1987), *Office without Power: Diaries 1968–72* (1988), *Against the Tide: Diaries 1973–76* (1989), *Conflicts of Interest: Diaries 1977–80* (1990), *The End of an Era: Diaries 1980–90* (1992).

Benn, William Wedgwood (Viscount Stansgate) (1877–1960)   Cabinet minister and recruit from the Liberals. Educated Lycée Condorcet, Paris, and London University. First World War service in Royal Naval Air Service. Liberal MP for Tower Hamlets, 1906–18; Leith, 1918–27. Junior Lord of the Treasury and Whip, 1910–15. Joined Labour Party, 1927. Labour MP for Aberdeen North, 1928–31; Manchester Gorton, 1937–42. Secretary of State for India, 1929–31. Vice-president, Allied Control Commission in Italy, 1943–44. Secretary of State for Air, 1945–46. Created a Viscount, 1942.

Bevan, Aneurin ('Nye') (1897–1960)   Party deputy leader, left-wing orator and creator of the National Health Service. Educated elementary school and Central Labour College. Miner at the age of 13. Tredegar councillor and chairman of the South Wales Miners' Federation Lodge. Active in General Strike, 1926; abandoned syndicalism following the strike's defeat. Independent Labour Party (ILP) MP for Ebbw Vale,

1929–31, Labour MP, 1931–60. Expelled from the party for advocating a Popular Front, 1939; re-admitted, 1940. Minister of Health 1945–51, with responsibility for establishing health service and the government's house-building programme. Minister of Labour and National Service, 1951. Resigned over imposition of NHS charges (and disappointment at not receiving higher office), 1951, opening up fundamental divisions in the party. *In Place of Fear* (1952) set out his fundamentalist socialist beliefs but contained little practical policy. Defeated by Gaitskell for party leadership, 1955. Party treasurer, 1956–60. Shadow Foreign Secretary, 1956. Broke with unilateral nuclear disarmament at 1957 party conference. Deputy party leader, 1959–60.

Bevin, Ernest (1881–1951)   Trade union leader and Cabinet minister. Educated elementary school. Casual worker at age 13; Baptist lay preacher until 1905. Joined Social Democratic Federation (SDF); active in Right to Work movement, 1908. Founding chairman, Bristol branch of Dockers' Union, 1911; full-time official, 1911; assistant national organiser, 1913; national organiser, 1914; assistant general secretary, 1920. Member of the Council of Action against British intervention in Russia, 1920. Nicknamed 'dockers' KC' for effective representation at wages tribunal, 1920. Founding general secretary Transport and General Workers' Union, 1922–40. Trades Union Council (TUC) General Council member, 1924–40; TUC president, 1936–37. Strong supporter of the Mond–Turner talks, 1927. Member of Macmillan Committee on Finance and Industry, 1929–31. Increasingly influential in party affairs after 1931 collapse; advocate of re-armament. Unsuccessful Labour candidate at 1918 and 1931 general elections. MP for Central Wandsworth, 1940–50, East Wandsworth, 1950–51. Minister of Labour and National Service, 1940–45. Foreign Secretary, 1945–51. Lord Privy Seal, 1951. Published *The Job to be Done* (1942).

Blair, Anthony Charles Lynton (Tony) (born 1953)   Prime minister and leading architect of 'New Labour'. Educated Fettes College and Oxford. Called to the Bar, 1976. Lost deposit as unsuccessful candidate for Beaconsfield, 1982. MP for Sedgefield since 1983. Opposition spokesperson on Treasury and economic affairs, 1984–87; trade and industry, 1987–88; energy, 1988–89; employment, 1989–92 (where he ended party support for the trade union closed shop and backed retention of Conservative legislation on strike ballots and secondary action); home affairs, 1992–94 (where his slogan 'Tough on crime, tough on the causes of crime' undermined Conservative dominance over the issue). He did not include opposition posts in *Who's Who* entry on the grounds that they were not 'real jobs'. Party National Executive Committee member since 1992. Emerged as one of the party's leading 'modernisers'; frustrated at the slower pace of party reform under Smith's leadership, 1992–94. Following withdrawal of Gordon Brown from the contest (with alleged souring of relations), elected Labour's youngest ever leader, 1994. As opposition leader, continued reforms initiated by Kinnock to build a 'New Labour' capable of winning office; fundamentally revised Clause Four, 1995. While Labour benefited from his remarkable popularity, the vagueness of his policies (variously called the 'project', the 'stakeholder society' and the 'Third Way') led to him being described as Tony 'Blur'; the Labour left accused him of being 'tough on socialism, tough on the causes of socialism'. Prime Minister of a Labour government with an impregnable majority, and determined to be leader of the only Labour government ever to win a second complete term, 1997–.

Blatchford, Robert Peel Glanville (1851–1943)   Influential socialist journalist who wrote under the pen name Nunquam. Elementary education; indentured brushmaker at 14. Army service, 1871–78. Timekeeper; became journalist, 1885. Dismissed from *Sunday Chronicle* for being a socialist, 1891; established the *Clarion*. His *Merrie England* (1893) popularised the *Clarion* and socialism. Supported the Boer War and the First World War. Contributed to the *Sunday Chronicle*, 1916–24; *Sunday News*, 1924–27. Among his other publications are *Britain for the British* (1902), *The Sorcery Shop* (1907), *My Eighty Years* (1931).

Blunkett, David (born 1947)   Cabinet minister and local government leader. Educated Sheffield University and Holly Bank College of Education. Clerk/typist; industrial relations lecturer. Deputy chairman, Association of Municipal Authorities, 1984–87. Sheffield City councillor, 1970–88; leader, 1980–87. MP for Sheffield Brightside since 1987. Opposition spokesperson on the environment, 1988–92; on health, 1992–94; education, 1994–95; education and employment, 1995–97. Secretary of State for Education and Employment, 1997–. Party National Executive member, 1983–; chairman, 1993–94. Among his jointly-written publications are *Democracy in Crisis: The Town Halls Respond* (1987), *On a Clear Day* (1995).

Boateng, Paul Yaw (born 1951)   Born in Ghana, became one of Labour's first ethnic minority MPs in 1987. Educated Apsley Grammar School and Bristol University. Solicitor, 1976. National Council for Civil Liberties activist. Greater London Council member, 1981–86. MP for Brent South since 1987. Appointed Parliamentary Under Secretary, Department of Health, 1997.

Bondfield, Margaret Grace (1873–1953)   Trade unionist and first woman Cabinet minister. Educated elementary school. Assistant general secretary,

National Union of Shop Assistants, 1898. Seconded motion calling on Trades Union Congress (TUC) to support establishment of the Labour Representation Committee (LRC), 1899. Co-founder with Mary Macarthur of National Federation of Women Workers, 1906; assistant general secretary, 1916–21. Elected to Independent Labour Party (ILP) National Administrative Council, 1913. Chief Woman Officer, General and Municipal Workers' Union, 1921. Chair of Standing Joint Committee of Industrial Women's Organisations, 1921. First woman TUC General Council president, 1923. MP for Northampton, 1923–24; Wallsend, 1926–31. Discredited on left for supporting Blanesburgh Report on National Insurance, 1927. Parliamentary Secretary, Ministry of Labour, 1924. Minister of Labour, 1929–31. Supported MacDonald but did not join his National Government, 1931. Vice-president, National Council of Social Service. Companion of Honour, 1948.

Boothroyd, Betty (born 1929)   First woman Speaker of the House of Commons. Educated Dewsbury Technical College. Hammersmith councillor, 1965–68. MP for West Bromwich, 1974; West Bromwich West, since 1974. MEP, 1975–77. Assistant government whip, 1974–75. Deputy Speaker, 1987–92; Speaker, 1992–. Party NEC member, 1981–87.

Bowden, Herbert William (Baron Aylestone) (1905–94)   Cabinet minister, Educated Canton High School, Cardiff. Leicester councillor, 1938–45. MP for Leicester South, 1945–50; Leicester South West, 1950–67. Parliamentary Private Secretary to Minister of Pensions, 1947; Parliamentary Private Secretary to Postmaster-General, 1947–49; assistant government whip, 1949–50; Lord Commissioner of the Treasury, 1950–51. Lord President of the Council and Leader of the House of Commons, 1964–66; Secretary of State for Commonwealth Affairs, 1966–67. Independent Television Authority chairman, 1967–72; Independent Broadcasting Authority chairman, 1972–75.

Braddock, Elizabeth Margaret ('Bessie') (née Bamber) (1899–1970)   MP and dominant personality in Liverpool politics. Educated elementary school. Clerk in Warehouse Workers' Union. Independent Labour Party (ILP) member; Communist Party member, 1920–24; became strenuously anti-Communist. Liverpool City councillor, 1930–61; alderman, 1955–61; her partner, Jack, was council leader until 1963. Faced accusations of misuse of patronage and organisational malpractice in Liverpool. MP for Liverpool Exchange, 1945–70; first woman member for a Liverpool seat. Party National Executive member, 1947; anti-Bevanite. First woman MP to be suspended from a Commons sitting, 1952. Declined offer of a post in 1964 Labour government. Published *The Braddocks* (1963).

Brockway, (Archibald) Fenner (Baron Brockway) (1888–1988)   Left-wing anti-colonialist activist. Educated School for the Sons of Missionaries, Blackheath. Joined Independent Labour Party (ILP), 1912; editor ILP paper, *Labour Leader*. Active in No Conscription Fellowship in the First World War; imprisoned as conscientious objector, 1917–19. MP for East Leyton, 1929–31; Eton and Slough, 1950–64. ILP organising secretary, 1922; leader, ILP organisation, 1926–29; editor *New Leader*, 1926–29. Secretary of League against Imperialism, 1929. Chair at ILP meeting which voted to disaffiliate from Labour, 1932. Visited Spain during civil war, 1937. Rejoined Labour Party following 1945 election. Supporter of anti-colonialist and independence campaigns and of anti-racism in Britain. Life peer, 1964. Among his publications are *Inside the Left* (1942), *Socialism over Sixty Years* (1946), *Outside the Right* (1963), *Towards Tomorrow* (1977), *98 Not Out* (1986).

Brown, George Alfred (Baron George-Brown of Jevington) (1914–85)   Party deputy leader and Cabinet minister. Educated West Square Central School, Southwark. Fur salesman; Transport and General Workers' Union official. Labour League of Youth activist. MP for Belper, 1945–70. Parliamentary Private Secretary to Minister of Labour and National Service, 1945–47; to Chancellor of Exchequer, 1947. Joint Parliamentary Secretary, Minister of Agriculture and Fisheries, 1947–51. Minister of Works, 1951. Party deputy leader, 1960; supported Gaitskell against unilateralism. Defeated by Wilson in party leadership contest, 1963; remained deputy leader until 1970. First Secretary of State for Economic Affairs, 1964–66; introduced National Plan, 1965; hopes for economic expansion thwarted. Foreign Secretary, 1966–68. Resigned following dispute with Wilson, 1968. Lost seat in general election, 1970. Life peer, 1970. Left party to form a social democratic organisation, 1976. Published *In My Way* (1985).

Brown, (James) Gordon (born 1951)   Cabinet minister. Educated Kirkcaldy High School and Edinburgh University; PhD, 1982. Lecturer, 1975–80; head of Scottish TV current affairs, 1980–83. MP for Dunfermline East since 1983. Member Scottish Labour Party executive, 1977–83; chairman of the party's Scottish Council, 1983–84; chairman, Labour Party in Scotland, 1987. Shadow Chief Secretary to the Treasury, 1987–89. Shadow trade and industry spokesperson, 1989–92. Shadow Chancellor, 1992–97. Chancellor of the Exchequer, 1997–. Among his publications are *Maxton* (1986), *Where There is Greed* (1989), *John Smith: Life and Soul of the Party* (1994), *Values, Visions and Voices: An Anthology of Socialism* (1995).

Buchanan, George (1880–1955)   A Clydesider who became a minister in the 1945–51 government. Engineering worker. Joined Independent

Labour Party (ILP); street orator; trade union activist. Glasgow councillor, 1918. Labour MP for Gorbals, 1922–32; ILP MP, 1932–39; Labour MP 1939–48. President, Patternmakers' Union, 1932–48. Joint Under Secretary for Scotland, 1945–47; Minister of Pensions, 1947–48. First chairman, National Assistance Board, 1948–53.

Buxton, Noel (Baron Noel-Buxton of Aylsham) (1869–1948)   Cabinet minister and recruit from the Liberals. Educated Harrow and Cambridge. Aide-de-camp to Governor of South Australia, 1895–98. Badly wounded on peace mission to Bulgaria, 1914. Member, Whitechapel Board of Guardians. Liberal MP for Whitby, 1905–6; North Norfolk, 1910–18. Joined Labour Party, 1919. Labour MP for North Norfolk, 1922–30. Minister of Agriculture, 1924. President of the Board of Agriculture and Fisheries, 1929–30. Created Baron, 1930. President, Save the Children Fund, 1930–48.

Callaghan, (Leonard) James (Baron Callaghan of Cardiff) (born 1912)   Prime minister and holder of all the major offices of state. Educated Portsmouth Northern Secondary School. Began work in Inland Revenue, 1929. Assistant secretary, Inland Revenue Staff Federation, 1936–47. Second World War service in the Navy. MP South Cardiff, 1945–50; South East Cardiff, 1950–83; Cardiff South and Penarth, 1983–87. Parliamentary Secretary, Minister of Transport, 1947–50. British delegate to the Council of Europe, 1950. Parliamentary and Financial Secretary, the Admiralty, 1950–51. Chancellor of the Exchequer, 1964–67. Home Secretary, 1967–70 (deployed troops in Northern Ireland, 1969; opposed trade union legislation). Secretary of State for Foreign and Commonwealth Affairs, 1974–76. Party leader 1976–80. Prime Minister, 1976–79; negotiated pact with Liberals, 1977–78. Leader of the Opposition, 1979–80. National Executive member, 1957–80; party treasurer, 1967–76. Life peer, 1987. Among his publications are *A House Divided: The Dilemma of Northern Ireland* (1973), *Time and Chance* (1987).

Castle, Barbara Anne (*née* Betts) (Baroness Castle of Blackburn) (born 1911)   Cabinet minister. Educated Bradford Girls' Grammar School and Oxford. Journalist. St Pancras Borough councillor, 1937. Metropolitan Water Board member, 1940–43. Second World War civil servant and writer for *Daily Mirror*. MP for Blackburn, 1945–50, 1955–79; Blackburn East, 1950–55. Leading Bevanite in the 1950s. Party chair, 1958–59. Minister of Overseas Development, 1964–65. Minister of Transport, 1965–68. Secretary of State for Employment and Productivity, 1968–70; unsuccessfully attempted union reform on lines of *In Place of Strife*, 1969. Secretary of State for Social Services, 1974–76. Left government when Callaghan became prime minister. MEP for Greater Manchester North,

1979–84; Greater Manchester West, 1984–89. Leader, European Parliament British Labour Group, 1979–85; vice-chair of European Parliament Socialist Group, 1979–84. Life peer, 1990. Among her publications are *The Castle Diaries, 1974–76* (1980), *The Castle Diaries, 1964–70* (1984), *Fighting All the Way* (1993).

Citrine, Walter McLennan (1st Baron Citrine of Wembley) (1887–1983)   Influential Trades Union Congress (TUC) general secretary. Electrician. First full-time Electricians' Trade Union (ETU) district official, 1914. President, Mersey district Federated Engineering and Shipbuilding Trades, 1917. Unsuccessful Labour candidate, 1918 general election. ETU assistant general secretary, 1920. TUC assistant general secretary, 1924–26; general secretary, 1926–46. Welded relationship between party and unions; combated Communist influence. President, International Federation of Trades Unions, 1928–45. Knighted, 1935. Appointed to Royal Commission on Economic and Social Conditions in the West Indies, 1938. Member of World Anti-Nazi Council. Member of National Coal Board, chairman of Miners' Welfare Commission, 1946–47. Peer, 1946. Chairman, Central Electricity Authority, 1947. Among his publications are *I Search for Truth in Russia* (1936), *Men and Work* (1964), *Two Careers* (1967).

Clynes, Joseph Robert (1869–1949)   Cabinet minister. Elementary education. Textile worker at 10. District organiser of Lancashire Gasworkers' Union, 1891. Founder member of Independent Labour Party (ILP), 1893; Lancashire district secretary, 1895. Chairman of Labour Party Organisation, 1908. Vice-chairman of Labour in the Commons, 1910–11, 1918–21; chairman, 1921–22. Party deputy leader, 1929–31. Oldham Trades Council president, 1892; secretary, 1894–1912. President of General and Municipal Workers' Union (GMWU), 1912–37. MP for North East Manchester, 1906–18; Manchester Platting, 1918–31, 1935–45. Parliamentary Secretary, Ministry of Food, 1917–18. Food Controller, 1918–19. Lord Privy Seal, 1924. Home Secretary, 1929–31. Refused to join National Government, 1931. Published *Memoirs* (1937).

Cole, George Douglas Howard (1889–1959)   Socialist activist, theoretician and advocate of guild socialism. Educated St Paul's School and Oxford. Became a socialist, 1906. Fabian Society member, 1908; elected to executive, 1914. Social Democratic Federation (SDF) member, 1913–14; critical of Labour's links with Liberals, left Fabians in 1915 (rejoined 1928). Joined Fabian Research Department, 1913; honorary secretary, 1916; secretary of renamed Labour Research Department, 1919–24. Writer for the *New Statesman* from 1918. Workers' Education Association (WEA) tutor; London University lecturer, 1921–24; appointed reader in economics, Oxford, 1924. Member of Economic Advisory Council, 1930.

Founder, Society for Socialist Inquiry and Propaganda (SSIP), 1931. Established New Fabian Research Bureau, 1931; secretary, 1931–35; chairman, 1937–39. Supporter of the Popular Front. Restored influence of Fabian Society as chairman, 1939–46, 1948–50, 1952–59. Chichele Professor of social and political theory, 1944–57. Unofficial and unsuccessful Labour candidate for Oxford University, 1945. Among his many publications are *The World of Labour* (1913), *Self-Government in Industry* (1917), *Guild Socialism Re-stated* (1920), *Workshop Organisation* (1923), *The Next Ten Years in British Social and Economic Policy* (1929), *The Intelligent Man's Guide through World Chaos* (1932), *What Marx Really Meant* (1934), *The Condition of Britain* (with M.I. Cole, 1937), *The Common People* (with R.W. Postgate, 1938).

Cole, (Dame) Margaret Isabel (née Postgate) (1893–1980)   Educated Roedean School and Cambridge; a teacher. Joined Fabian Society Research Department; with husband, G.D.H. Cole, founded Labour Research Department; left because of Communist control, 1925. Organised strike committee in Oxford in General Strike, 1926. Workers' Education Association (WEA) lecturer, 1925–49. Co-founder, New Fabian Research Bureau, 1935. London County Council (LCC) member, 1943–65; alderman, 1952–65; Inner London Education Authority (ILEA) member, 1965–67. Fabian Society president, 1963–80. Among her many publications are *Makers of the Labour Movement* (1948), *Beatrice and Sidney Webb* (1955).

Cook, Arthur James (1883–1931)   Miners' leader during the 1926 General Strike. Elementary education. Farmworker at 12; miner for 21 years. Preacher; joined Independent Labour Party (ILP), 1905. Attended Central Labour College, 1911–12. South Wales Miners' Federation (SWMF) official, 1919; Welsh representative to Miners' Federation of Great Britain (MFGB). MFGB secretary, 1924; secretary, International Miners' Federation. Rhondda Urban District councillor. Imprisoned for agitation, 1918 and 1921. A syndicalist; involved in the production of *The Miners' Next Step*, 1912. Led the MFGB through the General Strike and the coal strike, 1926. TUC General Council member, 1927. Involved in production of radical ILP Cook–Maxton Manifesto, 1928. Signed Mosley Manifesto, 1930.

Cook, Robert Finlayson (Robin) (born 1946)   Cabinet minister. Educated Aberdeen Grammar School and Edinburgh University. Workers' Education Association (WEA) tutor-organiser, 1970–74. Edinburgh Corporation member, 1971–74. MP for Edinburgh Central, 1974–83; Livingston since 1983. Opposition Treasury spokesperson, 1980–83. Party leadership campaign manager for Kinnock, 1983. Spokesperson on Europe,

1983–84; Parliamentary Labour Party (PLP) campaign co-ordinator, 1984–86. Spokesperson on trade, 1986–87; health, 1987–92. Party leadership campaign manager for Smith, 1992. Spokesperson on trade and industry, 1992–94; on foreign affairs, 1994–97. Foreign Secretary, 1997–.

Cousins, Frank (1904–86)   Trade union leader and Cabinet minister. Educated elementary schools. Miner at 14; lorry driver. Transport and General Workers' Union (TGWU) official, 1938; national officer, 1944; national secretary, 1948; general secretary, 1956. Left-winger; led defeat of Gaitskell on unilateralism at party conference, 1960. Labour MP for Nuneaton, 1964–66. Minister of Technology, 1964–66; resigned in disagreement with incomes policy. Founding chairman, Community Relations Commission, 1969–70.

Creech Jones, Arthur (1891–1964)   Trade union leader and minister; particular interest in colonial affairs and the international movement. Elementary education; solicitor's clerk and civil servant. Camberwell Independent Labour Party (ILP) secretary, 1911–15. Anti-conscription activist in the First World War; imprisoned, 1916–19. Secretary, National Union of Docks, Wharves and Shipping Staffs, 1919–22. A joint author of the ILP's 'Living wage' programme, 1926. Organising secretary, Workers' Travel Association, 1930. MP for Shipley, 1935–50; Wakefield, 1954–64. Parliamentary Secretary to the Minister of Labour, 1940–44. Toured West Africa as member of a Royal Commission, 1944. Parliamentary Under Secretary of State, Colonial Office, 1945–46; Secretary of State for the Colonies, 1946–50. Governor of Ruskin College, 1923–56; vice-president, Workers' Education Association (WEA); executive member of the International Federation of Clerical Employees and Technicians.

Cripps, Charles Alfred (1st Baron Parmoor of Frieth) (1852–1941) Cabinet minister and recruit from the Conservatives. Educated Winchester and Oxford. Called to the bar, 1877. Conservative MP for Stroud (1895–1900); Stretford, 1901–6; Wycombe, 1910–14. Created Baron, 1914. Opposed British entry into the First World War; supported peace attempts, 1917. Accepted offer of post in first Labour government. Lord President of the Council (and British representative at League of Nations), 1924; 1929–31. Retired from politics on formation of National Government, 1931. Chancellor and Vicar-general of York, 1900–14. Vicar-general of Canterbury, 1902–24. Published *A Retrospect* (1936).

Cripps, (Sir) (Richard) Stafford (1889–1952)   Cabinet minister and 1930s Popular Front advocate known as 'The Red Squire'. Educated Winchester and London University. Called to the bar, 1913. Served with Red Cross in France in the First World War. Treasurer, World Alliance for Promoting International Friendship through the Churches. Persuaded by Herbert Morrison to join Labour Party, 1921. MP for East Bristol, 1931–50; South East Bristol, 1950. Knighted, 1930. Solicitor-General, 1930–31. Founder member of Socialist League, 1932. Argued for anti-fascist United Front and then Popular Front with Communists throughout 1930s. Expelled from party, 1939; re-admitted, 1945. Ambassador to Soviet Union, 1940–42. Lord Privy Seal and Leader of the Commons, 1942. Minister of Aircraft Production, 1942–45. President of the Board of Trade with responsibility for transforming industry from a war to peace footing, 1945–47; led Cabinet mission to India, 1946. Involved in unsuccessful attempt to remove Attlee as leader, 1947. Minister for Economic Affairs, 1947; Chancellor of the Exchequer, 1947–50. Wrote *Towards a Christian Democracy* (1945).

Crooks, William (Will) (1852–1921)   Labour pioneer. A cooper; lectured and taught in Poplar; his Sunday morning open air addresses at East India Docks were called 'Crooks' College'. London County Council (LCC) member, 1893. First Labour mayor in London (and first working-class mayor in England), Poplar, 1901. MP for Woolwich, 1903–18.

Crosland, (Charles) Anthony Raven (1918–77)   Cabinet minister and revisionist theoretician. Educated Highgate School and Oxford. Second World War service in the army. MP for South Gloucester, 1950–55; Grimsby, 1959–77. Minister of State, Economic Affairs, 1964–65. Secretary of State for Education and Science, 1965–67. President of the Board of Trade, 1967–69. Secretary of State for Local Government and Regional Planning, 1969–70. Secretary of State for the Environment, 1974–76. Foreign Secretary, 1976–77. Among his publications are *The Future of Socialism* (1956), *The Conservative Enemy* (1962), *Socialism Now* (1974).

Crossman, Richard Howard Stafford (1907–74)   Cabinet minister whose diaries revealed many of the tensions of the 1964–70 Labour government. Educated Winchester and Oxford. Fellow and tutor, New College, 1931–37; Workers' Education Association (WEA) tutor. Journalist, working for *Spectator* and *New Statesman*. Labour leader on Oxford City Council. Second World War service as political and psychological warfare specialist. MP for Coventry East, 1945–70. Bevanite. Minister of Housing and Local Government, 1964–66. Lord President of the Council and Leader of the House of Commons, 1966–68. Secretary of State for Social Services, 1968–70. Editor, *New Statesman*, 1970 until his dismissal in 1972. Among his many publications are *Government and the Governed* (1939), *Planning for Freedom* (1965), and the revealing *Diaries of a Cabinet Minister* (1975–77).

Cunningham, John Anderson (Jack) (born 1939)   Cabinet minister. Educated Jarrow Grammar School, Durham University; PhD. Research chemist; teacher; trade union official. Chester-le-Street councillor, 1969–74. MP for Whitehaven, 1970–83; Copeland since 1983. Parliamentary Under Secretary, Department of Energy, 1976–79. Opposition spokesperson on Industry, 1979–83; Environment, 1983–92; Shadow Leader of the House of Commons and campaign co-ordinator, 1989–92; Opposition spokesperson on foreign affairs, 1992–94; on Trade and Industry, 1992–97. Minister of Agriculture and Fisheries, 1997–98. Chancellor of the Duchy of Lancaster, 1998–.

Dalton, (Edward) Hugh John Neale (Lord Dalton of Forest and Frith) (1887–1962)   Cabinet minister and theoretician. Educated Eton, Cambridge and London School of Economics (LSE). Called to the Bar, 1914. LSE lecturer, then reader, 1919–36. MP for Peckham, 1924–29; Bishop Auckland, 1929–31, 1935–59. Party National Executive member, 1926–27, 1928–52; party chair, 1936–37. Parliamentary Under Secretary, Foreign Office, 1929–31. Travelled in Germany, Italy and Russia, 1932–33. Outspoken opponent of appeasement in 1930s. Minister of Economic Warfare, 1940–42; President of the Board of Trade, 1942–45; Chancellor of the Exchequer, 1945–47; resigned following inadvertent budget leak. Chancellor of the Duchy of Lancaster, 1948–50; Minister of Town and Country Planning, 1950–51; Minister of Local Government and Planning, 1951. Peerage, 1960. Among his publications are *Some Aspects of the Inequality of Incomes in Modern Communities* (1920) and *Practical Socialism for Britain* (1935), a forerunner of Labour's 1945 programme.

Dewar, Donald Campbell (born 1937)   Cabinet minister. Educated Glasgow Academy and Glasgow University. MP for Aberdeen South, 1966–70; Glasgow Garscadden since 1978. Opposition spokesperson on Scottish affairs, 1981–92; on social security, 1992–95; Opposition Chief Whip, 1995–97. Secretary of State for Scotland with responsibility for devolution campaign, 1997–.

Dobson, Frank (born 1940)   Cabinet minister. Educated Archbishop Holgate's Grammar School, York, and London School of Economics (LSE). Worked in local government; assistant secretary for Commission for Local Authorities, 1975–79. MP for Holborn and St Pancras since 1979. Opposition spokesperson on education, 1981–83; on health, 1983–87; energy, 1989–92; Shadow leader of House of Commons and party campaign co-ordinator, 1987–89; Opposition spokesperson on employment, 1992–93; transport, 1993–94; environment and London, 1994–97. Secretary of State for Health, 1997–.

Ede, James Chuter (Baron Chuter-Ede of Epsom) (1882–1965)   Cabinet minister. Educated Dorking High School, Battersea Pupil Teachers Centre, Cambridge University. Teacher, 1905–14. A Liberal; joined the Labour party during the First World War. MP for Mitcham, 1923; South Shields, 1929–31, 1935–64. Parliamentary Secretary, Board of Education, 1940–45; played a central part in shaping the 1944 Education Act. Home Secretary, 1945–51. Leader of the House of Commons, 1951. Life peer, 1964.

Feather, Victor Grayson Hardie (1908–76)   Trades Union Congress (TUC) general secretary in a period of difficult relations with the Labour government. Co-op grocery worker at 14. Union of Shop, Distributive and Allied Workers (USDAW) steward; wrote for local Independent Labour Party (ILP) newspaper. Joined TUC Organisation Department, 1937; TUC assistant secretary, 1947; assistant general secretary, 1960; general secretary 1969–73. Leading opponent of Labour's attempt at trade union legislation based on *In Place of Strife*, 1969; offered a 'solemn and binding' undertaking on unofficial strikes. Led campaign against Conservative 1971 Industrial Relations Act which was repealed by Labour in 1974.

Fitt, Gerard (Gerry) (Baron Fitt of Bell's Hill) (born 1926)   Northern Ireland political leader. Educated Christian Brothers School, Belfast. Merchant seaman, 1941–53. Belfast Corporation councillor, 1958–61. Republican Labour MP for Belfast Dock in Northern Ireland Parliament, 1962–72. Republican Labour MP for Belfast West, 1966–70; Social Democratic and Labour Party (SDLP) MP for Belfast West, 1970–79; Socialist, 1979–83. Northern Ireland Civil Rights Association activist. Founding leader, SDLP, 1970. Deputy chief executive, Northern Ireland Executive, 1973–74. Member of the Northern Ireland Constitutional Convention, 1975–76. Resigned from SDLP, 1979. Life peer, 1983.

Foot, Michael Mackintosh (born 1913)   Party leader and prominent left-wing activist. Educated Leighton Park School and Oxford. Initially a Liberal. Journalist; assistant editor *Tribune*, 1937–38; managing director, 1945–74; editor 1948–52, 1955–60. Editor of the London *Evening Standard*, 1940–44; *Daily Herald* columnist, 1944–64. Unsuccessful Labour candidate, 1945. MP for Plymouth Devonport, 1945–55; Ebbw Vale, 1960–83; Blaenau Gwent, 1983–92. Campaign for Nuclear Disarmament (CND) activist from 1958. Party whip withdrawn, 1961–63. Unsuccessfully stood as party deputy leader, 1971. Secretary of State for Employment, 1974–76. Lord President of the Council and Leader of the House of Commons, 1976–79. Deputy party leader, 1976–80; party leader and leader of the Opposition, 1980–83. Among his many publications are Guilty *Men* (with others, 1940), *Trial of Mussolini* (1943), *Aneurin Bevan* (2 volumes, 1962, 1973).

Gaitskell, Hugh Todd Naylor (1906–63)   Party leader, Cabinet minister and thwarted party reformer. Educated Winchester and Oxford. Lecturer, 1928–39. New Fabian Research Bureau assistant secretary, 1930–33. Principal Private Secretary, Ministry of Economic Warfare, 1940–42. Principal assistant secretary, Board of Trade, 1942–45. Unsuccessful candidate at 1935 general election. MP for Leeds South, 1945–63. Parliamentary Under Secretary, Ministry of Fuel and Power, 1946–47. Minister of Fuel and Power, 1947–50. Minister of State for Economic Affairs, 1950. Chancellor of the Exchequer, 1950–51. Party leader, 1955–63. Criticised use of force at Suez, 1956. Insisted on need to re-evaluate party's ideology, 1959; criticised for, and failed in, his attempt to remove or reform Clause Four of the party constitution in the interests of modernisation. Successfully reversed policy of unilateral nuclear disarmament, 1961.

Gallacher, William (1881–1965)   Communist activist and MP. Educated board school. Began work as delivery boy at age of 12; engineering apprentice, 1895. Joined Social Democratic Federation (SDF), 1906. Chairman of Clyde Workers' Committee in the First World War; imprisoned for one year for sedition, 1916; imprisoned for three months for rioting, 1919. Founder member, Communist Party of Great Britain (CPGB), 1920. Imprisoned for one year for seditious libel on eve of General Strike, 1925. Communist MP for West Fife, 1935–50. CPGB chairman, 1943–56; president, 1956–63. Among his publications are *Revolt on the Clyde* (1936), *The Case for Communism* (1949), *Last Memoirs* (1966).

Gosling, Harry (1861–1930)   Trade union activist, Labour pioneer and minister. Thames waterman from 1875; secretary of Watermans' Union, 1890. London County Council (LCC) alderman, 1898–1925. Trades Union Congress (TUC) president, 1916. President of the Transport Workers' Federation and then the Transport and General Workers' Union. MP for Whitechapel and St George's, 1923–30. Minister of Transport and Paymaster-General, 1924.

Graham, William (1887–1932)   Cabinet minister. Educated George Heriot's School and Edinburgh University. Journalist from 1905. Edinburgh councillor, 1913–19. MP for Edinburgh Central, 1918–31. Financial Secretary to the Treasury, 1924. President of the Board of Trade, 1929–31.

Grant, Bernard Alexander Montgomery (Bernie) (born 1944)   Prominent black MP and local government leader. Educated Stanislaus College,

Guyana, and Tottenham Technical College. Analyst, 1961–63; British Rail clerk, 1963–65; international telephonist, 1969–78; National Union of Public Employees (NUPE) official, 1978–83; Black Trade Unionists Solidarity Movement development worker, 1983–84; Newham housing officer, 1985–87. London Borough of Haringey leader, 1985–87. MP for Tottenham since 1987. Founder member and chairman, party Black Caucus, 1987. Anti-apartheid National Executive member, 1988. Founding editor, *The Black Parliamentarian*, 1989. Chairman, Standing Conference on Racial Equality in Europe, 1990; Socialist Campaign Group of Labour MPs, 1990; National Committee on Reparations for Africa, 1993.

Greenwood, Arthur (1880–1954)   Party deputy leader and Cabinet minister. Educated elementary school and Yorkshire College. Teacher; active in the Workers' Education Association (WEA); lecturer at Leeds University, 1913. General secretary, Council for the Study of International Relations, 1914. Member of the Fabian Society. Founder and president until 1940 of the University Labour Federation. Member of Lloyd George's secretariat during the First World War; assistant secretary to Ministry of Reconstruction, 1917; involved in establishment of Whitley Councils. Labour Party research department secretary, 1920–43. MP for Nelson and Colne, 1922–31; Wakefield, 1932–64. Parliamentary Secretary, Ministry of Health, 1924. Minister of Health, 1929–31. Refused to join National Government; involved in development of post-1931 Labour party ideology. Parliamentary party deputy leader, 1935. Strongly anti-appeasement. Minister without Portfolio (economic affairs, then reconstruction), 1940–42. Lord Privy Seal, 1945–47. Minister without Portfolio, 1947. Party treasurer, 1943. Party National Executive chair, 1952.

Griffiths, James (1890–1975)   Trade union leader and Cabinet minister. Educated at elementary school and Central Labour College. Miner; miners' agent, 1925–36; President of South Wales Miners' Federation (SWMF), 1934–36. MP for Llanelli, 1936–50. Party National Executive member, 1939–40, 1941–59; chairman, 1948. Minister of National Insurance, 1945–50. Secretary of State for the Colonies, 1950–51. Deputy leader of the Opposition, 1956–59. Advocate of Welsh devolution; opposition spokesman on Welsh affairs, 1959–64. First Secretary of State for Wales, 1964–66.

Haldane, Richard Burden (Viscount Haldane of Cloane) (1856–1928)   Labour Lord Chancellor and recruit from the Liberals. Educated Edinburgh Academy, Universities of Edinburgh and Göttingen. Called to the bar, 1879; KC, 1890. Liberal MP for East Lothian, 1898–1912. Secretary of State for War, 1905–12; Lord Chancellor, 1912–15;

1924 after joining Labour. Co-founder, London School of Economics (LSE). Chairman, Royal Commission on University Education in London, 1909–13; in Wales, 1916–18.

Hardie, James Keir (1856–1915)   Party leader and pioneer; an agitator uncomfortable in the role of party chair. Self-educated. Converted to Christianity, 1878. Began work at seven as a messenger and then a miner. Union and strike leader; writer and agitator for socialism. Secretary, Ayrshire Miners' Federation; President, Ayrshire Miners' Union. Dismissed for agitation. Assistant editor *Cumnock News*. Initially a radical Liberal; failure of 1887 miners' strike led to his attack on the pro-Liberal TUC leadership. His first report to the Ayrshire Miners' Federation called for 'the complete emancipation of the workers from the thraldom of wagedom' and 'co-operative production under state management'. Stood unsuccessfully as independent miners' candidate for Mid-Lanarkshire, 1888. Co-founder and secretary Scottish Parliamentary Labour Party, 1889. Socialist MP for West Ham South, 1892–95; defeated following his attack in the Commons on the Royal Family. Founded and became editor of the *Labour Leader*, later the ILP paper, 1893. Founder and chairman of the Independent Labour Party (ILP), 1894–1900, 1913–14. Steered Labour Representation Committee (LRC) away from class-war position of the Social Democratic Federation (SDF). Opposed Boer war as a pacifist. MP for Merthyr, 1900–15. Put motion in the Commons for a 'Socialist Commonwealth founded upon the common ownership of land and capital, production for use and not for profit, and equality of opportunity for every citizen'. Led 29 members in Commons following 1906 general election; Labour Party chairman, 1906–8, 1909–10. Attempted to rouse international Socialist movement to oppose war before 1914. Chair, London Inter-Allied Socialist Conference, 1915.

Harman, Harriet (born 1950)   Cabinet minister. Educated St Paul's Girls' School and York University. Solicitor at Brent Community Law Centre, 1975–78. National Council for Civil Liberties (NCCL) legal officer, 1978–82. MP for Peckham since 1982. Opposition spokesperson on health and social security, 1984–89; on health, 1989–92; on treasury affairs, 1992–94; on employment, 1994–95; on health, 1995–96; social security, 1996–97. Secretary of State for Social Security and Minister for Women's issues, 1997–98. Returned to back-benches. Party National Executive member, 1993. Among her publications are *Justice Deserted: The Subversion of the Jury* (1979), *The Century Gap* (1993).

Hart, (Dame) (Constance Mary) Judith (Baroness Hart of South Lanark) (1924–91)   Cabinet minister and anti-colonialist activist. Educated Clitheroe Grammar School and London School of Economics (LSE).

MP for Lanark, 1959–83; Clydesdale, 1983–87. Joint Parliamentary Under Secretary, Scottish Office, 1964–66; Minister of State, Commonwealth Relations Office, 1966–67; Minister of Social Security, 1967; Paymaster-General, 1968–69; Minister of Overseas Development, 1969–70, 1974–75, 1977–79. Party NEC member, 1969–83; party chair, 1981–82. Among her publications is *Aid and Liberation: A Socialist Study of Aid Policies* (1973).

Hattersley, Roy Sydney George (Baron Hattersley of Sparkbrook) (born 1932)   Party deputy leader and Cabinet minister. Educated Sheffield City Grammar School and Hull University. Journalist, health service executive, 1956–64. Sheffield City councillor, 1957–65. MP for Sparkbrook Birmingham, 1964–97. Parliamentary Private Secretary to Minister of Pensions and National Insurance, 1964–67. Joint Parliamentary Secretary, Department of Employment and Productivity, 1967–69. Minister of Defence (Administration), 1969–70. Minister of State, Foreign and Commonwealth Office, 1974–76. Secretary of State for Prices and Consumer Protection, 1976–79. Party deputy leader, 1983–92. Director, Campaign for a European Political Community, 1966–67. Life peer, 1997. Prolific journalist and writer; among his publications are *Choose Freedom: The Future of Democratic Socialism* (1987), *Economic Priorities for a Labour Government* (1987), *Who Goes Home? Scenes from a Political Life* (1995).

Healey, Denis Winston (Baron Healey of Riddlesden) (born 1917)   Party deputy leader and Cabinet minister. Educated Bradford Grammar School and Oxford. Communist Party member, 1937–39. Second World War service in the army. Secretary of party International Department, 1945–52; wrote for Norwegian Labour paper *Arbeiderbladet* until 1964. MP for South East Leeds, 1952–55); Leeds East, 1955–92. Secretary of State for Defence, 1964–70. Chancellor of the Exchequer, 1974–79. Unsuccessful candidate for party leadership against Callaghan in 1976 and Foot in 1980. Deputy leader, 1980–83. Resigned from Shadow Cabinet, 1987. Member of Fabian Society executive, 1954–61. Party NEC member, 1970–75. Life peer, 1992. Described by his supporters as 'the best leader Labour never had'. Among his many publications are *Labour Britain and the World* (1963), *The Time of My Life* (1989).

Henderson, Arthur (1863–1935)   Party leader and Cabinet minister. Educated at elementary school. Iron moulder; Methodist lay preacher. Initially a Liberal; elected as Newcastle City councillor with Labour support, 1894. Elected as Lib-Lab councillor in Darlington, 1898; mayor, 1903. Labour MP for Barnard Castle, 1903–18; Widnes, 1919–22; Newcastle East, 1923; Burnley, 1924–31; Clay Cross, 1933–35. Party chairman, 1908–10, 1914–17, 1931–32; Secretary, 1912–34; leader in the House of Commons, 1908–10, 1914–17. Chief Whip, 1914. Supported British entry into the First World War; member of Parliamentary Recruiting Committee. President of the Board of Education, 1915–16. Minister without Portfolio and War Cabinet member, 1916–17. Resigned from War Cabinet, 1917. Key figure in revising party Constitution, 1918. Chief Whip, 1920–24, 1925–27. Home Secretary, 1924. Foreign Secretary, 1929–31. Refused to join the National Government, 1931. Leader of the Opposition, 1931–32. Party Treasurer, 1931–35. President of the World Disarmament Conference, 1932. Awarded Nobel Peace Prize, 1934. Among his publications is *Labour's Way to Peace* (1935).

Herbison, Margaret McCrorie ('Peggy') (1907–96)   Minister who resigned from the Labour government because of objections to threats to the Welfare State. Educated Bellshill Academy and Glasgow University; teacher and voluntary tutor with the National Council of Labour Colleges. MP for North Lanark, 1945–70. Joint Parliamentary Under Secretary of State, Scottish Office, 1950–51; Minister of Pensions and National Insurance, 1964–66; Minister of Social Security, 1966–67. Chair of the Select Committee on Overseas Aid, 1969–70. Refused the offer of a peerage. Lord High Commissioner to the Church of Scotland General Assembly, 1970–71.

Hodge, John (1855–1937)   Trade union activist and First World War coalition minister. Steelworker at age of 11; founding secretary of British Steel Smelters' Association, 1886; president, Iron and Steel Trades Confederation until 1931. Trades Union Congress (TUC) president, 1892. Labour National Committee member, 1900–15. Manchester city councillor; MP for Gorton, 1906. First Minister of Labour, 1916–17; Minister of Pensions, 1917–19. Opposed his union's participation in the General Strike, 1926. His autobiography was entitled *Workman's Cottage to Windsor Castle* (1931).

Houghton, (Arthur Leslie Noel) Douglas (Baron Houghton of Sowerby) (1898–1996)   Trade union official, Cabinet minister and Parliamentary Labour Party chairman. Inland Revenue Staff Federation secretary, 1922–60; Trades Union Congress (TUC) General Council member, 1952–60. London County Council (LCC) alderman, 1957–59. MP for Sowerby, 1949–74. Chancellor of the Duchy of Lancaster, 1964–66; Minister without Portfolio, 1966–67. Parliamentary Labour Party chairman, 1967–74. Member, Commission on the Constitution, 1969–73.

Hughes, Cledwyn (Baron Cledwyn of Penrhos) (born 1916)   Cabinet minister and Parliamentary Labour Party chairman. Educated Holyhead Grammar School and University College of Wales, Aberystwyth; a solicitor. Second World War service in the Royal Air Force. MP for Angelsey,

1951–79. Minister of State, Commonwealth Relations Office, 1964–66; Secretary of State for Wales, 1966–68; Minister of Agriculture, Fisheries and Food, 1968–70. Parliamentary Labour Party chairman, 1974–79.

Hume, John (born 1937)   Northern Ireland Social Democratic and Labour Party leader who played central part in the Northern Ireland peace process, 1994–98. Educated St Patrick's College, Maynooth, and Queen's University, Belfast. Teacher and businessman; President of the Credit Union League of Ireland, 1964–68. Northern Ireland Civil Rights Association activist. Co-founder and vice-chair Derry Citizens' Action Committee, 1968. Elected Stormont MP for Foyle, 1969. SDLP founder member, 1970. SDLP member of Northern Ireland Assembly for Londonderry, 1973–74. Minister of Commerce in power-sharing executive, 1974. SDLP leader, 1979. MEP from 1979. Talks with Sinn Fein culminated in the IRA ceasefires of 1994–96, 1997 and the 1998 peace agreement.

Hyndman, Henry Mayers (1842–1921)   Wealthy socialist pioneer. Educated privately and at Cambridge. Journalist and businessman, 1866–80. Became a socialist after reading Marx's *Das Kapital* on an Atlantic crossing, 1880. Formed radical Democratic Federation, 1880; renamed Social Democratic Federation (SDF), 1884. Founding editor of *Justice*, 1884. Led unemployed agitation; opposed imperialism and the Boer War. As the Social Democratic Party (SDP – formerly the Social Democratic Federation) weakened in face of ILP expansion, merged SDP with the British Socialist Party (BSP), 1911. Left BSP over his enthusiastic support for British participation in the First World War; formed National Socialist Party, 1916. Among his many publications are *The Historical Basis of Socialism* (1883), *The Economics of Socialism* (1896), *The Record of an Adventurous Life* (1911), *Further Reminiscences* (1912).

Isaacs, George Alfred (1883–1979)   Trade union leader and minister. Elementary education; a printer at the age of 12. General secretary, NATSOPA, 1909–49. Trades Union Congress (TUC) General Council member, 1931–45. MP for Gravesend, 1923–24; North Southwark, 1929–31, 1939–50; Southwark, 1950–59. Parliamentary Private Secretary to Secretary of State for the Colonies, 1924; Parliamentary Private Secretary to Secretary of State for the Dominions, 1929–31. Parliamentary Private Secretary to First Lord of the Admiralty, 1942–45. Minister of Labour and National Service, 1945–51, with responsibility for demobilisation; Minister of Pensions, 1951. TUC General Council chairman, 1945. President, World Conference of Trade Unions, 1945.

Jay, Douglas Patrick Thomas (Baron Jay) (1907–96)   Cabinet minister and strong opponent of Britain's entry into Europe. Educated Winchester and Oxford. A journalist. Assistant secretary, Ministry of Supply, 1940–43; Principal assistant secretary, Board of Trade, 1943–45. Personal assistant to prime minister, 1945–46. Elected MP for Battersea North, 1946. Parliamentary Private Secretary to the Chancellor of the Exchequer, 1947. Economic Secretary to the Treasury, 1947–50. Financial Secretary to the Treasury, 1950–51. President of the Board of Trade, 1964–67. Chairman, Common Market Safeguards Campaign, 1970–76. Among his many publications are *The Socialist Case* (1937) and *Socialism in the New Society* (1967).

Jenkins, Roy Harris (Baron Jenkins of Hillhead) (born 1920)   Party deputy leader, Cabinet minister, European Community official and defector from Labour. Educated Abersychan Grammar School, University College, Cardiff, and Oxford. Second World War service in the army. Worked for Industrial and Commercial Finance Corporation, 1946–48. Labour MP for Central Southwark, 1948–50; Stechford Birmingham, 1950–76. Social Democratic Party (SDP) MP for Glasgow Hillhead, 1982–87. Parliamentary Private Secretary to Secretary of State for Commonwealth Relations, 1949–50. Minister of Aviation, 1964–65. Home Secretary, 1965–67, 1974–76. Chancellor of the Exchequer, 1967–70. Deputy party leader, 1970–72; resigned over party's support for referendum on Europe. Fabian Society executive committee member, 1949–61; chairman, 1957–58. President of the European Economic Commission, 1977–81; architect of European Monetary System, 1978. Unsuccessful party leadership candidate, 1976. Proposed realignment in British politics in televised lecture, 1979. SDP joint leader, 1981–82; leader, 1982–83. Life peer 1987. Leader, Social and Liberal Democratic Party peers, 1988. Among his many publications are *Pursuit of Progress* (1953), *Sir Charles Dilke* (1958), *Asquith* (1964), *Baldwin* (1987), *A Life at the Centre* (1991).

Johnstone, Thomas (1882–1965)   Cabinet minister. Educated Lenzie Academy and Glasgow University. Founded *Forward*, 1906; editor, 1919–46. MP for Stirling and Clackmannan, 1922–24, 1929–31, 1935–45; Dundee, 1924–29. Secretary of State for Scotland, 1929–31. Lord Privy Seal, 1931. Regional Commissioner, Civil Defence for Scotland, 1939–41. Secretary of State for Scotland, 1941–45. Chairman, Scottish National Forestry Commission, 1945–48; Scotland Hydro-Electricity Board, 1946–59; Scottish Tourist Board, 1945–55. Companion of Honour, 1953.

Jones, James Larkin (Jack) (born 1913)   Trade union leader and an influential figure in the 1974–79 Labour government's 'social contract'. Educated at elementary school. Worked in docks and engineering, 1927–39. Liverpool city councillor, 1936–39. Fought for Republic in Spanish

Civil War; wounded, 1938. Transport and General Workers' Union (TGWU) district secretary, 1939–55; regional secretary, 1955–63; executive officer, 1963–69; general secretary, 1969–78. Chairman of Labour Party Working Party on Industrial Democracy, 1967. TUC General Council member, 1968–78. Labour NEC member, 1969–78. Founder member, European TUC, 1973. Persuaded unions to accept incomes restraint, 1975. Chairman of National Pensioners' Convention, 1992–. Among his publications is *Union Man* (1986).

Jowett, Frederick William (1864–1944)   Cabinet minister. Elementary education. Textile worker and manager. Bradford councillor, 1892–1907. MP for West Bradford, 1906–18; East Bradford, 1922–24, 1929–31. First Commissioner for Works, 1924. Independent Labour Party (ILP) chairman, 1909–10, 1914–17. Labour Party NEC chairman, 1921–22. Unsuccessful ILP candidate, 1931 and 1935 general elections.

Jowitt, William Allen (1st Earl Jowitt, Viscount Stevenage) (1885–1957)   Labour and National Government Cabinet minister and recruit from the Liberals. Educated Marlborough and Oxford. Called to the bar, 1909; KC, 1922. Liberal MP for Hartlepool, 1922–24; Preston, 1929. Joined Labour Party on appointment as Attorney-General and resigned seat. Labour MP for Preston, 1929–31; Ashton-under-Lyme, 1939–45. Expelled from Labour Party on joining National Government, 1931; defeated as National Labour candidate for Combined Universities, 1931. Readmitted to Labour, 1936. Solicitor-General, 1940–42. Paymaster-General, 1942–43. Minister without Portfolio, 1943–44. Minister of National Insurance, 1944–45. Lord Chancellor, responsible for piloting legislation through a predominantly Conservative House of Lords, 1945–51. Among his publications are *The Strange Case of Alger Hiss* (1953), *Some Were Spies* (1954).

Kinnock, Neil Gordon (born 1942)   Party leader and European Union official. Educated Lewis School, Pengam, and University College, Cardiff. Workers' Education Association (WEA) tutor-organiser, 1966–70. Welsh Hospital Board member, 1969–71. MP for Bedwelty, 1970–83; Islywn, 1983–95. Parliamentary Private Secretary to Secretary of State for Employment, 1974–75. Member of party National Executive, 1978–95. Opposition spokesperson on education, 1979–83. Party leader and leader of the Opposition, 1983–92, during which period he abandoned unilateral nuclear disarmament, drove Militant entryists from the party and began reforms to make the party electable. Director, Tribune Publications, 1974–82. European Commissioner for Transport, 1995–. Among his publications are *Wales and the Common Market* (1971), *Making our Way* (1986), *Thorns and Roses* (1992).

Lansbury, George (1859–1940)   Party leader and prominent pacifist. Educated elementary schools. Railway worker at 14. Emigrated to Australia, 1884; returned to sawmill business, 1885. Established Emigration Information Department, 1886. Became a Christian socialist, 1890. Bow Liberal agent, 1886–92. Joined Social Democratic Federation (SDF), 1892. Unsuccessful SDF candidate for Walworth, 1895; Socialist candidate for Bow, 1900. Elected to Poplar Board of Guardians, 1892; Poplar borough councillor, 1903. Member of the Central (Unemployed) Body for London. Member of Royal Commission on the Poor Laws, 1905–9; signed Minority Report. Unsuccessful Independent Labour Party (ILP) candidate for Middlesborough, 1906. Socialist London County Council (LCC) member for Poplar, 1909–12. MP for Bow and Bromley 1910–12; defeated when resigned to stand on women's suffrage platform; 1922–40. Co-founder *Daily Herald*, 1912; editor, 1912–22. Pacifist in the First World War. Mayor of Poplar, 1919. Imprisoned with other Poplar councillors for refusing to pay LCC precept, 1921. Refused offer of Ministry of Transport in first Labour government, 1924. Edited *Lansbury's Labour Weekly*, 1925–27. First Commissioner of Works, 1929–31. Party leader and leader of the Opposition, 1932–35; resigned at party conference over Labour support for sanctions against Italy. Among his publications are *My Life* (1928), *Looking Backwards and Forwards* (1935), *My Quest for Peace* (1938).

Laski, Harold Joseph (1893–1950)   Prominent activist and theoretician. Educated Manchester Grammar School, London University and Oxford. *Daily Herald* journalist. Lecturer at Harvard, 1916–20; London School of Economics (LSE), 1920–26; Professor of Political Science, 1926–50. Increased Marxist emphasis in views following the 1931 Labour government collapse. Associated with Left Book Club in the 1930s; active in the Socialist League and the Unity Campaign. Fabian Society executive committee member, 1921–36. Party NEC member, 1936–49. Party chairman, 1945; attacked by Conservatives as advocate of violent change. Member of Lord Chancellor's Committee on Ministers' Powers, 1929–32; on Legal Education, 1932–34. Among his many publications are *Studies in the Problem of Sovereignty* (1917), *Authority in the Modern State* (1919), *A Grammar of Politics* (1925), *Liberty in the Modern World* (1930), *The Crisis and the Constitution, 1931 and After* (1932), *Parliamentary Government in England* (1938), *The American Democracy* (1948), *Reflections on the Revolution of Our Time* (1943).

Lawrence, (Arabella) Susan (1871–1947)   Recruit from the Conservatives who went on to become one of the first woman Labour MPs. Educated home, London University and Cambridge. Member of the Conservative Primrose League, 1891–1901. Member of London School Board, 1900; London County Council (LCC) Education Committee, 1904.

Municipal Reform (Conservative) LCC councillor, 1907–11; resigned to join Independent Labour Party (ILP). National Federation of Women Workers organiser, 1912–22. LCC councillor for Poplar, 1913–28. Poplar borough councillor, 1919; imprisoned with other councillors for refusing to pay LCC precept, 1921. MP for East Ham North, 1923–24, 1926–31. Parliamentary Private Secretary to President of the Board of Trade, 1924. Parliamentary Secretary to the Ministry of Health, 1929–31. Refused to support National Government. Member of Fabian Society executive, 1913–45. Party National Executive member, 1918–41; first woman party chair, 1929–30.

Lee, Frederick (Baron Lee of Newton) (1906–84)   Cabinet minister. Elementary education. An engineer. Salford councillor, 1941–45. MP for Manchester Hulme, 1945–50; Newton, 1950–74. Parliamentary Private Secretary to the Paymaster-General, 1947; to the Minister of Economic Affairs, 1947; to the Chancellor of the Exchequer, 1947–50. Parliamentary Secretary to the Minister of Labour and National Service, 1950–51. Unsuccessful candidate for the party's deputy leadership, 1960. Minister of Power, 1964–66. Secretary of State for the Colonies, 1966–67. Chancellor of the Duchy of Lancaster, 1967–69.

Lee, Jennie (Baroness Lee of Asheridge) (1904–88)   Left-wing MP and first Minister for the Arts. Educated Moray House College and Edinburgh University. Writer and lecturer. A founding director of *Tribune*, 1937. MP for North Lanarkshire, 1929–31; Cannock, 1945–70. Party National Executive member, 1958–70; chair, 1967–68. Parliamentary Private Secretary to the Minister of Public Building and Works, 1964–65. Minister for the Arts, 1965–70, as Parliamentary Under Secretary, Department of Education and Science, 1965–67; Minister of State, 1967–70.

Lees-Smith, Hastings Bertrand (1878–1941)   Cabinet minister and recruit from the Liberals. Educated Aldenham, Royal Military Academy, Woolwich, and Oxford. London School of Economics (LSE) lecturer, 1906–41; reader, 1924–41. Chairman Ruskin College executive committee, 1907–9. Liberal MP for Northampton, 1910–18. Joined Independent Labour Party (ILP), 1919. MP for Keighley, 1922–23, 1924–31, 1935–41. Postmaster-General, 1929–31. President of the Board of Education, 1931. Acting Parliamentary Labour Party chair and leader of the Opposition, 1940–41.

Livingstone, Kenneth Robert (Ken) (born 1945)   Local government leader and radical activist. Educated Tulse Hill Comprehensive School and Philippa Fawcett College of Education. Laboratory technician.

Lambeth borough councillor, 1971–78. Camden borough councillor, 1978–82. Greater London Council (GLC) member, 1973–86; radical, and last, leader, 1981–86; attempted to construct a 'Rainbow Coalition' of minority and radical groups. MP for Brent East since 1987. Party National Executive member, 1987–89, 1997–98. Among his publications are *If Voting Changed Anything They'd Abolish It* (1987), *Livingstone's Labour: A Programme for the Nineties* (1989).

MacDonald, James Ramsay (1866–1937)   Party pioneer, prime minister in first and second Labour governments who left the party to form a National Government. Educated at elementary school. Journalist; editor of *The Socialist Review*. London County Council (LCC) member, 1901–4. Labour MP for Leicester, 1906–18; Aberavon, 1922–29; Seaham Harbour, 1929–31. National Labour MP for Seaham Harbour, 1931–35; Scottish Universities, 1936–37. Secretary of Labour Representation Committee and Labour Party, 1901–12. Party treasurer, 1919–29. Independent Labour Party (ILP) chairman, 1906–9. Labour Party chairman, 1911–14. Opposed British entry to the First World War and resigned, 1914. Member of Union of Democratic Control (UDC). Chairman of Parliamentary Party and leader of the Opposition, 1922. Party leader, 1922–31. Prime Minister and Foreign Secretary, 1924. Labour Prime Minister, 1929–31; formed National Government following Cabinet disagreement on benefit reductions; Prime Minister, 1931–35. Lord President of the Council, 1935–37. National Labour Party leader, 1931–37.

McNeil, Hector (1907–55)   Minister in the 1945–51 governments. Educated secondary school and Glasgow University. Journalist, *Scottish Daily Express*. Glasgow city councillor, 1929–35. MP for Greenock, 1941–55. Parliamentary Private Secretary to Parliamentary Secretary for War Transport, 1942–45. Minister of State, Foreign Office, 1946–50, with United Nations responsibilities; Secretary of State for Scotland, 1950–51.

Mandelson, Peter Benjamin (born 1953)   Minister and influential campaigns organiser. Educated Hendon Senior High School and Oxford. Chairman, British Youth Council, 1977–80; television producer, 1982–85. Lambeth borough councillor, 1979–82. Party director of campaigns and communications, 1985–90; leading figure in the party's modernisation. MP for Hartlepool since 1992. Minister without Portfolio, 1997–98. Secretary of State for Trade and Industry, 1998–. Unsuccessful candidate for election to the party National Executive, 1997. Responsible for Millennium celebrations.

Martin, (Basil) Kingsley (1897–1969)   Labour activist and influential editor of the *New Statesman*. Educated Mill Hill School and Cambridge.

Conscientious objector in the First World War; served in Friends' Ambulance Unit, 1917–18. London School of Economics (LSE) lecturer, 1918–27. Worked on *Manchester Guardian*, 1927–30; co-founder of the *Political Quarterly*. Editor of *New Statesman & Nation*, 1931–60; increased circulation from 14,000 to 60,000. Active in the Union of Democratic Control (UDC), National Council for Civil Liberties (NCCL) and the Campaign for Nuclear Disarmament (CND).

Mason, Roy (Baron Mason of Barnsley) (born 1924)   Cabinet minister. Educated Royston Senior School and London School of Economics (as a mature student). Miner, 1938–53. National Union of Mineworkers (NUM) branch official, 1947–53. MP for Barnsley, 1953–83; Barnsley Central, 1983–87. Minister of State, Board of Trade (Shipping), 1964–67. Minister of Defence (Equipment), 1967–68. Postmaster-General, 1968. Minister of Power, 1968–69. President of the Board of Trade, 1969–70. Secretary of State for Defence, 1974–76. Secretary of State for Northern Ireland, 1976–79. Life peer, 1987.

Maxton, James (1885–1946)   Radical Independent Labour Party (ILP) leader; a legendary orator and agitator. Educated Hutcheson's Grammar School and Glasgow University. Teacher. Joined ILP, 1904; National Administrative Council Scottish representative, 1914. Conscientious objector in the First World War. Imprisoned for one year for organising attempted shipyard strike, 1916; worked as a labourer on release. ILP paid organiser, 1918. Elected to Glasgow education committee, 1919. Labour MP for Bridgeton, 1922–31; ILP MP, 1931–46. ILP chair, 1926–31, 1934–39. Involved in production of the radical ILP Cook–Maxton Manifesto, 1927; attempted to develop links with Communist Party, 1934–39. Among his publications are *Lenin* (1932), *If I were Dictator* (1935).

Mellish, Robert Joseph (Baron Mellish of Bermondsey) (1913–98) Cabinet minister and defector from Labour. Transport and General Workers' Union (TGWU) official, 1938–46. Second World War service in the army. Labour MP for Bermondsey Rotherhithe, 1946–50; Bermondsey, 1950–74; Southwark Bermondsey, 1974–82; Independent MP, 1982. Parliamentary Private Secretary to Minister of Supply, 1950–51; to Minister of Pensions, 1951. Parliamentary Secretary, Minister of Housing, 1964–67. Minister of Public Building and Works, 1967–69. Government Chief Whip, 1969–70, 1974–76. London Regional party chairman, 1956–77. Chairman, London Docklands Development Corporation, 1981–85. Life peer, 1985.

Middleton, James Smith (1878–1962)   A leading figure in the early development of Labour. Elementary education; left school at 12 to work on father's newspaper. Secretary, Workington Trades Council; Independent Labour Party (ILP) branch secretary. Moved to London, 1902; part-time assistant to MacDonald in his role as Labour Representation Committee (LRC) secretary. Prominent in the transformation of the LRC into the party, 1906. Secretary, War Emergency Workers' National Committee, 1914–18. Labour Party assistant secretary, 1924; close to MacDonald. Labour Party secretary, 1934–44.

Morris, William (Bill) (born 1938)   Trade union leader. Born in Jamaica; educated Handsworth Technical College. Transport and General Workers' Union (TGWU) shop steward, 1963–73; regional official, 1973–79; National Secretary, 1979–86; Deputy Secretary, 1986–92; General Secretary, 1992–. TUC General Council member, 1992. Member, Commission for Racial Equality (CRE), 1977–87. Member, Employment Appeals Tribunal, 1988–.

Morrison, Herbert Stanley (Baron Morrison of Lambeth) (1888–1959) A leading figure in Labour's revival from 1931–45; deputy leader and minister in Labour and wartime Coalition governments. Educated at elementary school. Shop assistant; telephone operator; circulation manager for Labour *Daily Citizen*, 1912. Co-founder, London Labour Party, 1913; secretary, 1915. Conscientious objector in the First World War despite immunity on health grounds. Mayor of Hackney, 1920–21. London County Council (LCC) member, 1922–45; leader, 1934–40 with the slogan 'Labour Gets Things Done'. MP for South Hackney, 1923–24, 1929–31, 1935–45; East Lewisham, 1945–50; South Lewisham, 1950–59. Party chair, 1928–29. Minister of Transport, 1929–31. Declined office in National Government, 1931. Unsuccessful candidate for party leadership, 1935. Minister of Supply, 1940. Home Secretary and Minister of Home Security, 1940–45. War Cabinet member, 1942–45. Lord President of the Council, Leader of the House of Commons and deputy Prime Minister, 1945–51; advocate of 'consolidation' in 1947. Foreign Secretary, 1951. Deputy leader of the Opposition, 1951–55. Defeated in party leadership contest by Gaitskell, 1955. Life peer, 1959. Among his publications are *Socialisation and Transport* (1933), which set the corporate model for Labour's post-war nationalisation, *The Peaceful Revolution* (1949), *Government and Parliament* (1954), *Autobiography* (1960).

Mosley, (Sir) Oswald Ernald (1896–1980)   Junior minister and fascist leader. Educated Winchester and Royal Military Academy, Sandhurst. First World War service in the army, Royal Flying Corps and civil service. Conservative MP for Harrow, 1918–22; Independent, 1922–24. Opposed Coalition government's Ireland policy; secretary, Peace with Ireland Council, 1920. Joined Independent Labour Party (ILP), 1924. Labour

MP for Smethwick, 1926–31; New Party, 1931. Chancellor of the Duchy of Lancaster, 1929–30; resigned after Cabinet rejection of Memorandum on unemployment. Launched New Party with four other MPs, 1931; all lost seats in general election. Visited Italy; formed British Union of Fascists (BUF), 1932; renamed British Union of Fascists and National Socialists, 1936. Conducted anti-war campaign; imprisoned, 1940–43; under house arrest, 1943–45. Led Union Movement, emphasising united Europe and anti-immigration, 1948–66. Among his publications are *My Answer* (1946), *My Life* (1980).

Mulley, Frederick William (Baron Mulley of Manor Park) (born 1918) Cabinet minister. Educated Warwick School and Oxford (as mature student). Clerk. Second World War service in the army; prisoner of war, 1940–45. Called to the bar, 1954. MP for Sheffield, Park, 1950–83. Parliamentary Private Secretary to Minister of Works, 1951. Deputy Defence Minister and Minister for the Army, 1964–65. Minister of Aviation, 1965–67. Joint Minister of State, Foreign and Commonwealth Office (Minister for Disarmament), 1967–69. Minister of Transport, 1969–70. Minister for Transport, Department of the Environment, 1974–75. Secretary of State for Education and Science, 1975–76. Secretary of State for Defence, 1976–79. Vice-President, Western European Union Assembly, 1960; President, 1980–83. Party National Executive member, 1957–58, 1960–64, 1965–80. Party chairman, 1974–75. Life Peer, 1985. Among his publications are *The Politics of Western Defence* (1962).

Nathan, Harry Louis (1st Baron Nathan) (1889–1963) Liberal convert and minister. Educated St Paul's School. Solicitor, 1913; 'Poor Man's Lawyer' in East End of London. Army service in the First World War. Liberal MP for North East Bethnal Green, 1929–31; Independent Liberal, 1931–35; supported National Government, 1931. Active in the League of Nations Union and involved in the Peace Ballot, 1934–35. Joined Labour Party, 1935; MP for Central Wandsworth, 1937–40; created Baron to allow Bevin to take seat, 1940. Parliamentary Under Secretary of State, War Office, 1945–46; Minister of Civil Aviation, 1946–48.

Noel-Baker, Philip (Baron Noel-Baker) (1889–1982) A leading party internationalist referred to between the wars as 'MP for the League of Nations'. Educated Bootham School and Cambridge. First World War service in Friends' Ambulance Unit. Member of Versailles Peace Conference secretariat, 1919; League of Nations secretariat, 1919–22. MP for Coventry, 1929–31; Derby, 1936–77. Specialist in international affairs and disarmament. International relations professor, London University, 1924–29; lecturer at Yale, 1934. Private secretary to Henderson at Disarmament Conference. Parliamentary Secretary, Ministry of War Transport,

1942–45. Minister of State, Foreign Office, 1945–46. Secretary of State for Air, 1946–47; for Commonwealth Relations, 1947–50. Minister of Fuel and Power, 1950–51. Awarded Nobel Peace Prize, 1959. Life peer, 1977. Among his many publications are *Disarmament* (1926), *The Arms Race* (1958).

Olivier, Sydney Haldane (Baron Olivier of Ramsden) (1859–1943)   A leading figure in the early Fabian Society while a colonial civil servant. Educated Tonbridge School and Oxford. Joined Colonial Office, 1882. Joined Fabian Society, 1885; secretary, 1886–89. Assistant Colonial Secretary, Honduras, 1890–95. Secretary, West Indies Royal Commission, 1897. Colonial Secretary, Jamaica, 1899–1904; Governor, 1907–13. Permanent Secretary, Board of Agriculture, 1913–17. Assistant comptroller and auditor of Exchequer, 1917–20. Secretary of State for India, 1924. His publications include *The Anatomy of African Misery* (1927), *White Capital and Coloured Labour* (1929) and the controversial *Jamaica, The Blessed Island* (1936).

Owen, David Anthony Llewellyn (Baron Owen of Plymouth) (born 1930)   Cabinet minister, defector from Labour and Social Democratic Party (SDP) leader. Educated Bradfield College, Oxford and St Thomas' Hospital. Doctor. Labour MP for Plymouth Sutton, 1966–74; Plymouth Devonport, 1974–81. SDP MP for Plymouth Devonport, 1981–92. Parliamentary Private Secretary to the Minister of Defence (Administration), 1967. Parliamentary Under Secretary for Defence (Navy), 1968–70. Resigned from Opposition front bench over issue of Europe, 1972. Parliamentary Under Secretary, Department of Health and Social Security (DHSS), 1974; Minister of State, 1974–76; Minister of State, Foreign and Commonwealth Office, 1976–77. Foreign Secretary, 1977–79. SDP co-founder, 1981; deputy leader, 1982–83; leader, 1983–87, 1988–92. Life peer, 1992. Appointed European Community Co-chairman, International Conference on Former Yugoslavia, 1992. Among his publications are *Personally Speaking to Kenneth Harris* (1987), *Time to Declare* (1991).

Pankhurst, Emmeline (née Goulden) (1858–1928)   Women's suffrage activist. Registrar of births and deaths, 1907. Joined Independent Labour Party (ILP), 1893; elected to National Administrative Council, 1904. Founded Women's Social and Political Union (WSPU) with daughter Christabel, 1903, largely because of the indifference of male-dominated socialist organisations to the issue; took up radical agitation, 1905; withdrew WSPU from ILP, 1907; imprisoned for activities, 1909 and intermittently 1912–14. Suspended agitation during the First World War. Co-founder of the Women's Party, 1917–18. Conservative prospective parliamentary candidate, 1926.

Parmoor, Lord   See Cripps, Charles Alfred.

Peart, (Thomas) Frederick (Baron Peart) (1914–88)   Cabinet minister and party leader at the Council of Europe. Educated Durham University. Teacher. Rural district councillor, 1937–40. Second World War service in the army. MP for Workington, 1945–76. Parliamentary Private Secretary to the Minister of Agriculture, 1945–51. Minister of Agriculture, Fisheries and Food, 1964–68; Lord Privy Seal and Leader of the House of Commons, 1968–70. Leader, Labour delegation to the Council of Europe and Council vice-president, 1973–74. Unsuccessful candidate for the party's deputy leadership, 1970. Minister of Agriculture, Fisheries and Food, 1974–76; Lord Privy Seal and Leader of the House of Lords, 1976–79; Opposition leader in the House of Lords, 1979.

Pethick-Lawrence, Frederick William (1871–1961) (1st Lord Pethick-Lawrence of Pealake)   Minister. Women's suffrage and First World War peace activist. Educated Eton and Cambridge. Called to the bar, 1899; 'Poor Man's Lawyer' in East End of London, 1899–1901. Founder and editor, the *Echo*, 1902–5. Joined Independent Labour Party (ILP) and Fabian Society, 1906. Co-editor (with wife Emmeline Pethick) of *Votes for Women*, 1907; imprisoned for nine months, 1912. Conscientious objector in the First World War. Union of Democratic Control treasurer. Unsuccessful peace candidate in South Aberdeen by-election, 1917. MP for West Leicester, 1923–31; East Edinburgh, 1935–45. Financial Secretary to the Treasury, 1929–31. Leader of the Opposition in the Commons, 1941. Secretary of State for India and Burma, 1945–47; led Cabinet mission to India, 1946.

Pollitt, Harry (1890–1960)   Communist Party leader. Educated elementary schools and evening classes. Millworker at the age of 12; apprentice boilermaker, 1905–12. Joined Independent Labour Party (ILP), 1909; British Socialist Party (BSP), 1911. National organiser, Hands off Russia Committee, 1919; encouraged *Jolly Roger* incident, 1920. Founder member Communist Party of Great Britain (CPGB), 1920. Secretary, National Minority Movement, 1924. Imprisoned for one year for seditious libel on eve of General Strike, 1926. CPGB general secretary, 1929–39; removed for supporting war with Germany; restored to office, 1941–56; chairman, 1956–60. Among his publications is *Serving My Time* (1940).

Prescott, John Leslie (born 1938)   Party deputy leader and Cabinet minister. Educated Ellesmere Port Secondary Modern, Ruskin College, Hull University. Trainee chef, 1953–55; steward in merchant navy, 1955–63. General and Municipal Workers' Union (GMWU) official, 1965; National Union of Seamen official, 1968–70. MP for Kingston upon

Hull East, 1970–83; Hull East since 1983. Parliamentary Private Secretary to Secretary of State for Trade, 1974–76. Opposition spokesperson on regional affairs and development, 1981–83; on transport, 1983–84, 1988; employment, 1984–87; energy, 1987–88. Council of Europe member, 1972–75. Member of the European Parliament, 1975–79; leader of the Labour Group, 1976–79. Party National Executive member, 1989–. Stood unsuccessfully for deputy Labour Party leadership, 1988. Deputy leader, 1994. Deputy Prime Minister and Secretary of State for the Environment, Transport and the Regions, 1997–. Among his publications are *Not Wanted on Voyage* (1966), *Planning for Full Employment* (1985), *Full Steam Ahead* (1993), *Jobs and Social Justice* (1993).

Rees, Merlyn (Baron Merlyn-Rees of Morley and Cilfynydd) (born 1920)   Cabinet minister. Educated Harrow Weald Grammar School and London School of Economics. Second World War service in the Royal Air Force, 1941–46. Teacher and lecturer, 1949–53. MP for South Leeds, 1963–83; Morley and Leeds South, 1983–92. Parliamentary Private Secretary to the Chancellor of the Exchequer, 1964. Parliamentary Under Secretary, Ministry of Defence (Army), 1965–66; Ministry of Defence (RAF), 1966–68; Home Office, 1976–79. Secretary of State for Northern Ireland, 1974–76. Home Secretary, 1976–79. Life peer, 1992. Among his publications are *The Public Sector of the Modern Economy* (1973), *Northern Ireland: A Personal Perspective* (1985).

Robens, Alfred (Lord Robens of Woldingham) (born 1910)   Cabinet minister and businessman. Educated Manchester Secondary School. Union of Shop, Distributive and Allies Workers' (USDAW) official, 1935–45. Manchester city councillor, 1942–45. MP for Wansbeck, 1945–50; Blyth, 1950–60. Parliamentary Private Secretary, Ministry of Transport, 1944–47. Parliamentary Secretary, Ministry of Fuel and Power, 1947–51. Minister of Labour and National Service, 1951. Influential party figure during the 1950s and seen as a potential successor to Attlee as leader; a critic of Bevanism. Shadow Foreign Secretary, 1955–56; stood down following criticisms of his performance in Suez crisis. Left politics, 1960; peer, 1961. Chairman, National Coal Board, 1961–71. National Economic Development Council member, 1962–71. Member, Royal (Donovan) Commission on Trade Unions and Employers' Associations, 1965–68. Chairman of Vickers, 1971–79; held wide range of other directorships. Among his publications are *Industry and Government* (1970), *Ten Year Stint* (1972).

Ross, William (Baron Ross of Marnock) (1911–88)   Cabinet minister. Educated at Ayr Academy and Glasgow University. Teacher. Second World War service in the army. MP for Kilmarnock, 1946–79. Secretary of State for Scotland, 1964–70, 1974–76. Lord High Commissioner to General Assembly of the Church of Scotland, 1978–79.

Scargill, Arthur (born 1938)   Trade union leader who advocated industrial action for political objectives in 1970s and 1980s. Educated secondary school and Leeds University. Miner, 1953; National Union of Mineworkers (NUM) branch official, 1960. Young Communist League (YCL) member, 1955–62; Co-operative Party member, 1963; joined Labour Party, 1966. NUM national executive member, 1972; led successful 'flying pickets' during 1972 miners' strike. Yorkshire NUM president, 1973. Critic of the unions' 'social contract' with the 1974–79 Labour government. NUM president, 1981–. Led unsuccessful miners' strike which divided the Labour Party and trade union movement, 1984–85. Member, TUC general council, 1986–88. Founded Socialist Labour Party, 1996.

Shackleton, (Sir) David Thomas (1863–1938)   Important figure in drawing early Labour and trade union groups in the House of Commons together. Cotton worker; secretary Darwen Weavers' Association, 1894–1907. MP for Clitheroe, 1902–10. Labour Party chair, 1905. Effective campaigner against Labour Exchanges acting as recruiters of undercutting workers, 1907–8. TUC president, 1908–9. Home Office principal labour adviser, 1910. National health insurance commissioner, 1911–16. Ministry of Labour's first Permanent Secretary, 1916–21; chief labour adviser, 1921–25.

Shaw, George Bernard (1856–1950)   Writer and political activist. Elementary education; left school at 15 to become a clerk in Dublin. Moved to London, 1876; worked as journalist and continued self-education. St Pancras Liberal and Radical Association executive member in 1880s. Joined Fabian Society, 1884; recruited Sidney Webb. Prolific speaker and writer for Fabians. Founder member of the Socialist Defence League, 1887. Fabian delegate to Independent Labour Party (ILP) inaugural conference, 1893. St Pancras councillor, 1897–1903; unsuccessful London County Council (LCC) candidate, 1904. Resigned from Fabian Society executive, 1911; continued to speak and write on political issues. Among his many publications on political themes are *Commonsense about the War* (1914), *The Intelligent Woman's Guide to Socialism, Capitalism, Sovietism and Fascism* (1928), *Everybody's Political What's What* (1944), *Sixteen Self Sketches* (1949).

Shaw, Thomas (1872–1938)   Trade union activist and Cabinet minister. Elementary education. Textile worker at the age of 10. Secretary of the Colne Weavers for 18 years. Secretary, International Textile Workers'

Federation, 1911–29, 1931–38. West Midland region director of National
Service in the First World War. MP for Preston, 1918–38. Secretary of
the Socialist International, 1922–24. Minister of Labour, 1924. Secretary
of State for War, 1929–31.

Shawcross, (Sir) Hartley William (Baron Shawcross of Friston) (born 1902)
Cabinet minister best known for not having said in 1945: 'We are the
masters now.' Educated Dulwich College. Called to the bar, 1925. Law
lecturer, 1927–34. MP for St Helens, 1945–58. Attorney-General, 1945–51.
Chief British prosecutor at Nuremburg Trials, 1945–46. Chief investiga-
tor in Lynskey Tribunal, 1948. President of the Board of Trade, 1951.
Resigned as MP, 1958. Life peer, 1959. Pursued business career after
retirement from politics.

Shinwell, Emmanuel ('Manny') (Baron Shinwell of Easington) (1884–
1986)   Cabinet minister and orator who turned against Labour at the
end of his life. Educated at elementary school. Apprentice tailor's cutter
at 11. Joined Independent Labour Party (ILP), 1903. Elected to Glasgow
Trades Council, 1912; supported campaign for a negotiated peace, 1917.
Imprisoned for incitement to riot during 40-hour week demonstration,
1921. MP for Linlithgow, 1922–24, 1928–31. Defeated MacDonald to
take Seaham Harbour, 1935, holding the seat until 1970. Parliamentary
Secretary, Mines Department, 1924, 1930–31. Financial Secretary to the
War Office, 1929–30. Refused invitation to join National Government,
1931. Paid party propagandist, 1931–35. Refused offer of post in Coalition government, 1940. Chairman of committee drafting Labour manifesto, 1942–45. Minister of Fuel and Power (with responsibility for coal
nationalisation), 1945–47; moved following criticisms of his handling of
fuel crisis. War Minister, 1947–50. Secretary of State for Defence, 1950–
51. Party National Executive member, 1941–50. Parliamentary Labour
Party Chairman, 1964–67. Life peer, 1970. Resigned Labour Whip in
Lords because of the party's alleged move to the left, 1982.

Shore, Peter David (Baron Shore of Stepney) (born 1924)   Cabinet
minister. Educated Quarry Bank Grammar School and Cambridge. Head
of party research department, 1959–64; responsible for 1964 general
election manifesto. MP for Stepney, 1964–74; Stepney and Poplar,
1974–83; Bethnal Green and Stepney, 1983–97. Parliamentary Private
Secretary to Prime Minister, 1965–66; Minister of Technology, 1966–
67; Parliamentary Secretary, Department of Economic Affairs, 1967;
Secretary of State for Economic Affairs, 1967–69. Minister without Portfolio, 1969–70. Deputy leader, House of Commons, 1967–70. Secretary
of State for Trade and Industry, 1974–76; Secretary of State for the
Environment, 1976–79. Among his publications is *Entitled to Know* (1966).

Short, Clare (born 1946) Cabinet minister. Educated St Paul's Grammar School, Birmingham, Keele University. Civil servant, 1970–75; director, Youth Aid and the Unemployment Unit, 1979–83. MP for Birmingham Ladywood since 1981. Chair, All Party Parliamentary Committee on Race Relations, 1985–86. Opposition spokesperson on employment, 1985–88; on social security, 1989–91; on environmental protection, 1993–95; on transport, 1995–96; on overseas development, 1996–97. Party National Executive member, 1988–. Secretary of State for International Development, 1997–. Among her publications is *Talking Blues: A Study of Young West Indians' Views on Policing* (1978).

Smillie, Robert (1857–1940) Trade union leader and an influential early party member. Elementary education. Mineworker at 12. President, Scottish Miners' Federation, 1894–1918, 1922–31. Miners' Federation of Great Britain (MFGB) president, 1912–21. Founder member of Scottish Labour Party (SLP), 1888; and of the Independent Labour Party (ILP), 1893. Member of the Royal Commission on Safety in Mines, 1906. Pacifist in the First World War; refused offer of post as Minister of Food, 1917. Member of the Sankey Commission on the coal industry which recommended nationalisation, 1919. Labour MP for Morpeth, 1923–29; refused to accept office in 1924 Labour government. Published *My Life for Labour* (1924).

Smith, John (1938–94) Party leader and Cabinet minister. Educated Dunroon Grammar School and Glasgow University. Called to Scottish bar, 1967; QC, 1983. MP for Lanarkshire North, 1970–83; Monklands East, 1983–94. Parliamentary Private Secretary to the Secretary of State for Scotland, 1974; Parliamentary Under Secretary, Department of Energy, 1974–75; Minister of State, 1975–76; Minister of State, Privy Council Office, 1976–78; Secretary of State for Trade, 1978–79. National President, Industrial Common Ownership Movement, 1988–94. Party leader and leader of the Opposition, 1992–94. President, Socialist International, 1992–94. His lasting achievement was the introduction of one member one vote (OMOV), 1993.

Snell, Henry (Baron Snell) (1865–1944) A leading figure in the ethical and early socialist movement. Self-educated man who worked as a farm servant and bar worker and went on to Nottingham University College, the London School of Economics (LSE) and Heidelberg University. Worked for Charity Organisation Society and as secretary to the first director of the LSE. Joined Fabian Society and Independent Labour Party (ILP); secularist activist and Fabian lecturer. Secretary, Union of Ethical Societies; secretary, Secular Education League, 1907–31. London

County Council (LCC) member, 1919–25; LCC chair, 1934–38. MP for East Woolwich, 1922–31. Deputy Labour leader in House of Lords, 1940–44.

Snowden, Philip (Viscount Snowden of Ickornshaw) (1864–1937)   A socialist evangelist who became a leading figure in Labour and National governments, finally turning against his party. Educated at board school and privately. Teacher; insurance clerk, 1879; Inland Revenue clerk, 1886. Independent Labour Party (ILP) propagandist and journalist, 1894. Keighley councillor, 1899. ILP representative at Labour Representation Committee (LRC) founding conference, 1900. Member, ILP National Administrative Council; chair, 1904–7, 1917–20. MP for Blackburn, 1906–18; Colne Valley, 1922–31; National Labour in 1931. Critic of 1911–14 syndicalist activity. Opposed Britain's entry into the First World War and Labour's participation in Coalition government. Resigned ILP treasureship because of party's leftwards move, 1921; left the ILP, 1927. Chancellor of the Exchequer, 1924, 1929–31. Lord Privy Seal, 1931–32. Attacked former Labour colleagues in October 1931 general election. Resigned from National Government over abandonment of free trade, 1932. Supported Lloyd George's 'New Deal', 1935. Among his publications are *Socialism and Syndicalism* (1913), *An Autobiography* (1934).

Soper, Donald Oliver (Lord Soper of Kingsway) (born 1903)   Methodist minister and Christian Socialist. Educated Aske's School, Cambridge and London School of Economics. Minister, South London Mission, 1926–29; Central London Mission, 1929–36. Superintendent, West London Mission, 1936–78. Joined Labour Party, 1926. Columnist for *Tribune*, 1953–73. Member of the Peace Pledge Union during 1930s. Chairman, Hydrogen Bomb National Campaign, 1954. Led first Campaign for Nuclear Disarmament (CND) Aldermaston March, 1958. Chairman, Christian Socialist Movement, 1960. Lifelong speaker at Hyde Park and Tower Hill, London. Among his publications on religion and socialism is *Calling for Action* (1984).

Soskice, (Sir) Frank (Baron Stow Hill) (1902–79)   Cabinet minister. Educated St Paul's School and Oxford. Called to the bar, 1926; KC, 1945. Second World War service in the army. MP for Birkenhead East, 1945–50; Sheffield Neepsend, 1950–55; Newport, 1956–66. Solicitor-General, 1945–51. Attorney-General, 1951. Home Secretary, 1964–65. Lord Privy Seal, 1965–66.

Stewart, (Robert) Michael Maitland (Baron Stewart of Fulham) (1906–90)   Cabinet minister and Labour leader in the European Parliament. Educated Christ's Hospital and Oxford. Teacher and Workers' Education

Association (WEA) tutor. Army service in the Second World War. MP for Fulham East, 1945–55; Fulham, 1955–79. Government whip, 1945–47. Parliamentary Under Secretary for War, 1947–51. Parliamentary Secretary, Minister of Supply, 1951. Secretary of State for Education and Science, 1964–65. Secretary of State for Foreign Affairs, 1965–66. Secretary of State for Economic Affairs, 1966–67. Secretary of State for Foreign and Commonwealth Affairs, 1968–70; supported US involvement in Vietnam and opposed use of force against Rhodesian regime. Leader, European Parliament British Labour Group, 1974–75. Life peer, 1979. Published *Life and Labour: An Autobiography* (1980).

Strachey, (Evelyn) John St Loe (1901–63)   Cabinet minister and left-wing theoretician. Educated Eton and Oxford. Edited *The Miner* and *Socialist Review*. MP for Aston, 1929–31. Resigned from the Labour Party, 1931. Council member of Mosley's New Party, 1931; then an active Communist sympathiser. Secretary, Co-ordinating Committee for Anti-Fascist Activities; refused entry into the United States as a revolutionary, 1938. Second World War service in Royal Air Force. Parliamentary Under Secretary for Air, 1945–46. Minister of Food, 1946–50. Secretary of State for War, 1950–51. Among his many works are *The Coming Struggle for Power* (1932), *The Menace of Fascism* (1933), *The Theory and Practice of Socialism* (1936), *Contemporary Capitalism* (1956), *The Strangled Cry* (1962).

Straw, John Whitaker (Jack) (born 1946)   Cabinet minister. Educated Brentwood School and Leeds University. President, National Union of Students, 1969–71. Called to the bar, 1972. Islington borough councillor, 1971–78. ILEA deputy leader, 1973–74. Political adviser to Secretary of State for Social Services, 1973–74; to Secretary of State for the Environment, 1976–77. MP for Blackburn since 1979. Opposition spokesperson on Treasury and economic affairs, 1981–83; on the environment, 1983–87; education, 1987–91; environment and local government, 1992–93; local government, 1993–94; home affairs, 1994–97. Home Secretary, 1997.

Tawney, Richard Henry (1880–1962)   Historian, Christian Socialist and Labour activist. Educated Rugby and Oxford. Educational social work at Toynbee Hall; Glasgow University lecturer; Workers' Education Association (WEA) tutor, 1908. Army service in the First World War; invalided out, 1917. Unsuccessful parliamentary candidate four times. Member, Board of Education Consultative Committee, 1912–31. Trade union representative on Sankey Commission on mining industry, 1919. London School of Economics (LSE) economics history lecturer, 1919–31; professor, 1931–49. Drafted party's programme *Labour and the Nation*, 1928; repudiated it later. Among his publications are *The Acquisitive Society* (1921), *Religion and the Rise of Capitalism* (1926), *Equality* (1931).

Tewson, (Harold) Vincent (1898–1981)   Trade union leader. Elementary education. Office boy for the Amalgamated Society of Dyers at 14.
Army service in the First World War. Local trade union and party activist
in Blackburn. Secretary, Trades Union Congress (TUC) Organization
Department, 1925–31. TUC assistant general secretary, 1931–46; general
secretary, 1946–60. Sought co-operation between unions and Labour
government. Played leading role in establishment of anti-Communist
International Confederation of Free Trade Unions, 1949; president,
1951–53.

Thomas, James Henry ('Jimmy') (1874–1949)   Trade union leader and
minister in Labour and National governments who left the party and was
expelled by the union he had led. Educated board school. Rail worker at
12. Amalgamated Society of Railway Servants (ASRS) president, 1904–6.
National Union of Railwaymen (NUR) president, 1910; general secretary,
1918–24, 1925–31; led railway strikes, 1911 and 1919. Supported entry
into the First World War but declined office in Coalition government.
Swindon councillor. MP for Derby, 1910–31; National Labour, 1931–36.
Secretary of State for the Colonies, 1924. Lord Privy Seal (Minister for
Employment), 1929–30. Secretary of State for the Dominions, 1930–35.
Secretary of State for the Colonies, 1935–36. Disowned by his union
on joining the National Government, 1931. Resigned from office after
revealing budget secrets. TUC president, 1920–21. President of the International Federation of Trades Unions, 1920–24.

Thomas, (Thomas) George (Baron Thomas of Tonypandy) (1909–97)
Cabinet minister and first Labour Speaker of the House of Commons.
Educated at secondary school and University College, Southampton. A
teacher. National Union of Teachers executive member, 1940–45. MP
for Cardiff Central, 1945–50; Cardiff West, 1950–83. Parliamentary Private
Secretary to the Minister of Civil Aviation, 1951. Parliamentary Under
Secretary, Home Office, 1964–66. Minister of State, Welsh Office, 1966–
67. Minister of State, Commonwealth Office, 1967–68. Secretary of State
for Wales, 1968–70. Deputy Speaker, 1974–76; Speaker of the House of
Commons, 1976–83.

Thorne, William (Will) James (1857–1940)   Union leader and Labour
pioneer. Began work at the age of 6. Joined Social Democratic Federation (SDF), 1884. Taught to read and write by Eleanor Marx. Founded
National Union of Gasworkers and General Labourers (later NUGMW),
1889; general secretary, 1889–1934. Led dockworkers' campaign for eight-
hour day, 1889. Member, TUC Parliamentary Committee, 1894–1933;
TUC president, 1912. West Ham councillor, 1890–1946; mayor, 1918–
19. MP for West Ham South, 1906–35.

Tillett, Benjamin (Ben) (1860–1943)   Union leader, Labour pioneer and self-proclaimed agitator. Joined the Navy at 14. Founded Dockers' Union, 1887; secretary until amalgamation into Transport and General Workers' Union (TGWU), 1922. London dock strike leader, 1889. Member of the TUC Parliamentary Committee from 1892. Active in formation of National Transport Workers' Federation, 1910. TGWU political department, 1922–31. TUC general council member, 1921–31; TUC president, 1929. MP for North Salford, 1917–24, 1929–31.

Tomlinson, George (1890–1952)   Minister in Coalition and Labour governments. Educated at elementary school and evening classes. Cotton mill worker at the age of 11. Rushton urban district councillor, 1912; Lancashire county councillor, 1931. MP for Farnworth, 1938–52. Joint Parliamentary Secretary, Ministry of Labour and National Service, 1941–45. Minister of Works, 1945–47. Minister of Education, 1947–51.

Trevelyan, (Sir) Charles Philips (1870–1958)   Radical Liberal recruit to Labour who became a minister in the first Labour government. Educated Harrow and Cambridge. Secretary to Lord Lieutenant of Ireland, 1892–93. London School Board member, 1896–97. Liberal MP for Elland, 1899–1918; Labour MP for Newcastle, 1922–31. Parliamentary Secretary, Board of Education, 1908–14; resigned from government over opposition to Britain's declaration of war, 1914. Active in the Union of Democratic Control; advocate of a negotiated peace, 1917. Joined Labour Party and Independent Labour Party (ILP), 1919. President of the Board of Trade in first Labour government, 1924. President of the Board of Education, 1929–31; left in protest against proposed cuts in education. Active supporter of the Soviet Union in the 1920s and 1930s.

Vaz, (Nigel) Keith Anthony Standish (born 1956)   One of the first ethnic minority Labour MPs. Educated Aden, Latymer Upper School and Cambridge. Solicitor, Islington Borough Council; Highfields and Belgrave Law Centre. Unsuccessfully contested Richmond and Barnes, 1983. MP for Leicester East since 1987.

Walsh, Stephen (1859–1929)   Minister in Coalition and Labour governments. Educated Kirkdale School, Liverpool. A miner at the age of 14. Co-founder of the Lancashire and Cheshire Miners' Federation. Vice-chair, Miners' Conciliation Board. President, Wigan and District Trades Council. Ashton-in-Makerfield district councillor, 1894–1901. MP for Ince, 1906–29. Parliamentary Secretary, Ministry of National Service, 1917. Local Government Board, 1917–19. Resigned from the Coalition Government, 1919. Vice-president, Miners' Federation of Great Britain, 1922–24. Secretary of State for War, 1924.

Webb, (Martha) Beatrice (née Potter) (1858–1943)   Socialist theoretician and activist. Educated privately. Became associate in father's railway business, 1872. Charity Organization Society visitor and rent collector in London. Worked with Charles Booth on *Life and Labour of the People in London,* published in 1887. Gave evidence to the House of Lords Committee on the Sweating System, 1888–89. Declared herself a socialist, 1890. Member of War Cabinet Committee on Women in Industry, 1918–19. Much of her activity was jointly undertaken with her partner Sidney Webb, whom she married in 1892. Launched London School of Economics (LSE), 1895; drafted minority report of Royal Commission on Poor Laws, of which she was a member, 1905–9; founded *New Statesman,* 1912. Joined Independent Labour Party (ILP), 1912. Among the Webbs' joint works were *The History of Trade Unionism* (1894), *Industrial Democracy* (1897), *English Local Government* (1906–29). Among her publications were *Wages of Men and Women – Should They be Equal?* (1919), *A Constitution for the Socialist Commonwealth of Great Britain* (1920), *My Apprenticeship* (1926), *Our Partnership* (1948), and her *Diaries 1912–24* (1952).

Webb, Sidney James (1st Lord Passfield) (1859–1947)   Socialist theoretician and Cabinet minister. Educated in Europe, Birkbeck Institute, City of London College. Civil service clerk, 1878–91; called to the bar, 1885. Joined Fabian Society, 1885; saw social progress as generated by an elite and attempted to permeate ideas through influential people. Progressive London County Council (LCC) councillor (member of Labour and Socialist Group), 1892–1910. Much of his activity was jointly undertaken with his partner Beatrice Webb whom he married in 1892. Launched London School of Economics (LSE), 1895; drafted Royal Commission on Poor Laws minority report, 1909; founded *New Statesman,* 1912. Labour National Executive Committee member, 1915–25. Worked with War Workers' National Emergency Committee. Drafted party policy document *Labour and the New Social Order,* 1918. MP for Seaham, 1922–29. President of the Board of Trade, 1924. Created a Baron, 1929. Secretary of State for the Dominions and Colonies, 1929–30; for the Colonies, 1930–31. Refused to service in the National Government, 1931. Visited Russia with Beatrice in 1932; published *Soviet Communism: A New Civilisation?* (1935). Among other joint works were *The History of Trade Unionism* (1894), *Industrial Democracy* (1897), *English Local Government* (1906–29).

Wedgwood, Josiah Clement (Baron Wedgwood) (1872–1943)   A self-proclaimed 'philosophic anarchist', initially a Liberal who became a Labour minister. Educated Clifton College and Royal Naval College, Greenwich. Naval architect. Served in the army in the Boer War and the First World War. Resident magistrate, Transvaal, 1902–4. Staffordshire county councillor, 1910–18; deputy lieutenant for Staffordshire. Liberal

MP for Newcastle-under-Lyme, 1906–18; left Liberals to join Labour Party, 1918. Labour MP for Newcastle-under-Lyme, 1918–31; independent Labour member, 1931–42. Parliamentary Labour Party vice-chair, 1921–24; party NEC member, 1924. Chancellor of the Duchy of Lancaster, 1924. Mayor, Newcastle-under-Lyme, 1930–32. Among his publications are *The Future of the Indo-British Commonwealth* (1921), *The Seventh Dominion* (1928), *Memoirs of a Fighting Life* (1940).

Wheatley, John (1869–1930)   A Clydeside activist who became one of the most successful ministers in the first Labour government. Elementary education. Began work as a miner at 12; shop assistant. Joined Independent Labour Party (ILP), 1908; formed a Catholic Socialist Society. Lanarkshire county councillor, 1910–12; Glasgow councillor, 1912–22. Pacifist in the First World War and an advocate of peace by negotiation, 1917. MP for Glasgow Shettleston, 1922–30. Minister of Health, 1924; piloted a successful Housing Bill. Criticised the Trades Union Congress for ending the General Strike, 1926; withdrew from the Opposition front bench.

Wilkinson, Ellen Cicely ('Red Ellen') (1891–1947)   A left-wing activist who became the first woman Minister of Education. Educated secondary school and Manchester University. Joined Independent Labour Party (ILP), 1912. Election organiser for National Union of Women's Suffrage Societies 1913–15. National organiser, Amalgamated Union of Co-operative Employees (later USDAW), 1915. Founder member of Communist Party of Great Britain (CPGB), 1920; resigned, 1924. Member of Labour committee investigating Black and Tans' conduct in Ireland. Manchester city councillor, 1923–26. MP for Middlesborough East, 1924–31; Jarrow, 1935–47. President, Conference of Labour Women, 1925. Parliamentary Private Secretary to Minister of Health, 1929. Led investigatory missions to Germany, India and Spain, 1933–34. Played leading part in organising the Jarrow unemployed march, 1936. A co-founder of *Tribune*, 1937. Visited Spain during civil war, 1937. Parliamentary Secretary, Ministry of Pensions, 1940; to Minister of Home Security (with responsibility for civil defence), 1940–45. First woman Minister of Education, 1945–47. Among her publications are *Peeps at Politicians* (1930), *Why Fascism?* (co-author, 1934), *The Town that was Murdered* (1939).

Williams, Shirley Vivien Teresa Brittain (Baroness Williams of Crosby) (born 1930)   Educated St Paul's Girls' School, Oxford and Columbia. Labour MP for Hitchin, 1964–74; Hertford and Stevenage, 1974–79. Social Democratic Party (SDP) MP for Crosby, 1981–83. Parliamentary Private Secretary to Minister of Health, 1964–66. Parliamentary Secretary to Minister of Labour, 1966–67. Minister of State, Department of

Education and Science, 1967–69; Home Office, 1969–70. Secretary of State for Prices and Consumer Protection, 1974–76. Secretary of State for Education and Science and Paymaster-General, 1976–79. Fabian Society general secretary, 1960–64; chairman, 1980–81. Labour Party National Executive member, 1970–81. SDP co-founder, 1981; president, 1982–88; led SDP merger with Liberals, 1987–88. Appointed Professor of Politics, Harvard University, 1988. Life Peer, 1993. Among her publications are *Politics is for People* (1981), *A Job to Live* (1988).

Williams, Thomas (Baron Williams of Barnburgh) (1888–1967)   Union activist who became a minister in the 1945 Labour government. Elementary education and evening classes. A miner at the age of 11. Union branch secretary, 1908; urban district councillor, 1919. MP for Don Valley, 1920–59. Parliamentary Private Secretary to the Minister of Agriculture, 1924. Parliamentary Private Secretary to the Minister of Labour, 1929–31; opposed formation of the National Government. Joint Parliamentary Secretary to the Ministry of Agriculture, 1940–45. Minister of Agriculture, 1945–51.

Wilson, (James) Harold (Baron Wilson of Rievaulx) (1916–95)   Prime minister. Educated Wirral Grammar School and Oxford. Economics lecturer, 1937. Economic Assistant to War Cabinet, 1940–41; Director of Economics and Statistics, Ministry of Fuel and Power, 1943–45. MP for Ormskirk, 1945–50; Huyton, 1950–83. Parliamentary Secretary, Ministry of Works, 1945–47. Secretary for Overseas Trade, 1947. President of the Board of Trade, 1947–51; resigned over imposition of NHS charges, 1951. Party NEC chairman, 1961–62. Party leader, 1963–76. Leader of the Opposition, 1963–64, 1970–74. Prime Minister, 1964–70, 1974–76. Life peer, 1983. A complex figure, discredited as merely a party tactician by the 1970s but whose reputation (and that of his period in office from 1964 to 1970) appeared on the verge of rehabilitation in the 1990s. Among his publications are *New Deal for Coal* (1945), *In Place of Dollars* (1952), *The Labour Government 1964–70* (1971), *Final Term: The Labour Government 1974–76* (1979), *Harold Wilson Memoirs 1916–64* (1986).

21 Glossary

ACAS. See Advisory Conciliation and Arbitration Service.

Advisory Conciliation and Arbitration Service (ACAS). Statutory body established in 1975 by the Labour government as part of its 'social contract' agreement with the trades unions. ACAS is empowered to encourage negotiation and agreement between employers and unions, to prevent and to intervene in industrial disputes.

Bennites. Left-wing supporters of Tony Benn, minister in the 1966–70 and 1974–79 Labour governments, who argued, following Labour's 1979 general election defeat, for a more fundamentalist socialist approach and for greater influence of party activists in policy formulation. Benn's influence, at its height in 1981 when he was narrowly defeated by Denis Healey for the post of deputy party leader, waned following the election of Neil Kinnock as leader in 1983 and the defeat of the 1984–85 miners' strike.

Berlin Airlift. The first major confrontation of the Cold War between the Soviet and Western blocs, which took place from June 1948 to May 1949 under the 1945–51 Labour government. Berlin was under four-power control and the Soviet Union, alleging that the Western powers had reneged on agreements on German status, attempted to force Britain, France and the United States out of their sectors of Berlin by blocking road and water transport into the city. The Western powers mounted a round-the-clock airlift of essential provisions to preserve control. Britain introduced bread rationing – something that had not happened in wartime – to ensure food supplies to the city.

Bevanites. Members of a loose, left-wing alliance of backbenchers and constituency activists which grouped around Aneurin Bevan (1897–1960) following his resignation as Minister of Labour in 1951 in protest against the levying of NHS charges and increased spending on rearmament. The Bevanites – many of whom had been members of the Keep Left group – mounted a challenge to the party leadership in the 1950s, favouring a less Cold War-oriented defence policy and a more emphatic socialist policy domestically. Although Bevanism represented a series of temporary alliances on the left, at the 1952 party conference six of the seven Bevanite candidates were elected to the National Executive's constituency section. In May 1952, 57 backbenchers backed Bevan's opposition to Labour's support for the Conservative government's defence policy. In 1955, the party whip was temporarily withdrawn from Bevan when 62 Labour MPs abstained in a vote on Labour's amendment to the Conservative government's Defence White Paper. He came second to Gaitskell in the party leadership contest of that year. Bevan effectively split with his supporters when, appearing at the 1957 party conference as shadow Foreign Secretary, he abandoned his opposition to British nuclear weapons.

Beveridge Report.   The *Report on Social Insurance and Allied Services*, presented by the Liberal economist William (later Lord) Beveridge (1879–1963) in 1942, which provided the framework for the post-war Labour government's Welfare State programme (and more specifically the National Insurance Act 1946). Beveridge proposed a reorganisation of social insurance to provide support 'from the cradle to the grave', based on family allowances, unemployment and sickness benefits and retirement pensions through the National Insurance system, and a national health service, against the background of economic and fiscal policies which guaranteed full employment.

Bevin Boys.   Second World War conscripts sent to work in the mines as an alternative to service in the armed forces. The term derived from Ernest Bevin (1881–1951), Minister of Labour and National Service in the 1940–45 Coalition government.

Big Five, the.   The prominent figures in the earliest and most active phase of the 1945 Labour government – Clement Attlee (1883–1955), Ernest Bevin (1881–1951), Sir Stafford Cripps (1889–1952), Hugh Dalton (1887–1962) and Herbert Morrison (1888–1959). The Five become the Four when Dalton was forced to resign as Chancellor of the Exchequer in 1947 following an inadvertent budget leak to a journalist.

Bingham Report.   A report issued in September 1978 on the breaking of oil sanctions imposed on the white regime in Southern Rhodesia following its unilateral declaration of independence in 1965. The enquiry – chaired by Thomas Bingham QC – found that Wilson's Labour government had been aware, despite denials, that the illegal regime had been helped to survive by Shell–BP and Total oil supplies.

Black Sections.   Black and Asian party members argued in the 1980s that the establishment of Black Sections was necessary to encourage ethnic minority participation in party activity and policy formulation. Proposals for the formation of Black Sections first emerged in 1981 and initially met with a favourable response from the party's NEC. Diane Abbott, Paul Boateng and Sharon Atkin were among the founding members at a conference held in 1984. Supporters argued that while 13% of the Labour vote at the 1983 general election had come from black and ethnic minorities, there were no black MPs. However, the post-1983 party leadership refused to accept the formation of groups 'based on race' within the party and proposals to establish Black Sections were overwhelmingly rejected at the 1984 and 1986 party conferences. Nonetheless, over 30 constituency sections were established. Although agitation waned after the election of four ethnic minority MPs in 1987, some of the arguments put forward by the supporters of Black Sections were acknowledged by the establishment of a Black Socialist Society in 1993.

Black Socialist Society.   Party grouping formed in 1993 as an alternative to Black Sections, the establishment of which had been rejected by Labour. The majority of leading positions in the society was taken by former Black Sections members. However, in 1997 – when estimated membership was in hundreds rather than thousands – there were complaints from TGWU general secretary Bill Morris that the society was being denied adequate support by Labour's leadership.

Block vote.   The system under which votes were distributed at the Labour Party conference based on an organisation's affiliated membership, the most notable and controversial of which were the trade unions, largely because of the numbers they wielded. Votes were cast by union officials in a block total through a show of hands from delegates or by the use of voting cards. In each case the total affiliated membership was represented as taking one point of view and minority opinion in any block was never registered. The mechanism had been created by the trade unions at the Trades Union Congress (TUC) annual conference in 1894. The introduction of one member, one vote at the 1993 Labour Party conference began the process of ending the block vote with organisations' votes becoming more representative of differing opinions within them. The block vote was replicated at party constituency level.

'Bonfire of controls'.   The beginning, on 5 November 1948, of the abolition by President of the Board of Trade Harold Wilson of restrictions on business activity that required the issue of 200,000 licences and permits a year. Wilson announced that he intended to remove as many controls as possible except those seen as necessary for national recovery. By March 1949 the Labour government had relaxed controls on consumer goods, industrial equipment and the purchase of overseas goods. Although criticised by the left as the beginning of an abandonment of socialist planning, the policy was intended to allay Conservative criticisms of unnecessary bureaucracy.

British Socialist Party (BSP).   Formed as a revolutionary Marxist party in 1911–12 by the Social Democratic Party (SDP) and members of the Independent Labour Party (ILP) with an initial membership of almost 40,000. The party's dominant figure, H.M. Hyndman (1842–1921), left with his followers in 1916 over his support for British participation in the First World War. The BSP reverted to a more pacifist attitude and from January 1916 was affiliated to the Labour Party. In 1920 the BSP broke away to become the major section of the newly-formed Communist Party of Great Britain, following the rejection of its proposal to the Labour Party conference that Labour should leave the Second International and join the Third (Communist) International.

British Workers' League.   See National Democratic Party.

BSP.   See British Socialist Party.

Budget leak.   Hugh Dalton was forced to stand down as Chancellor of the Exchequer in November 1947 after giving details to a journalist of the budget he was about to present. A report of some of the measures he was proposing appeared in an evening newspaper while he was still addressing the Commons. Dalton's position in the government had already been weakened by austerity measures required to counter a balance of payments crisis. He returned to the Cabinet as Chancellor of the Duchy of Lancaster in 1948 with much reduced influence.

Bullock Report.   A report on Industrial Democracy produced by a committee appointed in December 1975 and chaired by the historian Alan Bullock. The report, which was issued in April 1977, recommended a system of worker representatives on company boards. Although supported by the Labour government, the recommendations were shelved following demands by trade union leaders that representatives should be union nominees rather than directly elected by the workforce as a whole, and criticism from the employers' organisation, the Confederation of British Industries.

Butskellism.   Expression used to denote the post-Second World War consensus between Labour and Conservative governments on maintenance of full employment based on a mixed economy and the Welfare State. The term derived from R.A. Butler (1902–82), Conservative

Chancellor of the Exchequer, 1951–55, and Hugh Gaitskell (1906–63), Labour Chancellor, 1950–51.

Campaign for Democratic Socialism (CDS).   A grouping formed in 1960 by right-wing Labour MPs associated with party leader Hugh Gaitskell (1906–63), academics and party members in Oxford, and parliamentary candidates in London. Originally established to counter left-wing influence in the constituency parties and trade unions, and to press for a revisionist socialist programme, the CDS concentrated on defence policy following Gaitskell's defeat on unilateral nuclear disarmament at the 1960 party conference. There were allegations that the CDS was helped with finance, indirectly, by the US Central Intelligence Agency. Following the reversal of the party's line on nuclear weapons at the 1961 conference, the CDS reduced its activity and was formally dissolved in 1964.

Campaign for Labour Party Democracy (CLPD).   A pressure group established by the Labour left in 1973 in an attempt to make the Parliamentary party more accountable to constituency activists' power. The CLPD called for the mandatory reselection of MPs by party members once in each Parliament, voting for the party leader and deputy leader by activists and the trade unions and for control of the contents of general election manifestos by the party conference. The CLPD succeeded in imposing the mandatory reselection policy and came close to winning the party's deputy leadership for Tony Benn in 1981 but its successes were partly responsible for the breaking of the Gang of Four with Labour and, ultimately, for the formation of the Social Democratic Party.

Campaign for Nuclear Disarmament (CND).   Movement formed in February 1958 to agitate for unilateral nuclear disarmament and a reduction in arms expenditure. CND mounted an annual protest march against nuclear weapons from 1958 to 1964. Much of the movement's membership looked to a Labour government to achieve its objectives and in 1960 the party conference passed a resolution in favour of unilateralism (although this was reversed the following year). CND rapidly declined in membership and influence following the election of the 1964 Labour government and the growth in other radical left organisations. The movement briefly revived in campaigning against the deployment of Cruise missiles in Western Europe in the early 1980s. Leading members of the Labour Party who were CND members include Tony Blair, Neil Kinnock and Michael Foot.

Campaign Group.   Left-wing section of the Labour Party which broke away from the Tribune Group in 1982. The Campaign Group's influence weakened following the 1983 general election defeat, which was partly blamed on Labour's left-wing policies. The group, which had become known as the Socialist Campaign Group, supported Margaret Beckett's candidacy for the party leadership in 1994. The group lost influence with the establishment in the mid-1990s of New Left in New Labour.

Campbell case.   In July 1924 the Communist *Workers' Weekly* published an 'Open Letter to the Fighting Forces' in which troops were called upon to 'let it be known that neither in the class war nor in a military war, will you turn your guns on your fellow workers'. The paper's acting editor, J.R. Campbell – a decorated First World War veteran – was charged under the Incitement to Mutiny Act 1797, but the charge was withdrawn. The Conservative opposition suggested that Communist sympathies among the Labour rank and file had forced the withdrawal, and moved a censure motion which, together with a Liberal amendment calling for a select committee of enquiry, MacDonald said he would treat as a confidence vote. The Liberal amendment was carried by 364 votes to 198 and MacDonald called a general election. The suggestion that Labour was sympathetic to Communism bore fruit during the election campaign in the Zinoviev letter.

Card vote.   The method of voting at Labour Party (and Trades Union Congress) conferences which symbolised the power of the block vote, particularly that of the trade unions. Delegates used a book containing 'for' and 'against' votes which were torn out and placed in ballot boxes circulated by tellers. At the TUC the cards were held up to be counted. In the case of the largest trade union delegations, vote papers represented millions of members affiliated to the Labour Party.

CDS.   See Campaign for Democratic Socialism.

Christian socialism.   A strand of thought which emerged in the mid-nineteenth century as an attempt to counterpose the ethical principles of the New Testament to the excesses of *laissez-faire* capitalism. Its leading proponents were Charles Kingsley (1819–75) and Thomas Hughes (1822–96). Early Christian socialists pressed for the establishment of industrial co-operatives and were involved in the setting up of the Working Men's College in 1854. Many of the Labour Party's pioneers, including Hardie, MacDonald, Snowden, Henderson and Lansbury, were active Christians, and Lansbury wrote: 'Socialism is to me the finest and fullest expression of religion.' Among later adherents were Stafford Cripps (Chancellor of the Exchequer in the 1945–51 Labour government) and R.H. Tawney (author of the 1928 party programme *Labour and the Nation*).

In 1923 the Society of Socialist Churches (SSC) affiliated to the Labour Party and set out as one of its objectives to 'work as part of the Labour movement'. The SCC developed into the Socialist Christian League (SCL) which disaffiliated from the party in 1933. In 1960 the SCL merged with the Society of Socialist Clergy and Ministers to form the Christian Socialist Movement, chaired by Donald Soper. Labour leader John Smith, a Movement member since the early 1980s, encouraged a renewed interest in Christian socialism with an address he gave in 1993. From 1,200 members in 1993 the Movement rapidly grew to 5,000 members at the beginning of 1997, among them party leader Tony Blair, and Gordon Brown, Jack Straw, Chris Smith and Paul Boateng, all of whom were to become ministers in the 1997 Labour government. Blair declared that it was his intention to re-unite the ethical code of Christianity with the basic values of democratic socialism.

Clarion, **the**.   Socialist newspaper established in December 1891 by Robert Blatchford (1851–1943), together with Alexander Mattack Thompson and Edward Francis Hay. The first issue sold 4,000 copies and sales then rose to an average 34,000. A series of articles by Blatchford were reprinted in book form as *Merrie England* and proved a valuable means of propagating socialism in England. However, much of the popularity of the *Clarion* itself derived from Hay's talents as a journalist and sales fell following his death in 1896. The paper survived another three years but was able to provide the basis of the Clarion Movement.

Clarion Movement.   Emerging from the *Clarion* newspaper, established by Robert Blatchford (1851–1943) in 1891, the associated movement stressed Labour's cultural aspects, with an emphasis on 'fellowship and brotherhood'. Blatchford consistently declared: 'We cannot have socialism without Socialists.' The movement established a network of choirs, cycling clubs, scouts groups, and formed associations with local religious groups, particularly in Lancashire, where Blatchford formed alternative socialist Sunday schools. In the 1890s the movement was an important focus for generalised debate about forms of socialism and in 1894 Blatchford proposed that the Clarion Scouts, the Independent Labour Party (ILP) and the Social Democratic Federation (SDF) should amalgamate in a single socialist party. The proposal was, however, resisted by Hyndman of the SDF and Hardie of the ILP. In their view, the advance to socialism would be by a political route rather than cultural and social one. A Clarion Van Movement was established shortly before the First World War to disseminate socialist literature throughout Britain but the movement had lost much of its moral fervour following Blatchford's vociferous support for the 1899–1902 Boer War.

Clause Four.   The section of the 1918 Constitution (revised in 1928) which set out Labour's ultimate, if imprecise, objective as being to 'secure for the workers by hand or by brain the full fruits of their industry and the most equitable distribution thereof that may be possible upon the basis of common ownership of the means of production, distribution, and exchange, and the best obtainable system of popular administration and control of each industry or service'. Though partly a reaction to the successful Bolshevik seizure of power in Russia in 1917, the very vagueness of the clause helped unite the differing strands of socialism in the party, particularly between the individualist and cultural view and the statist view. By 1945 the clause was interpreted as a programme for nationalisation, although some on the left of the party criticised the form this took, particularly the absence of workers' control. In 1959 Gaitskell, party leader from 1955 to 1963, failed in his hopes to modernise the party on the lines of the German Social Democrats by abandoning the clause, but in practice it was simply ignored by subsequent Labour governments. However, at a special party conference in April 1995 the party's new leader, Tony Blair, won support for a re-wording of the clause by 65.23% of those voting to 34.66%. The new wording says: 'The Labour Party is a democratic socialist party. It believes that by the strength of our common endeavour, we achieve more than we can achieve alone so as to create for each of us the means to realise our true potential and for all of us a community in which power, wealth and opportunity are in the hands of the many not the few, where the rights we enjoy reflect the duties we owe, and where we live together, freely, in a spirit of solidarity, tolerance and respect.' The revised clause also promises 'a dynamic economy', 'a just society', 'an open democracy' and 'a healthy environment'.

CLP.   See Constituency Labour Party.

CLPD.   See Campaign for Labour Party Democracy.

Clydesiders.   Also known as the 'Clydeside Brigade', the Clydesiders were a loosely organised group of left-wing Independent Labour Party (ILP) MPs elected from the area around Glasgow in the November 1922 general election. Among the most prominent were James Maxton (1885–1946), David Kirkwood (1872–1955), John Wheatley (1869–1930), Emanuel Shinwell (1884–1986), and George Buchanan (1890–1955). Four members, including Maxton, were almost immediately suspended from the Commons because of their disruptive tactics. Their influence had been long established through industrial activity and support of rent strikes and housing issues during the First World War and, once in Parliament, they agitated for a rapid advance to socialism. Wheatley proved a successful

Minister of Health in the 1924 Labour government, but the Clydesiders' continuing confrontational actions intensified tensions with the Labour leadership, particularly MacDonald and Snowden, and played some part in encouraging the ILP's eventual disaffiliation from the Labour Party.

CND.   See Campaign for Nuclear Disarmament.

Cole Group.   Informal weekly discussion group for radical and socialist students established by G.D.H. Cole (1889–1959) following his appointment as Reader in economics at Oxford in 1924 and continued for the remainder of his active academic life. Among those who attended the group and who were to become prominent in public life were W.H. Auden, Colin Clark, Evan Durbin, Hugh Gaitskell, John Parker and Michael Stewart. During the 1926 General Strike, members of the group were actively involved in the formation of a university strike committee.

'Commanding heights'.   Expression used, generally (but not exclusively) by the left of the Labour Party, to describe the elements of industry – particularly the core elements of coal, iron and steel – that were to be nationalised in order to ensure popular control over the working of the economy and to bring Labour governments closer to achieving the goals of Clause Four of the party's 1918 Constitution. The expression derived from the Bolshevik leader Lenin.

Commission on Social Justice.   Established in 1992 by Labour leader John Smith (1938–94) to conduct an enquiry into and make recommendations on the party's policies on the welfare state and social security. The Commission, which was chaired by Sir Gordon Borrie and administered by the Institute of Public Policy Research, issued its final report in October 1994. Among the Commission's recommendations were a commitment to restore full employment, a minimum wage, subsidised wages to assist the long-term unemployed, a new top rate of income tax, restoration of benefits to 16 and 17 year olds, increased child benefit, and guaranteed nursery education for all three and four year olds. Some, but not all, of the proposals were ignored by the party leadership as it prepared a restructuring of the welfare state following Labour's 1997 general election victory.

Common Wealth.   An idealist left-wing party combining Christian, radical Liberal and Marxist strands, formed in 1942 by the merger of Forward March – led by Liberal MP Sir Richard Acland (1906–90) – and the 1941 Committee (groupings of sympathisers with the radio broadcasts made by the radical writer J.B. Priestley). The party's supporters were generally middle class. Common Wealth broke the wartime electoral truce, standing in seats uncontested by Labour and was successful in by-elections in 1943, 1944 and 1945. Membership of the party was pro-scribed by Labour in 1943. Common Wealth fielded 23 candidates in the 1945 general election, one of whom – R.W.G. McKay – was elected and immediately joined the Labour Party. Acland himself joined the Labour Party in 1945 and became an MP in 1947. As Labour members, both were active in Keep Left. Common Wealth contested no more elections but survived briefly as a discussion group.

Communist Party of Great Britain (CPGB).   Formed in July–August 1920 by the British Socialist Party (which provided the bulk of its early membership), the Communist Unity Group of the Socialist Labour Party, the Communist Party and shop stewards' movement activists. The Com-munists – in contrast to Labour – accepted the establishment of a dict-atorship of the proletariat through armed revolution and affiliated to the Third International (Comintern). Throughout its existence, the party had a fraught and ambivalent relationship with the Labour Party, denoun-cing the leadership for the weakness of its commitment to socialist trans-formation but at the same time attempting to influence the membership. A request for affiliation to Labour shortly after the CPGB's foundation was rejected, as were further attempts in 1935, 1943 and 1946. Labour's attitude – given the tortuous tactical turns taken by the Communists, largely in response to demands from the Soviet Union – appeared justi-fied. In 1924 the Labour Party conference barred Communists from individual membership and from standing as Labour candidates. In 1927 trade unions were prevented from sending Communists as delegates to Labour conferences. In electoral terms, the Communists were persist-ently unsuccessful. Two Communist MPs returned in 1922, J.T. Walton Newbold (Motherwell) and S. Saklatvala (North Battersea), were both Labour members. Saklatvala, running as a Communist from 1924, re-mained an MP until 1929. In 1935 William Gallacher was elected and held his seat until 1950. Phil Piratin was a Communist MP from 1945 to 1950. Generally, however, Communist candidates lost their deposits. It was at rank-and-file level that the party found its more significant suc-cesses, often in areas neglected by the Labour Party and the trade unions such as among the unemployed and in tenants' organisations, as well as through industrial militancy. In 1929 the Communists adopted the 'class against class' line in which the Labour Party was denounced as 'social fascist' and the 'third party of capitalism'. But with the rise of fascism, the Communists attempted to renew association with Labour, first in the United Front period of 1933–35, with party members, and then, in the Popular Front period from 1935, with the Labour Party itself. Neither yielded much success for the Communists. Having first opposed the Second World War, the party changed its attitude when the Soviet Union was attacked by Germany in 1941 and found a new popularity, with membership rising to 56,000. But with the onset of the Cold War the party's strength waned and the attitude of the Labour Party leadership hardened. Communists, however, remained prominent as trade union activists. With the collapse of the Soviet Union in 1991 – after a period in which the party in Britain had moved steadily towards a less rigorously Leninist 'Euro-communism' – the Communists renamed themselves the Democratic Left and expressed less interest in a rigid class-based politics and more in building alliances with feminism and the Green Movement.

Constituency Labour Party (CLP).   Introduced by the Labour Party's 1918 Constitution when party membership was opened to individuals. From that date there has been a CLP in each constituency. Until the 1937 party conference members of the constituency section of the National Executive Committee (NEC) were elected annually by conference as a whole. From that date the seven-strong constituency section was elected by constituencies alone. In practice, power in the CLP lay with the General Committee (formerly the General Management Committee). In 1994 one member, one vote was introduced in the election and the party's *Partnership into Power* in 1997 introduced further reforms.

Constitution.   See 1918 Labour Party Constitution.

Contracting-in.   See Political levy.

Contracting-out.   See Political levy.

Cook–Maxton Manifesto.   Produced by the Independent Labour Party (ILP) MP James Maxton and the non-aligned Miners' Federation of Great Britain leader A.J. Cook (1883–1931) in June 1928, the Manifesto, which criticised the direction in which the Labour leadership appeared to be moving, raised the possibility of a new alliance between the Labour left, the ILP and non-aligned socialists. The Manifesto attacked MacDonald's attempt to transform Labour into a party of all classes and argued for the establishment of a new socialist party based in the working class. However, the Manifesto aroused criticism from the *Daily Herald* on the right and the Communist Party on the left. The Communists said Maxton and Cook were advocating a form of 'managed capitalism' rather than socialism. The Manifesto was a stark revelation of the underlying antagonism which led to the ILP's disaffiliation from the Labour Party in 1932.

Co-operative Party.   Formed in 1918 (following a decision at the 1917 Co-operative Congress) to obtain direct representation in Parliament. One Co-operative MP was elected in 1918 and joined Labour in the Commons. Under an agreement made with Labour in 1926, local

Co-operative parties became eligible for affiliation to divisional Labour parties and from 1941 the party's representatives attended meetings of the National Council of Labour. The 1926 agreement was revised in 1946 to provide for the nomination for elections of Co-operative and Labour candidates and from 1960 the number of candidates was limited to 30. Following growing Communist influence in the Co-operative movement, the party adopted a new constitution in 1951 banning membership of bodies proscribed by Labour. There were 15 Co-operative MPs in the 1992–97 Parliament and the party fielded 26 candidates at the 1997 general election.

CPGB. See Communist Party of Great Britain.

Cunningham amendment. An amendment proposed by Labour (later SDP) MP George Cunningham to the Scottish Devolution Bill in January 1978 which effectively torpedoed the Labour government's intentions. The amendment, which was passed by 166 votes to 151, made a 'Yes' vote in Scotland invalid unless 40% of the country's registered voters supported it. In the March 1979 referendum, only 32.9% of registered votes were in favour of the devolution proposals. The dissatisfied Scottish National Party put down a no confidence motion which the Labour government lost, leading to the 1979 general election.

Daily Citizen. The pre-First World War moderate trade union-sponsored organ of the Parliamentary Labour Party, a rival to the more radically agitational *Daily Herald*. The *Daily Citizen* ceased publication during the war.

Daily Herald. Established as a single-sheet strike bulletin by London printers in April 1912, the Herald quickly became a rival to the official Labour *Daily Citizen* following the appointment of George Lansbury as editor in October 1913. The paper, which regularly attacked the official Labour and trade union leadership before the First World War, was chronically unprofitable and relied for survival on voluntary subsidies. During the war it became a weekly and was increasingly sympathetic to guild socialism. Reverting to daily publication in 1919, with a circulation of over 300,000, the *Herald* faced financial difficulties following a boycott by advertisers and in 1922 the TUC and the Labour Party became partners in maintaining the paper's solvency. In 1930 Odham's Press took half the paper's shares and transformed the *Herald* into a popular daily, with the TUC retaining editorial control. By 1937 circulation had risen from one million to 2,033,000. However, sales slumped in the 1950s and 1960s and in 1964 the *Herald* ceased publication.

DEA.   See Department of Economic Affairs.

Democracy versus Dictatorship.   A document published by the National Joint Council of Labour in May 1933 following an invitation from the Communist Party and the ILP for Labour and the trade unions to participate in a United Front against fascism. The document rejected the invitation, equating fascism and Communism as dictatorial systems which had nothing in common with Labour's democratic socialism. *Democracy versus Dictatorship* was endorsed at the October 1933 Labour Party conference and resolutions in favour of the United Front were rejected.

Department of Economic Affairs (DEA).   The establishment of a Department of Economic Affairs was advocated in Labour's 1964 general election manifesto as a means of reviving Britain's stagnant economy through planning. The DEA was intended to counterbalance what was seen as the negative influence of the Treasury. More cynically, commentators suggested that a further attraction for Labour leader Harold Wilson (1916–95) was that the DEA provided a way of diverting his two main rivals through 'creative tension' – James Callaghan (born 1912) became Chancellor following Labour's 1964 general election victory while George Brown (1914–85) became first Secretary of State for Economic Affairs. No real agreement was ever reached on a demarcation of responsibilities between the Treasury and the DEA but in 1965 the DEA published a five-year National Plan which aimed at a 25% increase in domestic output by 1970. The deflationary package of July 1966 confirmed the Treasury's dominance and in August Brown left to become Foreign Secretary. He was succeeded at the DEA by Michael Stewart (1966–67) and Peter Shore (1967–69) before the Department was finally wound up in 1969.

Deselection.   See Reselection.

'Desiccated calculating machine'.   An expression used by Labour left-winger Aneurin Bevan (1897–1960) on 29 September 1954 which was assumed to refer to his ideological opponent Hugh Gaitskell (1906–63). Gaitskell's introduction of NHS charges in 1951 had provoked Bevan's resignation from the Labour government. The term was a further revelation of the bitter internecine struggles over Labour's policies which contributed to the party's defeat in the 1955 and 1959 general elections.

Devaluation.   The reduction in value of a currency in relation to those of other countries. The intended effect is to ease persistent trading deficits by reducing the price of exports and increasing the price of imports. Two Labour Chancellors have devalued the pound, Stafford Cripps (from

$4.03 to $2.80 in September 1949) and James Callaghan (to $2.40 in November 1967). Labour's fear of being accused of being unable to sustain the value of sterling prevented what many commentators saw as a necessary devaluation following the party's general election victory of 1964. Prime Minister Wilson, Economic Affairs Secretary Brown and Chancellor Callaghan decided against devaluation in October 1964 and thereafter devaluation was known as 'the Unmentionable'.

Devolution.   Decentralisation of power falling short of complete independence, usually referring to Scotland and Wales. Labour's Scotland Act 1978 and the Wales Act 1978 provided for the establishment of assemblies in Edinburgh and Cardiff but in referendums held in March 1979 Wales rejected the devolution proposals while Scotland failed to give a sufficient majority in favour. The Labour government elected in 1997 presented further proposals which were put to referendums in September 1997. On a 60% turnout, Scotland voted in favour of a devolved Parliament by 74.3% to 25.7% and in favour of the Parliament having tax-raising powers by 63.5% to 36.5%. Wales voted in favour of a representative assembly by 50.3% to 49.7% on a 50% turnout. The results encouraged demands for devolution to the English regions, particularly in the North East and Yorkshire. In May 1998 London voted in favour of the setting up of a Greater London Authority (GLA) with an elected mayor.

'Dog licence speech'.   A warning made by Labour prime minister Harold Wilson (1916–95) on 2 March 1967 following the refusal of a number of left-wing backbenchers to support the government's Defence White Paper. Wilson told a Parliamentary Labour Party meeting: 'Every dog is allowed one bite, but a different view is taken of a dog that goes on biting all the time. He may not get his licence returned when it falls due.' The warning had little effect. On 10 May, 34 Labour MPs voted against proposals to apply for EEC entry and 51 abstained. On 17 July, 22 Labour MPs abstained in a vote on wages restraint and ten days later 19 failed to support the government's defence policy.

Donovan Report.   The report of the Royal Commission on Trade Unions and Employers' Associations, chaired by Lord Donovan, which was appointed in April 1965 and reported in June 1968. The report recognised the increased decentralisation of pay bargaining and the growing influence of shop stewards in industrial relations, and recommended plant level rather than nationally negotiated agreements. Donovan rejected legal or penal sanctions to discourage strikes, preferring voluntary reform instead. The report suggested the appointment of an Industrial Relations Commission to investigate problems in industry and Labour Tribunals to deal with individual grievances. The report was shelved by the government, which went on in 1969 to formulate its own proposals in a document entitled *In Place of Strife.*

Dream ticket.   The optimistic description of the combination of Neil Kinnock as party leader and Roy Hattersley as his deputy, elected in 1983 to unite Labour's left and right following the turmoil of the early 1980s and the 1983 general election defeat. The combination went on to defeat in the 1987 and 1992 general elections.

Eaton Lodge conferences.   Meetings held in the 1930s by, among others, future party leader Clement Attlee, G.D.H. Cole and Stafford Cripps which attempted to absorb the lessons of the increasing disappointment felt in the conduct of the Labour government elected in 1929 and to formulate a radical application of socialist principles by a future govern-ment. The conferences – which were held at the home of the Countess of Warwick – formed the basis of the Society for Socialist Inquiry and Propaganda (SSIP), formed in 1930.

Ebbw Vale.   The South Wales constituency represented by Aneurin Bevan (1897–1960) from 1929 until his death, and inherited by his biographer Michael Foot (born 1913, party leader 1980–83).

Eccleston Square.   The site in London of the headquarters of the Labour Party and the Trades Union Congress from 1918 to 1929 when both moved to Transport House.

Economic Advisory Council.   Established by Labour prime minister MacDonald in January 1930 to provide the government with wide-ranging advice. The 1929 policy document *Labour and the Nation* had proposed the creation of such a committee to act as the 'eyes and ears' of a future Labour prime minister on economic questions. The Council, which MacDonald chaired, was made up of ministers, economists and other figures from outside politics and included Maynard Keynes, G.D.H. Cole, Ernest Bevin and the TUC general secretary Walter Citrine. Meet-ing approximately every month, the Council achieved little.

Electoral College.   The party body established under the influence of left-wing Bennites in 1981–82 through which party leaders were to be elected with trade union representation of 40%, with the remaining votes shared equally between constituency parties and Labour MPs. Per-haps ironically, the first leader to be elected under the system was the anti-Bennite Neil Kinnock, following Labour's 1983 general election defeat.

Entryism. Tactic of joining the Labour Party in order to subvert its policies, capture influential positions and, ultimately, to destroy what is seen as a reformist obstacle to revolutionary socialism. Entryist organisations maintain their own political programme and objectives but attempt to gain greater influence by operating within the Labour Party. In the 1930s members of the Communist Party often joined in order to further their party's Popular Front line. Among post-Second World War entryists have been the Socialist Labour League, which captured the Young Socialist movement in the 1960s, forcing its abandonment by the Labour Party, and Militant Tendency. Militant supporters dominated Liverpool City Council in the mid-1980s and four members were elected as Labour MPs. In 1985, the Labour Party expelled prominent Militant figures. Entryism was also attempted in 1978 by the International Marxist Group (later called Socialist Action). Entryism became easier in the 1970s following the abolition in 1973 of the 'proscribed list' which set out the names of organisations whose membership was incompatible with that of the Labour Party.

Fabian Research Department. Established in 1912 by Beatrice (1858–1943) and Sidney Webb (1859–1947), with George Bernard Shaw (1856–1950) as chairman until 1918 and G.D.H. Cole (1889–1959) as honorary secretary from 1916 to 1924. The Department became a focal point for guild socialists who gave the body its ideological colouring. In 1918 the Department was renamed the Labour Research Department and came under Communist Party control, prompting Cole's resignation in 1924. The Department remains in existence as an independent body providing information to trade unionists and activists and is financially supported by part of the trade union movement. The Labour Party established its own research department in 1921.

Fabian Society. A largely middle-class group established in November 1883 to disseminate socialist ideas in Britain and which had its greatest influence into the 1920s. The group, which derived its name from Quintus Fabius Maximus Cunctator, a Roman general known for his cautious manoeuvring against Hannibal, favoured gradual rather than radical social reform. Among its early leading figures were Sidney Webb (1859–1947), George Bernard Shaw (1856–1950) and Beatrice Potter (Mrs Webb) (1858–1943). Fabians rejected Marxist materialism and the class struggle and were initially against the formation of a specifically socialist party, preferring to influence established parties with their views. An early statement of aims said: 'The object of the Fabian Society is to persuade the English people to make their political constitution thoroughly democratic, and so to socialise their industries as to make the livelihood of the people entirely independent of private capitalism. . . . It does not propose that the practical steps towards social democracy should be carried out by itself, or by any other specially organised society or party.' However, Fabians were present at the foundation of the Labour Representation Committee in 1900 and acted as the Labour Party's research body. The Constitution adopted by the Labour Party in 1918 was an essentially Fabian programme drafted by Sidney Webb.

Fearless talks.   Final and unsuccessful attempt by Labour prime minister Harold Wilson to negotiate a settlement of the illegal unilateral declaration of independence made by white Rhodesian leader Ian Smith, held on the cruiser *Fearless* in October 1968.

Fellow-traveller.   Expression generally used (particularly from the 1930s to the 1950s) to describe people who, while supporting the policies of the Communist Party, did not become members. In the 1930s John Strachey was accused of fellow-travelling while in the late 1940s and early 1950s Labour backbenchers often faced the accusation when they criticised the party's Cold War defence policies.

'Fight and fight and fight again'.   Phrase from a speech made on 5 October 1963 by party leader Hugh Gaitskell (1906–63) following a vote in favour of nuclear unilateralism at the Scarborough party conference. He declared that the policy was opposed by a majority of Labour MPs and that the party was not composed of unilateralists, pacifists and fellow-travellers and went on: 'There are some of us, Mr Chairman, who will fight and fight and fight again to save the party we love. We'll fight and fight and fight again to bring back sanity and honesty and dignity . . .'.

For Socialism and Peace.   Policy document published by the Labour National Executive Committee in July 1934 and adopted by the party conference in October. The policy, the most radical ever adopted by Labour, called for the immediate public ownership of banking and credit, transport, water, coal, electricity, gas, agriculture, iron and steel, shipbuilding, engineering, textiles, chemicals, insurance, all with workers taking a share in control and direction. The House of Lords was to be abolished in a Labour government's first term and, if necessary, Emergency Powers were to be taken to counter any resistance to the government's measures.

Forward March of Labour Halted?   A seminal document produced by the Marxist historian Eric Hobsbawm in 1981 in which he argued that the base on which the Labour Party had been built and survived – a working class based in labour-intensive industries with a distinct culture – had been eroded by post-war economic and social development (much of it the achievement of Labour governments). He argued that Labour needed to respond to change with greater flexibility to survive as a coherent political party and that it should embrace electoral reform and build alliances with the environmental and peace movements and with the devolutionary demands inherent in Scots and Welsh nationalism.

Future of Socialism, The.   Major work of revisionist theory by Anthony Crosland (1918–77), published in 1956. *The Future of Socialism* set out the argument for socialism as equality. Crosland's view that public owner-ship on the Morrisonian model as undertaken by the 1945–51 Labour government was irrelevant to the objective of equality antagonised the left in the party. Criticism centred on Crosland's optimistic view that world economic expansion would continue and, as he acknowledged, his neglect of the problems of sterling and the exchange rate which would confront a future Labour government.

Gaitskellites.   Supporters of the social democratic tradition of moderate reformism (right-wing to their opponents) advocated by Hugh Gaitskell (1906–63), Labour leader from 1955 to 1963. The Gaitskellites were successful in their campaigns against Bevanism, the challenge of Harold Wilson for the party leadership and unilateral nuclear disarmament. However, divisions between the Gaitskellites and the Bevanites contrib-uted towards keeping Labour in opposition from 1951 to 1964. Follow-ing the 1959 general election defeat, Gaitskell unsuccessfully attempted to modernise Labour's image by proposing the abandonment of Clause Four. In 1960, the left succeeded in winning conference support for a policy of nuclear unilateralism, only to see the Gaitskellites reverse the decision at the following party conference. Prominent Gaitskellites Roy Jenkins and Bill Rodgers were instrumental in the split from Labour which resulted in 1981 in the formation of the Social Democratic Party (SDP).

Gang of Four.   The group of senior Labour members – Roy Jenkins, David Owen, Bill Rodgers and Shirley Williams – who announced the formation of a Council for Social Democracy in the Limehouse Declara-tion of 25 January 1981. The move came in response to what the Gang saw as increased left-wing dominance in the Labour Party, particularly in the left's successful campaigns for an electoral college to select the party leader and mandatory reselection of sitting MPs. The Council was not ostensibly intended to threaten Labour's unity but became the forerunner to the Social Democratic Party (SDP) which was launched two months later.

General Management Committee (GMC).   Renamed General Committee in the party reforms of the 1990s. The GMC in each Constituency Labour Party (CLP) was made up of delegates from party branches, local affiliated trade union branches and Socialist Societies and monitored MPs' activities, elected delegates to the annual party conference and formulated resolutions. The introduction of one member one vote (OMOV) reduced the influence of activists as the right to vote was shifted to individual members rather than being restricted to those willing to attend meetings.

General Strike.   The 'national strike' organised by the Trades Union Congress on 3–12 May 1926 in support of coal miners who had been locked out on 30 April following their refusal to accept longer hours and a reduction in pay. The Conservative government declared a State of Emergency as workers were withdrawn from the railways, road transport, iron and steel, construction, gas and electricity. The miners remained out for a further six months until forced back to work. The Labour leadership's view was summed up by MacDonald when he said: 'With the discussion of general strikes and Bolshevism and all that kind of thing, I have nothing to do at all. I respect the Constitution.' One result of the strike was the Trade Disputes and Trade Union Act 1927, which introduced 'contracting-out' and seriously affected Labour Party finances.

Gladstone–MacDonald Pact.   A secret agreement reached in 1903 between Liberal and Labour leaders by which the Liberal Party headquarters promised to use its influence on local parties to give Labour Representation Committee candidates a free run in 30 constituencies at the next general election. The agreement explicitly states that Labour candidates so helped would be those who supported the general objects of the Liberal Party. In addition, Labour would have to show an equal solicitude towards Liberals in constituencies in which it had influence. Only MacDonald and Hardie knew of the agreement and persistently denied its existence. In the 1906 general election 24 of the successful 29 Labour candidates were unopposed by Liberals, although a further five Labour candidates were elected despite Liberal opposition. Labour remained weak in parliamentary terms but the Liberals had undermined their own position as the sole opposition to Conservatism.

GLC.   See Greater London Council.

Gradualism.   The measured progress towards a socialist society through constitutional rather than revolutionary methods, associated particularly with the Fabians. The leading Fabian Sidney Webb declared at the 1925 Labour Party conference: 'Let me insist on what our opponents habitually ignore, and indeed what they seem intellectually incapable of understanding, namely the inevitable gradualness of our scheme of change.'

Grant affair. A source of embarrassment for Labour prime minister MacDonald (1866–1937) when it was revealed in September 1924 that he has been given a Daimler car by his friend, the wealthy Scottish biscuit magnate Alexander Grant. Shortly afterwards Grant had been given a baronetcy. MacDonald suffered the indignity of being harried with shouts of 'Biscuits, biscuits' in the House of Commons. Although nothing untoward had in fact occurred (Grant had been nominated for the honour by the previous Conservative government), the irritation of publicity over the affair allegedly affected MacDonald's judgement in dealing with the far more serious Campbell case.

'Great betrayal'. The formation of a predominantly Conservative National Government by Ramsay MacDonald (1866–1937) and his associates in 1931 which scarred the Labour Party for many years and influenced its attitude towards co-operation with other parties. In response to Trades Union Congress opposition to a cut in unemployment benefit, MacDonald had told the Labour Cabinet: 'If we yield to the TUC now, we shall never be able to call our bodies or souls or intelligence our own.' There was, however, an implication in the phrase that as MacDonald had betrayed the party it was unnecessary to consider how far the weakness of the 1929–31 Labour government had been a failure of the party's conception of socialism.

Greater London Council (GLC). The governing body for London from 1963 to 1986, established as an enlarged London County Council (LCC). Labour complained that the inclusion of the outer suburbs was intended to ensure a Conservative majority but Labour secured control of the GLC for most of its existence. The GLC had strategic authority over housing, planning and later took responsibility for London Transport. Under the leadership of Ken Livingstone from 1981, the GLC initiated radical transport and equal opportunities policies. The GLC's strident anti-government stance (County Hall, for example, faced Parliament across the Thames and displayed London's unemployment figures prominently) prompted its abolition in 1986. In May 1998 Londoners voted in a referendum for the establishment of a Greater London Authority (with far fewer powers than the GLC).

Groundnuts scheme. Attempt initiated by the Labour government in 1947 to use unproductive land in the colony of Tanganyika (now Tanzania) for groundnut production. The project – administered by the Overseas Food Corporation – was abandoned in 1950, having lost £30 million, with criticisms that the scheme had been undertaken with no serious analysis of soil or weather conditions in East Africa. The term was used for many years after by the party's opponents as an example of

Labour's overall economic incompetence. There was a similarly unsuccessful eggs scheme in the British colony of Gambia.

Guild socialism.   A form of syndicalism based on the medieval guild system which had some influence in sections of the Labour movement in the early twentieth century. A.J. Penty's *The Restoration of the Guild System*, published in 1906, was an influential text and its ideas were developed by A.R. Orage (through his journal *New Age*) and S.G. Hobson. Guild socialism feared the bureaucratisation apparently inherent in state nationalisation of industry and advocated workers' control through the trade unions. Guild socialism envisaged a society in which unions would represent working-class interests by control of industry while the state would protect the interests of the consumer through Parliament. A National Guilds League was formed in 1915 by 500 defectors from the Fabian Society, with G.D.H. Cole (1866–1937) and Harold Laski (1893–1950) among its prominent supporters. A number of trade unions became affiliates. A nation-wide National Building Guild was established in 1920 to construct houses under government contract but its collapse provoked the end of the movement and the League was dissolved in 1925. However, closer links with the Labour Party which grew from the increasing politicisation of the trade unions, together with the 1917 Bolshevik revolution and the rise of the Communist Party, had already weakened the attraction of direct workers' control.

Hard left.   Term used to describe a broad alliance of Labour Party groups in the late 1970s and early 1980s, including the Campaign for Labour Party Democracy (CLPD), the overtly Trotskyist Socialist Organiser and the Labour Co-ordinating Committee, together with many non-aligned socialists. The hard left operated at a national level for party constitutional reforms which would give greater influence to activists, and at constituency level against what was seen as the paternalism of Labour local authorities. The hard left was able to alter policy on reselection of Labour MPs, the establishment of an electoral college to choose the party leader, and came close to winning the deputy leadership for Tony Benn in 1981. The hard left found its greatest strength in local government, particularly in inner London, and led to the formation of the Campaign Group of Labour MPs. Hard-left influence declined after the 1983 general election defeat, the election of Neil Kinnock as party leader and the defeat of the 1984–85 miners' strike.

ILP.   See Independent Labour Party.

Independent Labour Party (ILP).   Formed in 1893, the ILP was one of the important founding members of the Labour Representation Committee (LRC) in 1900. From that point the ILP was the main area of activity for the left in the Labour Party and, although affiliated to Labour, maintained its own conferences and political agenda and fielded its own parliamentary candidates. Many of the most prominent Labour Party leaders – including MacDonald and Snowden – were ILP members. There were, however, early difficulties in the relationship between the ILP and Labour and by 1907 the ILP's left wing was threatening to disaffiliate from the Labour Party because of dissatisfaction with its achievements. ILP membership increased after 1918, as did clashes over policy. Although the ILP rejected affiliation to the Third (Communist) International in 1920, it did leave the Second International, becoming for a short period a member of the Second-and-a-Half International, which attempted to reconcile the chasm between revolutionary and parliamentary socialism. The election of the left-wing Clydeside group of MPs intensified divisions between the ILP and Labour. By 1925 membership of the increasingly radical ILP was estimated at approaching 50,000. At its conference, the ILP declared its role in the Labour Party to be the development 'in detail the Socialist objectives of the movement'. The ILP's radical programme *Socialism in Our Time* of 1926 provided a marked contrast to the Labour Party's attempt to be a cross-class party of the nation. In 1929 37 ILP MPs were elected and they proved to be among the most vociferous critics of the 1929–31 Labour government. At the ILP's 1930 conference, delegates agreed that ILP MPs should vote against the government where it acted in conflict with ILP policy. In 1932 the ILP voted to disaffiliate from Labour, although a significant minority chose to leave the ILP and remain Labour Party members. As the ILP attempted to work with the Communists in anti-fascist activity (and the Communists saw the ILP as an area to recruit supporters for itself), membership declined rapidly from 17,000 in 1932 to 11,000 in 1933. By 1935 it had fallen to a little over 4,000. In 1935, of 17 candidates only four were returned, all in what had become its Glasgow heartland. After the death of their leader James Maxton (1885–1946), the two remaining ILP MPs rejoined Labour. In the 1950 and 1951 general elections, the ILP fielded three candidates and two in 1955 and 1959. All lost their deposits.

In Place of Fear.   A testament of socialist faith produced by Labour left-winger Aneurin Bevan (1897–1960) in 1952 – much of which was made up of earlier writings – which revealed his (and the Labour left's) difficulty in coming to terms with changes wrought by post-war affluence and the transformation for which he himself had been responsible in developing the Welfare State. Bevan summed up the left-wing position when he wrote: 'The socialist party . . . rushes to the defence of state spending; their supporters are the poor and the defenceless who most need it.'

In Place of Strife.   White Paper on industrial relations reform introduced by the left-wing Employment Secretary Barbara Castle in January 1968, drafted by – among others – Tony Benn and Peter Shore. The document's proposals divided the Labour Party and threatened relations between the party and the trade union movement. The main purpose of the reforms was to stem the growing incidence of unofficial strikes and the power of shop stewards, and there were provisions in subsequent draft legislation to take both strikers and unions to court. Home Secretary James Callaghan emerged as the leading opponent in the Labour Cabinet and legislation was dropped when the Trades Union Congress promised to develop machinery to police disputes.

'Irreversible shift of power and wealth'.   A misquotation of a term used in the party's radical document, *Labour's Programme, 1973*, adopted at the October 1973 conference. The document, on which Labour fought the February 1974 general election, promised an 'irreversible transfer of wealth and power to working people and their families'. The expression was used by the party's left into the 1980s to push for more fundamentalist socialist policies.

John Smith House.   Headquarters of the Labour Party in Walworth Road, South London, named after John Smith (1938–94), leader of the party from July 1992 until his sudden death in May 1994. In the run-up to the 1997 general election the party's administrative machinery was moved closer to Parliament at Millbank Tower.

July measures.   Financial programme announced by the Labour government on 20 July 1966 designed to support sterling and avoid devaluation as Britain faced an estimated £350 million deficit in the balance of payments. The crisis was intensified by a seamen's strike. The measures included stricter hire purchase controls, higher duties on alcohol, tobacco and petrol, curbs on overseas civilian and military expenditure, and a six-month wage and price freeze. July 1966 was seen as a turning point for the Labour government which had been elected with an increased majority in the spring. The measures were attacked by the left of the party; the hopes for economic expansion represented by the setting up of the Department for Economic Affairs in 1964 (and the subsequent expansionist National Plan of 1965) were dashed; and the government became increasingly unpopular with the electorate. Despite the measures, the pound was devalued in November 1967.

Keep Left.   A left-wing grouping in the Parliamentary Labour Party (PLP) which emerged in November 1946. The group produced a pamphlet of the same name in April 1947 written by Richard Crossman,

Michael Foot and Ian Mikardo and signed by 12 other Labour MPs. Keep Left opposed what it called the Labour government's 'Cold War' policies and advocated a 'third force' position built on a European socialist alliance which would reduce Britain's dependence on the United States while keeping a distance from the Communist bloc.

Labour and the Nation.   Labour's programme drafted by R.H. Tawney (1880–1962) and endorsed by the 1928 Birmingham party conference. The document, which was a longer but less precise version of *Labour and the New Social Order*, declared that Labour was a socialist party which intended to organise industry in the interest 'not of the small minority (less than 10 per cent of the population) who own the greater part of the land, the plant and the equipment without access to which their fellow countrymen can neither work nor live, but of all who bring their contribution of useful service to the common stock'. Socialism was equated with an extension of state intervention in economic and social affairs. A Labour government would 'end the capitalist dictatorship in which democracy finds its most insidious and most relentless foe'. In his introduction, party leader MacDonald said that Labour 'is not concerned with patching the rents in a bad system, but with transforming Capitalism into Socialism'. Among the practical proposals were the repeal of the 1927 Trade Disputes and Trade Union Act, increased unemployment benefit, the restoration of the seven-hour working day in the mining industry, and a statutory maximum 48-hour working week. The programme continued the longstanding Labour view that crises and depression were inherent in the capitalist system but put forward no proposals for what a Labour government confronted by crisis would do, as the events of 1929–31 demonstrated graphically. Snowden, Chancellor in the 1929–31 Labour government, later revealed that he had never read the document.

Labour and the New Social Order.   Party programme written by Sidney Webb (1st Lord Passfield, 1859–1947) and adopted at a special conference in Nottingham in February 1918. The 27-point programme proposed a new social order based on the 'socialisation of industry' and 'deliberately planned co-operation in production and distribution for the benefit of all who participate by hand or brain'. The first point described the 'gradual building up of a new social order based not on internecine conflict, inequality of riches and dominion over subject classes, subject races or a subject sex, but on deliberately planned co-operation in production and distribution, the sympathetic approach to a healthy equality, the widest possible participation in power both economic and political and the general consciousness of consent which characterises a true democracy'. The new order was to be based on 'four pillars':

(1) universal enforcement of a national minimum (through increased social security and full employment; (2) democratic control of industry through the nationalisation of the railways, coal mining, electricity, industrial life insurance, and alcohol manufacture and retailing (the form democratic control should take was not specified and workers' control was mentioned only in passing); (3) a revolution in national finance (through equality in taxation and a capital levy to reduce the National Debt); and (4) the use surplus wealth for the common good.

Labour Co-ordinating Committee. A 'hard left' grouping within the Labour Party formed in 1978 as a wide alliance of socialists committed to inner-party constitutional reform to strengthen the authority of activists and to encourage extra-parliamentary political militancy. Following the election of Neil Kinnock as leader in 1983, the group supported his modernising programme and became increasingly 'soft left'.

Labour Electoral Association. Formed at the TUC's Southport conference in 1886 as the Labour Electoral Committee and renamed in the following year, the Association was intended to encourage support for politically independent working-class candidates at parliamentary and municipal elections. The Association was, however, unsuccessful, particularly because of the failure of the 12 Lib-Lab MPs elected at the 1885 general election to assert themselves as anything more than a section of the Liberal Party.

Labour Independent Group. A Labour left-wing grouping formed in 1949 following the expulsion of MPs John Platts Mills and Konni Zilliacus for what were alleged to be persistent attacks on the party's foreign policies, with suggestions that they were Communist sympathisers. The expulsions were intended as a warning to Labour dissidents to follow the leadership's line, particularly in the area of foreign policy. The Group, the central figures of which were Mills, Zilliacus, D.N. Pritt and Lester Hutchinson, advocated co-operation with Communists and was particularly impressed by Yugoslavia's assertion of independence from Soviet domination in 1949.

Labour Leader. The newspaper of the Independent Labour Party (ILP) which was renamed the *New Leader* in 1922 and came under the dynamic editorship of H.N. Brailsford (1873–1958) from 1922 to 1926. In 1926 the ILP announced in the *New Leader* that it had set 'before itself the object of winning Socialism for this generation' as a preliminary to issuing the document *Socialism in Our Time.* The paper, which appeared weekly, had a literary as well as political influence.

Labour Representation Committee (LRC). The forerunner to the Labour Party formed at a meeting at the Memorial Hall in London on 27 February 1900 with the sole objective of securing independent representation of working men in Parliament. The founding conference had arisen as the result of a gradual shift towards socialist parties by trade unions which felt under increasing legal pressure. A Trades Union Conference (TUC) resolution in 1898 had called for the working class to support socialist parties. The conference was made up of 129 delegates representing 570,000 trade unionists (less than a quarter of TUC membership) together with the 861-strong Fabian Society (one delegate), the Independent Labour Party (ILP), with seven delegates for its 13,000 members, and the Social Democratic Federation (SDF), with 9,000 members represented by four delegates. An SDF resolution calling for a 'distinct party' with a programme of 'class war' was rejected, with the ILP leading the opposition. Ramsay MacDonald of the ILP was appointed LRC secretary. The LRC was fundamentally an organisation of reformists and evolutionary socialists allied in Parliament to the Liberals and intent on winning trade union support. The LRC's pledge to seek reversal of the 1901 Taff Vale judgment encouraged trade union support and by 1903 there were 861,000 affiliated trade union members. By 1905 there were only five LRC MPs but the 1903 Gladstone–MacDonald Pact helped increase this to 30 following the 1906 general election. In 1906 the LRC became the Labour Party.

Labour Research Department. See Fabian Research Department.

Labour's Immediate Programme. Policy document largely drafted by Hugh Dalton (1887–1962) and adopted unanimously at the 1937 Labour Party conference. The document, though marking a step back from the radicalism of *For Socialism and Peace,* provided a blueprint for the 1945–51 Labour government, with a commitment to schemes of social welfare and full employment, the public ownership of the Bank of England, electricity and gas supply, the mines, the railways and sections of transport, and the state-directed location of industry. On rearmament, the document committed a future Labour government to maintain forces adequate for the defence of Britain and its obligations to the Commonwealth and the League of Nations.

LCC. See London County Council.

Left Book Club. Radical imprint launched by the publisher Victor Gollancz in May 1936. The club's books were selected by Gollancz and the prominent Labour Party members John Strachey and Harold Laski to avoid criticisms that the choice was dominated by Communist interests. However, the first book offered by the club was *World Politics 1918–1935* by the leading Communist theoretician Rajani Palme Dutt and many of the succeeding books argued for the Communist Popular Front tactic. The club had 57,000 members at its peak with an estimated readership of half a million for each title. One-third of the titles published were written by Communists. In 1938 the club established a thousand local discussion groups and began producing the monthly *Left News*. The club was wound up in 1945 when, according to Gollancz, Labour's general election victory made its existence no longer necessary. The Labour Party set up its own Labour Book Service which failed to achieve an equivalent success.

Lib-Lab Pact. (1) The Gladstone–MacDonald Pact of 1903; (2) the agreement which kept Callaghan's government in power in 1977–78 with Liberal support. In return for their support, the Liberals were consulted on major issues and allowed a partial veto over policy. Labour had been elected with a majority of three in October 1974 but suffered a number of defeats at the hands of the Opposition. In March, having negotiated the pact with the Liberals, the government survived a Conservative censure motion by 322 votes to 298. In January 1978 the Liberal leader, David Steel, announced his party's intention to continue the pact into the summer. The agreement was terminated in August but the government was able to survive until May 1979. In July 1997, Blair invited the Liberal Democrats to sit on a Cabinet committee to discuss constitutional reform and other issues of mutual interests. Both parties denied that this represented the opening of a new Lib-Lab Pact. In November 1998 the Labour and Liberal Democrat leaders issued a joint statement extending co-operation into other areas.

Lib-Labs. Trade union representatives elected as Liberal MPs before the formal establishment of the Labour Party. Lib-Labs, with their roots in nonconformity, temperance and Liberal Radicalism, dominated working-class politics from 1860 but were gradually undermined by the economic instability which manifested itself in unemployment, the extension of the franchise to male manual workers in 1867 and 1884 and the perceived failure of the Liberals to meet the needs of an increasingly class conscious working class, all of which culminated in the formation of the Labour Representation Committee (LRC) in 1900 and the Labour Party in 1906.

Living wage. See *Socialism in Our Time*.

London County Council (LCC). The government of inner London, the capture of which by Labour under Herbert Morrison (Baron Morrison of Lambeth, 1888–1959) in 1934 marked a revival in the party's fortunes following the 1931 collapse. Labour went on to hold power on the LCC for much of the period until its replacement by the Greater London Council (GLC) in 1965.

London Labour Briefing.   The principal organisation of the Labour left in London in the early 1980s, launched in February 1980 and including Ken Livingstone, Ted Knight (leader of Lambeth Council) and Jeremy Corbyn (later an MP). The organisation's first campaign – to win control of the Greater London Council (GLC) for the left – succeeded in 1981 when Livingstone ousted Andrew Macintosh to become GLC leader. Briefing then launched Target 82 to encourage Labour-controlled local authorities to confront the Conservative government, encouragement that bore particular fruit in Lambeth and on the GLC.

'Longest suicide note in history'.   Expression used by the Labour MP Gerald Kaufmann (born 1930) to describe the manifesto on which the party fought the 1983 general election, *The New Hope for Britain*. The document – at over 30 pages – included every policy proposal issued by Labour in the previous four years during a period of intense left-wing influence and promised to end unemployment with an 'emergency programme of action', to repeal Conservative trade union legislation, increase benefits, extend the rights of women and ethnic minorities, and to carry out a policy of unilateral nuclear disarmament.

Loony left.   Pejorative description used by opponents (and sometimes within the Labour Party itself) in the 1980s and 1990s of left-wing-controlled Labour local authorities – specifically Brent, Haringey, Lambeth and (until its abolition in 1986) the Greater London Council (GLC). The loony left was alleged to be over-concerned with the interests of ethnic minorities, gays and lesbians and feminists and prone to socialist rhetoric. The authorities concerned were generally in office in areas of intense inner-city deprivation.

Low Pay Commission.   Appointed in June 1997 by the Labour government and chaired by Professor George Bain of the London Business School to recommend the level at which the national minimum wage promised in the party's general election manifesto should be set. In May 1998 the Labour government set a minimum hourly wage for adults of £3.60.

Lynskey Tribunal.   Established by the Labour government in 1948 under the chairmanship of Mr Justice Lynskey to investigate allegations that Board of Trade ministers and civil servants had taken bribes. The main charges were made by Sidney Stanley, a businessman who had attempted to profit by his alleged influence with important figures. Although Stanley was exposed as a liar and no evidence of bribery was found, junior trade minister John Belcher resigned for accepting gifts and a trade union-nominated Bank of England director was reprimanded. The enquiry also had an adverse effect on the career of Hugh Dalton (1887–1962) who, though not involved in the main case, had been offered a directorship by Stanley following his resignation as Chancellor of the Exchequer over a budget leak.

Lyons v Wilkins.   One of a series of cases which convinced the trade unions of the need for independent political organisation. In 1896 Lyons – a leather goods manufacturer – took action against Wilkins – general secretary of the Amalgamated Trade Society of Fancy Leather Workers – over picketing at his factory during a strike. The judge in the case ruled that picketing, which had become legal in the 1870s, that went beyond merely communicating information was illegal. A High Court case in 1899 confirmed that picketing to encourage workers to strike was against the law. The perception of many trade unionists that cases of this kind were in the interests of employers pushed them towards political activity and co-operation with socialist parties.

Marshall Aid.   Post-Second World War aid to Europe from the United States offered by Secretary of State George C. Marshall (1880–1959) and administered by the Organisation for European Economic Co-operation which began functioning in April 1948. Between 1948 and 1952 Europe received US$17,000 million to assist its economic recovery. The Soviet bloc's refusal to accept assistance helped entrench Cold War divisions. Aid to Britain ended in December 1950. One US politician objected to the provision of aid to a Labour government which, he said, intended to use it to preserve the British Empire abroad and finance socialism at home.

May Report.   The report issued by a Committee on National Expenditure, appointed by the Labour government in February 1931 under Sir George May, former chairman of the Prudential Assurance Company. Chancellor Snowden saw the committee as providing a useful background to the cuts in public expenditure which he regarded as necessary. The committee consisted of two representatives of Labour, two Conservatives and two Liberals. May's report predicted a budget deficit of £120 million for the year 1932–33 and recommended a £24 million increase in taxation combined with £96 million reductions in public spending. Among the cuts were to be 20% reductions in unemployment benefit and public service wages. The report, which the *Economist* at the time said 'seriously overpaints the gloom', heightened an already serious financial crisis. The Cabinet's failure to agree even on a compromise 10% unemployment benefit cut led directly to the August 1931 collapse and the formation of the National Government.

'Memorandum on the Causes and Remedies for Labour Unrest'. A text produced by G.D.H Cole (1889–1959) and leading Labour figure Arthur Henderson (1863–1935) to the National Industrial Conference in March 1919. Cole was secretary of the workers' side of the conference. The memorandum was a clear statement of Cole's guild socialist views and referred to a 'desire to substitute a democratic system of public ownership and production for use with an increasing element of control by the organized workers themselves for the existing capitalist organization of industry'. The conference of employers' and trade union representatives had been called by Lloyd George's Coalition government and was intended to meet regularly. The trade union representatives withdrew in July 1921.

Merrie England. Written by Robert Blatchford (1851–1943) as a series of articles for his socialist newspaper the *Clarion* and published in book form in 1893, *Merrie England* was the first popular socialist work and sold over two million copies in Britain and the United States. The work's popularity took the circulation of the *Clarion* up to 60,000. The prominent Labour Party pioneer J.R. Clynes (1869–1949) described *Merrie England* as 'the most original contribution to the making of socialists in this country which had ever been known.'

Militant Labour. See Militant Tendency.

Militant Tendency. A Trotskyist grouping – emerging from schisms in the Revolutionary Communist Party of the 1940s to become the Revolutionary Socialist League and then Militant in the 1960s – which claimed descent from the Fourth International. Militant began a policy of entryism into the Labour Party in 1964 when its weekly newspaper came under the editorship of Peter Taafe. Ted Grant was another major figure. Militant had an unvarying programme built on the imminent collapse of capitalism and called for nationalisation of 250 major monopolies, banks and insurance companies under workers' control. Militant was, however, out of sympathy with many of the concerns of the Labour left, for example, equal opportunities for women and ethnic minorities and community and sexual politics. However, through the tactic of entryism, the group was able to build a national organisation using constituency Labour parties as a source of recruitment, particularly among younger members of the party. Warnings to the Labour Party National Executive – particularly in the Underhill Report – appeared to be largely ignored but in 1982 membership of Militant – its members always denied any membership and claimed to be simply 'supporters' of the newspaper – was ruled to be incompatible with Labour Party membership. Long-drawn-out proceedings were begun to expel the five-strong editorial board of the newspaper. At the 1983 general election, two Militant supporters – Terry Fields and Dave Nellist – were elected as Labour MPs. In addition, Militant supporters won control of the Labour group on Liverpool City Council, with council deputy leader Derek Hatton as the dominant figure. The council began systematic confrontation with the Conservative government which embarrassed the Labour Party leadership. In 1985 Labour leader Neil Kinnock launched a dramatic attack on Militant's conduct in Liverpool at the Labour Party conference and an enquiry – followed by a National Constitutional Committee – was set up to organise expulsions from the Labour Party. Nevertheless, two further Militant supporters were elected as Labour MPs at the 1987 general election. The Labour leadership's opportunity to move firmly against Militant came in 1990 when a Militant candidate opposed a Labour Party candidate in Liverpool and suffered a decisive defeat. With its leading figures expelled from the Labour Party, Militant split between those who advocated continuing the tactic of entryism and those favouring the formation of a new revolutionary socialist party – Militant Labour. In Scotland, a new party won council seats in 1992, largely because of the effective organisation of an anti-poll tax campaign, but lost all but one in 1995. In January 1997 Militant relaunched itself as the Socialist Party.

Millbank.   Headquarters of the Labour Party at Millbank Tower, a short distance along the River Thames from Parliament, to which the party moved from its former offices in Walworth Road during the run-up to the 1997 general election.

Mond–Turner conference.   Post-general strike renewal of relations between employers and the TUC prompted by Sir Alfred Mond (Lord Melchett, 1868–1930), founder and head of Imperial Chemical Industries (ICI). The talks brought together a representative group of employers and members of the Trades Union Congress (TUC) General Council, including Ben Turner, Ernest Bevin, Walter Citrine and J.H. Thomas, to discuss industrial relations and issues raised by the 'rationalisation' of industry. The discussions, which were denounced by the left as collaborationist, achieved little in immediate practical terms but influenced the attitude of sections of the unions and the Labour Party in the 1930s.

Mosley Memorandum.   The radical proposals to combat unemployment presented to the Labour Cabinet by Chancellor of the Duchy of Lancaster Sir Oswald Mosley (1896–1980) in February 1930. The proposals included increased pensions to encourage early retirement and expand purchasing power; the protection of industry through import controls; bulk purchase agreements with overseas producers, particularly in the Colonies and Dominions; the development of British agriculture; and the rationalisation of industry under public control. The abandonment of free trade and the inevitable increases in public expenditure aroused intense opposition from the Treasury and Chancellor of the Exchequer Snowden. The Labour Party conference in October narrowly rejected Mosley's motion that his proposals should be examined by the National Executive.

Municipal socialism. The policy adopted by Labour councillors returned in 1919 – particularly in London boroughs – of using their powers to apply collective solutions to the problems of bad housing, poor health and general insecurity. Labour local government attempted to create a proto-welfare state through, for example, the elected Boards of Guardians, paying higher levels of poor relief to the unemployed, and encouraging the construction of municipal baths, housing and clinics which – as well as providing necessary services – boosted local employment. The expression was briefly revived by left-wing Labour councils in the 1980s during a period of Conservative dominance in national politics.

'Naked into the conference chamber'. Dismissive expression used by Labour left-winger (and Shadow Foreign Secretary) Aneurin Bevan (1897–1960) at the 1957 Labour Party conference which marked his break with his allies over the issue of unilateral nuclear disarmament. Bevan described calls for unilateral nuclear disarmament as an 'emotional spasm' and said that the policy would send a British Foreign Secretary 'naked into the conference chamber'. The party conference went on to reject the policy overwhelmingly.

National Board for Price and Incomes. Established by the Labour government in 1965, the board had no statutory powers to set prices or incomes but, by being requested by the government to investigate a proposed increase and issue a report, acted as a delaying device. The board was abolished by the Conservative government in 1972.

National Council of Labour. Formed in 1920 as part of the reorganisation of the Trades Union Congress (TUC), the Council replaced the former Joint Board and included representatives of the newly formed TUC General Council, the Labour Party National Executive and the Parliamentary Labour Party.

National Democratic Party (NDP). Section of the British Socialist Party (BSP) which supported participation in the First World War, forming the Socialist National Defence Committee which became the British Workers' League and then the NDP. Formed in 1915 by anti-Socialist members of the Labour movement who went on to support Lloyd

George's Coalition government, the party was led by G.N. Barnes, who succeeded Henderson in the War Cabinet when Henderson withdrew in 1917. Among its leading members were Robert Blatchford, Ben Tillett and Will Thorne. When Labour ended its support for the Coalition, NDP members remained in the government. The party fielded 28 candidates in the 1918 general election, 15 of whom were returned, but was dissolved in 1923.

National Enterprise Board.   Set up by the Labour government in 1975 under its Industry Act, the board was part of Labour's attempt to extend public ownership by buying shares to give a controlling interest in private companies or lending money for investment. In 1977 the government took a majority shareholding in the ailing car manufacturer British Leyland and vested the share in the Board.

National Executive Committee (NEC).   Elected annually at the party conference, the NEC acts as Labour's ruling body and is made up of representatives from the constituency parties, the trade unions, socialist societies and the women's section. The party treasurer is also a member, as are the party leader and deputy leader. The National Executive's composition and the methods of its election were drastically transformed by *Partnership into Power*, adopted at the 1997 party conference.

National Guilds League.   See Guild socialism.

National Health Service (NHS).   The crowning achievement of the 1945–51 Labour government, established in 1948 by Minister of Health Aneurin Bevan (1897–1960). The NHS amalgamated hospitals administered by charities, the private sector and local authorities into a single organisation financed through the National Insurance system and taxation. Facing resistance from the medical profession, Bevan was forced to compromise on the continuation of private medical treatment and the status of doctors. The NHS was intended to be free at the point of delivery but in 1951 Chancellor Gaitskell imposed charges on spectacles and false teeth to meet the needs of an expanding arms programme. Bevan, together with junior ministers Wilson and Freeman, resigned from the Labour government. One of the first acts of the 1964 Labour government was to abolish prescription charges imposed by the Conservatives but these were then reimposed in the long campaign to defend the pound. By the 1960s the NHS had become Europe's largest employer outside the Red Army and, popular though it remained, there were criticisms of its bureaucracy and sluggishness. The Conservative governments of the 1980s and 1990s introduced an internal market which the Labour government elected in 1997 promised to dismantle.

National Joint Council.   See National Council of Labour.

National Labour Party.   The grouping set up by the 20 Labour MPs who supported Ramsay MacDonald's formation of the National Government in 1931. At the October 1931 general election, 20 National Labour candidates took 341,370 votes and 13 were elected. In the 1935 general election, the party fielded 20 candidates, gaining 340,000 votes and the election of eight MPs. When the party dissolved itself in 1945, seven MPs remained, three of whom retired. In the general election, two were defeated as National Labour candidates, while of the two who stood as Independents, one was elected.

National Left-Wing Movement.   Body set up by the Communist Party in December 1925 to extend its influence in constituency parties when the Labour Party nationally was making strenuous efforts to remove Communists. A number of constituency Labour parties refused to accept the decision of the 1925 conference to exclude Communists and 54 local Labour parties were represented at the Movement's second conference in September 1927. The Movement was dissolved in 1929 when the Communists took on a political line which involved refusing to co-operate with Labour members. The Movement had some success in London and in South Wales and by 1927, following the collapse of the General Strike, claimed 150,000 members. In the period 1926–29 Labour's NEC had dissolved 27 constituency parties for their involvement with the Movement and had warned a number of others. The Communists made a parallel attempt to influence the trade unions through the National Minority Movement.

National Plan.   Introduced by deputy party leader George Brown (1914–85) and his Department of Economic Affairs in September 1965, representing for the first time in Britain, in the words of its introduction, 'a statement of Government policy and a commitment to action by the Government'. The plan was intended to achieve a 25% increase in national output by 1970, with an annual average growth of 3.8%. There was a commitment to keep public expenditure growth at 4.25% a year, to increase export volume by 5.25% annually and to make necessary improvements in management training. There were, however, few examples of how the planning process would function or be managed. Even before the plan's launch, Brown had admitted in Cabinet that growth in 1965–66 would only be 1% and that unemployment would increase by almost half a million. Any hopes the plan had of fulfilment were dashed by the deflationary July 1966 measures which put defence of the pound before expansion.

Nationalisation.   The taking into public ownership or control of an industry or enterprise with – in the British case – compensation for the former private owners. Clause Four of the Labour Party's 1918 Constitution set out the objective of the 'common ownership of the means of production, distribution, and exchange, and the best obtainable system of popular administration and control of each industry or service'. Although this did not necessarily imply state ownership, the 1945–51 Labour government – which nationalised the Bank of England, coal, cables and wireless, electricity, iron and steel, transport and civil aviation – adopted what was described as the Morrisonian model (after Herbert Morrison, 1888–1959), with a centralised hierarchy of management and no element of workers' participation or consumer consultation.

NATO.   See North Atlantic Treaty Organisation.

NDP.   See National Democratic Party.

New Fabian Research Bureau.   Established in April 1931 by G.D.H. Cole with himself as secretary, Clement Attlee as chairman and Hugh Gaitskell as assistant secretary, and the membership of a new generation of economists, including Evan Durbin. Cole remained secretary until 1935, serving as chairman from 1937 to 1939. The 1932 party conference accepted the Bureau's proposal that the nationalisation of joint-stock banks was an essential precondition for socialist planning. This had been in 'A Labour Programme for Action', produced by Harold Laski and William Mellor, which caused some controversy by arguing for arming against possible capitalist resistance to a Labour government. In 1939 the Bureau amalgamated with the Fabian Society with a revised constitution.

New Labour.   Term used to describe the project of Tony Blair (born 1953, party leader from 1992, prime minister from 1997) to continue the modernisation of the Labour Party to enable it to win power following four successive general election defeats. New Labour attempted to break with 'old Labour' by revising Clause Four, weakening links with the trades unions, and accepting the Thatcherite agenda of low non-wage labour costs, lower levels of social protection and deregulated labour markets. The party went on to gain a landslide victory in the 1997 election but there were criticisms that New Labour had abandoned the historic aim of an equal society.

New Leader.   See *Labour Leader.*

New Left in New Labour.   An informal left grouping in the Labour Party which emerged in the mid-1990s. Unlike the Campaign Group,

New Left attempted to work with the grain of New Labour reforms rather than against, and appeared to be gaining greater influence because of this. In July 1997 the group responded to the party leadership's *Partnership into Power* proposals for inner-party reform by calling for the retention of a substantial element of trade union influence in party affairs and for the continuation of genuine debate at party conferences.

New Party.   Set up by the former Labour minister Sir Oswald Mosley (1896–1980) in February 1931. In May 1930 Mosley resigned from the government following the rejection by the Cabinet of his Memorandum setting out proposals to combat rising unemployment. In December he published his proposals in a Manifesto which was signed by 17 Labour MPs. Six of these – Mosley himself, Lady Cynthia Mosley, Oliver Baldwin, W.J. Brown, Robert Forgan and John Strachey – became the founding members of the New Party. Brown and Baldwin left almost immediately and Strachey in June. At the 1931 general election, the New Party fielded 24 candidates. All the New Party's MPs lost their seats and the party's candidates – except Mosley – lost their deposits. In 1932, impressed by the apparent success of Mussolini in Italy and increasingly contemptuous of parliamentary politics, Mosley transformed the party into the British Union of Fascists.

New Statesman and Nation.   A journal founded as the *New Statesman* in 1913 by Sidney and Beatrice Webb and which amalgamated with the Liberal *Nation* in 1930. The *New Statesman* – nicknamed the 'Staggers and Naggers' – was at its most influential under the editorship of Kingsley Martin (1897–1969), from 1931 to 1960 when it had a distinctively Fabian and moderate socialist tone. The journal's highest circulation was 93,000 in 1966 under the editorship of Paul Johnson. The *New Statesman* then went into decline and, following a shift to the radical left in the 1980s, was relaunched in 1993, becoming supportive but not uncritical of the Blairite New Labour project.

1918 Labour Party Constitution.   The Constitution transformed the Labour Party from a loose association of trade unions and socialist societies into a nationally-organised party with individual members in local branches with implementation Clause Four as the party's ultimate objective. The provision for a new category of individual membership reflected the concern of Sidney Webb (1st Lord Passfield, 1859–1947) that Labour should not be an exclusively working-class party and opened up Labour's potential to become a mass party. Previously, the only route into the party for a non-trade unionist had been through a socialist society. In 1918, the membership of the main affiliated societies – the British Socialist Party (BSP), Fabian Society and the Independent Labour

Party (ILP) – totalled only 75,000. The new Constitution also made it easier for women to become active in the party. The annual party conference was to comprise delegates from nationally-affiliated organisations and from local parties with strength in proportion to affiliated membership; membership of a new National Executive (all members of which were to be elected by the conference) was increased to 23, with 13 places allocated to the unions, five to constituency parties and four to women. The party's object was defined as 'to give effect as far as may be practicable to the principles from time to time approved by the Party Conference'. The Constitution was discussed at the party's conference in Manchester in January 1918 and adopted at a special conference in Nottingham in February. In June the party went on to adopt *Labour and the New Social Order* as its formal programme, with a commitment to a new order based on the 'socialisation of industry' and planned production and distribution 'for the benefit of all who participate by hand or brain'.

North Atlantic Treaty Organisation (NATO).   An alliance of the United Kingdom, the United States, Belgium, Canada, Denmark, France, Iceland, Luxembourg, the Netherlands and Portugal formed at the beginning of the Cold War for the collective defence of the West against what was seen as Soviet aggressive intentions. Labour Foreign Secretary Ernest Bevin (1891–1951) was a prominent proponent of the alliance which came into effect in August 1949.

'Nye'.   The affectionate nickname for the left-wing Labour MP Aneurin Bevan (1897–1960), Minister of Health from 1945 to 1951, Minister of Labour and National Service, 1951, party deputy leader from 1959 to 1960.

OMOV.   See One member one vote.

One member one vote (OMOV).   A central part of the attempt at constitutional reform in the Labour Party from the mid-1980s which culminated in the 1993 party conference. Supporters of the principle of OMOV argued that at the constituency level the system would allow the wider membership to participate more effectively in the selection of candidates, voting for the party leadership and for constituency representatives on the National Executive Committee (NEC), rather than limiting influence to activists willing to attend meetings. A further effect of this would be to weaken what was seen as the influence of the left at constituency level. But at the heart of debate over the issue was whether the trade unions would relinquish their use of the block vote at the party's annual conference, in elections to the party leadership and the selection of party candidates.

Open University.   Originally proposed as a 'University of the Air', the Open University was set up by the Labour government and began functioning in 1969 to encourage people without a formal educational background to take part-time university degrees through correspondence courses and televised lectures. One of the notable successes of the 1964–70 Labour government, the project was particularly associated with Arts Minister Jennie Lee (1904–88).

Osborne judgment.   A decision by the House of Lords in 1909 which outlawed the use of trade union payments from their funds for political campaigning and financing the Labour Party. Walter Osborne – an anti-socialist member of the Amalgamated Society of Railway Servants – had objected to his union imposing a levy on members to support the Labour Party. By August 1913, as a result of the judgment, 13 unions had been restrained from using their funds for political purposes, including the support of 16 Labour MPs. The dilemma for the Liberal government in the face of union appeals for the decision to be reversed was that this would strengthen links between the unions and the Labour Party. To refuse, however, would undermine support for the Liberals among trade unionists. The 1913 Trade Union Act did not entirely reverse the judgment but allowed unions to hold secret ballots on whether to set up political funds and allowed individual union members to 'contract-out' of contributing. By the beginning of 1914 over 400,000 trade unionists from unions with membership of 1,200,000 had voted for establishment of political funds – 298,702 for and 125,310 against.

Parliament Act 1949.   Under this legislation, the Labour government curbed the delaying powers of the House of Lords, reducing its right to hold up legislation which had been accepted by the House of Commons from two years to one year.

Parliamentary Labour Party (PLP).   The Labour Party in Parliament, consisting of all Labour MPs. The PLP meets twice weekly when the House of Commons is sitting to discuss party and policy matters. Until 1981 the PLP elected the party leader and deputy leader.

Partnership into Power.   Policy document accepted by the 1997 Labour Party conference which set out a radical programme to reform the party's decision-making processes. Policy formulation was to be removed from the conference and placed in the hands of a 175-strong National Policy Forum which would discuss policies under a two-year rolling programme. There were to be drastic changes in the composition and election of the National Executive Committee (NEC). The women's section was to be abolished and trade union representation reduced from 17 to 12, although six of these were to be women. Three places were reserved for members of the government (nominated by the prime minister), three for MPs (elected by the Parliament Labour Party) and one for the leader of the Labour Group in the European Parliament. Six were set aside for representatives elected by postal ballot of all members. Opponents on the left criticised the plan for weakening the influence of the party conference.

Plant Commission.   See Proportional representation.

PLP.   See Parliamentary Labour Party.

Policy review.   A reassessment of Labour's policy which followed the party's third successive general election defeat in 1987. The most fundamental changes which resulted were the abandonment of unilateral nuclear disarmament and nationalisation. Although the review was seen as successfully narrowing the gap between Labour and the Conservatives at the 1992 general election, there were accusations that it had become increasingly difficult to see what the Labour Party stood for.

Political levy.   Money raised by trade unions from their members to be devoted to political campaigning and, in the case of affiliated unions, providing financial support to the Labour Party. The 1909 Osborne judgment barred unions from contributing to the party from their general funds but the subsequent 1913 Trade Union Act allowed unions to establish a separate fund to which members contributed through the political levy in addition to their normal subscriptions. A member had the right to choose to 'contract-out' of paying the levy. In 1927 the Conservative government's Trade Disputes and Trade Union Act reversed the position, with members having specifically to 'contract-in' to pay the levy. The effect on the Labour Party's finances was immediate, with a fall in contributions from the unions of over a quarter. In 1946 the Labour government restored 'contracting-out'. Conservative legislation in the 1980s forced trade unions to hold ballots on the retention of political funds. By 1986 the members of 37 unions had voted to retain them.

Poplarism.   Term used to describe the form of 'municipal socialism' operated in the East End of London borough of Poplar in the 1920s. In September 1921, the borough's mayor, George Lansbury (1859–1940, party leader from 1932 to 1935), and 29 other councillors were imprisoned for refusing to levy precepts to the London County Council (LCC) on the grounds that the cost of supporting the local unemployed made this an unbearable burden on the rates. The councillors demanded that the burden should be more fairly shared between prosperous and poor boroughs. The actions of the Poplar councillors were disapproved of by the Labour Party's national leadership but left-wing MP John Wheatley (1869–1930) said their policy should be more accurately described as 'popularism'. The longer-term effect of their actions was legislation providing for the greater equality between boroughs that they had demanded.

Popular Front. Policy proposed by the Communist International in 1935 calling for co-operation of Communist, socialist and other democratic parties against fascism. As well as resistance to fascism, the Popular Front was intended to encourage radical democratic reforms stopping short of socialism. Although Popular Front governments were formed in France and Spain in 1936, the policy was regarded with suspicion by the Labour leadership in Britain where – in any case – the Communist Party was too weak to wield any significant influence. Sir Stafford Cripps and a number of his supporters were expelled from the Labour Party at the 1939 conference for supporting the Popular Front.

'Pound in your pocket'. Expression used in a television broadcast by Labour prime minister Harold Wilson on 19 November 1967 following the previous day's devaluation of the pound from $2.80 to $2.40. Wilson feared a repetition of the events following the 1949 devaluation when the public went to banks to withdraw savings. He said: 'From now on the pound abroad is worth 14% or so less in terms of other currencies. It does not mean, of course, that the pound here in Britain in your pocket or in your purse or in your bank has been devalued.' The effect, however, was to build on growing disillusionment with Wilson.

'Prawn cocktail offensive'. Term used by the media to describe a campaign of lunches held by Labour Shadow Chancellor John Smith in the run-up to the 1992 general election in which he attempted to persuade City figures that a future Labour government would be friendly to business interests.

Proportional representation. Advocates of proportional representation have had a long history in the Labour Party although, until recently, they were in a minority. The 1929 Labour government – depending on the Liberals for survival – appointed a three-party conference under former Speaker Lord Ullswater to consider electoral reform in December 1929 but this was abandoned following the refusal of both the Conservative and Labour representatives to accept a change in the first-past-the-post system. Labour appointed a commission under Professor Raymond Plant in 1991 to examine the arguments for and against and the Liberals were invited to participate in 1992. Plant's interim report in 1993 proposed proportional representation for elections to the European Parliament and to a future Scottish Parliament. Labour leader John

Smith promised a referendum on the issue when Labour returned to office. In October 1997, the Labour government announced proposals to introduce proportional representation for European Parliamentary elections and in December appointed an Electoral Reform Commission chaired by former Labour Minister Lord Jenkins to devise a system for Westminster elections in preparation for a referendum on the issue. His report in October 1998 recommended a new Alternative Vote Top-up System. A partial proportional representation system has been introduced by Labour for elections to the Scottish Parliament and Welsh Assembly.

Proscribed list.   A list of organisations, largely Communist-front bodies, membership of which was incompatible with membership of the Labour Party. The list was abolished in 1973 and replaced by a rule that party members could not be members of organisations which ran candidates against Labour at elections. Organisations within the Labour Party were required to register and problems in relations were referred to a National Constitutional Committee. However, the ending of the list eased the process of entryism conducted by, for example, Militant Tendency and led to crisis for Labour in the mid-1980s.

Reading resolution.   A composite resolution (based on a motion from the Reading constituency Labour Party) presented by left-winger Ian Mikardo at the 1944 party conference which, when passed by a show of hands, attempted to commit a future Labour government to extensive public ownership. A National Executive motion, based on the policy document *Economic Controls, Public Ownership and Full Employment*, had made no specific reference to public ownership. Mikardo's motion called for the nationalisation of banking, land, large-scale building, gas and electricity supply, heavy industry, transport, fuel and power, 'democratically controlled and operated in the national interest, with representation of the workers engaged therein and consumers'. Although some of the provisions were included in the 1945 manifesto, *Let Us Face the Future*, campaign manager Herbert Morrison told Mikardo after the conference vote: 'You realise, don't you, that you've lost us the general election?'

Red Flag, The.   The Labour Party's anthem, the words of which were written in 1889 by James Connell (1852–1929), traditionally sung at the end of each annual party conference. Labour members sang it in the Commons when their party took office in 1924 and 1945. The first verse and chorus are:

> The people's flag is deepest red:
> It shrouded oft our martyr'd dead.
> And ere their limbs grew stiff and cold,
> Their hearts' blood dyed its ev'ry fold.

Then raise the scarlet standard high,
Beneath its shade we'll live or die.
Tho' cowards flinch and traitors sneer,
We'll keep the red flag flying here.

Reselection. The system by which a sitting Labour MP had to be reselected by her or his constituency party before each general election. The system is also known, where an MP is removed, as 'deselection'. The issue provoked intense inner-party conflict from 1979 to 1981. The success of the Campaign for Labour Party Democracy (which intended to use reselection as a means of removing MPs seen as unsatisfactory by the left of the party) in winning support for the policy at the 1980 conference played a part in persuading the Gang of Four to leave Labour and form the Social Democratic Party (SDP). No more than a dozen MPs were deselected before the 1983 and 1987 elections, although the practice encouraged some MPs to exaggerate their sympathy for left-wing policies in the face of pressure from constituency activists. However, perhaps ironically, the first two MPs to be deselected were left-wingers replaced by ethnic minority candidates. The introduction of one member one vote (OMOV) in which all constituency members were able to take part in the choice of candidate weakened the power of small groups of activists to reselect.

Scottish Labour Party (SLP). Formed in January 1976 by Scots who objected to Labour's devolution proposals. The bulk of SLP members were from the Labour Party, including two MPs, Jim Sillars and John Robertson. In July 1976 both announced that they would sit as independents in the Commons. At the party's first conference in October 1976, one-third of delegates left following the expulsion of members alleged to be supporters of the far left. The SLP unsuccessfully contested three seats in the 1979 general election.

SDF.   See Social Democratic Federation.

SDP.   See Social Democratic Party.

Second International.   See page 190.

Shadow Communications Agency.   Grouping of sympathetic market researchers, psephologists and advertising professionals who provided their services free to Labour to assist with attempts at modernising the party's image from the mid-1980s onwards. The appearance of Labour publications and conference decor drastically improved and the red rose (the symbol of a number of European social democratic parties) replaced the red flag as the party emblem.

SLP.   See Scottish Labour Party.

Social compact.   See Social contract.

Social contract.   An agreement between the Labour government elected in 1974 and the Trades Union Congress (TUC) under which the unions accepted restrictions on wage increases to assist in the reduction of inflation. In return the government offered the repeal of the Conservative Industrial Relations Act 1971, price controls, and improved benefits and measures through the 'social wage' which effectively guaranteed improvements for the lower paid. The expression had first been used by James Callaghan at the 1972 Labour Party conference and agreement was reached on the outlines of the policy in 1973. The social contract's left-wing opponents criticised it as the 'social con-trick'. By 1978 the policy was faltering and its collapse led to the 'Winter of Discontent' and, effectively, to the fall of the Labour government in 1979.

Social Democratic Alliance.   Formed in June 1975 by right-wing Labour Party members to work against what they saw as growing left-wing influence and to further the aims of social democracy. Alliance attacks in October 1975 on National Executive members who spoke on platforms for the Communist *Morning Star* led to the group's denunciation by Labour leader Wilson as 'anti-party'.

Social Democratic Federation (SDF).   One of the participants in the founding conference of the Labour Representation Committee (LRC) in February 1900. The SDF derived from H.M. Hyndman's Democratic Federation, formed in March 1881, and which in 1883 adopted nationalisation as the means of production and exchange as a central objective. The SDF, which found the bulk of its strength in London and Lancashire, was represented by four delegates at the LRC founding conference. A motion it put forward calling for a 'distinct party' with a programme of 'class war' was rejected, with the Independent Labour Party (ILP) leading the opposition. Within a year, the SDF had broken with the LRC. In 1911–12, the SDF fused with a number of ILP members to form the British Socialist Party (BSP) and affiliated to the Labour Party in 1916. The BSP went on to become a founding grouping in the Communist Party of Great Britain in 1920.

Social Democratic Party (SDP).   Breakaway party formed on 16 March 1981 by the 'Gang of Four' – former Labour ministers Roy Jenkins, David Owen, Bill Rodgers and Shirley Williams. The four had been provoked into forming a 'Council for Social Democracy' – while remaining in the party – following the constitutional changes made at a special Labour Party conference in January. The SDP soon had the backing of

30 MPs (29 Labour and one Conservative) and reached 50% in opinion polls, draining off many traditional Labour Party supporters. Despite spectacular by-election victories by Shirley Williams at Crosby (Nov. 1981) and Roy Jenkins at Glasgow Hillhead (Mar. 1982), the SDP – in an Alliance with the Liberals formed in September 1981 – was able to capture only six seats at the 1983 general election (after, however, taking 25.4% of the vote with their Liberal allies to Labour's 27.6%). There were also continuing tensions with the Liberals, particularly over defence policies. The party lost further ground at the 1987 general election, despite capturing Greenwich from Labour at a by-election shortly before, and despite taking 22.6% of the vote with the Liberals. Following the general election, the SDP merged with the Liberals in January 1988 to form a Social and Liberal Democratic Party. Members opposed to the merger – led by Owen – continued with a rump SDP which collapsed in 1990. However, much of the SDP's policy appeared to pre-figure the direction taken by the Labour Party in the 1990s, particularly under the leadership of Tony Blair.

Socialism in Our Time. Independent Labour Party (ILP) policy document written by J.A. Hobson, H.N. Brailsford, E.F. Wise and A. Creech Jones and published in September 1926. Its main recommendation, based on Hobson's 'underconsumptionist' theories, was for a 'living wage' to be introduced by a future Labour government to create full employment by maintaining overall demand. The 'living wage', combined with the introduction of family allowances, was intended effectively to double average working-class income. This was to be combined with the nationalisation of basic industries. The document's sub-text was that wages would be set at a level no employer could afford, so opening the way to wider nationalisation of industry. The proposals were opposed by the Labour leadership and the trade unions. MacDonald objected that such a programme would commit a future Labour government to specific policies. The trade union objection was that the institution of family allowances could interfere with wage bargaining.

Socialist Charter. A group of activists (the 'Chartists') formed in 1968 – as dissatisfaction increased with the Labour government elected with an increased majority in 1966 – to exert constituency pressure on the Parliamentary Labour Party (PLP) and to encourage the formation of a new non-parliamentary left in the Labour Party. The group was supported in Parliament by the Tribune Group and found some support among trade union leaders. Within a year of its establishment, Socialist Charter claimed the support of over 180 party and trade union bodies. However, a combination of relative inactivity, tension between the parliamentary and extra-parliamentary strands and the activity of Trotskyists in the group, led to an early demise. The group represented an early foretaste of the divisions within the party that were to become more open in the early 1980s.

Socialist Fellowship. Founded in 1949 by, among others, Fenner Brockway (1888–1988) to work in constituency parties and trade unions for a more active socialist policy. Trotskyists practising entryism were attracted to the Fellowship which argued that only a vigorous socialist policy could save the economy and advocated sweeping state ownership of large-scale industry under workers' control. The organisation, which had the support of a small number of Labour MPs, was proscribed in April 1951 and dissolved itself soon after. Its journal, *Socialist Outlook*, continued publication until 1954.

Socialist International.   See page 190.

Socialist Labour Party.   Formed by National Union Mineworkers' president Arthur Scargill (born 1938) in May 1996 when he left the Labour Party. However, the grouping had already fielded a candidate against Labour in the Hemsworth by-election in February, taking 5.4% of the vote. The party fielded 64 candidates at the 1997 general election, all of which lost their deposits. However, party members won a number of influential trade union positions including, in May 1998, the general secretaryship of the train drivers' union.

Socialist League.   Founded as an agitational socialist ginger group in the Labour Party in succession to the Society for Socialist Inquiry and Propaganda (SSIP), with the inclusion of Independent Labour Party members who disagreed with the ILP's disaffiliation from the Labour Party in 1932. The League's inaugural meeting was held on the eve of the 1932 Labour Party conference. Its first chairman, Frank Wise, was succeeded by Stafford Cripps in 1933. Among other prominent figures associated with the League were G.D.H. Cole, Harold Laski, Sir Charles Trevelyan, William Mellor, H.N. Brailsford, Clement Attlee, Aneurin Bevan, R.H. Tawney and Ellen Wilkinson. By 1933 the League had over 2,000 members and was allowed to affiliate to the Labour Party. Problems began for the League when it flouted Labour Party policy by supporting a Communist Party/Independent Labour Party Unity Manifesto for working-class unity against 'fascism, Reaction and War, and for the immediate demands of the workers' in 1937. Threatened with disaffiliation by Labour, the League voluntarily disbanded in May 1937.

Socialist Medical Association.   Established in 1930 as a successor to the defunct State Medical Service Association, a body formed by Labour supporters in the medical profession in 1912. The Association, which argued for the establishment of a state medical service, affiliated to the Labour Party on its foundation and in 1943 published proposals for a future service entitled *The Socialist Programme for Health.*

Society for Socialist Inquiry and Propaganda (SSIP).   Founded in 1930 by G.D.H. Cole and members of the by then moribund Fabian Society, with Ernest Bevin as chairman, in an attempt to provide a resource to the Labour Party for policy formulation. SSIP grew out of weekend discussion meetings held by Cole at Eaton Lodge, the home of the Countess of Warwick. In 1932, SSIP was absorbed into the Socialist League – to Cole's disapproval, although he became a member.

Soft left.   Section of the Labour Party in the 1980s which, although willing to support the attempts of Neil Kinnock (born 1942, party leader 1983–92) to increase the party's electoral chances by modernising its image, remained loyal to Clause Four as Labour's ultimate socialist objective. The soft left emerged as a traditional democratic left counterpart to the hard left and was represented by the Tribune Group, which split in 1982 when a minority formed the hard left Campaign Group of Labour MPs.

Solidarity.   Grouping formed by right-wing Labour MPs in 1981 who preferred to stay in the party to confront left-wing influence rather than leave to join the newly-formed Social Democratic Party (SDP). Among the most prominent members were future Labour leader John Smith, Jack Cunningham and Roy Hattersley.

Taff Vale case.   The House of Lords decision in July 1901 that a trade union was liable for the acts of its agents, effectively limiting the ability of unions to take industrial action. The Taff Vale Railway Company had sued the Amalgamated Society of Railway Servants (ASRS) for breach of contract under the Protection of Property Act 1875 for mounting pickets at Cardiff Station. In December 1902 the ASRS was fined £23,000 plus costs. The decision exposed all union funds to similar claims and, coming as it did under a Conservative government, encouraged demands for independent working-class parliamentary representation and strengthened the position of the newly formed Labour Representation Committee (LRC). As a result, between 1901 and 1903, affiliated trade union membership of the LRC increased from 350,000 to 861,000. Trade union immunity while conducting a dispute was restored by the Liberal government's Trade Disputes Act 1906.

Third Way.   An expression introduced by the Labour prime minister Tony Blair in 1998 which sought to define the ideological framework of his administration. In May 1998 Blair convened a meeting of 36 left-wing academics in an attempt to provide substance to what remained a vague slogan. In his 1998 pamphlet, *The Third Way,* Blair wrote that the policy 'draws vitality from the uniting of the two great streams of left-of-centre thought – social democracy the liberalism – whose divorce did so much to weaken progressive polities across the West.' He said there was no conflict between 'the primacy of individual liberty in the market economy' and the social democratic belief in 'social justice with the state as the main agent'.

***Tiger* talks.**   First attempt to end white Rhodesia's unilateral declaration of independence. Prime Minister Wilson met Ian Smith on the cruiser *Tiger* off Gibraltar. Wilson offered a deal that would prevent majority African rule until the end of the twentieth century. Nonetheless it was rejected by Smith's colleagues in Salisbury.

'tightly knit group of politically motivated men'.   Phrase used by Labour prime minister Harold Wilson to blame Communists, without referring to the party by name, for a strike for higher wages and a 40-hour week mounted by the National Union of Seamen (NUS) from May to July 1966. The strike, which came shortly after Labour's general election victory, had a drastic impact on British trade and sterling's position, and a state of emergency was declared to meet its effects on 23 May. Wilson's charges, which were based on buggings of NUS meetings carried out by MI5, revealed to trade union leaders that their telephones were being tapped.

Trade Disputes and Trade Union Act 1927.   Legislation introduced by the Conservative government following the 1926 General Strike, seen, in part, as a punishment for the strike. The Act outlawed large-scale sympathetic strikes and imposed heavy penalties for instigating, assisting or participating in them. Picketing was curtailed and civil service unions forced to end affiliation to the Trades Union Congress (TUC). More fundamentally for the Labour Party, 'contracting-out' of payment of the political levy by trade union members was replaced by 'contracting-in'. Affiliated membership of the party fell from 3,388,000 in 1926 to 2,077,000 in 1928 and the party lost a quarter of its income from affiliation fees between 1927 and 1929. A side effect, however, was that the party made greater efforts to secure individual members. Depending on Liberal support, the 1929–31 Labour government was unable to repeal the legislation. The Act was repealed by the Labour government in 1946.

Transport House.   Headquarters in Smith Square, London, of the Transport and General Workers' Union (TGWU) from 1928, of the Trades

Union Congress (TUC) from 1928 to 1960, and of the Labour Party from 1928 to 1980, built under the influence of TGWU leader Ernest Bevin (1881–1951). The sharing of Transport House symbolised the intimate connection between the political and industrial wings of the Labour movement.

Tribune. Left-wing Labour weekly founded in January 1937 by, among others, Aneurin Bevan (1897–1960), Stafford Cripps (1889–1952) and Ellen Wilkinson (1891–1947), and known originally as *The Tribune.* The paper initially took a Popular Front line, supporting Communist calls for unity against the threat of fascism. *Tribune* then developed into a left-wing weekly newspaper aimed at party and trade union activists. While not an official party paper, it was described as 'the unofficial house magazine for the Labour Party'.

Tribune Group. Parliamentary Labour Party grouping named after the weekly newspaper, founded in 1966 as a successor to the left-wing Bevanite grouping of the 1950s. Some left-wingers had already been referred to as 'Tribunites' in the 1950s. The Tribune Group operated in the House of Commons on the principle of not voting against any decisions made at the Labour Party conference and saw itself as defending the conference's central policy-making role. Its strong support in the constituency parties was reflected by the group's domination of the National Executive constituency section until the late 1980s. With the splitting-off of the more radically left Campaign Group in 1982, the Tribune Group became less influential.

Underhill Report. The 1979 report to the Labour Party National Executive by party national agent Reg (later Lord) Underhill (1914–93) which revealed the depth of entryism into the party by the Trotskyist Militant Tendency. Following discussion by the National Executive in February 1980, no action was taken against Militant, although the report's contents were leaked to the media.

Unilateralism. Expression usually meaning that Britain should abandon its nuclear weapons regardless of whether or not other states retain theirs. In the moral sense, the policy was seen as a gesture towards encouraging multi-lateral disarmament and was advocated by the Campaign for Nuclear Disarmament (CND) and much of the Labour left. Unilateralism was adopted as party policy in 1960, reversed in 1961, re-adopted in 1980 and reversed once more in 1989.

Union of Democratic Control (UDC). Grouping of socialists, radicals and pacifists formed in September 1914, shortly after the outbreak of the First World War. The UDC advocated political control over foreign policy, a negotiated peace, open diplomacy to prevent the secret alliances which were believed to be one of the causes of the outbreak and spread of the war. Among the founding members was Ramsay MacDonald. Much of the UDC programme was adopted by Labour after the First World War. Nine appointees to Labour's first Cabinet in 1924 had been UDC members.

Unity Campaign.   Attempt in the late 1930s by the Socialist League, the Independent Labour Party (ILP) and the Communist Party to encourage unity against fascism and to shift politics – particularly in the Labour Party – to the left. The Campaign's supporters held regular meetings in the offices of *Tribune*, the left-wing weekly founded in 1937, and issued a Manifesto in 1937 calling for working-class unity against 'fascism, Reaction and War, and for the immediate demands of the workers'. The campaign effectively ended when the Socialist League, threatened with disaffiliation by the Labour Party, voluntarily dissolved itself in May 1937.

Unity Group.   Left-wing Labour group formed as a successor to Victory for Socialism, Unity emerged in 1961 in the wake of the publication the previous year of an Appeal for Unity in Support of Conference Decisions following the party conference's rejection of the leadership's defence policy. Unity claimed the support of over 2,000 Labour Party members and attempted a more centralised left alliance than Victory for Socialism. The Group was dissolved in 1964 although informal activity continued until 1967.

VFS.   See Victory for Socialism.

Victory for Socialism (VFS).   Formed by left-wing activists in 1944 to press for a Left Labour policy, VFS was strengthened when Bevanite MPs Michael Foot and Ian Mikardo joined in 1958. Membership was estimated at 1,000. VFS held annual conferences, established an executive committee and 14 area groups throughout Britain. There were, however, constant internal political divisions and an unwillingness on the part of some area groups to accept central direction. VFS was succeeded in 1961 by the Unity Group.

Walworth Road.   The thoroughfare in south London in which Labour had its headquarters after moving from Transport House in 1980. The building was renamed John Smith House in memory of the party's leader from 1992 until his death in 1994. In the run-up to the 1997 general election much of the party's administrative machinery was moved closer to Parliament at Millbank Tower.

War Emergency Workers' National Committee.   Formed to defend working-class interests in wartime at a meeting called by party secretary Arthur Henderson (1863–1935) on 5 August 1914. Initially comprising the Labour Party and the Co-operative Movement, the Committee rapidly incorporated pro-war and anti-war organisations, including representatives from the trade unions, the ILP, the BSP and the Fabian Society. The Committee protested against wartime inflation and rent increases and campaigned to ensure adequate food distribution. As part of its protests against military conscription in 1916, the Committee demanded a 'Conscription of Riches', to ensure sacrifices were equally shared. The Committee also demanded that industries under government control for the duration should be nationalised. Some historians have suggested a line running from the Committee and the adoption of Clause Four by Labour in 1918.

'We are the masters now'.   A misquotation of a remark made in the House of Commons by Attorney-General Hartley Shawcross (born 1902) on 2 April 1946, often used by Labour's opponents at the time to show its inherently undemocratic authoritarianism. Shawcross actually said: 'We are the masters at the moment, and not only at the moment, but for a very long time to come.' Following the party's 1997 general election landslide victory, Tony Blair attempted to quell any fears of Labour triumphalism by declaring to the Parliamentary Labour Party: 'The people are the masters. We are the servants of the people.'

'Weeks rather than months'.   Prime minister Wilson, criticised for Britain's refusal to use force against the illegal white Rhodesian unilateral declaration of independence, declared at the Commonwealth Conference in Lagos on 11 January 1966 that economic sanctions would bring the regime down in 'a matter of weeks rather than months'. Following the 11 November 1965 declaration, the Labour government had banned Rhodesian imports on 16 November and imposed an oil embargo on 16 December.

Welfare State.   The comprehensive social welfare provision proposed in the Beveridge Report and introduced by the 1945–51 Labour governments, largely continued by the Conservatives until the Thatcher and Major governments of the 1980s and 1990s. The term itself was first used by the Archbishop of Canterbury, William Temple (1881–1944) in 1943 when he said: 'In place of the conception of the Power State, we are led to that of the Welfare State.'

'White heat of the technological revolution'.   The core of a speech made by Harold Wilson (1916–95, party leader from 1963 to 1976) at the

Scarborough conference on 1 October 1963 in which he attempted to set the scene for a coming Labour government. Wilson said: 'We are redefining and we are restating our socialism in terms of the scientific revolution. . . . The Britain that is going to be forged in the white heat of this revolution will be no place for restrictive practices or outdated methods on both sides of industry.' The attraction of Wilson's rhetoric served to intensify the disappointment many of Labour's supporters felt with the actual achievements of Labour in office from 1964 to 1970.

Winter of Discontent.   Term coined by the Conservative-supporting tabloid newspaper *The Sun* to describe a wave of private and public sector strikes over the winter of 1978–79 against the Labour government's attempt to impose a 5% ceiling on wage increases. The period of disruption marked the end of two decades of corporatism, the attempt by both the Conservative and Labour parties to combine deals over wages with an expansionist economic policy. The effect of action by local government manual workers, together with picket-line violence, reputedly played a part in Labour's 1979 general election defeat and persistent use of the expression undermined the party in successive elections.

Women's Labour League.   Established in 1906, the League was the only autonomous women's group that has ever existed in the Labour Party. A supporter of female suffrage, one of the League's central objectives was to 'obtain direct representation in Parliament and on local bodies'. The League was unable to co-operate with the leading suffrage organisation, the Women's Social and Political Union (WSPU), because of the latter's opposition to working with Labour. Active in social policy, the League established a child welfare clinic in Kensington before the First World War. The League affiliated to the Labour Party during the First World War and in 1918 amalgamated with the party to form the basis of Women's Sections established under the new constitution. By 1922 over 100,000 women had joined the 650 Women's Sections in local Labour parties.

Zinoviev letter.   Allegedly written by Zinoviev, president of the Communist International (Comintern) to British Communists shortly before the 1924 general election calling on them to campaign for ratification of an Anglo-Soviet treaty to further 'the revolutionizing of the international and British proletariat', to create Communist cells in the armed forces to spread disaffection, to encourage anti-colonial agitation and to prepare for a revolutionary seizure of power in the event of war. Labour had recently recognised the Soviet Union and was attempting to improve relations and the charge that the party's policy was in some way linked to Communist ambitions was therefore potentially damaging to the minority government. J.H. Thomas reputedly said on reading the first newspaper report: 'We're sunk.' Official response to publication of the letter was delayed and Snowden, with whom MacDonald's relations were never easy, later criticised MacDonald's mishandling of the issue. Arguments continue over how far Labour was affected by the affair in the general election (Labour's vote increased but the number of seats it won fell) and whether or not the document was a forgery (documents released by the Public Record Office in 1998 finally confirmed that it was a forgery).

22 Bibliography

Topics

Introductory Note

This bibliography provides an introduction to the main areas covered in this *Companion* but, given the large amount of material that has been produced on the Labour Party, is not exhaustive. Although the bibliography under topic headings is wider than is normally necessary for an essay, a reader with a deeper interest will want to consult the bibliographies in each of the suggested works. The reader consulting a particular theme bibliography should also consult the section on autobiographies and biographies for references to individuals.

Unless otherwise stated, the place of publication is London.

1   General Works

A useful recent study – with an excellent bibliography – is A. Thorpe, *A History of the British Labour Party* (1997). Among other general accounts are H. Pelling, *A Short History of the Labour Party* (11th edn, 1996), K. Laybourn, *The Rise of Labour: The British Labour Party, 1890–1979* (1988), and C.F. Brand, *The British Labour Party: A Short History* (Stanford, CA, 1965). P. Adelman, *The Rise of the Labour Party 1880–1945* (3rd edn, 1996) is concise and contains basic documents. K. Laybourn, *The Labour Party 1881–1951: A Reader in History* (Gloucester, 1991) also has useful documents. R. Miliband, *Parliamentary Socialism* (2nd edn, 1972) is very critical but has a mass of fascinating detail and argument. J. Hinton, *Labour and Socialism: A History of the British Labour Movement* (Brighton, 1983), and D. Howell, *British Social Democracy: A Study in Development and Decay* (1976), both take a critical position. For the cultural background against which Labour developed – in England at least – R. McKibbin, *Classes and Cultures: England 1918–51* (Oxford, 1998) is valuable. K. Burgess, *The Challenge of Labour. Shaping British Society 1850–1930* (1980) provides an economic and industrial as well as political background. G.D.H. Cole, *History of the Labour Party from 1914* (1948) gives useful coverage of the 1920s and 1930s. Moving the story forward are C. Cook and I. Taylor (eds), *The Labour Party: An Introduction to its History, Structure and Politics* (1980), K. Jefferys, *The Labour Party since 1945* (1992) and E. Shaw, *The Labour Party since 1945* (Oxford, 1996), which gives a decidedly critical view. See also, A. Warde, *Consensus and Beyond: The Development of Labour Party Strategy since the Second World War* (Manchester, 1982).

It is worth consulting S. Fielding, *Labour: Decline and Renewal* (Manchester, 1994), J. Saville, *The Labour Movement in Britain* (1988), and A. Briggs and J. Saville (eds), *Essays in Labour History* (1967), *Essays in Labour History, 1886–1923* (1971), *Essays in Labour History, 1920–1939* (1977). For views set against a wider post-Second World War background see, K.O. Morgan, *The People's Peace* (Oxford, 1990) and A. Sked and C. Cook, *Post War Britain* (Harmondsworth, 1993), which covers similar ground. D.E. and G. Butler, *British Political Facts, 1900–1994* (1994), is invaluable for the basics, as are the Nuffield general elections series on Labour's performance at the polls since 1945.

On socialism and on the party's ideology, see A. Wright, *British Socialism: Socialist Thought from the late 1880s to the 1960s* (1983), G. Foote, *The Labour Party's Political Thought: A History* (1985), J. Callaghan, *Socialism in Britain since 1884* (Oxford, 1990), K. Laybourn, *The Rise of Socialism in Britain* (Gloucester, 1997), H.M. Drucker, *Doctrine and Ethos in the Labour Party* (1979), the intensely critical R. Miliband, *Parliamentary Socialism* (2nd edn, 1972) and W. Thompson, *The Long Death of British Labourism*

(1993). See also R. Desai, *Intellectuals and Socialism – Social Democrats and the Labour Party* (1994).

On guild socialism – a not unimportant strand in the party's early history – see A. Wright, *G.D.H. Cole and Socialist Democracy* (Oxford, 1979). For documents, see F. Bealey (ed.), *The Social and Political Thought of the Labour Party* (1970) and A. Wright (ed.), *British Socialism: Socialist Thought from the 1880s to the 1960s* (1983). C.A.R. Crosland's *The Future of Socialism* (1956) presents the important 1950s revisionist view and S. Holland, 'Keynes and the socialists', in R. Skidselsky (ed.), *The End of the Keynesian Era* (1977) makes some interesting points. R.K. Middlemas, *Politics in Industrial Society: The Expansion of the British System since 1911* (1979) is useful on the mid-century move to corporatism, while D. Kavanagh and P. Morris, *Consensus Politics from Attlee to Thatcher* (1989) looks at the broad post-war experience. See also L. Panitch, *Working Class Politics in Crisis: Essays on Labour and the State* (1986) and N. Thompson, *Political Economy and the Labour Party* (1996). For Christian socialism, a recurring theme in the party's history, see C. Bryant, *Possible Dreams: A Personal History of the British Christian Socialists* (1996).

2   Organisation, Membership and Electoral Base

R.T. McKenzie, *British Political Parties: The Distribution of Power within the Conservative and Labour Parties* (1955) remains a valuable account of a particular phase. L. Minkin, *The Labour Party Conference* (1978) has a wealth of interesting detail not only on the conference but on where power and influence lay. There is useful material in E.G. Janosik, *Constituency Labour Parties in British Politics* (1968), and M. Rush, *The Selection of Parliamentary Candidates* (1966). More general studies of the relationship between the party and the working class can be found in B. Hindess, *The Decline of Working Class Politics* (1971), T. Forrester, *The Labour Party and the Working Class* (1976) and the seminal E. Hobsbawm, 'The forward march of Labour halted?', in M. Jacques and F. Mulhern (eds), *The Forward March of Labour Halted?* (1981). At a more detailed level, see H. Jenkins, *Rank and File* (1981), an oral history of a constituency party, P. Whiteley, 'The decline of Labour's local party membership and electoral base, 1945–79', and I. Crewe, 'The Labour Party and its electorate', both in D. Kavanagh (ed.), *The Politics of the Labour Party* (1982), and P. Seyd and P. Whiteley, *Labour's Grass Roots* (Oxford, 1992), a national survey of members. See also for the reforms of the early 1980s, A. Young, *The Reselection of MPs* (1983). For an earlier period, see C. Howard, 'Expectations born to death: local Labour Party expansion in the 1920s', in J. Winter (ed.), *The Working Class in Modern British History* (Cambridge, 1983). Discussions of electoral performance and base can be found in A. Heath, R. Jowell and J. Curtice, *Labour's Last Chance? The 1992*

Election and Beyond (1994) and E. Shaw, *Discipline and Discord in the Labour Party* (Manchester, 1989). Among useful articles are D.V. Donnison and D.E.G. Plowman, 'The function of local Labour parties', in *Political Studies*, 2, 2 (1954) and N. Hart, 'Gender and the rise and fall of class politics', in *New Left Review*, 175 (1989).

3   Forerunners, Foundation and Early Years

H. Pelling, *The Origins of the Labour Party, 1880–1900* (2nd edn, Oxford, 1966) remains the outstanding introduction to the party's formation. Useful background material can be found in E. Hobsbawm (ed.), *Labour's Turning Point, 1880–1900* (2nd edn, Hassocks, 1974), E.F. Biagini and A.J. Reid (eds), *Currents of Radicalism: Popular Radicalism, Organized Labour and Party Politics in Britain, 1850–1914* (Cambridge, 1991), R. Harrison, *Before the Socialists: Studies in Labour and Politics 1861–1881* (1965), H.V. Emy, *Liberals, Radicals and Social Politics 1892–1912* (Cambridge, 1973) and in J. Lawrence, 'Popular radicalism and the socialist revival in Britain', *Journal of British Studies*, 31 (1992). R. Dowse, *Left in the Centre. The Independent Labour Party, 1893–1940* (1966) is useful on the main socialist grouping at the party's birth, as is D. Howell, *British Workers and the Independent Labour Party 1888–1906* (Manchester, 1983). On another important contemporary grouping, see M. Crick, *The History of the Social Democratic Federation* (Keele, 1994). C. Tsuzuki considers contemporary tensions in *H.J. Hyndman and British Socialism* (Oxford, 1961), while a different emphasis can be found in H. Pelling, *Popular Politics and Society in Late Victorian Britain* (1968). For the role of Fabianism, see A.M. McBriar, *Fabian Socialism and English Politics, 1884–1918* (Cambridge, 1962).

On the party's earliest period, see F. Bealey and H. Pelling, *Labour and Politics, 1900–1906: History of the Labour Representation Committee* (1958) and R. McKibbin, *The Evolution of the Labour Party 1910–1924* (Oxford, 1974). K.D. Brown, *Essays in Anti-Labour History: Responses to the Rise of Labour* (1974) is interesting, as is his edited collection, *The First Labour Party, 1906–1914* (1985). D. Powell, 'New Liberalism and the rise of Labour, 1886–1906', *Historical Journal*, 29 (1986) is also valuable. On the pressures on the unions which encouraged support for the party, see J. Saville, 'Trade unions and Free Labour: the background to the Taff Vale decision', in A. Briggs and J. Saville (eds), *Essays in Labour History: In Memory of G.D.H. Cole* (1967) and H. Pelling, 'The politics of the Osborne Judgment', *Historical Journal*, 25 (1982). B. Pribicevic, *The Shop Stewards' Movement and Workers' Control 1910–22* (Oxford, 1959) gives an insight into a possible alternative to purely parliamentary politics. For an examination of the pre-First World War relationship between Labour and the Liberal government, see C.J. Wrigley, *Lloyd George and the British*

Labour Movement (Hassocks, 1976). D. Tanner, *Political Change and the Labour Party, 1900–18* (Cambridge, 1990) takes the party to the end of the First World War. For relations with the suffrage movement and feminism, see the section of this bibliography on Labour and women.

On the impact of the war, see J. Turner, *British Politics and the Great War: Coalition and Conflict, 1915–1918* (1992), J. Hinton, *The First Shop Stewards' Movement* (1973), C. Howard, 'MacDonald, Henderson, and the outbreak of war, 1914', *Historical Journal*, 20, 4, (1977), R. Harrison, 'The War Emergency Workers' National Committee', in A. Briggs and J. Saville (eds), *Essays in Labour History, 1886–1923* (1971), R. Davidson, 'War-time Labour policy, 1914–1916: a reappraisal', *Journal of Scottish Labour History Society*, 8 (1974), and J.M. Winter, *Socialism and the Challenge of War: Ideas and Politics in Britain 1912–18* (1974). For an important effect of events outside Britain, see M. Winter, 'Arthur Henderson, the Russian Revolution, and the reconstruction of the Labour Party', *Historical Journal*, 15, 4 (1972). M. Cowling, *The Advent of Labour 1920–24: The Beginning of Modern British Politics* (Cambridge, 1971) takes the story to the first Labour government as its subject. On Labour's supersession of the Liberals, see P.F. Clarke, 'The electoral position of the Liberal and Labour parties, 1910–14', *English Historical Review*, 90 (1975) and K. Laybourne, 'The rise of Labour and the decline of Liberalism: the state of the debate', *History*, 80 (1995). C.A. Cline, *Recruits to Labour: The British Labour Party, 1914–1931* (Syracuse, NY, 1963) remains interesting. K.O. Morgan, *Consensus and Disunity: The Lloyd George Coalition Government, 1918–22* (Oxford, 1979) and C.J. Wrigley, *Lloyd George and the Challenge of Labour: The Post-War Coalition, 1918–22* (Hemel Hempstead, 1990) are useful on Labour's move to becoming the main opposition party. On foreign policy, see H.R. Winkler, 'The emergence of a Labor foreign policy in Great Britain, 1918–1929', *Journal of Modern History*, XXVIII (1956).

4 Labour in the 1920s and 1930s

G.D.H. Cole, *History of the Labour Party from 1914* (1948) remains useful on this period. On Labour's short-lived first administration, see R.W. Lyman, *The First Labour Government* (1963), and on the second, see R. Skidelsky, *Politicians and the Slump: The Labour Government of 1929–31* (1994 edn). In this he answers some of the criticisms made in R. McKibbin, 'The economic policy of the second Labour government, 1929–31', *Past and Present*, 78 (1975). On foreign policy, see D. Carlton, *MacDonald versus Henderson: The Foreign Policy of the Second Labour Government* (1970). For a consideration of the party's development in the 1920s, see C. Howard, 'Expectations born to death: local Labour Party expansion in the 1920s', in J.M. Winter (ed.), *The Working Class in Modern British History: Essays in Honour of Henry Pelling* (Cambridge, 1983).

The crisis which faced the second Labour government is dealt with in P. Williamson, *National Crisis and National Government: British Politics, the Economy and Empire, 1926–32* (Cambridge, 1992). On the collapse of the Labour government in 1931, see R. Bassett, *Nineteen Thirty-one: Political Crisis* (1958), A. Thorpe, *The British General Election of 1931* (Oxford, 1991), and P. Williamson, 'A "Bankers' Ramp"? Financiers and the British political crisis of 1931', *English Historical Review*, 99 (1984). On the contrasting impact on two individuals, see A. Thorpe, 'Arthur Henderson and the British political crisis of 1931', *Historical Journal*, 31 (1988), and '"I am in the Cabinet": J.H. Thomas's decision to join the National government in 1931', *Historical Research*, 64 (1991).

For developments in the party after the 1931 collapse, see B. Pimlott, *Labour and the Left in the 1930s* (Cambridge, 1977), E. Durbin, *New Jerusalems: The Labour Party and the Economics of Democratic Socialism* (1985), and two older works which remain of interest, C.R. Attlee, *The Labour Party in Perspective* (1937) and D.E. McHenry, *The Labour Party in Transition, 1931–1938* (1938). T. Buchanan, *The Spanish Civil War and the British Labour Movement* (Cambridge, 1992) is important, as is J.F. Naylor, *Labour's International Policy: The Labour Party in the 1930s* (1969). Among articles worth looking at are R. Eatwell and A. Wright, 'Labour and the lessons of 1931', *History*, 63 (1978), R. Dare, 'Instinct and organisation: intellectuals and British Labour after 1931', *Historical Journal*, 26 (1983), and B.C. Malament, 'British Labour and Roosevelt's New Deal', *Journal of British Studies*, 17 (1977–78).

5   Coalition and Government, 1940–51

On the party and the Second World War, see S. Brooke, *Labour's War: The Labour Party during the Second World War* (Oxford, 1992). For contrasting views of the opportunity presented by participation in the Coalition, see P. Addison, *The Road to 1945: British Politics and the Second World War* (1975) and K. Jefferys, *The Churchill Coalition and Wartime Politics, 1940–45* (Manchester, 1991). See also T. Burridge, *British Labour and Hitler's War* (1976). H. Pelling, 'The impact of war on the Labour Party', in H.L. Smith (ed.), *War and Social Change: British Society in the Second World War* (Manchester, 1986) is also useful, as is I. Taylor, 'Labour and the impact of war, 1939–44', in N. Tiratsoo (ed.), *The Attlee Years* (1991). A. Bullock, *The Life and Times of Ernest Bevin, Volume 2: Minister of Labour, 1940–1945* (1967) is vital for a major Labour figure in the Coalition. On specific themes, see S. Brooke, 'Revisionists and fundamentalists: the Labour Party and economic policy during the Second World War', *Historical Journal*, 32 (1989), L. Johnman, 'The Labour Party and industrial policy, 1940–45', in N. Tiratsoo (ed.), *The Attlee Years* (1991), and S. Fielding, 'Labourism in the 1940s', *Twentieth Century British History*,

3 (1992). C. Barnett, *The Audit of War* (1986) is critical of the Coalition and of the subsequent Labour government. See also R. Lowe, 'The Second World War, consensus, and the foundation of the welfare state', *Twentieth Century British History*, 1 (1990). S. Fielding, P. Thompson and N. Tiratsoo, *England Arise! The Labour Party and Popular Politics in 1940s Britain* (Manchester, 1995), is stimulating.

On the 1945 Labour landslide, as well as R.B. McCallum and A. Readman, *The British General Election of 1945* (Oxford, 1947), see H. Pelling, 'The 1945 election reconsidered', *Historical Journal*, 23 (1980) and S. Fielding, 'What did "the people" want? The meaning of the 1945 general election', *Historical Journal*, 35 (1992).

Labour's first majority administration is well covered in K.O. Morgan, *Labour in Power, 1945–1951* (1983), H. Pelling, *The Labour Governments, 1945–51* (1984), and K. Jefferys, *The Attlee Governments 1945–51* (1992). P. Hennessy, *Never Again: Britain, 1945–51* (1992) is remarkably evocative. See also R. Eatwell, *The 1945–1951 Labour Governments* (1979). There are a number of valuable pieces in N. Tiratsoo (ed.), *The Attlee Years* (1991). D. Steel, 'Labour in office: the post-war experience', in C. Cook and I. Taylor (eds), *The Labour Party: An Introduction to its History, Structure and Politics* (1980), and P. Hennessy and A. Seldon (eds), *Ruling Performance: British Governments from Attlee to Thatcher* (1987) make some useful points. For an important aspect of what Labour did at home, see J.C. Hess, 'The social policy of the Attlee government', in W.J. Mommsen (ed.), *The Emergence of the Welfare State in Britain and Germany* (1981). There is also an interesting view in D. Rubinstein, 'Socialism and the Labour Party: the Labour left and domestic policy, 1945–50', in D.E. Martin and D. Rubinstein (eds), *Ideology and the Labour Movement: Essays in Honour of John Saville* (1979). M. Sissons and P. French (eds), *The Age of Austerity* (1963) remains entertaining.

The economic background is dealt with in A. Cairncross, *Years of Recovery: British Economic Policy, 1945–51* (1985) and J. Fyrth (ed.), *Labour's High Noon: The Government and the Economy, 1945–51* (1993). For specific aspects, see J. Tomlinson, 'The Attlee government and the balance of payments, 1945–51', *Twentieth Century British History*, 2 (1991), and S. Brooke, 'Problems of socialist planning: Evan Durbin and the Labour government of 1945', *Historical Journal*, 34 (1991). See also, A. Rogow and P. Shore, *The Labour Government and Industry, 1945–51* (Oxford, 1955).

Foreign policy is well covered in R. Ovendale, *The Foreign Policy of the British Labour Governments, 1945–51* (1984) and V. Rothwell, *Britain and the Cold War, 1941–47* (1983). See also, A. Bullock, *The Life and Times of Ernest Bevin, Volume 3: Foreign Secretary, 1945–51* (1983). On the development of nuclear weapons, see M. Gowing and L. Arnold, *Independence and Deterrence: Britain and Atomic Energy, 1945–51* (1974) and M. Gowing

'Britain and the bomb', *Contemporary Record*, 2 (1988). For critical views of Labour's foreign policy, see R. Saville, 'Politics and the Labour Movement in the early Cold War', *Our History Journal*, 15 (1990) and J. Saville, 'Labour and foreign policy 1945–1947: a condemnation', *Our History Journal*, 17 (1991). See also R. Ovendale, 'Britain, the USA and the European Cold War, 1945–48', *History* (1982).

On Labour's colonial policies, see P.S. Gupta, *Imperialism and the British Labour Movement 1914–64* (1975), S. Howe, *Anti-Colonialism in British Politics: The Left and the End of Empire, 1918–64* (Oxford, 1993) and J. Kent, 'Bevin's imperialism and the idea of Euro-Africa', in M. Dockrill and J.W. Young (eds), *British Foreign Policy, 1945–56* (1989).

6 Opposition, 1951–64

Much of Labour's 13 years in opposition was marked by conflict between right and left. For an outline, see V. Bogdanor, 'The Labour Party in opposition, 1951–64', in V. Bogdanor and R. Skidelsky (eds), *The Age of Affluence, 1951–1964* (1970). On the left, M. Jenkins, *Bevanism: Labour's High Tide* (Nottingham, 1979) includes interesting material on activism outside Parliament. M. Foot, *Aneurin Bevan: A Biography, Volume 2: 1945–60* (1973) is an adulatory study of the leading figure on the left, while J. Campbell, *Aneurin Bevan and the Mirage of British Socialism* (1987) is far less so. For the basic ideology, see R.H.S. Crossman (ed.), *New Fabian Essays* (1952) and A. Bevan, *In Place of Fear* (1952, reissued 1978), which is loose but revealing. For an apparent member of the left, see B. Pimlott, *Harold Wilson* (1992).

For a sympathetic view of the right, see S. Haseler, *The Gaitskellites: Revisionism in the British Labour Party, 1951–1964* (1969) and P. Williams, *Hugh Gaitskell: A Political Biography* (1979). R. Desai, *Intellectuals and Socialism. Social Democrats and the Labour Party* (1994) is useful. C.A.R. Crosland, *The Future of Socialism* (1956) is central to the revisionist position. Gaitskell's supporters are sympathetically examined in B. Brivati, 'The campaign for democratic socialism', in *Contemporary Record*, 4 (1990). It is also worth looking at 'Hugh Gaitskell: 1955–1963', in P. Shore, *Leading the Left* (1993) and 'Hugh Gaitskell: the Social Democrat as hero', in D. Marquand, *The Progressive Dilemma* (1991). N. Tiratsoo, 'Popular politics, affluence and the Labour Party in the 1950s', in A. Gorst, L. Johnman and W.S. Lucas (eds), *Contemporary British History 1931–61* (1991) is interesting on the political impact of a changing society, as is J.H. Goldthorpe, D. Lockwood, F. Bechhofer and F. Platt, *The Affluent Worker: Political Attitudes and Behaviour* (Cambridge, 1968). On the argument over nationalisation, see T. Jones, 'Labour revisionism and public ownership, 1951–63', *Contemporary Record*, 8, 3 (1991) and, for a longer view, K.O. Morgan, 'The rise and fall of public ownership in Britain', in J.M. Bean (ed.), *The Political Culture of Modern Britain* (1987).

L. Minkin, *The Labour Party Conference: A Study in the Politics of Intra-Party Democracy* (1978) contains much interesting material on Labour's functioning in the later 1950s, as does E. Shaw, *Discipline and Discord in the Labour Party* (Manchester, 1989). For the party's early difficulties with Europe, see L.J. Robbins, *The Reluctant Party: Labour and the EEC 1961–1975* (Ormskirk, 1975). The party's persistent electoral failure is competently covered in D.E. Butler, *The British General Election 1955* (1955) and D.E. Butler and R. Rose, *The British General Election of 1959* (1960).

7   Government, 1964–70

The Wilson governments have had mixed reviews. C. Ponting, *In Breach of Promise* (1989) is, as its title suggests, critical, D. Coates, *The Labour Party and the Struggle for Socialism* (Cambridge, 1975) is strongly critical, while B. Lapping, *The Labour Government 1964–70* (Harmondsworth, 1970) takes a more sympathetic view. The essays in R. Coopey, S. Fielding and N. Tiratsoo (eds), *The Wilson Governments, 1964–1970* (1993) are balanced but not uncritical. See also D. McKie and C. Cook (eds), *The Decade of Disillusion: British Politics in the 1960s* (1972), and B. Donoghue, *Prime Minister: The Conduct of Politics under Harold Wilson and James Callaghan* (1987). D. Walker, 'The first Wilson governments, 1964–70', in P. Hennessy and A. Seldon (eds), *Ruling Performance: British Governments from Attlee to Thatcher* (Oxford, 1987) is useful. A.H. Albu, J. Bray and R. Prentice, 'Lessons of the Labour government', *Political Quarterly*, 41, 3 (1970) presents an early view.

For Labour's narrow victory in 1964, see D.E. Butler and A. King, *The British General Election of 1964* (1965); on the expanded majority of 1966, D.E. Butler and A. King, *The British General Election of 1966* (1966); and the defeat of 1970, D.E. Butler and A. King, *The British General Election of 1970* (1971).

On divisions inside the party, see N. Tiratsoo, 'Labour and its critics: the case of the May Day Manifesto Group', in R. Coopey, S. Fielding and N. Tiratsoo (eds), *The Wilson Governments, 1964–1970* (1993). Further information on the party in this period can be found in L. Minkin, *The Labour Party Conference: A Study in the Politics of Intra-Party Democracy* (1978), and E. Shaw, *Discipline and Discord in the Labour Party* (Manchester, 1989). On a particular government failure, see M. Surrey, 'The National Plan in retrospect', *Oxford Bulletin of Economics and Statistics*, 34 (1972), and on the failure of Wilsonian rhetoric, see R. Clarke, 'The white heat of the scientific revolution', *Contemporary Record*, 5 (1991). On the economy, see also P. Browning, *The Treasury and Economic Policy, 1964–1985* (1986) and W. Beckerman (ed.), *The Labour Government's Economic Record 1964–70* (1972).

Much useful material can be found in the biographies, autobiographies and diaries of leading Labour figures of the period. The reader is referred to that section of this bibliography for, in particular, Wilson, Callaghan, Jenkins, Brown, Benn, Crossman, Castle and Stewart.

For the collapse of the government's attempt at industrial relations reform, see K. Middlemas, *Power, Competition and the State, Volume 2: Threats to the Post-War Settlement* (1990), and L. Panitch, *Social Democracy and Industrial Militancy: The Labour Party, the Trade Unions and Incomes Policy, 1945–1974* (Cambridge, 1976). On the party's continuing difficulties with Europe, see U. Kitzinger, *The Second Try: Labour and the EEC* (1973), and on the crisis over Britain's overseas commitments, C.J. Bartlett, *British Defence Policy East of Suez 1947–1968* (Oxford, 1973).

8   Opposition and Government, 1970–79

M. Hatfield, *The House the Left Built: Inside Labour Policy-making 1970–75* (1978) describes the path to Labour's 1974 return to office. D. Coates, *Labour in Power? A Study of the Labour Government, 1974–1979* (1980) is decidedly critical, and the title of K. Coates (ed.), *What Went Wrong: Explaining the Fall of the Labour Government* (Nottingham, 1979) is self-explanatory. M. Holmes, *The Labour Government, 1974–79: Political Aims and Economic Reality* (1985) is more sympathetic. P. Whitehead, 'The Labour governments, 1974–79', in P. Hennessy and A. Seldon (eds), *Ruling Performance: British Governments from Attlee to Thatcher* (Oxford, 1987) is useful, and his *The Writing on the Wall: Britain in the Seventies* (1985) provides a valuable background. See also B. Donoghue, *Prime Minister: The Conduct of Politics under Harold Wilson and James Callaghan* (1987), and, for the birth and progress of the 1977–79 Lib-Lab Pact, D. Steel, *A House Divided* (1980) together with A. Michie and S. Hoggart, *The Pact: The Inside Story of the Lib-Lab Government, 1977–78* (1978).

On economic management, see M. Artis and D. Cobham (eds), *Labour's Economic Policies, 1974–1979* (Manchester, 1991) and also E. Dell, *A Hard Pounding: Politics and Economic Crisis, 1974–1976* (1980). For the social contract with the trade unions, see W.J. Fishbein, *Wage Restraint by Consensus* (1984), and on its breakdown, 'The Winter of Discontent', Symposium, *Contemporary Record* (1987). R. Taylor, 'The uneasy alliance, Labour and the unions', *Political Quarterly* (Oct. 1976) provides some background.

The rise of nationalism and moves towards devolution are covered in V. Bogdanor, *Devolution* (Oxford, 1979), M. Keating and D. Bleiman, *Labour and Scottish Nationalism* (1979), A. Butt Philip, *The Welsh Question: Nationalism in Welsh Politics, 1945–70* (Cardiff, 1975), and, more broadly,

in *T. Nairn, The Break-up of Britain: Crisis and Neo-Nationalism* (1977). For
a particular Scottish problem for Labour, see H.M. Drucker, *Breakaway!*
The Scottish Labour Party (Edinburgh, 1979).

9   Opposition, 1979–97

On this difficult period in Labour's history, see the contemporary
D. Kogan and M. Kogan, *The Battle for the Labour Party* (1987), E. Shaw, *The
Labour Party since 1979: Crisis and Transformation* (1994), and P. Whiteley,
The Labour Party in Crisis (1983). M.J. Smith and J. Spear (eds), *The
Changing Labour Party* (1992) is a collection of essays on the 1980s and
1990s. See also G. Hodgson, *Labour at the Crossroads: The Political and
Economic Challenge to the Labour Party in the 1980s* (Oxford, 1981). On the
pressure from the right, see S. Hall, *The Hard Road to Renewal: Thatcherism
and the Crisis of the Left* (1988).

The record of Labour's long-running electoral failure is in D.E. Butler
and D. Kavanagh, *The British General Election of 1983* (1984), *The British
General Election of 1987* (1988) and the *British General Election of 1992*
(1992). M.N. Franklin, *The Decline of Class Voting in Britain: Changes in
the Basis of Electoral Choice, 1964–1983* (Oxford, 1985) and A. Heath,
R. Jowell and J. Curtice, *Labour's Last Chance. The 1992 Election and Beyond*
(Aldershot, 1994) provide some useful background.

C. Hughes and P. Wintour, *Labour Rebuilt: The New Model Party* (1990)
is sympathetic to the first wave of party reform, while R. Heffernan and
M. Marqusee, *Defeat from the Jaws of Victory: Inside Kinnock's Labour Party*
(1992) takes an oppositional position. See also N. Kinnock, 'Reforming
the Labour Party', *Contemporary Record*, 8, 3 (1994). On local government, which played a part in Labour's crisis, see S. Lansley, S. Goss and
C. Wolmar, *Councils in Conflict: The Rise and Fall of the Municipal Left*
(1989). On the left in the party, see P. Seyd, *The Rise and Fall of the
Labour Left* (1987) and H. Wainright, *Labour: A Tale of Two Parties* (1987).
See also P. Seyd, 'Bennism without Benn – realignment on the Labour
left', *New Socialist*, 17 (1985) and M. Rustin, 'Different conceptions of
party: Labour's constitutional debate', *New Left Review*, 126 (1981).

On the split which led to the Social Democratic Party (and influenced
the direction Labour took), see I. Crewe and A. King, *SDP: The Birth, Life
and Death of the Social Democratic Party* (Oxford, 1995), I. Bradley, *Breaking
the Mould? The Birth and Prospects of the SDP* (1981), and H. Stephenson,
Claret and Chips: The Rise of the SDP (1982). See also, for the views of the
leading figures, R. Jenkins, *Life at the Centre* (1991) and D. Owen, *Time to
Declare* (1991).

For the more recent wave of party reform, see L. Panitch and C. Leys,
The End of Parliamentary Socialism: From New Left to New Labour (1997).
There are contrasting views in M.J. Smith, 'Understanding the "politics

of catch-up": the modernisation of the Labour Party' and C. Hay, 'Labour's Thatcherite revisionism: playing the "politics of catch-up"', both in *Political Studies*, 42, 4 (1994). P. Mandelson and R. Liddle, *The Blair Revolution – Can New Labour Deliver?* (1996) gives a bland exposition of the Blair project, while A. McSmith, *Faces of Labour – The Inside Story* (1996) is an intelligent personality-based account of the 1980s and 1990s. See also J. Rentoul, *Tony Blair* (1995), P. Anderson and N. Mann, *Safety First: The Making of New Labour* (1997) and D. Draper, *Blair's Hundred Days* (1997).

10   Labour and the Trade Unions

Although a central component in the establishment of the Labour Party, the relationship with the trade unions has been complex. On the difficulties of the relationship between the two wings, see L. Minkin, *The Contentious Alliance: Trade Unions and the Labour Party* (Edinburgh, 1991) and A.J. Taylor, *The Trade Unions and the Labour Party* (1987). For a valuable background, see H. Pelling, *A History of British Trade Unionism* (4th edn, Harmondsworth, 1987) and for a broader view, see B. Pimlott and C. Cook, *Trade Unions in British Politics: The First 250 Years* (2nd edn, 1991). See also H.A. Clegg, A. Fox and A.F. Thompson, *A History of British Trade Unions since 1889, Volume I, 1889–1910* (Oxford, 1964), H.A. Clegg, *A History of British Trade Unions since 1889, Volume II, 1911– 1933* (Oxford, 1983), and *Volume III, 1934–51* (Oxford, 1994), and C. Wrigley (ed.), *A History of British Industrial Relations 1939–1979* (Aldershot, 1995). K. Burgess, *The Challenge of Labour. Shaping British Society 1850–1930* (1980) has some interesting views, as does J.E. Cronin, *Labour and Society in Britain, 1918–1979* (1984). On legal measures against the unions which promoted support for the party, see J. Saville, 'Trade unions and Free Labour: the background to the Taff Vale decision', in A. Briggs and J. Saville (eds), *Essays in Labour History: In Memory of G.D.H. Cole* (1967) and H. Pelling, 'The politics of the Osborne Judgment', *Historical Journal*, 25 (1982).

For the relationship with Labour in office, see, as well as works on Labour governments cited elsewhere in this bibliography, E.L. Wigham, *Strikes and the Government 1893–1974* (1976), J. Phillips, *The Great Alliance: Economic Recovery and the Problems of Power 1945–51* (1996), J. Davis-Smith, *The Attlee and Churchill Administrations and Industrial Unrest 1945–55* (1990), and R. Taylor, *The Trade Union Question in British Politics: Government and Unions since 1945* (Oxford, 1993). Also useful are M. Harrison, *Trades Unions and the Labour Party since 1945* (1960), G.A. Dorfman, *Government versus Trade Unionism in British Politics since 1968* (1979) and D. Barnes and E. Reid, *Government and the Trade Unions: The British Experience 1964–1979* (1980). See also L. Panitch, *Social Democracy and Industrial*

Militancy: The Labour Party, the Trade Unions and Incomes Policy (Cambridge, 1976) and V.L. Allen, *Militant Trade Unionism: A Re-analysis of Industrial Action in an Inflationary Situation* (1966). W.J. Fishbein, *Wage Restraint by Consensus* (1984) deals with the 1970s social contract between the Labour government and the unions, and 'The Winter of Discontent', Symposium, *Contemporary Record* (1987) on its breakdown. R. Taylor, 'The uneasy alliance, Labour and the unions', *Political Quarterly* (Oct. 1976) is worth looking at. For the awkward events of the mid-1980s, see M. Adeney and J. Lloyd, *The Miners' Strike: Loss without Limit* (1986).

Biographies of individual trade union leaders also provide some insight into the relationship, among them A. Bullock, *The Life and Times of Ernest Bevin, Volume 1 Trade Union Leader 1881–1940* (1960) and G. Goodman, *The Awkward Warrior: Frank Cousins, His Life and Times* (1979). There is also the autobiography of a significant figure of the 1960s and 1970s, J. Jones, *Union Man: The Autobiography of Jack Jones* (1986).

11   Labour and the Left

C. Tsuzuki, *H.J. Hyndman and British Socialism* (Oxford, 1961) provides an interesting early view and R.I. McKibbin, 'Why was there no Marxism in Great Britain?', *English Historical Review*, 99, 2 (1984) considers the left broadly. On the left inside the Labour Party, R. Dowse, *Left in the Centre. The Independent Labour Party, 1893–1940* (1966) is still worth reading. See also R.K. Middlemas, *The Clydesiders – A Left-wing Struggle for Parliamentary Power* (1965), A. McKinley and R.J. Morris (eds), *The ILP on Clydeside, 1893–1932: From Foundation to Disintegration* (Manchester, 1991), which is wider than its title suggests, and D. James, T. Jowitt and K. Laybourn (eds), *The Centennial History of the Independent Labour Party* (Keele, 1992). J. Jupp, *The Radical Left in Britain, 1931–41* (1982) is informative on the ILP after its disaffiliation. On the left-wing ILP leader of the 1920s–40s, see G. Brown, *Maxton* (1986). D. Blaazer, *The Popular Front and the Progressive Tradition: Socialists, Liberals, and the Quest for Unity 1884–1939* (Cambridge, 1991) is also interesting. The left and the 1945–51 Labour government is dealt with in J. Schneer, *Labour's Conscience: The Labour Left, 1945–51* (1988), and D. Rubinstein, 'Socialism and the Labour Party: the Labour left and domestic policy, 1945–50', in D.E. Martin and D. Rubinstein (eds), *Ideology and the Labour Movement: Essays in Honour of John Saville* (1979). M. Jenkins, *Bevanism, Labour's High Tide* (Nottingham, 1979) examines the left in the 1950s. P. Seyd, *The Rise and Fall of the Labour Left* (1987) deals with the increasingly bitter turmoil of the 1970s and 1980s. Also on this period, see M. Hatfield, *The House the Left Built: Inside Labour Policy-making 1970–75* (1978).

Useful information and insights into attitudes and personality clashes can be found in the autobiographies and biographies of the leading figures involved, including – most importantly – on Bevan, M. Foot, *Aneurin Bevan, 1897–1945* (1962) and *Aneurin Bevan, 1945–60* (1973), and J. Campbell's *Nye Bevan and the Mirage of British Socialism* (1987), together with J. Lee, *My Life with Nye* (1960). I. Mikardo, *Back-Bencher* (1989) is the autobiography of a figure influential in the 1940s and 1950s. The left over a longer period can be examined in A.F. Brockway, *Inside the Left* (1942), *Outside the Right* (1963), and *98 Not Out* (1986). More recently, Benn's *Against the Tide: Diaries 1973–76* (1989), *Conflicts of Interest, Diaries 1977–80* (1990), *The End of an Era, Diaries 1980–90* (1992) are important. E. Heffer, *Never a Yes Man* (1991), the autobiography of a contemporary left-wing working-class MP, is valuable.

On the Communist Party, which created problems for the leadership – and attempted to offer opportunities to the membership – of the Labour Party from 1920 until the late 1960s, H. Pelling, *The British Communist Party* (1958) remains an interesting introduction. W. Kendall, *The Revolutionary Movement in Britain 1900–21* (1969), R. Challinor, *The Origins of British Bolshevism* (1978), and L.J. MacFarlane, *The British Communist Party, Its Origins and 'Development until 1929* (1966) are useful for its early days. S. Bornstein and A. Richardson, *Two Steps Back: Communists and the Wider Labour Movement 1935–45* (1982) takes the story a stage further. R. Martin, *Communism and the British Trade Unions 1924–33* (Oxford, 1969) is a study of the National Minority Movement, the Communist attempt to gain a foothold in the official Labour movement. For the inter-war period, see also H.J.P. Harmer, 'The failure of the Communists: the National Unemployed Workers' Movement, 1921–1939: a disappointing success', and A. Thorpe, ' "The only effective bulwark against reaction and revolution": Labour and the frustration of the extreme left', both in A. Thorpe, *The Failure of Political Extremism in Inter-war Britain* (Exeter, 1989). The 'official' Communist histories – J. Klugmann, *History of the Communist Party of Great Britain, Volume 1: Formation and Early Years, 1919–1924* (1969) and *Volume 2: The General Strike, 1925–1926* (1969) – are dull, although N. Branson, *History of the Communist Party of Great Britain 1927–41* (1985) is readable and generally reliable. A more recent study is F. Beckett, *Enemy Within: The Rise and Fall of the British Communist Party* (1995). The biography of the party leader from the 1920s to the 1950s – K. Morgan, *Harry Pollitt* (Manchester, 1993) – is also useful.

Trotskyism, another brand of revolutionary socialism, created problems for the Labour Party from the 1960s to the 1980s, particularly in the form of the Militant Tendency. T. Grant, *The Unbroken Thread – The Development of Trotskyism over 40 Years* (1989) gives the Militant view, while A. Smith, *Faces of Labour – The Inside Story* (1996) presents an interesting portrait of Grant himself. Also worth looking at are J. Callaghan, *British Trotskyism* (Oxford, 1984), J. Callaghan, *The Far Left in British Politics*

(Oxford, 1987), M. Crick, *The March of Militant* (1986) and – from the group's supporters – P. Taffe and T. Mulhearn, *Liverpool: A City that Dared to Fight* (1988). R. Groves, *The Balham Group: How British Trotskyism Began* (1973) covers an earlier period.

12 Labour and Women

On the relationship between the Labour Party and women, P.M. Greaves, *Labour Women: Women in British Working-class Politics 1918–1939* (Cambridge, 1994), L. Middleton (ed.), *Women in the Labour Movement: The British Experience* (1977), and P. Thane, 'The women of the British Labour Party and feminism, 1906–45', in H.L. Smith (ed.), *British Feminism in the Twentieth Century* (Aldershot, 1990) are useful. Also on the early period, see J. Hannam, 'Women and the ILP, 1890–1914', in D. James, T. Jowitt and K. Laybourn (eds), *Centennial History of the Independent Labour Party* (Keele, 1992). On Labour and the early twentieth-century women's suffrage movement, see S.S. Holton, *Feminism and Democracy: Women's Suffrage and Reform Politics in Britain, 1900–18* (Cambridge, 1986) and also C. Collette, *For Labour and For Women: The Women's Labour League, 1906–1918* (Manchester, 1989). N. Hart, 'Gender and the rise and fall of class politics', *New Left Review*, 175 (1989) considers Labour's relative unpopularity among women. On a specific period, see J. Hinton, 'Women and the Labour vote, 1945–1950', *Labour History Review*, 57 (1992). An informative account of the party and women in the 1980s and 1990s can be found in V. Atkinson and J. Spear, 'The Labour Party and women: policies and practices', in M.J. Smith and J. Spear, *The Changing Labour Party* (1992).

The following should be consulted for the experiences and careers of individual women: M. Bondfield, *A Life's Work* (1949) and M. Miliband, 'Margaret Grace Bondfield', in J. Bellamy and J. Saville (eds), *Dictionary of Labour Biography, Volume II* (1974); B. Braddock, *The Braddocks* (1963); B. Castle, *The Castle Diaries, 1974–76* (1980), *The Castle Diaries, 1964–70* (1984), and *Fighting All the Way* (1993); P. Hollis, *Jennie Lee: A Life* (Oxford, 1997); J. Lee, *My Life with Nye* (1960); B. Webb, *My Apprenticeship* (1926), *Our Partnership* (1948), M.I. Cole (ed.), *Beatrice Webb Diaries, 1912–24* (1952), N. Mackenzie, *The Letters of Sidney and Beatrice Webb* (Cambridge, 1978), and L. Radice, *Beatrice and Sidney Webb: Fabian Socialists* (1984); B.D. Vernon, *Ellen Wilkinson* (1982).

13 Labour, Decolonisation, Immigration and Ethnic Minorities

Studies of ethnic minorities and British politics generally, with references to relationships with the Labour Party, are M. Anwar, *Race and*

Politics: Ethnic Minorities and the British Political System (1986), M. Fitzgerald, *Black People and Party Politics in Britain* (1987), and Z. Layton-Henry and D. Studtler, *The Political Participation of Black and Asian Britons* (1984). P. Foot's *Immigration and Race in British Politics* (Harmondsworth, 1985) is also valuable. More specifically on ethnic minorities and the Labour Party, see T. Carter, *Shattering Illusions* (1986), and R. Ramdin, *The Making of the Black Working Class in Britain* (1987).

For a critical background view, see R. Clough, *Labour: A Party Fit for Imperialism* (1992). See also P.S. Gupta, *Imperialism and the British Labour Movement 1914–64* (1975), S. Howe, *Anti-Colonialism in British Politics: The Left and the End of Empire 1918–64* (Oxford, 1993), M. Edwards, *The Last Years of British India* (1963), and M. Zinkin and T. Zinkin, *Britain and India: Requiem for Empire* (1964). C. Holmes, *John Bull's Island: Immigration and British Society, 1871–1971* (1988) contains some valuable views. Among useful – and often critical – articles, are B. Newman and S. Joshi, 'The role of Labour in the creation of a racist Britain', *Race & Class*, XXV, 3 (1984), A. Sivanandan, 'Black sections and the Labour Party', *Searchlight* (Oct. 1985), D. Upshall, 'The Labour Party – an anti-racist dilemma', *New Socialist* (Dec. 1987), and – on an earlier period – D. Dean, 'Coping with colonial immigration, the Cold War and colonial policy – the Labour government and black communities in Great Britain 1945–51', *Immigration and Minorities*, 6 (Nov. 1987). See also K. Paul, ' "British subjects" and "British stock": Labour's postwar imperialism', *Journal of British Studies*, 34 (1995), V.G. Kiernan, 'India and the Labour Party', *New Left Review*, 42 (1967), and J.G. Darwin, 'The end of Empire', *Contemporary Record*, 1, 3 (1987).

14   Autobiographies, Biographies and Diaries

Biographies and diaries can provide a valuable background by placing the individual in the context of her or his period. Political autobiographies, though often self-serving, also have their uses. This section of the bibliography provides an outline of what is available on the main figures in the Labour Party's history. Many are also referred to in the appropriate sections throughout the bibliography. A stimulating introduction to the party's leading – or simply interesting – figures as far as Kinnock can be found in K.O. Morgan, *Labour People. Leaders and Lieutenants* (Oxford, 1987). This should be accompanied by J. Bellamy and J. Saville (eds), *Dictionary of Labour Biography*, 9 vols (1972–93).

.On Addison, a not untypical Liberal recruit to Labour who went on to become a minister, see K. and J. Morgan, *Portrait of a Progressive: The Political Career of Christopher, Viscount Addison* (Oxford, 1980). Attlee, the first Labour prime minister to hold office with a majority, is well covered in T. Burridge, *Clement Attlee* (1985), K. Harris, *Attlee* (1985). R. Pearce,

Attlee (1997) is concise. Attlee himself is typically unrevealing in F. Williams, *A Prime Minister Remembers* (1961) and his own *As It Happened* (1954). Benn, former Cabinet minister turned tribune of the left, provides a wealth of detail in *Out of the Wilderness: Diaries 1963–67* (1987), *Office without Power: Diaries 1968–72* (1988), *Against the Tide: Diaries 1973–76* (1989), *Conflicts of Interest: Diaries 1977–80* (1990) and *The End of an Era: Diaries 1980–90* (1992). R. Jenkins, *Tony Benn: A Political Biography* (1980) covers the earlier period, and J. Adams, *Tony Benn* (1992) should also be consulted. On Bevan, M. Foot's superbly written but perhaps over-sympathetic *Aneurin Bevan, 1897–1945* (1962) and *Aneurin Bevan, 1945– 60* (1973) need to be balanced with J. Campbell's *Nye Bevan and the Mirage of British Socialism* (1987). It is also worth consulting J. Lee, *My Life with Nye* (1960), the work of his partner and a significant political figure in her own right. Bevin, the heavyweight trade unionist who became an equally powerful political figure, is impressively covered in A. Bullock, *The Life and Times of Ernest Bevin*, 3 vols (1960, 1967, 1983). F. Williams, *Ernest Bevin* (1952) has less depth. It is far too early for a considered view of Blair, but for an interim outline of his rise, see J. Sopel, *Tony Blair: The Moderniser* (1995) and, perhaps more usefully, J. Rentoul, *Tony Blair* (1995). For Labour's first woman Cabinet minis-ter, see her autobiography, M. Bondfield, *A Life's Work* (1949) and M. Miliband, 'Margaret Grace Bondfield', in J. Bellamy and J. Saville (eds), *Dictionary of Labour Biography, Volume II* (1974). Although a minor figure, B. Braddock's *The Braddocks* (1963) is riveting on party and Liverpool in-fighting. Brockway, the left-winger whose activity spanned over 70 years, describes his life and times in A.F. Brockway, *Inside the Left* (1942), *Outside the Right* (1963), and *98 Not Out* (1986). The expansive but flawed right-winger George Brown makes his own case in *In My Way* (1971).

Callaghan, the tactician with the reassuring touch, is well covered by K.O. Morgan in *Callaghan, A Life* (1997), B. Donoghue, *Prime Minister: The Conduct of Policy under Harold Wilson and James Callaghan* (1987) and, on his rise to office, P. Kellner and C. Hitchins, *Callaghan: The Road to No. 10* (1976). Callaghan's version can be found in *Time and Chance* (1987). For Castle, the left-winger whose plans for trade union reform Callaghan helped shatter, see B. Castle, *The Castle Diaries, 1974–76* (1980), *The Castle Diaries, 1964–70* (1984), and her autobiography, *Fighting All the Way* (1993). W. De'ath (ed.), *Barbara Castle: A Portrait from Life* (Brighton, 1970) covers her most influential period. For a central figure in cementing the inter-war party–union link, TUC general secretary Citrine, see W. Citrine, *Men and Work* (1964) and *Two Careers* (1967). Independent Labour Party (ILP) pioneer and later Home Secretary and deputy Labour leader Clynes describes his life in *Memoirs* (1937). G.D.H. Cole is covered in M. Cole, *The Life of G.D.H. Cole* (1971), while his ideas are considered in more depth in L.P. Carpenter, *G.D.H. Cole:*

An Intellectual Biography (1973) and A.W. Wright, *G.D.H. Cole and Socialist Democracy* (1979). E. Estorick, *Stafford Cripps: A Biography* (1949) and C. Cooke, *The Life of Richard Stafford Cripps* (1957) deal with the inter-war left-winger and post-war Chancellor. The life and ideas of the 1950s revisionist Crosland are covered sympathetically in S. Crosland, *Tony Crosland* (1982) and the impact of his views in D. Lipsey and S. Leonard (eds), *The Socialist Agenda: Crosland's Legacy* (1981). For a revelation of how the 1964–70 Labour government worked, little can outdo R. Crossman, *The Diaries of a Cabinet Minister*, 3 vols (1975, 1976, 1977). A shorter alternative is J. Morgan (ed.), *The Crossman Diaries: Selections from the Diaries of a Cabinet Minister, 1964–1970* (1979). For an earlier period, J. Morgan (ed.), *The Backbench Diaries of Richard Crossman* (1981). See also A. Howard, *Crossman, The Pursuit of Power* (1990).

The life and times of Dalton, the theoretician and Cabinet minister, are superbly covered in B. Pimlott, *Hugh Dalton* (1985) and B. Pimlott (ed.), *The Political Diary of Hugh Dalton 1918–40, 1945–46* (1987). Another view of the latter part of the period can be found in K. Jefferys (ed.), *Labour and the Wartime Coalition from the Diary of James Chuter Ede 1941–54* (1988). The varied political career of the one-time maverick Foot, who became party leader, is described in S. Hoggart and D. Leigh, *Michael Foot: A Portrait* (1981). For Gaitskell, another, far different, party leader, see P. Williams's sympathetic *Hugh Gaitskell* (1979), P. Williams (ed.), *The Diary of Hugh Gaitskell 1945–56* (1983), and (particularly for a memoir by Roy Jenkins) W.T. Rodgers (ed.), *Hugh Gaitskell 1906–63* (1964).

Labour pioneer Hardie is well covered in E. Hughes, *Keir Hardie* (1956), I. McLean, *Keir Hardie* (1975), K.O. Morgan, *Keir Hardie: Radical and Socialist* (1975) and F. Reid, *Keir Hardie* (1978). Labour's deputy leader in the late 1980s, Hattersley, makes interesting and entertaining points in R. Hattersley, *Who Goes Home? Scenes from a Political Life* (1995). Information on a powerful right-wing figure of the 1960s and 1970s can be found in B. Reid and G. Williams, *Denis Healey and the Politics of Power* (1971) and his own *The Time of My Life* (1989). The career of Labour leader Henderson is examined in C.J. Wrigley, *Arthur Henderson* (Cardiff, 1990), and F.M. Leventhal, *Arthur Henderson* (Manchester, 1989), while M.A. Hamilton, *Arthur Henderson* (1938) remains interesting. The significant part of the career of a reforming Labour Home Secretary who defected to help form the SDP is set out in J. Campbell, *Roy Jenkins: A Biography* (1983) and in the autobiography *A Life at the Centre* (1991). An influential trade union figure of the 1960s and 1970s (particularly the 'social contract' period) gives his view in J. Jones, *Union Man: The Autobiography of Jack Jones* (1986). Assessments of Kinnock, the left-winger turned party moderniser, are in G.M.F. Drower, *Neil Kinnock – The Path to Leadership* (1984) and, more interestingly, in R. Harris, *The Making of Neil Kinnock* (1984). Labour's post-1931 crisis leader Lansbury is covered in R. Postgate, *The Life of George Lansbury* (1951) and M. Cole, 'Lansbury', in J. Bellamy and J. Saville (eds), *Dictionary of Labour Biography, Volume II* (1974), as well as his own *My Life* (1928) and *Looking Backwards and Forwards* (1935). The ideas and life of Laski, the party intellectual from a similar period, are examined in H.A. Deane, *The Political Ideas of Harold J. Laski* (New York, 1955), K. Martin, *Harold Laski: A Biographical Memoir* (1983) and, more recently, I. Kramnick and B. Sheerman, *Harold Laski: A Life on the Left* (1993). For a sympathetic view of a significant woman politician, and the wife of Bevan, see P. Hollis, *Jennie Lee: A Life* (Oxford, 1997). An interim view of Livingstone, the 1980s left-wing Greater London Council leader who may yet achieve greater significance, is in J. Carvel, *Citizen Ken* (1984).

The much-reviled MacDonald is comprehensively covered in D. Marquand, *Ramsay MacDonald* (1977; new edn, 1997), while L. MacNeill Weir, *The Tragedy of Ramsay MacDonald* (1938) remains an interesting work of its time and J.R. MacDonald, *Memoirs, 1869–1924* (1937) is worth consulting for the early period. Maxton, the popular – but ultimately ineffectual – Independent Labour Party leader of the 1920s–1940s is considered in G. Brown, *Maxton* (1986). For an influential figure on the Labour left from the 1940s, see I. Mikardo, *Back-Bencher* (1989). B. Donoghue and G. Jones, *Herbert Morrison: Portrait of a Politician* (1973) cover the career of the force behind the form the post-war nationalisation programme took. There is also his own *Autobiography* (1960). Mosley, an interesting if peripheral figure, sets out his position in O. Mosley, *My Life* (1980) and receives some sympathy in R. Skidelsky, *Oswald Mosley* (1981, rev. edn). Owen, one of the architects of the 1980s Social Democratic Party and a figure whose political career also ended in disappointment, sets out his case in D. Owen, *Time to Declare* (1991) and is the subject of K. Harris, *David Owen* (1987).

The short leadership career of the emollient figure Smith in the 1990s is covered in A. McSmith, *John Smith* (1994). Snowden, Labour's original 'iron chancellor' whose career ended in bitterness, has been dealt with by K. Laybourn and D. James, *Philip Snowden* (1987). C. Cross, *Philip Snowden* (1966) is still of interest, and see Philip, Viscount Snowden, *An Autobiography, Volume 2, 1919–1934* (1934) for his periods as Chancellor and for the early National government. For the life of a colourless but central figure in the 1964–70 governments, see M. Stewart, *Life and Labour: An Autobiography* (1980). The varied political career of Strachey is considered in H. Thomas, *John Strachey* (1979) and M. Newman, *John Strachey* (Manchester, 1989). Two useful works on the intellectual Tawney are R. Terrill, *R.H. Tawney and His Times* (1973) and A.W. Wright, *R.H. Tawney* (1987). Much valuable information on the central figures of the Webbs and their part in Fabianism, the rise of Labour and on the wider political scene can be found in B. Webb, *My Apprenticeship* (1926), *Our*

Partnership (1948); M.I. Cole (ed.), *Beatrice Webb Diaries, 1912–24* (1952); N. and J. Mackenzie, *The First Fabians* (1977); N. Mackenzie, *The Letters of Sidney and Beatrice Webb* (Cambridge, 1978) and L. Radice, *Beatrice and Sidney Webb: Fabian Socialists* (1984). B.D. Vernon portrays a vivid figure in Labour's history in *Ellen Wilkinson* (1982). B. Pimlott, *Harold Wilson* (1992) attempts, not unsuccessfully, to rehabilitate a figure whose reputation declined in the 1970s. See also P. Zeigler, *Wilson: The Authorized Life* (1993). P. Foot, *The Politics of Harold Wilson* (Harmondsworth, 1968) is a brilliant contemporary polemic. As well as *Harold Wilson Memoirs 1916–64* (1986), Wilson provided his own narrative of his periods as prime minister in *The Labour Government 1964–70* (1971) and *Final Term: The Labour Government 1974–76* (1979).

Index

Main entries are in bold. For reasons of space, entries appearing in lists (for example, of ministers) or where they are so numerous as to be impracticable to refer to (for example, trade unions) are not included in this index. An entry may appear more than once on a page.